THE ROMAN NOVEL

THE
ROMAN NOVEL

THE 'SATYRICON' OF PETRONIUS AND
THE 'METAMORPHOSES' OF
APULEIUS

BY

P. G. WALSH

*Reader in Humanity in the
University of Edinburgh*

CAMBRIDGE
AT THE UNIVERSITY PRESS
1970

Published by the Syndics of the Cambridge University Press
Bentley House, 200 Euston Road, London N.W.1
American Branch: 32 East 57th Street, New York, N.Y.10022

© Cambridge University Press 1970

Library of Congress Catalogue Card Number: 70-98700

Standard Book Number: 521 07658 7

Printed in Great Britain
at the University Printing House, Cambridge
(Brooke Crutchley, University Printer)

PARENTIBUS OPTIMIS

CONTENTS

Preface   *page* ix

List of abbreviations   xiii

1 Introduction   1

2 The formative genres   7

3 The literary texture   32

4 The 'Satyricon'   67

5 'Cena Trimalchionis'   111

6 The 'Metamorphoses'   141

7 'Cupid and Psyche'   190

8 'Nachleben': the Roman novel and the
   rebirth of the picaresque   224

Appendix 1   The date of the 'Satyricon'   244

*Appendix 2   The career of Apuleius and
   the date of the 'Metamorphoses'*   248

Appendix 3   The Isiac Aretalogy from Kyme   252

Select bibliography   254

Indexes   260

PREFACE

The comic fiction of Petronius and Apuleius is now increasingly studied in Britain and in North America, though (astonishingly) there are still universities in Britain where undergraduates are never introduced to the *Cena Trimalchionis* or to *Cupid and Psyche*. The aim of this book, begun several years ago before the recent proliferation of learned articles, was to attempt to orientate the student by some account of the theory of the comic romance, and of the particular ways in which Petronius and Apuleius made their original contributions. Since then, Perry's *The Ancient Romances* has been published. I have suggested in a review of this book that Perry's major achievement is in the discussion of the Greek romances rather than of the Roman. Perhaps this was an immodest way of stating that I differed almost *toto caelo* in my interpretation of the *Satyricon* and the *Metamorphoses*.[1]

My approach to Petronius reflects the conviction that the *Satyricon* is sophisticated *gaminerie*. In the spirit of Scarron's *Roman comique*, Petronius might well have written: 'If the courteous reader be offended at all the silly trifles he has already found in this book, he will do well not to go on with the reading of it; for upon my conscience, he must expect nothing else.' I have tried to demonstrate this by a systematic analysis of the book scene by scene, in an attempt to dispel the surprising theories that Petronius is a coherent moralist, or an author dominated by a tragic view of life. Sullivan's learned study, with which I find myself in substantial accord, appeared after I had completed my chapters on Petronius; I have confined myself to acknowledging some suggestive discussions in his book, and noting some differences of interpretation.

Critics in English have not devoted as much attention to the novel of Apuleius as to the *Satyricon*. I hope that my essays on

[1] As I write this Preface, I have heard of the death of Ben Edwin Perry; *requiescat in pace*. He would have welcomed the forthrightness of my reaction to his analysis of Petronius and Apuleius.

the *Metamorphoses*, which have exploited the work of continental scholars, may encourage some better-qualified critic to write a full study of this remarkable novel. I know of no extended discussion in English which demonstrates that the book is essentially a fable, or which relates the central myth of Cupid and Psyche to the experiences of Lucius; to this extent my analysis may be useful. My original contribution, which visualises the final book as reaction against the Christian witness in Africa, is necessarily speculative. But if, as I believe, the evidence favours a late date of composition in Africa, the meteoric growth of Christianity can hardly have failed to impinge on any religious testament.

Though I have lectured on the *Cena Trimalchionis* and *Cupid and Psyche* for some years in Edinburgh, this book achieved its shape during a year's visiting appointment at University College, Toronto, where I conducted a graduate class on Roman fiction. I am most grateful to Professors Leonard Woodbury, Niall Rudd, Mary White, and other colleagues there, now friends, for their courteous hospitality and intellectual stimulation. I must likewise signal the contribution by members of the class to useful discussion of Petronian and Apuleian questions.

It is agreeable to record my thanks also to helpful colleagues in the Departments of Greek, Humanity and Ancient History at Edinburgh. I must make particular mention of Mr J. R. G. Wright, with whom I have conducted a dialogue on Apuleian questions over several years, and who has scrutinised my typescript with his knowledgeable and intelligent eye. Mr E. J. Kenney of Cambridge has also read the typescript, and I have profited greatly from his criticism. Mr Stephen Ryle of the University of Liverpool has helped me with bibliography on Isis-worship, and has also allowed me to see his Oxford B.Litt. thesis, a useful commentary on *Metamorphoses* XI. For the final chapter on the later influence of Petronius and Apuleius, which is inevitably a rather superficial taxi-ride, I have to acknowledge the help of friends in other Departments at Edinburgh, especially Professor A. A. Parker, Professor C. P.

Brand, and Mr A. M. Freedman. Professors Ian Campbell and David West, as always unstinting of their time and help, removed blemishes and infelicities from the proofs. Miss Catherine Strathie and Mrs Sheila Webb have provided efficient typing assistance. Finally I must thank the helpful readers, expert staff, and indulgent Syndics of the Cambridge University Press for consenting to renew an association which has for me been both a pleasure and a privilege.

P. G. W.

University of Edinburgh

ABBREVIATIONS

Abh. Preuss. Akad.	*Abhandlungen der preussischen Akademie der Wissenschaft*
Abh. Sächs. Akad.	*Abhandlungen der philol.-histor. Klasse der Sächsischen Gesellschaft*
AJP	*American Journal of Philology*
Ant. Class.	*L'Antiquité Classique*
BCH	*Bulletin de correspondance hellénique*
CIL	*Corpus Inscriptionum Latinarum*
CLE	*Carmina Latina Epigraphica*
CP	*Classical Philology*
CQ	*Classical Quarterly*
CR	*Classical Review*
CW	*Classical World*
GR	*Greece and Rome*
H	*Hermes*
Hisp. Rev.	*Hispanic Review*
HSCP	*Harvard Studies in Classical Philology*
HThR	*Harvard Theological Review*
JHS	*Journal of Hellenic Studies*
JRS	*Journal of Roman Studies*
JTS	*Journal of Theological Studies*
Mus. Helv.	*Museum Helveticum*
NJb	*Neue Jahrbücher für das klassische Altertum*
Philol.	*Philologus*
PIR	*Prosopographia Imperii Romani*
PP	*Parola del passato*
Preuss. Jb.	*Preussische Jahrbücher*
RE	Pauly–Wissowa–Kroll, *Real-Encyclopädie*
REA	*Revue des études anciennes*
REG	*Revue des études grecques*

ABBREVIATIONS

REL	*Revue des études latines*
Rev. Hist. Rel.	*Revue de l'histoire des religions*
RhM	*Rheinisches Museum*
RPh	*Revue de philologie*
TAPA	*Transactions and Proceedings of the American Philological Association*
WS	*Wiener Studien*

1

INTRODUCTION

I think that this kind of writing falls under the heading of Milesian fables,
which are fantastic tales whose purpose is to amaze but not to instruct,
contrary to the fables called apologues, which delight as well as instruct...
CERVANTES, Don Quixote, ch. 47

'The Roman Novel' is perhaps a grandiose title under which to
present the comic romances of Petronius and Apuleius. Yet
these books can claim the title 'Roman' in a sense in which the
later serious romances cannot. *Apollonius, Prince of Tyre*, the
first extant love-romance in Latin, does not make its appearance
till the third century; and, like the *Recognitions* of Ps. Clement,
the Christian romance which Rufinus translated into Latin in
the later fourth century, it is better regarded as Greek ideal
fiction composed in Latin.[1]

The *Satyricon* and the *Metamorphoses*, on the other hand,
though differing considerably in theme and tone, show basic
affinities. Both can be seen to be related to the Greek satirical
fiction shaped partly by the Milesian tradition inaugurated by
Aristides, and also by the fictitious themes in Menippean
satire; yet both are endowed with an authentically Roman
flavour. Both authors present their tales in a literary texture in
which there are frequent reminiscences of Greek and Roman
poetry and constant parody of the conventions and styles of
the various prose-genres. Moreover, the two romances have a
similarity of structure all the more striking because no similarly
extended comic romances survive in Greek; this protracted,

---

[1] See now B. E. Perry's very useful survey, *The Ancient Romances*
(California 1967), which discusses *Apollonius* and the *Recognitions* in the
appendices, with citation of bibliography. Perry's book is one of the
major contributions to the study of the ancient romance in this century,
and though the present work differs considerably in its interpretation of
both the *Satyricon* and the *Metamorphoses*, it is appropriate at the outset
to acknowledge a general debt to his book.

episodic narrative-form, into which are inserted apposite *novelle* and mannered reflexions on life and literature, justifies the claim that the Romans rather than the Spaniards invented the picaresque novel around the travels and adventures of an anti-hero. For all these reasons it is profitable to study the two romances in harness.

It need occasion no surprise that the Romans inaugurated no traceable tradition of serious fiction in the classical period, and this for two reasons. First, though the Greeks had already developed the love-romance by the first century B.C., fiction was widely regarded as a sub-literary genre, as a disreputable pursuit for men with intellectual talent. The ancients had not come to visualise the possibility that fiction could be instructive about the human condition, as philosophical and historical studies were seen to be; it had the status merely of a form of relaxation or sport. When Plutarch at the outset of *The Virtues of Women* stresses that his work is historical and not composed merely to 'beguile the ear', he is drawing a distinction between what really happened and those semi-historical or wholly fictitious accounts of maidens' fortunes told to divert and titillate.[1] Fiction, it will be noted, does not qualify for inclusion in Quintilian's survey of the genres of ancient literature. This is why it should not surprise us that Tacitus' sketch of Petronius omits his role as comic novelist; likewise Apuleius' omission of the *Metamorphoses* from his lists of published work is a precarious argument for a later date of composition.[2]

Secondly, it may reasonably be argued that during the period of the early empire no mass readership yet existed for Latin fiction. Those attracted to literary pursuits addressed their efforts to astringently critical ears. In the comparatively narrow segment of Roman society which comprised the reading public, satirically comic fiction was inevitably preferred

---

[1] *Mul. Virt.* 1.1: πρὸς ἡδονὴν ἀκοῆς. Some of this fiction has a legendary or semi-historical base; Plutarch is doubtless relegating some allegedly historical accounts to the level of fiction (cf. Polybius 3.31.12).

[2] Quint. 10.1.46 ff.: Tac. *Ann.* 16.18: Apul. *Flor.* 9.27 ff., 20.5 ff. (but the *Metamorphoses* was probably not written then; see Appendix 2).

to sentimental romance. The only known purveyor of fiction in Latin before Petronius was the historian Sisenna, who wrote Milesian stories, and it is difficult to imagine any prominent Latin author before Apuleius with time to spare for idealised love-stories. It is no accident that the Greek writers of fiction are not men of social prominence like Petronius and Apuleius, but are representative of a wider literacy to which there is no parallel in the Latin-speaking areas of the early empire.

The comic romance was recommended to its literate readers specifically as the literature of relaxation. Since the opening of the *Satyricon* has been lost, no programmatic statement survives from it, but Apuleius makes the aim of the *Metamorphoses* manifest at the outset. He promises that his story will titillate in an elegant manner—'auresque tuas benivolas lepido susurro permulceam'. The sentiment is echoed in Macrobius' comment on the aim of Petronius' and Apuleius' fiction: 'hoc totum fabularum genus, quod solas aurium delicias profitetur...'[1]

This aim for the comic romance is expressed in a more detailed and explicit way by Lucian, who declares his programme at the beginning of the *Vera Historia*. He informs us that he is writing for the student at play,[2] whose ideal reading in relaxation will be of a literary and witty kind. So he promises a story which will incorporate elements strange (τὸ ξένον), elegant (τὸ χαρίεν), and mendacious (ψεύσματα ποικίλα), and adds that each part will subtly and wittily (οὐκ ἀκωμῳδήτως ᾔνικται) allude to the works of ancient poets, historians and philosophers.[3] So in Lucian's view the aim of the comic writer is τέρψις, but a pleasure at two levels, a combination of sensational content and a sophisticated literary texture. The constant literary evocation does not usually seek to ridicule the great classics, quotations from which continually stud the comic writers' narratives; the purpose is solely to add a more intellectual dimension of amusement for an educated audience.

[1] Apul. *Met.* 1.1.1; Macr. *In Somn. Scip.* 1.2.8.
[2] Compare likewise Ps. Lucian, *Erōtes* 1: Ἐρωτικῆς παιδιᾶς... πεπλή-ρωκας ἡμῶν τὰ κεκμηκότα πρὸς τὰς συνεχεῖς σπουδὰς ὦτα...
[3] *V.H.* 1.1.

The theme will be trivial and escapist, but the manner of expression elegant and bookish, so that the author provides simultaneously a cruder and a more refined pleasure.

Petronius and Apuleius in differing ways introduce important innovations to this programme for the comic romance. Petronius sets out deliberately to create a synthesis of Greek satirical fiction and Roman satirical characterisation; built into the sensational adventures of the Greek anti-hero is a series of vignettes of the types whom he encounters. This pattern is already a commonplace in the fiction of Petronius, Lucian and Apuleius some fifteen hundred years before it is 'invented' (according to some modern critics) in the first Spanish picaresque novel *Laẕarillo de Tormes*. Apuleius attempts a different kind of synthesis, by introducing into the comic romance some characteristic themes of the serious or ideal romance in a romanticising way and for an edifying purpose; in this sense he anticipates Cervantes' fruitful fusion of the romance of chivalry and the picaresque novel.

It is useful to approach the two Roman novels by preliminary study of the formative genres, and by analysis of the deployment of the literary texture. A recent study[1] has protested vehemently about the tendency to study the romance by tracing its genealogy from other genres. This objection may well be salutary when the Greek serious fiction is in question. But Petronius and Apuleius deliberately signal their exploitation of earlier genres, and it is impossible fully to measure their literary intentions without some account of the conventions which they exploit. Apuleius confesses his debt to the Milesian tradition of Greek satirical fiction; his novel incorporates also salient features of the love-romance. Petronius, it will be suggested, writes in reaction against this romantic Greek fiction, which inspires him to derisive burlesque. He also signals a debt to Roman satire—notably the Menippean, to which he signifies a kind of allegiance by the adoption of the 'prosimetric' form.

[1] So Perry, ch. 1. Rohde's *Der griechische Roman* is of course the main target, with his suggestion that the love-romance is a synthesis of erotic poetry and travel story.

Once the influence of these formative genres has been assessed, it is possible to grasp more clearly the nature and purposes of the literary evocations in the two authors. This in turn will assist us to demonstrate that Petronius and Apuleius stand within a common tradition of comic fiction, yet each makes a distinctively original contribution to that tradition. This originality is in each case partly shaped by the conditions of the age. Our discussion of the *Satyricon* starts from the assumption that the author was that Petronius who was *arbiter elegantiae* at the court of Nero.[1] The temptation to specify the precise circumstances attending its composition must be indulged with caution, for this inevitably leads to that kind of speculative biographical interpretation which may distort.[2] But the evidence of a date of composition about A.D. 65 makes it important to visualise the episodes against the backcloth of the later Neronian age, not merely because the social and economic conditions illuminate Petronius' choice of satirical targets, but also because our appreciation of the literary discussions and compositions is enhanced by some knowledge of the prevailing intellectual climate.

An awareness of the intellectual currents of Africa late in the second century is similarly rewarding for a study of Apuleius' *Metamorphoses*. At first sight this may appear a timeless story which might have been written at any time in the imperial period, but the realisation that it was written in an era of religious upheaval by an author in close touch with the philosophical and religious movements of the day may bring deeper understanding of his purposes.

[1] I share with Sullivan, *The Satyricon of Petronius*, ch. 1, and K. F. C. Rose, *Arion* (1966), 275 ff., the conviction that the arguments are overwhelming. See Appendix 1.

[2] I think not only of those like the seventeenth-century de Salas who believe that the *Satyricon* was the catalogue of Nero's sexual vices sent by Petronius from his death-bed (see now Rose's entertaining account, *Arion* (1966), 280), but those who like Bagnani, *Arbiter of Elegance* (Toronto 1954), 4 ff., suggest that the *Satyricon* was read at court for the amusement of Nero. As we shall see (ch. 5), the characterisation of Trimalchio makes that a dubious suggestion.

In this sense it can be claimed that both Petronius and Apuleius attempt to incorporate into their novels elements drawn from their own experience. Hazlitt's description of the novel as 'A close imitation of men and manners...the very web and texture of society as it really exists, and as we meet it when we come into the world' is applicable to Petronius as to none of his predecessors in ancient fiction. In such scenes as the *Cena Trimalchionis*, the author is satirically criticising the society of which he is himself a part. With Apuleius the personal involvement takes a different direction. Towards the close of the novel he identifies himself with the narrator not for a satirical but for an evangelical purpose. In portraying the progress of the hero to the mystical awareness of religious truth from a life of sensuality and unhealthy curiosity, he incorporates a detailed description of contemporary religious practice into the framework of his novel, which undergoes a metamorphosis from comic romance to moral fable and religious apologia.

2

THE FORMATIVE GENRES

Apuleius begins his *Metamorphoses* with a clear pointer to the genre and his intended treatment. 'It's a Greek story I'm embarking on,' he writes, adding that 'the language is that of the Milesian Tales.'[1] Even without this explicit assurance it is clear from the compendious *Lucius or the Ass* that the theme of Apuleius' tale had already been exploited in briefer compass in Greek comic fiction.[2] The same cannot, however, be said of Petronius' *Satyricon*. Nothing remotely comparable to its plot survives in Greek literature, and the Roman atmosphere of many of the episodes encourages the belief that he has brought to birth a new type of fiction. But he did not begin with a *tabula rasa*. He was well acquainted with the experiments in fiction already pioneered by his Greek and Roman predecessors in widely differing genres. The *Satyricon* is best regarded as a creative synthesis of Greek fiction with Roman satire and mimic motifs.[3]

Greek fiction as it has survived contains three categories[4] which may be seen to exert a formative influence on the Roman novelists. There is first the ideal romance, flourishing from the first century B.C. if not earlier. This is a stylised, artificial genre in which a highly moral love between boy and girl ultimately

[1] *Met.* 1.1.6 and 1: 'fabulam Graecanicam...sermone...Milesio'.
[2] See below, ch. 6.
[3] There is little point in retailing here the diverse theories on the subject of influences on the *Satyricon*; a useful summary may be found now in P. Veyne, *REL* (1964), 301 ff. Most scholars seek to align the book with either Greek fiction or Menippean satire, but the comment of U. Knoche, *Die römische Satire*, 75, is highly relevant: 'aufs Ganze gesehen, wird Petrons Werk aus mehreren Wurzeln gespeist, und die Frage nach der literarischen Gesamtform lässt sich für uns nicht im Sinne eines Entweder-Oder entscheiden'.
[4] I do not include the Menippean diatribe here, since it is convenient to consider it with Roman satire later.

triumphs with divine aid over a series of bizarre obstacles set up by malevolent fortune.[1] Pirates carry them off, soldiers attack them, bystanders honourable or lustful seek to seduce one or other of them. But the gods eventually reward their piety and loyalty to each other by bringing them together into perennial bliss. The notorious difficulty of dating the surviving romances underlines the fact that they are deliberately distanced from the immediate and real world.[2] Conventionally pious and unabashedly sentimental, such fiction (if we may infer the nature of earlier lost novels from the later)[3] must have afforded cynics like Petronius much amusement.

The theory that the *Satyricon* is a sustained skit on the Greek romance,[4] with the homosexual relationship between Encolpius and Giton replacing the chaste amour between boy and girl, is at present out of favour. It should however be noted that the love-romance is the sole type of extended episodic fiction in Greek for which any evidence exists before Petronius; there is no other Greek genre which can be proposed with confidence as having inspired the developed structure of the *Satyricon* and the *Metamorphoses*. It is instructive to observe how, in the later history of the picaresque in sixteenth-century Spain and of the comic romance in seventeenth-century France (and again in the case of Fielding in eighteenth-century England), the identical pattern of reaction against idealised romance is observable. It is important, however, to argue this

[1] The appearance of Perry's *The Ancient Romances* makes a detailed account here superfluous. While the summary of the stereotyped plot given here is justified in terms of the extant romances, Perry's comment on the variations (122 ff.) should be noted.

[2] A summary of tentative dating is offered by O. Weinreich (see p. 176 n. 1) and Perry, 350.

[3] The three papyrus fragments of the Ninus romance (usually dated to the first century B.C.) certainly suggest close similarities to the 'presophistic' novel; see Perry, ch. 4.

[4] Proposed by Heinze, *H* (1889), 494 ff., and supported by Reitzenstein, *Hellenistische Wundererzählungen*, 30, and Kroll, *Studien zum Verständnis der röm. Lit.* 224. Amongst recent scholars, Highet, *The Anatomy of Satire*, 114 f., remains open to the theory.

thesis for Petronius' novel on its own merits. The homosexual liaison, and the tensions it creates, are the unifying strand of the *Satyricon*, and there are certainly incidental motifs which indicate striking connexions with the love-romance.[1]

If Petronius' attitude towards the Greek ideal fiction inspires him to derisive burlesque, the influence which the Greek novels exercise on Apuleius is different but equally marked. The *Metamorphoses* takes its theme from a comic romance, but Apuleius grafts on to it a wholly original climax inspired by similar denouements in the love-romances. Moreover, much of the subsidiary characterisation in individual episodes bears a close resemblance to that of heroines in the Greek ideal stories.

A second type of influential Greek fiction is the comic travelogue, which we see perfected by Lucian in the second century A.D. This genre is inspired by weird and wonderful stories of poets, historians and travellers from the *Odyssey* to Strabo. The prevalence of such travellers' tales in the Hellenistic age after Alexander's expedition led to the development of the fictitious travelogue as 'the underside of geography'.[2] It has been suggested that the *Satyricon* is deliberately composed within this tradition as a burlesque *periplous*, but with an ironical twist. Instead of the usual setting of physical hazards—a fantastic journey along coasts unknown, where the narrator encounters monstrous beasts and bestial humans—the characters of Petronius travel along a coastline only too well known, where the Greek cities of southern Gaul and Italy offer the more pleasurable dangers of a decaying civilisation.[3] It is the influence of the autobiographical travelogue, it is suggested,

---

[1] Below, ch. 4.

[2] Tarn's picturesque phrase; his account of travel tales, factual and fictitious, should be consulted in *Hellenistic Civilisation*, ch. 8.

[3] Reitzenstein, *Hellenistische Wundererzählungen*, 30 f.: 'Es war ein glücklicher Gedanke für die Wunderbare Fahrt an unbekannten Küsten und die Abenteuer mit Fabelvölkern und Märchenwesen eine Reise längs der allbekannten Küste Galliens und Italiens einzusetzen, und jede neue Stadt zur typischen Vertreterin eines neuen Lasters zu machen.'

which encouraged Petronius to write his picaresque novel in the first person.[1]

Whilst this suggestion should not be dismissed out of hand, it is worth noting that the extant episodes of the *Satyricon* are enacted in two cities only, with an interlude on board ship between them. More important, the central theme of the affair between Encolpius and Giton reduces the importance of the 'sights and wonders', the description of which is the main end of the travel-narrative. Finally, the interpretation of the novel as Greek travel-story lays too much emphasis on the *Greekness* of the novel, whereas in fact the unholy Greek duo are confronted by a parade of unsavoury Roman *mores* personified in character-types familiar from both earlier literature and life. If we are to describe the *Satyricon* as a travel-story, the label must be interpreted to mean a journey through the world of Roman satire. The influence of the fictitious travel-story, then, may be present but not conspicuously present in the *Satyricon*, and its importance for Petronius should not be exaggerated. Nor did Apuleius draw much inspiration directly from the travelogue in his account of Lucius' journey from Hypata to Corinth, for the travels of his hero up to the final stage of the story are taken over from the comic romance which was the model for the *Metamorphoses*.

The comic romance is the third Greek formative genre to be considered. It is obvious that there are close affinities here with the comic travel-story. Any reconstruction of the development of the comic romance before Lucian is speculative. The problems centre on the precise nature of such collections as Aristides' *Milesiaka*; these 'Milesian Tales' presumably take their origin from the custom of story-telling as a social accomplishment in Hellenistic society. Theophrastus and Athenaeus reveal how private and club dinners exploited this type of oral entertainment.[2] There may possibly have been edifying stories

[1] See P. Veyne, *REL* (1964), 301 ff.
[2] See, for example, Theophrastus *Char.* 27.2; Athenaeus 614D, etc. I follow S. Trenkner, *The Greek Novella* (Cambridge 1958), ch. 7, in my

of true love and chaste wives, and innocent accounts of adventure, but the dominant type of anecdote reflected the seamier sexual proclivities of humankind, reinforced by spooky accounts of sorcery and witchcraft. Aristides of Miletus incorporated the spicier of these into a literary framework probably in the second century B.C., and the Roman historian Sisenna translated the collection into Latin in the first century B.C. The prevalence of eroticism in the book is certainly indicated by Plutarch in his account of the reactions of the Parthians to this bedside reading of Roman officers.[1] Aristides was the most celebrated editor of such collections, but Martial indicates that there were *Sybaritici libelli*, presumably of a similar type.[2]

The character of the individual anecdotes incorporated into their collections by Aristides and his Roman translator can be gauged only from the developed form of the Milesian tales inserted in the *Satyricon* and in the *Metamorphoses*. Those with a sexual theme have invariably ironical and indeed cynical undertones; their message is that 'no man's honesty and no woman's virtue are unassailable'.[3] The most celebrated is the story of the Widow of Ephesus, which Petronius' character Eumolpus claims as an event of which he had personal knowledge.[4] The significant feature of the story is that it deliberately undercuts the conventional praise of chastity and matrimonial *fides* enshrined in both historiography and the love-romance.

interpretation of the development of the *novella*. The popularity of such story-telling can be equally well documented in early imperial Rome. See Suet. *Aug.* 78; Pliny *Ep.* 2.20: Reitzenstein, *Das Märchen*, 32 f.

[1] Plut. *Crass.* 32. The origins of the *Milesiaka* can be further investigated by consulting Lucas, *Philol.* (1907), 16 ff.: the critical refutation of Lucas in Reitzenstein, *Das Märchen*, 49 ff.; von Fleschenburg, *Die griechische Novelle* (Halle 1913); Perry, *TAPA* (1926), 254 ff., and now *The Ancient Romances*, 94; E. H. Haight, *Essays on Ancient Fiction* (N.Y. 1936), 8.   [2] Mart. 12.95.2.

[3] The happy phrase is F. F. Abbott's, in *CP* (1911), 265.

[4] *Sat.* 111 f.: 'rem sua memoria factam'. But the story is found also in Phaedrus Appendix *Fab.* 15 Perry, and must have been a favourite in the Greek world. The claim of personal knowledge is in fact one of the conventions of the Tale; the speaker protests the truth of the story. See below, p. 14 n. 3.

This story of the grieving widow, who locks herself in her husband's vault for five days without food, is characteristically introduced by stress on her chaste loyalty to her husband in his life and after his death. Her chastity is so renowned that the local women flock to lay eyes on her;[1] and her loyalty to her husband makes her the talk of the town. She is the counterpart of the heroines so beloved of romantic historiography and of romantic fiction, a latter-day Lucretia, *singularis exempli femina*. A soldier guarding some crucified thieves enters the vault at the sound of her sobbing; out of pure goodness of heart he offers her conventional comfort[2] and food which she eventually accepts.

At this point the tone changes, and cynicism makes its entry introduced by specious generalisation. 'No one refuses to lend an ear when food or life is forced on him... You all know the temptation that usually comes over people after a good meal.' The maid plays Anna to the widow's Dido when the soldier begins to make advances.

> placitone etiam pugnabis amore?
> nec venit in mentem quorum consederis arvis?[3]

The widow yields. They close the doors—now the irony is undisguised. 'Anyone visiting the tomb would have thought that this most chaste of wives (*pudicissimam uxorem*) had died over her husband's corpse.' But the appalling and unexpected climax is still to come. During the dalliance, one of the corpses under the soldier's charge is spirited away, and the paramour prepares his own death to anticipate execution for dereliction of duty. But the widow, 'matching her chastity with pity', offers him her husband's body to attach to the vacant cross so that his delinquency may escape detection.

---

[1] So in the romances of Chariton and Xenophon, the heroine is the cynosure of all eyes, and people travel miles to gaze on her.

[2] 'Ne perseveraret in dolore supervacuo, ac nihil profuturo gemitu pectus diduceret; omnium esse eundem exitum et idem domicilium...'

[3] Bücheler, followed by K. Müller, excises the second line of the quotation from the text. But in the context of the crucifixion-field the line is so apt that if Petronius did not quote it one feels he ought to have done so.

This ghoulish story, later retold in many literatures,[1] has clearly been lent its artistic structure[2] and its Virgilian evocation by Petronius himself. But the essence of the story, the cynical affirmation that no *pudicitia* is unassailable, suggests that this type of tale takes its impetus in reaction from those stories of faithful love which are the staple of both romantic historiography and Greek romantic fiction.[3]

Apuleius' group of stories recording the infidelity of wives is likewise an ironical demonstration of the comfortless realities behind the façade of *pudicitia*. The tale of Barbarus, Arete ('Virtue') his wife, Myrmex ('Busy bee') the slave, and Philesitherus ('Lover of the chase') the gallant, is the best of these cuckold-stories. Barbarus departs on a journey, leaving the *pudicitia* of his wife in the charge of his slave, whose life depends on his stewardship. The story begins in the usual Milesian fashion; Myrmex is 'fidelitate praecipua cognitus' and Arete 'famosa castitate'. Philesitherus the gallant takes up the challenge. He relies on the frailty of human loyalty and on the all-conquering progress of money to subvert the slave's integrity; Myrmex is thus the battle-ground of loyalty and cupidity, greed and fear of torture. *Pestilens avaritia* prevails; Arete willingly 'hires out her *pudicitia* for the accursed metal'.

[1] See the literature cited in Sedgwick's edition of the *Cena Trimalch.* Appendix B: M. E. Grisebach, *Die Wanderung der treulosen Wittwe durch die Weltliteratur*[2] (Berlin 1889): P. Ure, 'The Widow of Ephesus: Some reflections on an international comic theme', *Durham Univ. Journ.* (Dec. 1956), 1 ff.

[2] The story has a structure similar to that of the episode in the Roman historians. The first sentence ('matrona quaedam Ephesi...') sets the stage with a description of the central character and the locale; the last sentence rounds off the episode. Compare Sallust *B.J.* 12, and many Livian scenes, on which see my *Livy*[3] (Cambridge 1967), 178 ff.

[3] Another variation of the ironical sexual story in Petronius is Eumolpus' experience with the *ephebus* at Pergamum (*Sat.* 85 ff.). Notice here that the irony is directed against the narrator. After Eumolpus overcomes the boy's scruples and the threat to wake his father ('aut dormi aut ego iam patri dicam'), the boy becomes so importunate that the exhausted Eumolpus repulses him with the same formula, 'aut dormi aut ego iam patri dicam'.

Philesitherus and Arete are just 'serving their first campaign in the service of Venus' when Barbarus unexpectedly returns. The gallant, an earlier-day Cinderella, flees without his sandals. When they are found, Myrmex is led in chains to the magistrates. But Philesitherus resourcefully rushes out to the procession and accuses the slave of stealing his sandals at the baths. By this 'opportuna fallacia' Myrmex is pardoned. 'No man's honesty and no woman's virtue are unassailable' is certainly the keynote of this story.[1]

Tales of sorcery and magic were also popular, and both Petronius and Apuleius incorporate such stories; the striking feature here is that in spite of their different themes the techniques of narration show clear similarities in the two authors. In the *Cena Trimalchionis*, one of the guests, Niceros, tells how a companion was transformed into a werewolf; at the beginning of the *Metamorphoses* Aristomenes tells of the fate which befell his friend Socrates at the hands of a witch called Meroë.[2] The narrator of each story claims to have witnessed the magic—it is no joke.[3] The audience is in each case compounded of sceptics and believers. Both episodes commence in darkness, and end in daylight. And though the central narratives are different, the magical practice of urination is prominent in both.[4] The surviving witnesses Niceros and Aristomenes both emphasise how the experience left them bathed in sweat and prostrate.[5] Though it is possible that Apuleius has exploited

---

[1] 9.17 ff. The other stories are those of the tradesman's wife (9.5 ff.), the baker's wife (9.14 ff., 26 ff.), and the fuller's wife (9.23 ff.). In the first, the *uxorcula* is at first believed *continens*: the baker's wife is (ironically) *pudica uxor*: and the fuller's wife is 'servati pudoris ut videbatur femina'.

[2] *Sat.* 61.6 ff.; *Met.* 1.6 ff.

[3] 'Nolite me iocari putare.' '. . .me vera comperta memorare.'

[4] In Petronius the soldier *circumminxit vestimenta* (62.6); in Apuleius the witches *vesicam exonerant* (1.13.8). For urination as a magical practice, see R. Muth, *RE Suppl.* 11, 1292 ff., s.v. 'Urin'.

[5] *Sat.* 62.5: 'mihi anima in naso esse, stabam tamquam mortuus...'; 62.10: 'sudor mihi per bifurcum volabat, oculi mortui, vix umquam refectus sum'. *Met.* 1.13.1: 'sudore frigido miser perfluo...', 14.2: 'semimortuus'.

the detail of the Petronian story, it is more likely that this type of story has stock motifs which both authors incorporate.[1]

Such, then, is the Milesian Tale, a mannered story[2] of bizarre adventure or sexual encounter. It may be an episode which had merely reached the ear of the narrator, who recounts it in an objective manner, or an experience allegedly suffered by the narrator himself, who tells the story in a tone of deprecating self-mockery.[3] In short, the collections may have incorporated a wide variety of adventure-fiction, and were narrated with the variations of narrative-technique evolved by the practised profession of story-telling.

The examples of the developed Milesian anecdote which have been examined here do not form part of the sequence of connected adventures experienced by Encolpius or Lucius, but are self-contained stories told in the presence of the hero-narrator to while away a journey or to entertain a company. It is important for our preliminary enquiry to investigate whether Aristides provided a narrative-link for his stories by the creation of a picaresque hero whose successive adventures might have afforded a framework for the *Milesiaka* similar to that of the *Satyricon* or the *Metamorphoses*. If such a central thread could be demonstrated, it would be possible to place Petronius and Apuleius in the Milesian tradition *tout court*. But such evidence as exists hardly supports the theory of an extended and episodic comic romance composed by Aristides. The most important testimony is the preface to the *Erōtes* of Ps. Lucian, where Aristides is depicted as a listener to a series of wanton stories.[4] The obvious inference is that Aristides recounted in the first person anecdotes allegedly related to him by others;

---

[1] For further detail, Ciaffi, *Petronio in Apuleio* (Turin 1960), 9 ff.

[2] Cf. E. Auerbach, *Mimesis* (N.Y. 1957), 26: the Milesian Tale is 'so crammed with magic, adventure, and mythology, so overburdened with erotic detail that it cannot possibly be considered an imitation of everyday life...'.

[3] Eumolpus' story (p. 13 n. 3 above) is a good example.

[4] *Erōtes* 1: πάνυ δή με ὑπὸ τὸν ὄρθρον ἡ τῶν ἀκολάστων σου διηγη-μάτων αἰμύλη καὶ γλυκεῖα πειθὼ κατεύφραγκεν, ὥστε ὀλίγου δεῖν Ἀριστείδης ἐνόμιζον εἶναι τοῖς Μιλησιακοῖς λόγοις ὑπερκηλούμενος.

the *Erōtes* may in fact be the best indication of how the *Milesiaka* were structured. The stories were doubtless all connected with Miletus, either in characters or in situations. But it is quite unnecessary to suggest that they were published under the pretext of 'scientific sociology, a documentary report...on the sexual behaviour of the Milesians'.[1] Much more probably they were, like the works of Lucian, designedly the literature of relaxation, a collection of ironically amusing stories told avowedly for their own sake.

Some verses of Ovid,

> iunxit Aristides Milesia crimina secum,
> pulsus Aristides nec tamen urbe sua est,[2]

have been cited to support the suggestion that the *Milesiaka* had a continuous narrative describing the adventures of the I-narrator, but the argument places too much weight on the phrase 'iunxit...secum'.[3] The thesis has gained support partly through a misunderstanding of Ovid's description of Sisenna's translation. The lines

> vertit Aristiden Sisenna, nec obfuit illi
> historiae turpis inseruisse iocos

do not mean that Sisenna wrote a story ('historia') interspersed with Milesian tales ('iocos') but that he turned from his serious occupation of writing history to recount the amusing stories of Aristides as relaxation,[4] just as Varro of Atax turned to light verses from epic with the same motive.[5]

Our direct knowledge of the works of Aristides and of Sisenna is restricted to one and ten fragments respectively, on

[1] Perry, 95: Kinsey here seems unnecessarily to raise his ugly head.
[2] *Tr.* 2.413 f.
[3] For the thesis, see Lucas's article (p. 11 n. 1 above): Cataudella, *La novella greca*, 152 ff.; and V. Ciaffi, *Petronio in Apuleio*. For the rebuttal, see the explanation of Reitzenstein, *Das Märchen*, 63: 'aller crimina seiner Heimat Milet stellte Aristides zusammen, und doch haben die Milesier ihn nicht verbannt.'
[4] *Tr.* 2.443 f. Wheeler's Loeb translation fails to pick up this nuance.
[5] Cf. Prop. 2.34.85: 'haec quoque perfecto ludebat Iasone Varro...'. Pliny, *Ep.* 8.21.2 affords another striking parallel.

the basis of which the bold theory has been advanced that these writers had indeed told a single extended story, and none other than that taken up in *Lucius or the Ass* and Apuleius' *Metamorphoses*. But though there are many stylistic borrowings from Sisenna in Apuleius, the theory that they handle the same fictional theme is precarious;[1] much more probably Aristides' book was a collection of lubricious anecdotes without a fictional framework, and Sisenna faithfully translated it into Latin.

By the second century A.D. a form of short comic story had developed in Greek, as *Lucius or the Ass* demonstrates. Though one should not be over-dogmatic about its precise relation to such collections as the *Milesiaka*, so witty and sophisticated an art-form could hardly have been perfected without experimentation, and one may reasonably assume a connexion with the Milesian tradition—especially as Apuleius boasts of writing 'Milesio sermone'. But the Greeks cannot be shown to have advanced beyond the short story, which was presumably developed from individual anecdotes in such collections as those of Aristides.[2]

Some scholars have indeed assumed that a continuous narrative-form had evolved before Petronius in Greek comic fiction. They regard the *Satyricon* as the adaptation of a lost romance perhaps called *Priapeia*.[3] It cannot be emphasised too

---

[1] The fragment of Aristides concerns the word δερμηστής, the worm that devours skin (Soph. fr. 449 Pearson; Harpocr. p. 88 Dindorf: μήποτε μᾶλλον ἂν εἴη ὅστις τὰ δέρματα ἐσθίει δερμηστής, ὡς ὑποσημαίνεται καὶ ἐν ἕκτῃ Μιλησιακῶν Ἀριστείδου. The suggestion that this is connected with Apul. *Met.* 6.32.1: 'et illa [*sc.* Charite sustinebit] morsus ferarum, cum vermes membra laniabunt' (cf. *Onos* 25) is clearly rash. Likewise the citation of Sisenna fr. 10 Bücheler, 'penitus utero suo recepit' side by side with *Met.* 10.22.3, 'totum me prorsus, sed totum recepit', even when supported by several stylistic parallels (see Reitzenstein, *Das Märchen*, 55 ff.), is inconclusive.

[2] Cf. K. Bürger, *H* (1892), 345 ff.

[3] A. Collignon, *Etude sur Pétrone* (Paris 1892), 323: 'Il n'y aurait nulle invraisemblance à supposer qu'un ou plusieurs romans érotiques, d'une couleur assez réaliste, satiriques au sens le plus large du mot sans aucune satire personnelle, se soient produits en Grèce aux environs du premier siècle de l'ère chrétienne. L'un d'eux, une Priapeia, aventures d'une

strongly, however, that many of the episodes of the *Satyricon* are emphatically Roman. If Petronius' central theme of a homosexual liaison, in which the hero and the slave are hounded by an angry Priapus, was inspired by a Greek predecessor, it could have been a composition no longer than *Lucius or the Ass*, transformed by Petronius into a wholly original story by a reconstruction far more radical than that of Apuleius.

A patient comparison of the structure and content of the *Satyricon* with these three formative kinds of Greek fiction inevitably supports the thesis that the influence of the love-romance is more important than is generally conceded. In the absence of any evidence of a Greek *Priapeia*, the only indubitable debt to the Milesian tradition is visible in the apposite and ironical anecdotes incorporated into the narrative of adventure. One may acknowledge also that Petronius exploits the tradition of the traveller's tale, developing it in a new and comic direction. But neither of these genres can be shown to have a framework of fiction remotely like that of Petronius, whereas the prior existence of the love-romance, with its similarly episodic structure, cannot be gainsaid—nor can the comic reorientation in Petronius of its characteristic themes and treatment.

Apuleius' *Metamorphoses*, as we have seen, has a much clearer genealogy. He has expanded a short Greek comic romance, itself doubtless 'Milesian' in origin, into an extended story of eleven books by the insertion of new episodes and appropriate anecdotes. This more ambitious structure, so familiar to us in the history of the picaresque from the sixteenth century onward, may well have been inspired by the *Satyricon*; to this suggestion we must presently return.

These connexions with divergent strands of Greek fiction do not exhaust the formative genres. Petronius' novel, unlike

victime de Priape, aurait fourni à Pétrone l'idée et quelques épisodes de son roman.' So also Perry, *CP* (1925), 39 ff., but he has changed his mind since (*The Ancient Romances*, 188).

Apuleius', must be visualised also within a Roman literary tradition. His decision to write in the form of Menippean satire, a genre established at Rome by the learned Varro of Reate, is a clear pointer to the audience envisaged, at once highly literate and Roman. It must be acknowledged that some themes of Varro's satires derive from the writings of Menippus of Gadara, the third-century Cynic preacher with whom Varro proclaims his fellow-feeling. Moreover, the general philosophical attitudes, which reflect the ethos of Cynicism, and the highly literary presentation likewise attest the influence of the Greek diatribe.[1] But Varro has so thoroughly adapted his themes to the Roman scene that his writings are essentially a 'prosimetric' contribution to the Roman satirical tradition inaugurated by Ennius and Lucilius.[2]

Varro's main preoccupation is with the decline in Roman morality. Repeatedly he contrasts the standards of behaviour prevailing in his day[3] with the old Roman *mores* of public and private life.[4] These attacks on the prevailing immorality of Roman society are underpinned by a severely practical philosophy which stresses the central importance of reason and virtue, and which more emphatically condemns avarice, prodi-

---

[1] See A. Oltramare, *Les origines de la diatribe romaine* (Lausanne 1926).

[2] Varro christened his satires after Menippus 'a societate ingenii' (Probus on Virg. *Ecl.* 6.31), but the differences in race, status, and profession between the two men makes the label less relevant to Varro's writings. I have found the summary discussion of U. Knoche, *Die röm. Satire²* (Göttingen 1957), 34 ff., a useful guide; Knoche owes much to A. Oltramare, *Les origines de la diatribe romaine* 97 ff. Cf. A. Marzullo, *Le satire menippee di M. Terenzio Varrone* (1958); and J. P. Cèbe, *La caricature*, 233 ff., 247 ff. There is a useful discussion of Menippus in J. W. Duff, *Roman Satire* (Cambridge 1937), 33 ff.; this book has also a section on Varro, Seneca, Petronius (ch. 5).

[3] The date of composition was about 80–67 B.C. (cf. Cichorius, *Röm. Stud.* 207 ff.).

[4] Cf. fr. 497 Bücheler: 'ubi tum comitia habebant ibi nunc fit mercatus'. 181: 'ergo tum sacra religio castaeque fuerunt res omnes'. So also 190, comparing the ancient matron and the modern hussy: 'sed simul manibus trahere lanam, nec non simul oculis observare ollam...'

gality and carousing.[1] Conspicuous in the attacks on *luxuria* are blistering comments on table-refinements, fondness for exotic dishes, ostentatious finery, and elaborately equipped houses.[2]

In other satires Varro airs his literary views. This literary theorising so characteristic of Roman satire is relevant to the role of the moralising preacher because good literature is the finest *magistra vitae*, as Horace observes.[3] So Varro adjudicates on the merits of the comic poets, and discusses general questions of literature and music.[4]

Several satires take the form of philosophical dialogues, in which a Cynic's attitude towards the professional philosophers is aired. The *Logomachia*, for example, satirically represents a dialogue between Stoics and Epicureans on the *summum bonum*. The *Skiamachia* and the *Armorum iudicium* may have had similar themes.[5] There are harsh attacks on Stoic self-sufficiency, on the Stoic doctrine of the philosopher-king ('Solus rex, solus rhetor, solus formonsus, fortis, aecus, vel ad aedilicium purus putus; ad hunc χαρακτῆρα Κλεάνθους conveniet. cave attigeris hominem'), on the theology of Stoics and others which seduces men from a life of practical virtue.[6]

These Varronian discussions on morality, literature and philosophy have many echoes in the *Satyricon*, and even more striking are the parallels between scenes in Petronius' novel

---

[1] Fr. 71: 'unam virtutem propriam mortalibus fecit'; 137: 'tu non insanis quom tibi vino corpus corrumpis mero?' Cf. 126, 252, etc.

[2] Cf. fr. 63, 313, 447, 524, etc.

[3] *Ep.* 1.2. The *sententia* inscribed on the old Edinburgh University building expresses the thesis succinctly: διπλοῦν ὁρῶσιν οἱ μαθόντες γράμματα.

[4] Fr. 385: 'in argumentis Caecilius poscit palmam, in ethesin Terentius, in sermonibus Plautus...'. Compare the theorising on epic at *Sat.* 118 in Petronius. For the general discussion, see fr. 348; the parallel with Petronius 83 ff. is striking.

[5] See fr. 43, 242; Porphyr. ad Hor. *Sat.* 2.4.1. (On which see K. Mras, *NJA* (1914), 400.)

[6] Fr. 583 (Sen. *Apocol.* 8): 'Stoicus deus—quomodo potest rotundus esse...sine capite sine praeputio?' (the vulgarity is characteristic of Menippean satire). Also fr. 122: 'nemo aegrotus quicquam somniat tam infandum quod non aliquis dicat philosophus'. See in general Cèbe, 252.

and the situations in the satires of Varro, which are encased in a variety of artistic frames. The theme of the conversational journey is found in both Menippean and Lucilian satire.[1] One Varronian satire is set in a school, like the first extant scene in Petronius;[2] another is a funeral feast, recalling the maudlin finale of the *Cena Trimalchionis*, where the host pronounces his own panegyric.[3]

In general, it should be noted that Varro took over from Menippus the exploitation of the satirical form for the purpose of fantastic fiction, as in the Rip van Winkle theme of the *Sexagesis*. Here is the genesis of the satirical short story in Latin, preparing the way for the *Apocolocyntosis* of Seneca, itself reminiscent of themes handled by Menippus. In this strand of the Menippean satire there exists in Latin before Petronius a form of satirical fiction.

Why did Varro diverge from the form of Lucilian satire and introduce the 'prosimetric' combination of prose and verse? He may have felt that prose as the staple medium was more suitable for realistic description and earthy moralising. But chiefly he was impressed with the enhanced possibilities for techniques of literary allusion, for a wider and more effective deployment of parody and burlesque. One sees the potential fully developed in the *Apocolocyntosis*, where the text is almost a mosaic of comic allusion, quotation and parody.[4] Moreover, in a predominantly prose form verses can be effectively introduced for a variety of structural and characterising purposes.

By his use of the 'prosimetric' form, Petronius wished his readers to associate him with Varronian satire. The main reason for this seems obvious. He sought to convey to them that his work was more than a mere Greek entertainment in

[1] See Varro, fr. 276; and compare Horace, *Sat.* 1.5 and its predecessor in Lucilius (fr. 94 ff. Warmington), on which see now Rudd, *The Satires of Horace*, ch. 3.

[2] Fr. 144: 'et ceteri scholastici saturis auribus scholica dape atque ebriis sophistice aperantologia consurgimus ieiunis oculis.' This reads like a barbed criticism of the teaching of rhetoric in the early first century B.C.; on which see M. L. Clarke, *Rhetoric at Rome* (London 1953), 11 ff.

[3] Below, ch. 5; the Varronian passage, fr. 516.   [4] Below, pp. 34 ff.

translation, but was also to be visualised as a satirical treatment of the world he describes. The ambivalent title *Satyricon* makes the same point,[1] proclaiming the work to be Roman as well as Greek; satirical vignettes directed against types already assailed by the Roman satirists will be incorporated into the adventures of the Greek hero. This treatment does not invest the novel with an integral purpose; the satirical observation is only intermittent, but the studied characterisation of Agamemnon, Trimalchio, Eumolpus, Lichas and Tryphaena reflects its important if subsidiary role. The Roman γελωτοποιός of literary bent harnesses the themes of the great satirists to present a complex entertainment—at once Greek and Roman, at once low and literary.

Yet Petronius' basic attitudes informing his satirical approach are wholly different from Varro's; he is much more a cynic in the modern sense than a Cynic preaching reasonable virtue. The result is that the employment of the Varronian form adds a fresh dimension of ironical comedy. The main characters of Petronius reflect the presuppositions of popular Epicureanism; as interpreters of the corrupt facets of Roman society which they encounter, they are scarcely appropriate mouthpieces for stern Varronian moralising. They are precisely the anarchistic outsiders condemned by Varro in his rhetorical questions:

> postremo quaero parebis legibus an non?
> anne exlex solus vives?[2]

Encolpius' *cri de cœur* at Croton emphasises this role—'quam male est extra legem viventibus'.[3] He and his associates are the antonym of the Varronian ideal of rational virtue, and the comic possibilities inherent in Varronian moralising uttered by Epicurean knockabouts on exotic table-fare or the great god money are considerable. The author is so far from being sincere in such sentiments that there are clear hints of self-mockery.[4]

---

[1] Below, p. 72.

[2] Varro, fr. 507. [3] *Sat.* 125.4.

[4] So in the first scene there are the verses which recommend to the student a life of austerity, avoiding the arrogance of palaces and also drinking-

The actual context of the moralising often makes it absurdly inappropriate.

The adoption of the Varronian form for his experiment in fiction also allowed easier entry to Petronius' literary discussions. Such topics were familiar to his sophisticated readers in Roman satire, and for them he made his fiction not only a narrative sequence of low adventures, but also a vehicle for judgments of forms of literature and art. There is almost a regular alternation between low episodes and discussions appropriate to the literary *salon*. Discursive dialogue takes over from scenes of bawdy humour, and in turn retires before them. Though the sophistic Greek romances of writers like Achilles Tatius likewise suspend the action with leisured reflexions,[1] nowhere is the contrast between racy narrative and cultural discussion so pronounced as in Petronius. In the course of these literary discussions conducted by his characters, Petronius introduced his longer poetic compositions, the *Halosis Troiae* and the *De Bello Civili*; the purpose of these poems, whose insertion represents an extension of the Menippean convention, will be examined in the next chapter.

Petronius, then, exploited the 'prosimetric' form chiefly to signal a formal connexion with Roman satire, and perhaps also to sustain in irony a Varronian pose. By his adoption of it he was able also to achieve special effects by introducing verse-sequences into the prose-narrative. These verses have often the structural function of rounding off an episode with a pithy summary of the lesson it teaches or a definition of the moral issue which it raises.[2] This functional purpose is explained in a different context by Seneca—'ipsa quae praecipiuntur per se

---

bouts and stage-shows. Agamemnon certainly does not practise what he preaches here, and Petronius himself, the *arbiter elegantiae*, may be also perpetrating irony at his own expense. See below, p. 86.

[1] Achilles Tatius comes especially to mind, e.g. 2.8, a treatise on the mouth as the fairest part of the body when Clitophon seeks the pretext for a kiss; 4.2: a learned *ekphrasis* on the hippopotamus; at 2.36 ff., a debate on whether love with boys is better than love with girls. On the topic generally, see Perry, *The Ancient Romances*, 106.

[2] So 80.9 on the hollowness of friendship, 137, etc.

multnm habent ponderis utique si aut carmini intexta sunt aut prosa oratione in sententiam coartata.'[1] The change from prose to verses may also signal an elevation in tone, for example in the expression of intense personal emotion, or again in a lyrical description of a landscape. Elsewhere the verses have a sophisticatedly comic purpose. They are reminiscences of earlier poets, or they parody genres, following the convention which obtains in both Greek fiction and Menippean satire, and which gives the Roman novel its characteristically bookish humour.[2]

The *Satyricon*, then, is set within the traditions of both Greek fiction and Roman satire. But one further influence is so pervasive and so frequently invoked that it must have been continually in the author's mind. This is the drama of the low stage; Petronius consistently compares the action of his story to scenes from the mime.[3] Perhaps the Greek comic romance before him had exploited the mime for particular episodes;[4] and likewise there are many similarities between Varronian satire and the low stage.[5] In Petronius almost every episode is at some point compared to a low comic drama. John of Salisbury puts it succinctly: 'Pretty well all the world, in the opinion of our Arbiter, seems to be performing a mime.'[6]

So when Quartilla and her maids visit Encolpius, and hoodwink the hero with a pretence of grief, 'omnia mimico risu exsonuerant'.[7] The slaves-at-table of Trimalchio, who sing as they work, are likened to a 'pantomimi chorus'; the charade in which a slave produces peahen's eggs from under a wooden hen

---

[1] *Ep.* 94.27.   [2] Below, ch. 3.

[3] For a useful discussion, see Rosenblüth, ch. 2. Inevitably, the influence of the mime has been on occasion exaggerated, being urged as the main formative genre; see e.g., F. F. Abbott, *Common People of Ancient Rome*, 143 f.

[4] The mime, like the Milesian Tale, drew upon stock literary motifs; there is a conveniently accessible account in W. Beare, *The Roman Stage*, ch. 18.

[5] A point well developed by Knoche, 43.

[6] *Policraticus* 3.8: 'fere totus mundus ex Arbitri nostri sententia mimmu videtur implere.'   [7] *Sat.* 19.1.

is called a *scaena*; moreover, Trimalchio takes off a Syrian performer, and murders the songs of Menecrates.[1] Encolpius' verses, uttered when Giton deserts him, express the thesis that all men are hypocrites and their lives a stage part:

> grex agit in scaena mimum; pater ille vocatur,
> filius hic, nomen divitis ille tenet...[2]

Later, when Encolpius is again threatened with the loss of Giton, and announces his intention of hanging himself, Giton decides to cut his throat. But the razor is blunt, and the attempt is called *mimica mors*, since this was the way violent death was simulated in the mime.[3] So too at Croton the characters decide to play stage-parts to obtain a favourable reception. 'Quid ergo' asks Eumolpus 'cessamus mimum componere? facite ergo me dominum.' And the narrator adds: 'et ne quid scaenae deesset...'.[4]

This deliberate alignment of Petronius' novel with the presentation of the mime and the low stage sheds an interesting light on the artistic level of his adventure-story. The Romans regarded the mime as entertainment, with no claim to serious dramatic status. Yet it was hugely popular at Rome, and there are many indications of its repercussions on the Neronian court and the life of the city.[5] The heterogeneous themes offer a striking parallel to the diversity of action in the Petronian novel, for the mime too could range from scenes of stupefying obscenity and disgusting sadism to the most decorous discussions containing mannered apothegms about the human con-

[1] 31.7; 33.5; 35.6; 73.3. Menecrates was a *citharoedus* who was a great favourite of Nero (Suet. *Nero* 30).

[2] 80.9.

[3] 94.15.

[4] 117.4, 10. Note also that the efforts at concealment on board ship are designated 'mimicae artes' (106.1). These passages are assembled by Collignon, 275 ff.

[5] Tacitus records how Nero encouraged 'impunitate et praemiis' brawling on the stage and fighting between rival supporters. But eventually he had to banish actors from Rome and patrol the theatre with soldiers in A.D. 56 (*Ann.* 13.25.4; cf. 14.21.7).

dition.[1] Sexual scenes were presented with the utmost licence, and on one occasion at least the realistic depiction of punishment extended to the actual crucifixion of a slave on the stage.[2] Some of these sexual and sadistic scenes are strikingly reflected in Petronius, and to a lesser extent in Apuleius.

The controlling theme of the *Satyricon* is the anger of Priapus, a character prominent on the mimic stage.[3] Again, the famous Oxyrhynchus mime[4] presents the theme of a mistress in love with her slave, whom she whips when he refuses her advances; the parallel with Tryphaena and Giton is the more arresting because the heroine of the mime, like Tryphaena, is most scrupulous in propitiating the gods. The characterisation of Trimalchio as astrologer may owe something to the themes of the popular stage; several literary mimes are named after the signs of the zodiac.

But the most striking similarity between the mimic performances and the *Satyricon* lies in the number of central performers. In the mime there were regularly three actors;[5] it is noteworthy that throughout the extant sections of Petronius' novel there are three characters at the centre—at first Encolpius, Giton and Ascyltus, and later Eumolpus replacing Ascyltus. The structural purpose of this constant number is to maintain as connecting motif the homosexual love of Encolpius and Giton under the stresses of the attempted seductions by Ascyltus and by Eumolpus. The homosexual theme was a favourite not only in the mime but also in the *fabula togata*; Quintilian

---

[1] The apothegms of Publilius Syrus need no exemplification here. In quoting some, Seneca, *Ep.* 108.8, comments: 'non vides quemadmodum theatra consonent quotiens aliqua dicta sunt quae publice agnoscimus et consensu vera esse testamur?' See Beare, 158.

[2] In the *Laureolus*; see J. Carcopino, *Daily Life in Ancient Rome* (London 1941), 231.

[3] Augustine, *C.D.* 6.75: 'numquid Priapo mimi, non etiam sacerdotes enormia pudenda fecerunt? an aliter stat adorandus in locis sanctis quam procedit ridendus in theatris?'

[4] Text conveniently in Beare's *Roman Stage*[3], 314 ff.; see earlier S. Sudhaus, *H* (1906), 247 ff.

[5] H. Reich, *Der Mimus* (Berlin 1903), 553 ff., 565.

is censorious about the plots of the second-century dramatist Afranius—'utinam non inquinasset argumenta puerorum foedis amoribus, mores suos fassus'.[1]

Reminiscent of the mime is the boisterous, slapstick element in so many Petronian scenes, as in the fracas between Eumolpus and the landlord of Encolpius' lodgings, when Eumolpus is struck by an earthenware jar, and a dog is set on him.[2] Characteristic too is the way in which episodes end on a sudden note of comic violence, as in the *Cena Trimalchionis* when the city-guards break into the villa with axes because they believe that fire has broken out. We are reminded of Cicero's distinction between the endings of a play and of a mime *cum clausula non invenitur*; in the mime, 'Someone makes good his escape, and at once the castanets sound and the curtain is rung down.'[3] This is precisely the end of the *Cena*, when Encolpius and Giton succeed in making their escape from the smothering morbidity of Trimalchio's drunken death-wish. The shipwreck off Croton likewise re-enacts what Seneca calls a *mimicum naufragium*.[4]

Finally, there is a connexion between the mime and the *Satyricon* in the exploitation of colloquial language. The celebrated mime-writer Decimus Laberius, we are told, incorporated the manner of speech of the lower stratum of society— *ex sordidiore vulgi usu*[5]—into his performances, just as Petronius in the *Cena* allows the dinner-guests to reveal their rusticity out of their own mouths.

This striking series of similarities to the action of the mime clearly indicates Petronius' attitude to his creation. He wishes to present the whole of life as a series of risible, unexpected happenings, in which nothing is taken seriously and no man's motives are what they seem. Every gesture is rehearsed, every attitude a studied pose.

The influence of the mime on Apuleius' *Metamorphoses* is

---

[1] Quint. 10.1.100.   [2] 95.5 and 8.

[3] *Pro Caelio* 65.   [4] *De Ira* 2.2.5.

[5] Gellius 16.7. For a detailed comparison between the Petronian language and that of the mimes of Laberius and Herodas, see Rosenblüth, 40 f.

less pronounced. Certain of the *novella*-themes, however, may have been inspired by performances on the low stage. The story of the stepmother's fatal passion for her stepson in the tenth book is found in a mime of Laberius ('domina nostra privignum suum amat efflictim'). Amongst the titles of Laberius' literary mimes is *Fullo*; one wonders if it had the theme of the cuckolded laundryman as in one of the comic anecdotes of Apuleius. Some critics go beyond these thematic parallels to claim that the mime may also have exercised a stylistic influence, as for example in the parody of the epic style.[1]

A host of other literary genres have been suggested as precursors of the Roman novel.[2] Some of them must be acknowledged for their general influence on the genre. Above all, there is the constant evocation of Greek and Roman epic. The picaresque novel of Petronius has as its hero a wanderer who is constantly and comically portrayed in the situations of the great wanderers of epic, Odysseus and Aeneas.[3] Again, the tradition of declamation as it develops in the schools of rhetoric, with special types of speech recommended for particular occasions, has clearly a subsidiary influence as in the Greek love-romance. In Petronius, for example, there was a court-scene now lost in which Encolpius was on trial, and there is a parody of another trial on board Lichas' ship, with Eumolpus defending his two friends before the tribunal of the stern captain. And at other points in the novel there are other stereotyped kinds of oration.[4] So too Apuleius, a professional barrister, sets within his adventure-story a full-scale trial in which the speeches of

[1] The Hippolytus-theme, *Met.* 10.2 (pp. 171 f., below), and Laberius 11. The laundryman, *Met.* 9.23 ff.; Laberius' title, Beare[3], 155. For parody of epic style, and general connexions between Apuleius and the mime, see Rosenblüth, ch. 3; Reich, 591 ('der Eselmimus').

[2] See in general the useful book of Cahen, *Le Satiricon et ses origines* (Paris 1925).

[3] Below, ch. 3.

[4] For the earlier lawsuit, see the reference at *Sat.* 81.3. The speech of Eumolpus is at 107.

prosecutor and defendant follow the structural conventions of the *genus iudiciale*.[1]

These and other influences are, however, indirect or incidental. For the main lines, Petronius has attempted a synthesis of the Greek comic romance with scenes and characters from Roman satire. The plot deliberately burlesques the Greek love-romance, and the episodes are enlivened with motifs from the low stage. It has been suggested that this synthesis is a wholly happy one, and that this alone entitles Petronius to his niche as an innovator of genius.[2] Yet it is precisely this synthesis which makes the purpose of the novel so ambivalent. In many narrative episodes the satirical vision is on holiday, in others it returns to bring the action of the story to a complete halt, so that all sense of dramatic illusion is lost. Though it is probable that the discussions on Roman education, on the decline of art, on the right way to write poetry are intended as part of the entertainment—an exposé of the superficial and cliché-ridden utterances of many contemporaries—the level of entertainment is so markedly at odds with that of the low episodes that the reader has constantly to adjust his sights.

There is in fact only one episode in the *Satyricon* in which the Greek picaresque and the Roman traditional satire happily merge, and that is the *Cena Trimalchionis*. Even here, as we shall see, there is a conflict, in the sense that the satirical portrayal of the boorish host is continually undercut by the presentation of Trimalchio as an amiable buffoon. As in other episodes, the satirist is secondary to the entertainer. Yet in this scene, which has as its theme the gargantuan dinner so beloved of the Roman satirists and the table-talk so frequently the staple in Greek humorous writing, a new type of satirical realism emerges in fiction. For, as we shall see, Petronius reinforces the traditional lines of characterisation of the tasteless

---

[1] *Met.* 3.3–6. One speech has *exordium, narratio, probatio, conclusio* as Quintilian demands; see below, p. 59.

[2] Collignon, 49: 'L'œuvre de Pétrone est une habile et originale combinaison de deux genres, et à ce seul titre déjà doit être considérée comme une véritable creation.'

host with sharp visual observation of his own; and since this observation relates to a social phenomenon of his age, the range of satirical vision goes beyond the criticism of an individual absence of taste and breeding to an implicit indictment of the social and economic conditions which buttress such manners.[1]

For Apuleius the problem of the formative influences is simpler. He had before him a short comic romance in Greek, written with the satirical verve of a Lucian, which was doubtless a developed version of a Milesian Tale. We shall see how he methodically converted this short story into a picaresque romance by the insertion of additional episodes and anecdotes. Whereas Petronius' novel is uniformly comic and derisive, Apuleius incorporates stories of wider emotional range, eliciting from the reader not only laughter but also horror, wonder and edification, and concluding on a note of high seriousness. The comic *novelle* reflect the influence of the Milesian Tales, and to a less extent mimic themes. The character of Psyche in the central story, the romantic episodes built round Photis and Charite, and the religious climax have a close affinity with facets of the ideal love-romance.

It seems certain that Apuleius was inspired to attempt this conversion from Greek short story to Latin picaresque by the pioneering venture of Petronius; at any rate, no other romance of comparable length has survived, and the *Metamorphoses* contains occasional similarities to the *Satyricon* in situations and in language.[2] Inevitably the comparison has been pushed too far. The claim that whenever Apuleius diverges from the theme of *Lucius or the Ass* he is inspired by Petronius is a palpable exaggeration, and the suggestion that the two authors share a similar attitude to life is little short of ludicrous.[3] Perceptible echoes of the *Satyricon* are heard in

[1] Below, ch. 5.

[2] On Petronius in Apuleius, see V. Ciaffi, *Petronio in Apuleio*; Collignon, Appendix 3; Paratore, *Il Satyricon* 1.90 ff.; Marmorale, *La questione petroniana*, 247 ff.

[3] So Ciaffi, 4: 'di Petronio [Apuleio] ha fatto suo lo spirito, la concezione della vita...'.

Apuleius' stories of magic, especially in the tale of Aristomenes, but even here there may be a common debt to the Milesian Tales and to the mime;[1] the thesis that Apuleius systematically exploits the Petronian vocabulary is even harder to sustain.[2] Petronius' direct influence is in fact peripheral, and confined to the stories in which Apuleius handles similar themes. In one episode at least the African writer reacts against Petronius' cynicism; his idealised account of a widow's loyalty to her dead husband contrasts strongly with the *novella* of the Widow of Ephesus.[3]

Apuleius does, however, share with Petronius the initial assumption that his task is to present an entertainment of a sophisticated kind, for which the key words are *lepos* and *venustas*. The theme at first appears trivial, but the tone is teasingly and mockingly literary, as if to emphasise the divorce of the narratives from life, and to soften the crudities of sexual encounter and violence with the amusing evocation of august poetry, and with the stock techniques of oratorical and historical presentation. This literary presentation must now be analysed in detail.

[1] Possible echoes of Petronius include *Met.* 1.21, Lucius' query to the inn-keeper (cf. *Sat.* 7.1); the attempted suicide at *Met.* 1.16 (*Sat.* 94.8 ff.). For the patterning of the Thelyphron story, and alleged similarities to that of Niceros at Trimalchio's table, see Ciaffi, 53 ff., which does not convince me. Cf. also the braggart soldier, *Met.* 9.39 and *Sat.* 82, and the hidden sneezing, *Met.* 9.24.3 and *Sat.* 98.

[2] It is instructive to peruse Bernhard, *Der Stil des Apuleius*, 130 ff., to observe how few identical *Vulgarismen* appear in both authors. The citation of alleged echoes like 'versipellis', 'circulator', 'utres inflati' is otiose; such expressions belong to the common stock. There are occasional words like *cucurbita*, 'blockhead', which may be borrowings (*Sat.* 39.13, *Met.* 1.15.2).

[3] Below, p. 164.

3

THE LITERARY TEXTURE

He may display the wiles of Ulysses, the piety of Aeneas, the prowess of Achilles...and in short all those attributes that contribute to create the model hero, sometimes placing them in one single man...The loose structure of those books gives the author a chance to display his talent in the epic, the lyric, the tragic, the comic, and all the qualities included in the pleasing sciences of poetry and rhetoric, for the epic may be written in prose as well as in verse.　　　　CERVANTES, *Don Quixote*, ch. 47

In the diction, I think, burlesque itself may be sometimes admitted, of which many instances will occur in this work, as in the description of the battles and some other places, not necessary to be pointed out to the classical reader, for whose entertainment those parodies or burlesque imitations are chiefly calculated.　　FIELDING, Preface to *Joseph Andrews*

We have seen that both the *Satyricon* and the *Metamorphoses* were written within a convention of comic fiction, the aim of which was sophisticated entertainment for the literary public. The programmatic statements of Lucian and Apuleius readily concede this limited purpose. Whilst the themes are of a trivial and sensational nature, the writer so structures and adorns the narrative with literary reminiscence that he simultaneously provides both a cruder and a more intellectual pleasure.[1]

The technique of constructing a fictitious narrative through the imitation or evocation of earlier writers is of course pervasive in all forms of fiction, Greek and Roman. The Greek love-romances, even the 'presophistic' like that of Chariton, constantly compare the situations of the protagonists with similar crises in earlier literature, especially epic.[2] Longus' romance

[1] In our own day a similar technique has been throughly exploited by the writers of the intellectual 'thriller'. It is almost a commonplace to find the plots of these based on the themes of Shakespearian plays and other classics of literature, a knowledge of which the author can assume in his audience.

[2] On romance as 'basically the same genre' as epic, see Perry, *The Ancient Romances*, 45 ff.

shows how the technique is exploited in its full sophistication. The story of Daphnis and Chloe is built up against the rural landscape, and Alexandrian pastoral poetry is repeatedly harnessed for the depiction of this background. There are hints of Theocritus everywhere, and Moschus and Bion are also exploited for the provision of the timeless atmosphere of the pastoral setting.[1] The development of the love-relationship itself invokes for its physical manifestations the poetry of Sappho,[2] and for its edifying spiritual tone the *Phaedrus* of Plato.[3] When a military operation is described, as in Mytilene's retaliatory expedition against Miletus, a Thucydidean flavour is perceptible.[4] Where such a literary flavour is apposite and carefully disciplined, it contributes to the appreciation of the literate reader, who readily identifies the reminiscence and its function in the particular scene.

In the comic fiction such as Lucian represents, the allusion to earlier authors has naturally a different, overtly comic purpose. It may take the form of relevant quotation or allusion not merely to lend an extra dimension of comedy but also to poke fun directly at the authors cited. The *Vera Historia*, for example, is an extended parody of those Hellenistic historians who palpably exaggerate the weird and wonderful in their accounts of foreign expeditions;[5] but there is also parody of other historical writing, for example when a peace-treaty is

---

[1] G. Dalmeyda's Budé edition (Paris 1934) notes the following echoes of Theocritus. Longus 1.31, lamentation of the cattle for the death of Dorco; cf. Theocr. 1.74–5. Longus 3.25.2, apples and roses; cf. Theocr. 11.10. 1.10 is an imitation of Theocr. 1.52. 1.14, 'Fair is the sound of Daphnis' pipe', echoes the first Idyll of Theocritus. For imitation of Moschus, compare 1.18 and Mosch. 1.27; for Bion, 2.5 and Bion 16 Gow.

[2] At 1.17, χλωρότερον τὸ πρόσωπον ἦν πόας καιρίμης clearly echoes Sappho's χλωροτέρα δε ποίας ἔμμι; and this chapter of Longus evokes the whole poem. There are other reminiscences of her elsewhere, e.g. 3.33–4, and Sappho 105 L–P (οἶον τὸ γλυκύμαλον . . .).

[3] So 1.22 echoes *Phaedr.* 255 D, and 3.7.1 is similar to 249 D.

[4] 3.2.

[5] Ctesias and Iambulus are cited as conspicuous offenders (1.3). Herodotus is also parodied (*V.H.* 1.16 and Herod. 3.102).

inserted into the narrative in obvious imitation of Thucydides —here not for the purpose of ridiculing Thucydides but merely to intensify the comic effect of the episode.[1] Again, there are philosophical allusions in Lucian's description of the Isle of the Blest, and here the author is both ridiculing the philosophers and enhancing the comedy of the narrative. He introduces jokes against Diogenes and the Stoics; he pokes fun at the Academics who won't go to the Isle because they can't be sure it exists; he ridicules the sociological theories of Plato (on the Isle all have wives in common, being in this respect μάλιστα Πλατωνικώτατοι).[2] Likewise literary jokes are incorporated, for example about the provenance of Homer and the problems of Homeric composition, where the butt of the humour is the pedantry of Homeric commentators.[3] In Lucian, then, the humour is frequently directed against the poets, philosophers and historians, but his purpose is not primarily to establish himself as literary critic, but rather to delight his readers by a mosaic of literary allusions which are introduced into his ridiculous narrative at the stage appropriate to each.

As in the Greek tradition of fiction, so too in the formative Roman genre; in Menippean satire also the elements of parody and literary allusions are prominent.[4] The fragments of Varro indicate that his satires incorporated both themes and actual verses from earlier authors. This had been the practice in the Greek diatribes of Menippus, who parodies for example the scene in the underworld in the eleventh *Odyssey* and the plot of Aristophanes' *Peace*. The *Apocolocyntosis* of Seneca is however the most revealing example of the literary texture characteristic of Menippean satire. The account of Claudius' arrival on Mount Olympus, the meeting of the gods' council to decide whether to elect him to the club, and his rejection and departure

---

[1] *V.H.* 1.20; cf. Thuc. 5.18.

[2] Diogenes is a changed man, 2.18; the Stoics are still on the way up, 2.18; the Academics, 2.18; Plato, 2.19.

[3] The hero questions Homer on his origin in 2.20. He then enquires περὶ τῶν ἀθετουμένων στίχων, which Homer claims as his own composition.

[4] For what follows, see especially E. Courtney, *Philol.* (1962), 86 ff.

to Hades as law-clerk is all punctuated with elaborately comic quotations from earlier authors which focus the mockery on Claudius' limp, stammer, and pedantic Latin.

The whole story is given the comic framework of an historian's account. The historian's solemn exordium is introduced to assure the reader of the sober verisimilitude of the proceedings in the Olympian senate: 'quid actum sit in coelo ...volo memoriae tradere.' Even the date is recorded—'ante diem tertium idus Octobris'; and the traditional reassurance is given that the author has no axe to grind ('nihil nec offensae nec gratiae dabitur').

Then, within this comically solemn historian's framework, can be found both malicious parody and more generally all manner of comic literary allusion. When the emperor Augustus speaks at the council, his words mirror the language of his *Res Gestae*, and here Augustus is clearly the butt of the joke. But the main purpose of the countless allusions and quotations is to add comic force to the description of the incidents themselves, to rouse in the reader what Meredith calls thoughtful laughter. For example, when the gods discuss whether Claudius can become an Epicurean deity or a Stoic one, it is suggested that he cannot be an Epicurean god since they cause no trouble to anyone, nor yet a Stoic god because he would have to be *rotundus, sine capite sine praeputio*—and yet, adds the spokesman meaningly, there is something of the Stoic god in him![1]

It is clear, therefore, that Petronius in his *mélange* of Greek fiction and Menippean satire was encouraged to regard the literary texture as a staple feature of his fiction. In fact the sophisticated presentation inherited from Greek and Roman predecessors was wholly suited to his wide literary interests. In a discussion of the inadequate formation which he claims is typical of many contemporary versifiers, Petronius' character Eumolpus makes this pompous pronouncement: 'No mind can conceive or bring to birth its offspring unless it has been flooded with a great river of literature.'[2] Perhaps Petronius

---

[1] *Apocol.* 8: 'est aliquid in illo Stoici dei, iam video; nec cor nec caput habet.'   [2] 118.3: 'ingenti flumine litterarum.'

intended the maxim to be referred to his own offspring. One cannot begin to appreciate the comic versatility of Petronius, or to savour the full flavour of the narrative, unless one is aware that scene after scene introduces echoes of earlier literature, especially of the Augustan poets Virgil, Horace and Ovid.

Petronius indeed seems to be signposting his purposes in this literary evocation, so that a persisting pattern is observable. It has earlier been suggested that the *Satyricon* is a deliberate attempt to synthesise the Greek comic romance with Roman satirical motifs; in some scenes the treatment focusses on the hero Encolpius and his intimates, in others on the persons they encounter. When Petronius amuses his readers with the comic and sensational adventures of Encolpius, no satirical effect is sought.[1] But when he concentrates our attention on the incidental characters, they are being held up as examples of what Petronius believes are the foolish or vicious elements of his world. The literary patterning reflects this alternation of the sensational and the satirical. When Encolpius is at the centre of the narrative, he is regularly compared, in the course of his mean and trivial progress, to the great epic heroes. But in other scenes the characters who briefly take the centre of the stage are frequently created in the recognisable likeness of figures from Roman satire.

This thesis can be firmly supported in several episodes. In the scenes which concentrate the attention on Encolpius, he is depicted successively as an Achilles, an Aeneas, an Odysseus. So, in the scene when Encolpius is deserted by Giton in favour of Ascyltus, the hero retires to brood morosely in lodgings by the sea, where he pines away reflecting on the ingratitude of his comrades. We are meant to envisage him as a comic reincarnation of the classic exemplar of solitary resentment, Achilles robbed of Briseis by Agamemnon. Homer too sets his hero away from human intercourse, moping in solitude on the shore.[2]

---

[1] So Perry, *The Ancient Romances*, 192 (and *CP* (1925), 31 ff.), against the mistaken view of Highet, *TAPA* (1941), 176 ff.

[2] *Sat.* 81: '...locumque secretum et proximum litori maestus conduxi'; *Iliad* 1.348 ff.

Achilles' conversation with Thetis, recounting the cause of his grief, is paralleled in the *Satyricon* by a soliloquy in which Encolpius recalls the history of his deprivation. Here, then, Encolpius is comically portrayed as a second Achilles; in the ensuing episode he becomes a second Aeneas. He marches out to fight, searching out his adversary as it were in fallen Troy; the language takes on a Virgilian tone, as he buckles on his sword ('gladio latus cingor') and rushes forth ('in publicum prosilio') stalking round the colonnades like a madman ('furentis modo omnes circumeo porticus');[1] the epic atmosphere is sedulously built up to accentuate the anticlimax, when the hero meekly surrenders his arms to a passing soldier.

Equally striking is the evocation of the *Aeneid* in the description of the shipwreck off Croton.[2] First a tempest is recounted in language similar to that which describes the storm at the beginning of Virgil's epic.[3] When Lichas is thrown overboard, the phraseology recalls the similar fate of Orontes. Next the heroes of the *Satyricon* are cast ashore, and spend the night in a fisherman's cottage, refreshing themselves with 'food spoiled in the wreck', just as Aeneas' comrades eat 'bread spoiled in the sea'.[4] On the following day Encolpius' reconnaissance round Croton is described in language similar to Aeneas' exploration near Carthage,[5] and finally the Petronian heroes climb the hill overlooking Croton and gaze down on the city with its lofty citadel. Petronius' words, 'destinatum carpimus iter, ac momento temporis in montem sudantes conscendi-

---

[1] *Sat.* 82.1. Cf. *Aen.* 2.314: 'arma amens capio', 2.671 f.: 'hinc ferro accingor rursus clipeoque sinistram / insertabam aptans meque extra tecta ferebam'. The *furor* of Aeneas (2.316, 595, 745) is of course a key motif of the second book. For the *porticus*, cf. 2.528, 761.

[2] Collignon, 126 ff.

[3] *Sat.* 114.1: 'inhorruit mare nubesque undique adductae obruere tenebris diem.' *Aen.* 1.88 f.: 'eripiunt subito nubes caelumque diem-que...'.

[4] *Sat.* 115.6 'cibis naufragio corruptis'; *Aen.* 1.177 'Cererem corruptam undis'.

[5] *Sat.* 115.7: 'cum poneremus consilium cui nos regioni crederemus...' *Aen.* 1.306 ff.: 'locosque / explorare novos, quas vento accesserit oras / qui teneant...'.

mus, ex quo haud procul impositum arce sublimi oppidum cernimus' are clearly meant to evoke the lines of the *Aeneid*:

> iamque ascendebant collem, qui plurimus urbi
> imminet, adversasque aspectat desuper arces...[1]

It will be recalled that Aeneas' exploration of Carthage is the prelude to the confrontation with Dido. Encolpius too is to meet his *femme fatale*, but now he changes his epic identity to become a second Odysseus. The lady's name is Circe, and Petronius allows the hero to name himself Polyaenus to indicate to the reader that he has now to keep in mind Odysseus' tarrying for a whole year in Aeaea.[2] As always, Encolpius is ludicrously unequal to his role. Later in the episode, he laments in verses the grievous anger of Priapus directed against him, and here also the epic evocation is clear.[3] Hence, in those scenes where Encolpius dominates the action, the episodes are structured after the familiar adventures of Homeric and Virgilian heroes. He is the anti-hero whose unheroic propensities are signalled by the successive identification with Achilles, Aeneas and Odysseus.

In the other episodes, where Encolpius retires to the sidelines to allow Petronius to present more prominently the objects of his satire, the switch from the narrative of rogue-adventure to satirical portrayal is signalled by a change in the literary patterning from reminiscences of epic to the evocation of Roman satire, Lucilian and Menippean.

The supreme example is Trimalchio. The characterisation of the Campanian millionaire is a complex creation, inspired not only by literary forbears but also by observation from life;[4] but in his role as lord of the feast, he is depicted as a second Nasidienus, who is the classical example of the boorish host in Roman satire.[5] True, Nasidienus is a wholly different social

---

[1] *Sat.* 116.1; *Aen.* 1.419 f.
[2] *Sat.* 126 ff. For πολύαινος 'Οδυσσεύς in the Circe episode, see *Od.* 12.184.   [3] Below, pp. 76 f.   [4] See below, pp. 136 ff.
[5] Hor. *Sat.* 2.8. On the connexion with Trimalchio, see L. R. Shero, *CP* (1923), 126 ff.; J. Révay, *CP* (1921), 202 ff.; and now Sullivan, *The Satyricon*, 126 ff.

type,[1] but this difference does not detract from the similarity of the two men visualised as hosts at table. Trimalchio, like his Horatian model, invites to his board guests much more literate than himself, yet dominates the conversation with banal observations and fatuous moralising. He demonstrates his cellar's prodigal range like Nasidienus, and the food too in part resembles that of the Horatian dinner.[2] Trimalchio, in violation of the canons of taste, asks Habinnas what the menu was at a friend's party, and here we are meant to recall Nasidienus' similar query to Fundanius.[3] In all these ways the *beatitudo Trimalchionis* is a re-creation of the *beatus Nasidienus*.[4]

But it is the attitude of the guests which above all evokes the dinner of Nasidienus. The temporary departure of the host brings relief to both tables.[5] When Trimalchio is bruised by a tumbling acrobat, his guests moralise on the human condition—'quam in praecipiti res humanae essent';[6] so Nasidienus' fellow-diners ironically commiserate with him on the iniquity of Fortune when the awning falls and ruins the meal.[7] And at the end of the episode in Petronius, the decision of Encolpius and Ascyltus to take to their heels recalls the similar Horatian finale.[8] In this sense the close structural connexion between the *Cena Trimalchionis* and the *Cena Nasidieni* is obvious. Encol-

---

[1] Nasidienus is an *ingenuus* and a social climber, whereas Trimalchio is a *libertus* with no aspirations beyond his social prominence in his *municipium*; see Bagnani, *Phoenix* (1954), 77 ff.

[2] Nasidienus' offer to provide an alternative to the Caecuban on the table (Hor. 2.8.16) is nicely labelled by Rudd the 'You name it we got it' strain in the vulgar host; cf. Petronius 48.1. On the food, note the wild boar (Hor. 2.8.6, Petr. 40.3), the fish in sauce (Hor. 2.8.45, Petr. 36.3) and the surprise items (Hor. 2.8.26 ff., and Petr. 33.4 ff., 69.8 ff.) in common.

[3] Petr. 66.1; Hor. 2.8.4. On the lapse of taste, Theophr. *Char.* 3.2.

[4] Hor. 2.8.1, Petr. 38.5 for these titles.

[5] Hor. 2.8.77 ff.; Petr. 41.9.

[6] Petr. 55.1—not a bad joke, as the acrobat has fallen *praeceps*.

[7] Hor. 2.8.61 ff.: 'heu, Fortuna, quis est crudelior in nos / te deus? ut semper gaudes illudere rebus / humanis.'

[8] Hor. 2.8.93 ff.; Petr. 78.8.

pius, Ascyltus, Agamemnon are cast in the roles of Varius, Vibidius, and Maecenas.[1]

A second clear example of the deployment of Roman satire for such literary modelling is found in the fragmentary episodes enacted at Croton. Here Petronius has satirised at some length the behaviour of the legacy-hunters in that town, who batten on to Eumolpus in the hope of inheriting his non-existent fortune.[2] We may assume that this portrayal was inspired by the Horatian criticism of the *captator* at Rome, or at any rate by the Roman satirical tradition generally, for the theme of the legacy-hunter is a popular one.[3]

These examples encourage us to investigate the possibility of literary antecedents for the other characters who are lent brief prominence. Agamemnon may well be a satirical portrayal, but owing to the loss of part of the episode in which he appears it is difficult to establish this beyond all doubt. However the comic name ('Wide-ruling lord of men') is one indication of Petronius' purpose; moreover, Agamemnon is depicted as an astute man perpetuating a vicious educational system out of self-interest.[4] The likelihood that Agamemnon is

[1] The pattern of literary evocation in the *Cena Trimalchionis* within this framework of Trimalchio as *Nasidienus alter* is varied and complex. Perhaps most notable is the sustained reminiscence of Plato's *Symposium* with the entrance of Habinnas. Habinnas as the ἄκλητος, who arrives when the evening is well advanced, comically evokes the entrance of Alcibiades in Plato's dialogue. Note the correspondence between the two as they make their way in, Alcibiades leaning on a flute-girl and Habinnas on his homely, fat spouse Scintilla. *Symp.* 212 D–E: καὶ οὐ πολὺ ὕστερον ᾿Αλκιβιάδου τὴν φωνὴν ἀκούειν ἐν τῇ αὐλῇ σφόδρα μεθύοντος καὶ μέγα βοῶντος... ἄγειν οὖν αὐτὸν παρὰ σφᾶς τήν τε αὐλητρίδα ὑπολαβοῦσαν καὶ ἄλλους τινὰς τῶν ἀκολούθων, καὶ ἐπιστῆναι ἐπὶ τὰς θύρας ἐστεφανωμένον αὐτὸν κιττοῦ τέ τινι στεφάνῳ δασεῖ καὶ ἴων, καὶ ταινίας ἔχοντα ἐπὶ τῆς κεφαλῆς πάνυ πολλάς... *Sat.* 65: 'ille autem iam ebrius uxoris suae umeris imposuerat manus, oneratusque aliquot coronis et unguento per frontem in oculos fluente...' For a perceptive treatment of this extended evocation, see Averil Cameron, 'Petronius and Plato', *CQ* (1969), 367–70.

[2] Petr. 124.2 ff., esp. 125.3, 141.2 ff.

[3] Hor. *Sat.* 2.5 (see Rudd, 224 ff.); cf. Juv. 5.98 and 12.93 ff.

[4] 3.3 ff.; below, pp. 85 ff.

being satirised is accentuated by the realisation that Varro had attacked the teaching in the school of rhetoric of the first century B.C.[1] Petronius may well be exploiting an accepted satirical motif in this scene.

Eumolpus, the manic poetaster with a chip on his shoulder about the exigent status of the literary genius, is also a stock satirical target. Juvenal's first and seventh satires are an indication of the popularity of the theme, and the first satire of Persius shows that, as one would expect, Juvenal's treatment is here derivative. Note the correspondence between Eumolpus— 'senex canus, exercitati vultus, et qui videretur nescio quid magnum promittere' and the sardonic depiction of Persius' literary circle:

> scribimus inclusi, numeros ille hic pede liber
> *grande aliquid,* quod pulmo animae praelargus anhelet. . .
> en *pallor seniumque*. . .[2]

Just as Eumolpus' name, as so often in Satire,[3] is an index to his character, so also the characters whom Encolpius encounters aboard ship, Lichas and Tryphaena, are personifications of cruelty and luxury.[4] But beyond these opposed traits of heartlessness and sexual promiscuity, this oddly assorted couple are depicted as dominated by the vice of superstition. We have noted the interesting parallel between Tryphaena and the heroine of the Oxyrhynchus mime;[5] but the foolishness of superstition connects her also with the satirists, for this is a subject dear to their hearts. Varro's practical philosophy recoils from it,[6] Horace condemns it, and Juvenal devotes a celebrated peroration to the subject of a right relation with the gods.[7] Here too one feels that Petronius is satirically handling a vicious trait with the aid of similar treatments in earlier satirists, but the

---

[1] Fr. 144, quoted on p. 21 n. 2.
[2] Pers. 1.13 f., 26. In Suetonius' *Vita* of Persius, we are told that the satirist attacked the poets and orators of recent days vehemently ('tanta recentium poetarum et oratorum insectatione').
[3] See Rudd, 143 ff.   [4] Below, pp. 100 ff.
[5] Above, p. 26.   [6] Fr. 181.
[7] Hor. *Sat.* 2.3.281 ff. (see Rudd, 180 f.); Juvenal 10.346 ff.

fragmentary nature of our evidence makes the suggestion difficult to confirm.

In general, however, the pattern seems clear enough—the evocation of epic to guide the main lines of the rogue-story, and reminiscences of characters and motifs from Roman satire where satirical vignettes are attempted. But Latin literature abounds in satirical portraiture outside the genre of satire itself, and other well-known authors are exploited for derisive effects. For example, the Circe–Polyaenus confrontation has only its token connexion with epic; the true literary model in this description of Encolpius' mysterious sexual enervation is Ovid's notorious and indelicate poem.[1] The affront expressed by Circe, the shame felt by the paramour, the girl's suggestion that her lover's failure is caused by another love-affair, and above all the pained *apostrophe* of the hero to his parts reveal clearly enough the literary model of Petronius here.[2]

Ovid is the inspiration too of the subsequent comic scene in which Oenothea is called in to succour the hero in his malady. The name of this priestess recalls Ovid's Dipsas, and there is more than a hint that the verses describing Oenothea's magic are recalling to the reader some similar sentiments in the *Amores*. For example, the refrain *cum volo* in this passage

> florida tellus
> cum volo siccatis arescit languida sucis,
> cum volo fundit opes...

echoes Ovid's *cum voluit*, likewise at the beginning of successive lines:

> cum voluit, toto glomerantur nubila caelo,
> cum voluit, puro fulget in orbe dies.[3]

Nor is this the sole echo of Ovid in the verses of this scene.[4]

---

[1] *Amores*, 3.7; *Satyricon*, 127 ff.

[2] *Sat.* 128.1: 'numquid te osculum meum offendit?' and *Amores* 3.7.1 and 37; *Sat.* 129.8 and *Amores* 3.7.80; *Sat.* 132.10 and *Amores* 3.7.69.

[3] *Sat.* 134.12.1–3; *Amores* 1.8.9–10.

[4] E.g., 134.12.8–10: 'Lunae descendit imago / carminibus deducta meis, trepidusque furentes / flectere Phoebus equos revoluto cogitur orbe.' Compare *Amores* 2.1.23 f.: 'carmina sanguineae deducunt cornua lunae / et revocant niveos solis euntis equos.'

More frequent, however, than the extended structuring of a scene after a model in Classical poetry is the continually employed technique of comic allusion to characters or events celebrated in Greek or Roman literature. These references are rarely subtle or learned; one might almost describe them as banal. Petronius does not wish to furrow the brows of his readers with esoteric allusions; the recognition is immediate, the smile instantaneous. So when Ascyltus, the unsavoury and unscrupulous friend of Encolpius, threatens violence against Giton unless the boy is complaisant to his advances, he evokes the rape of Lucretia immortalised in Livy's first book: 'Si Lucretia es, Tarquinium invenisti'.[1] Later, when Encolpius and Ascyltus are again contesting possession of Giton, their favourite begs them not to re-enact the duel of Eteocles and Polyneices.[2] There are numerous comic allusions to the *Odyssey*. Giton is strapped under a mattress to escape detection by Ascyltus, and Odysseus' escape from the Cyclops' cave is recalled both in the devising of the stratagem and in its detection.[3] So too in the ship-episode, when the heroes realise that the ship's captain is their enemy Lichas, Eumolpus visualises the ship as a Cyclops' cave from which they must escape;[4] and when they are finally brought before Lichas, Encolpius is recognised by his privates just as Ulysses was identified by his scar.[5]

Petronius exploits not only allusion but also extended quotation for comic effect, and again the quotations are such as any Roman with a pretence to a literary education would find familiar. Virgil is especially prominent in these. It has been noted how the anecdote of the Widow of Ephesus is invested

[1] 9.5.
[2] 80.3: 'ne Thebanum par humilis taberna spectaret.'
[3] 97.5: 'et Ulixem astu simillimo vicit.' 98.5: 'remota etiam culcita videt Ulixem.'
[4] 101.7: '"fingite" inquit "nos antrum Cyclopis intrasse".' One suggested means of escape is by the carpet method of Cleopatra (102.10: cf. Plut. *Caes.* 49).
[5] 105.10: 'miretur nunc aliquis Ulixis nutricem post vicesimum annum cicatricem invenisse [originis] indicem...'.

with a literary flavour by her maid's quotation from the fourth
book of the *Aeneid*; the comparison with Dido is all the more
apposite when we remember that the Carthaginian queen swore
that the dead Sychaeus would keep her love in his tomb—'ille
habeat secum servetque sepulcro'.[1] Surprisingly, Virgil is
quoted for a crudely comic effect in the account of Encolpius'
sexual tribulations with Circe. The hero, as we have seen,
evokes verses of Ovid in reproaching his parts for their failure;
their response is described with the Virgilian lines in which
Dido spurns Aeneas in the underworld:

> illa solo fixos oculos aversa tenebat
> nec magis incepto vultum sermone movetur

and a third line of Virgilian pastiche is added,

> quam lentae salices lassove papavera collo.[2]

Clearly this quotation does not intend to guy Virgil; it is an
attempt to introduce an element of sophistication to relieve
the sequence of crude sexual incidents, by the exploitation
of the exalted language of epic in the depiction of a mean
theme.

This raises the interesting question of parody of genres by
Petronius without the evocation of individual writers. It has
been noted how in Greek fiction the portrayal of a particular
type of scene or emotion challenges the author to exploit the
appropriate literary tone. So also in Petronius. When he
describes an exchange of fisticuffs on board ship, he slips into
the language of a Roman historian recounting a battle: '... illis
pro ultione, nobis pro vita pugnantibus. multi ergo utrimque
sine morte labuntur, plures cruenti vulneribus referunt pedem
... data ergo acceptaque ex more patrio fide. . .'[3] When peace
is agreed, the formula of the treaty is comically reproduced,
recalling the insertion by Livy of such antique documents, and

---

[1] *Aen.* 4.29; on the Widow of Ephesus anecdote, see above, pp. 11 ff.
[2] *Sat.* 132.11. For the first two lines, see *Aen.* 6.469 f. and cf. 1.482; for
the third line, *Ecl.* 3.83, 5.16, and *Aen.* 9.436.
[3] 108.9–12.

parodying the solemn oath taken on such occasions. '...tabulas foederis...quis haec formula erat. ex tui animi sententia ut tu, Tryphaena, neque iniuriam tibi factam a Gitone quereris... item, Licha, ex tui animi sententia ut tu Encolpion nec verbo contumelioso insequeris nec vultu...'[1]

But the most frequently invoked comic effect is the deployment of the epic tone. The heroes are in reality anti-heroes who meet situations demanding courage and intrepidity with acts of ludicrous cowardice, and who regard their trivial pains and quarrels as Homeric trials; and the language of epic is employed to make the subsequent deflation still more comic. One is reminded of the technique of Juvenal, who likewise raises the tone of his narration so that the anti-climax may strike home more sickeningly when it comes.[2] We have noted how Petronius accentuates the anti-climax in this fashion.[3]

Elsewhere Petronius incorporates verses which parody the epic style, again for the comic inflation of a mean episode. For example, during the fracas on the ship, Tryphaena urges peace in verses which are a pastiche of Virgil and Lucan:

> quis furor, exclamat, pacem convertit in arma?
> quid nostrae meruere manus? non Troius heros
> hac in classe vehit decepti pignus Atridae...
> cui non est mors una satis?[4]

Doubtless Petronius has Lucan directly in mind in this ridiculously inflated appeal for an armistice, for the *Pharsalia* begins with the same sentiments and the same two words:

> quis furor, o cives...[5]

---

[1] 109.1–3: note the archaic *quis*, and the solemn introduction to an oath, *ex animi sententia*. Cf. Livy 22.53.10.

[2] A good example is found in Satire 10, where the military glory of Hannibal is accentuated by the epic tone, the bubble of which is then devastatingly pricked with a single word: 'finem animae, quae res humanas miscuit olim / non gladii non saxa dabunt nec tela, sed ille / Cannarum vindex et tanti sanguinis ultor / anulus.'

[3] Above, p. 37.   [4] *Sat.* 108.14.

[5] Lucan, *Bell. Civ.* 1.8. For echoes of Virgil, cf. *Aen.* 8.115, 5.670, 9.139 f. See Collignon, 123.

but the humour of the situation derives more from the general epic tone here than from the citation of the poet whom elsewhere Petronius parodies with more derisive intent.

This is an apposite point at which to consider in some detail the purpose of the two lengthy poems, the *Halosis Troiae* and the *De Bello Civili*.[1]

The *Halosis Troiae* is declaimed by Eumolpus during a conversation with Encolpius in an art-gallery. As they inspect the statuary and the pictures, they chance upon a representation of the fall of Troy, which gives Eumolpus a pretext to declaim an impromptu composition in iambics on this most hackneyed of tragic subjects. Though the poem invites comparison with Virgil's treatment in the *Aeneid*, it is not only much shorter but also contains several variations in the theme by comparison with Virgil. Petronius has probably followed a standard mythological version from which Virgil has diverged, though his deep knowledge of Virgil's treatment is continually reflected in echoes of phraseology.[2]

These verses have frequently been regarded as a serious composition.[3] Yet we have seen how pervasive a role parody and comic evocation have in Roman fiction; moreover, this type of poem was utterly hackneyed, and the satirists claim that their ears are buffeted by the whole of Rome declaiming tragic lays:

[1] In spite of differing conclusions, my discussion has profited from H. Stubbe's useful commentary, *Die Verseinlagen im Petron* (Leipzig 1933). I have discussed the problem in greater detail in *CP* (1968), 208 ff.

[2] The variations between the two accounts are listed by Stubbe, 30 ff. (Petronius 1 ff. differs from Virgil *Aen.* 2.13 ff.; 'Delio profante' in Petr. 4 is a *lapsus memoriae*, 5 has detail not in Virgil; 12, 'titulus fero / incisus' is not in Virgil. 20 ff., esp. 22 'ictus resilit', differs from Virgil 50 ff.: 45 ff. lays emphasis on the children, Virgil 216 on Laocoon. In 57 the Greeks within open the horse, in Virgil Sinon does this (2.259). On the echoes of Virgil, see especially 'fero' (l. 12) echoing 'feri' (*Aen.* 2.51) as a description of the horse; 'iubae' (Petr. 38, Virgil, *Aen.* 2.206). On Virgil's independence of the tradition, see Austin's edition of *Aen.* 2, xii ff.

[3] E.g. by Collignon; and most recently by Perry, 197.

semper et adsiduo ruptae lectore columnae:
expectes eadem a summo minimoque poeta.[1]

Eumolpus is the manic poetaster; his character is boldly drawn.[2] The poem is the stock type of messenger speech which reports the remote disaster in the diction and metre of tragedy—'ein rhetorisches Prunckstück'.[3] Petronius is parodying here not Lucan, not Nero, and certainly not Virgil, but a contemporary phenomenon, a city of tragic versifiers of whom Seneca is the best-known representative. The connexion with Senecan tragedy is striking. The metrical canons observed by Petronius completely correspond to those of Seneca;[4] the diction too and the tricks of style recall Seneca. On four occasions in a poem of sixty-five lines a verse begins with *iam*;[5] the stock line-endings include the words *sacer*, *manus*, *motus* four times each.[6] This cannot be a careful or serious composition; Petronius is demonstrating how fatally easy it is to write tragedies like Seneca's. When at the close of his uninspired effort Eumolpus is showered by stones from the bystanders, the point is surely not the philistinism of the mob but the nuisance committed by Eumolpus; Encolpius certainly suggests that the hostile reception was deserved.[7]

There is another argument to support this claim that the *Troiae Halosis* is a deliberately mediocre poem inserted to ridicule the tragic declaimer. Encolpius labels the versifying tendencies of Eumolpus 'a disease', and tells his acquaintance 'saepius poetice quam humane locutus es'; and of this there is

---

[1] Juv. *Sat.* 1.13 f. (the nature of the poetry indicated in the lines preceding); cf. Pliny *Ep.* 1.13.

[2] Below, pp. 94 ff.   [3] So Deubner, *NJb* (1921), 367.

[4] On the metrical correspondence, see Stubbe, 93; for the Senecan iambics, L. Strzelecki, *De Senecae trimetro iambico quaestiones selectae* (Kraków 1938).

[5] For further detail, Walsh, *CP* (1968), 210.

[6] *Iubar*, *mare* and *mero* appear at the end of a line twice, and *iubae* and *iubar* end consecutive lines, the kind of jingle favoured by Seneca; Sullivan, *The Satyricon*, 188, well compares *Agamemnon* 406 ff. for such repetitions. See also *CP* (1968), 210.

[7] See Sage, *TAPA* (1915), 48.

an interesting echo in Lucian, where an exhibitionist is likewise told to 'come down from his iambics'.[1] The parallel suggests that Eumolpus, the man who can say nothing without mouthing verses, is a type belaboured in Menippean satire.

This demonstration that the *Halosis Troiae* is to be read in the context of the characterisation of Eumolpus, and regarded not as a serious composition but as a mediocre impromptu, provides us with an entry to the understanding of the longer poem, the *De Bello Civili*.[2] The poem is declaimed, again by Eumolpus, as the heroes make their way to Croton; it has the conventional status of an entertainment whiling away a journey.[3] Eumolpus prefixes it with some reflexions on the education requisite for a poet, and on the essential differences between epic and historiography. Whether this attack on Lucan's poem[4] represents substantially Petronius' own attitude or not is a question wholly unanswerable and in this context irrelevant; the importance of the disquisition lies in its characterising purpose. Eumolpus is depicted as a man who decries experimental novelty in poetry and proclaims the necessity for adhering to the traditional presentation of epic. But when he provides an example of his ideal, his traditionalist version is permeated with the *stylistic* vices of the poem which he condemns.

---

[1] *Sat.* 90.3; Lucian, *Menippus* 1: παῦσαι μακάριε, τραγῳδῶν, καὶ λέγε οὑτωσί πως ἁπλῶς καταβὰς ἀπὸ τῶν ἰαμβείων.

[2] Bibliography in Stubbe, 67; and see now A. F. Sochatoff in *Arion* (1966), 359 ff.; Sullivan, 170 ff. I find it strange that Sullivan accepts one of the long poems as parody, and the other as a serious composition.

[3] Publ. Syr. 104: 'comes facundus in via pro vehiculo est.' So the journey on the ship is whiled away with the story of the Widow of Ephesus; and in Apuleius the hero expresses his gratitude for a story which lightens the journey (1.20.5). See Stubbe, 69.

[4] *Sat.* 118.6: 'non enim res gestae versibus comprehendendae sunt, quod longe melius historici faciunt, sed per ambages deorumque ministeria et fabulosum sententiarum tormentum praecipitandus est liber spiritus, ut potius *furentis animi vaticinatio* appareat quam religiosae orationis sub testibus fides.' Eumolpus epitomises the *furens animus*.

For Petronius' poem, as many scholars have demonstrated, is in tone closely akin to Lucan's.[1] The poems do not, however, run along the same lines. Eumolpus, in harmony with his theory, incorporates more mythology and picturesque description, and is less concerned with historical events.[2] Several reminiscences of Virgil, and a deliberate evocation of Livy's narrative of Hannibal's Alpine journey,[3] are introduced to achieve this different purpose. So the poem is in content hardly comparable to Lucan's.

But the similarities in phraseology and metrical technique are such that Petronius must be characterising Eumolpus as a poet who succumbs to the flamboyancy of Lucan's poetic manner. The verbal echoes must be deliberate.[4] The adoption of the same irritating metrical mannerisms is also striking, especially the pause at the strong caesura in the third and fourth feet.[5] In Petronius' use of the hexameter, 'the great defect, as in Lucan, is want of variety'.[6]

The solution to Petronius' purpose thus seems clear. This is not a demonstration of how Petronius thought such a poem should be written; it is how Eumolpus thinks it should be

---

[1] For a list of parallels, see Stubbe, 74 n. 1; Sullivan, 174 f.

[2] See Ernout's edition, *ad loc.*: 'Eumolpe ajoute à son gré des développements mythologiques, des descriptions comme le passage des Alpes. Il supprime au contraire, conformément à ses principes, la partie historique...'

[3] On the reminiscences of Virgil, see Collignon, 154 ff.; for Livian echoes (l. 150 and Livy 21.36.8; 153 f. and 35.8, etc.) see Stubbe, 104 ff.

[4] Petr. 2: 'qua mare qua terrae' echoes Lucan 1.110, 'quae mare quae terras.' P. 216, 'ante oculos volitant' is close to L. 7.180: 'ante oculos volitare suos.' So also P. 225, 'maerentia tecta', reproduces L. 5.30: 'maerentia tecta.' See also P. 98 f. and L. 1.330 f.; P. 294 and L. 7.473. Voltaire, on his admission to the presidency of the Académie Française on 9 May 1746, called the *De Bello Civili* 'une déclamation pleine de pensées fausses'. Parody of Lucan is the obvious explanation.

[5] See *CP* (1968), 211, citing *Sat.* 122, 170 ff., 163 f., and Lucan 1.57 f., 81 ff. F. Baldwin, *The Bellum Civile of Petronius* (N.Y. 1911), 56 ff., provides further examples. Heitland, in his Introduction to Haskins' edition of Lucan (London 1887), xcv, demonstrates 'the artistic crudity' of the mannerism.   [6] Baldwin, 57.

written. In keeping with the characterisation of the conservative theorist of mediocre talent, the poem handles the theme of the civil war in a traditionalist manner, but in style echoes the stridency and monotonous versification of the poet whom Eumolpus is condemning.[1] The irony is characteristic of Petronius.

In these two poems, then, the chief purpose is derisive parody of the poetic styles of Seneca and Lucan, who represent the facile versifiers of the age.[2] But in other briefer poetic compositions the evocation of earlier poets has quite a different aim. The collection of these poems into a corpus may give a misleading idea of their purpose, for many of them must have appeared at apposite points of the novel. Originally they were enclosed within particular episodes as general judgments or reflexions on the action, and, since the tone of the book as a whole is in keeping with popular Epicureanism,[3] it is not surprising that the sentiment of many of the poems is likewise Epicurean. So Lucretius is the model for many of them.[4]

So, for example, this composition of Petronius,

> fallunt nos oculi vagique sensus
> oppressa ratione mentiuntur.
> nam turris prope quae quadrata surgit
> detritis procul angulis rotatur...

has a close relationship to a famous Lucretian passage on the fallibility of the senses.[5] In another poem Petronius takes up

---

[1] Mr E. J. Kenney (to whom here as elsewhere I am much indebted) remains unconvinced, arguing that the greater length of the *Bellum Civile* tells against the ideas of derisive parody expressed here. On this *quaestio disputata*, the reader of Sullivan's book will find this contrary view well set out.

[2] I find that the general ideas propounded here are also held by J. P. Cèbe, *La caricature et la parodie dans le monde romain antique* (Paris 1966), 332 ff.   [3] See ch. 4.

[4] I have benefited in what follows from O. Raith, *Petronius ein Epikureer* (Nürnberg 1963).

[5] Fr. 29 Müller; Lucr. 4.353 ff.; see Highet, *TAPA* (1941) 176 ff. Raith rightly regards the Petronian poem as a non-philosophical formulation of the doctrine of Lucretius.

the subject of dreams, and describes in sequence how the soldier, advocate, miser, hunter, sailor see in sleep the objects of their own activities; so too Lucretius had structured his explanation of dreams with a similar sequence of advocate, soldier, seaman, hunter.[1] Both poets handle the meaning of myths, and pass similar judgment on the Tantalus story. Again, in discussing Tityus, Petronius follows the guidance of Lucretius, who characteristically rationalises the myth by stating that Tityus everlastingly gnawed by birds symbolises man in the grip of passions. Petronius expresses a similar view more succinctly:

> cui voltur iecur intimum pererrat
> et pectus trahit intimasque fibras
> non est quem lepidi vocant poetae
> sed cordis mala, livor atque luxus...[2]

In these echoes of Lucretius, Petronius seeks to make it clear that he is motivated by a similar Epicurean spirit; this is not plagiarism, but a deliberate evocation of the lines of the *De Rerum Natura* which the reader is expected to recognise.

One sees therefore how pervasive the literary texture is in Petronius, and for what a variety of purposes it is deployed. First, the structuring of whole episodes after well-known passages of epic and satirical writing lends a comic literary dimension to the scenes as a whole, and indicates the lines of characterisation—on the one hand comically portraying the hero in epic terms, and on the other presenting the minor characters in a satirical framework. Secondly, this continual incorporation of literary allusions gives the narrative of sensational adventures a more sophisticated tone, and by such witty treatment helps to 'distance' and make less objectionable the account of the hero's scabrous progress. Thirdly, the long poems are closely interwoven into the characterisation of

---

[1] Lucr. 4.962 ff.; Petr. fr. 30.
[2] Lucr. 3.978 ff.; Petr. fr. 25. Other themes taken up by Petronius after the manner of Lucretius include the foolishness of those who worry about ritual burial; see Lucr. 3.888 ff. and Petr. *Sat.* 115.7 ff.

Eumolpus, and are a derisive imitation of the monotony and mediocrity of tragedy like Seneca's and epic like Lucan's. Finally, the shorter poems, some of which have as their function a commentary on the action portrayed, include several which reproduce the Epicurean philosophy of Lucretius as an indication of the author's attitude.

The narrative of Apuleius is not dominated to the same degree by successive evocations of classical poetry, yet the texture of the *Metamorphoses* is also highly literary. But there is not the same degree of literary *structuring* as in Petronius, and for an obvious reason. Apuleius is adapting a Greek story for Roman readers, and though he expands the narrative considerably, he is content to retain the main lines of the Greek plot up to the final scene. But in following this Greek story he constantly introduces literary motifs and comic conceits of a bookish kind.

We shall later see how Apuleius' novel in its adaptation reflects its author's more romantic temperament. In contrast to the derisive burlesque of the love-romance in Petronius, the *Metamorphoses* broadens the scope of the comic romance by including within its loose structure romantic and tragic episodes which derive much of their inspiration from Greek ideal fiction. It is precisely in these romantic scenes that Apuleius exploits the technique of literary evocation most extensively, and in contrast to the *Satyricon* for a serious and dramatic purpose. In general his method of literary allusion is much closer to that of a sophisticated Greek novelist like Longus than to that of Petronius. Wherever he describes a situation or a type of scene made familiar by the treatment of an earlier author, a reminiscence almost invariably appears; and unlike Petronius he invokes Greek writers as frequently as Roman—a factor of some significance in any assessment of the literary taste of the audience for whom he wrote.

The longest episode in the *Metamorphoses* provides the most extensive example of such literary allusion. Here the structuring cannot be doubted—Psyche in her wanderings is continually presented as a second Io.[1] The *Prometheus Vinctus* and the *Supplices* of Aeschylus were the main quarry in this depiction of a mortal maiden harried by a goddess.[2] Just as Io's father seeks the counsel of the oracles at Delphi and Dodona, so Psyche's father repairs to Miletus;[3] both fathers are bidden to abandon their daughters. Zeus falls in love with Io, Cupid with Psyche. When Hera and Venus remain ignorant of this development, they are informed by a bird.[4] Both girls wander pregnant through the world. Both seek the guidance of sympathetic advisers, Io of Prometheus, Psyche of Pan; ultimately both are delivered from their exile, and bear a divine child. If we are justified in assuming that Apuleius' version is an adaptation of a folk-tale,[5] it is clear that he will have introduced some of these similarities between the Aeschylean Io and Psyche. The joking comment with which he introduces the Milesian oracle suggests free adaptation at this point in the story.[6] And where Io threatens to throw herself off a rock, Psyche actually carries out a similar course—'per proximi fluminis marginem praecipitem se dedit'.[7]

A second clear example of how a whole episode is structured after a model in poetry is the story of Charite. Like those in Petronius, the literary exemplar is a celebrated one. This story of the virtuous wife avenging her husband's murder on the hunting-field by a lustful suitor probably derives from a synthesis of Herodotus' account of Atys and the true story of Camma,[8] but the literary model for the behaviour of Apuleius'

---

[1] See especially Helm, *NJb* (1914), 194; and K. Kerényi, *Die griechisch-orientalische Romanliteratur* (Tübingen 1927), 218 ff.

[2] *Suppl.* 291 ff.   [3] *P.V.* 658 ff.; *Met.* 4.32.5.

[4] Ps. Apollod. *Bibl.* 2.1.3; *Met.* 5.28.

[5] Below, ch. 7. It is possible, of course, to argue that both literary versions originate from the same basic folk-tale.

[6] 4.32.6: 'propter Milesiae conditorem'.

[7] *Met.* 5.25.1. Cf. *P.V.* 747 f.:

τί δῆτ' ἐμοὶ ζῆν κέρδος, ἀλλ' οὐκ ἐν τάχει
ἔρριψ' ἐμαυτὴν τῆσδ' ἀπὸ στύφλου πέτρας...

[8] W. Anderson, *Philol.* (1909), 537 ff., traces the main lines of the story to Euripides' lost *Protesilaus* and to Herod. 1.34 ff. as well as to Plutarch, *Mul. Virt.* 20.

heroine is the Virgilian Dido. Dido's situation is of course very different from Charite's, but Apuleius has incorporated from Virgil the epic framework and those psychological touches suited to the anguish of his heroine. It is Fama which first announces sad tidings to Charite as to Dido.[1] When Charite hears of the death of her husband, her emotional outburst and her nervous collapse are described in language recalling Dido's reaction on Aeneas' departure.[2] Next the ghost of her husband appears to her in a dream, as Sychaeus seems to speak to Dido in her sleep.[3] Both women in distraction kiss the marital couch, Charite 'toro faciem impressa', Dido 'os impressa toro'.[4] Both utter imprecations against the men who have wronged them, and Charite slays herself with Thrasyllus' sword as Dido with Aeneas'.[5] Apuleius has here adorned his tragic story with the evocation of the most celebrated suicide in Roman epic.[6]

Dido is again pressed into service as model for the infatuated stepmother of Book 10. Apuleius bids us prepare for a tragic story; the stepmother's passion is the *furor* and *dolor* of a Dido. Initially the stepmother readily controls her secret shame, just as Dido vows destruction on herself rather than violate her *pudor*. But the passion wells in both. In Virgil's fine description of Dido at sacrifice, deliberately searching for a divine sanction for a liaison she knows is sinful, we read:

> heu vatum ignarae mentes! quid vota furentem,
> quid delubra iuvant?

[1] *Met.* 8.6.4: 'fama dilabitur et cursus primos ad domum Tlepolemi detorquet, et aures infelicis nuptae percutit.' *Aen.* 4.298 f.: 'eadem impia fama furenti / detulit.'

[2] *Met.* 8.6.4 (Charite is *infelix*, one of Dido's key-epithets): 'quae quidem simul percepit tale nuntium...amens et vecordia percita cursuque bacchata furibundo per plateas populosas et arva rurestria fertur, insana voce casum mariti quiritans.' *Aen.* 4.300 f.: 'saevit inops animi, totamque incensa per urbem / bacchatur...' and at 4.68 ff. 'infelix Dido' wanders *furens*.

[3] *Met.* 8.8.6: *Aen.* 4.460.

[4] *Met.* 8.9.1: *Aen.* 4.659.

[5] *Met.* 8.12, *Aen.* 4.607; *Met.* 8.13.2 ff., *Aen.* 4.646 ff.

[6] See C. A. Forbes, *CW* (1943/4), 39.

For the stepmother in Apuleius it is the doctors who cannot help—'heu medicorum ignarae mentes!'[1] Into his creation of a Phaedra-figure, Apuleius has introduced a hint of Dido.

Still more striking is the way in which successive scenes of an individual episode are fittingly elaborated by reminiscences linking them with the appropriate literary genre. *Cupid and Psyche* is the supreme example of this, a fascinating demonstration of the conversion of a simple folk-tale into a mannered literary story. Apuleius begins the tale with an exordium adapted from the love-romance of the Greeks, a description of the superhuman beauty of the heroine.[2] The reactions of men and women far and near are so enthusiastic that the goddess Venus is ignored. Her angry soliloquy (throughout she is depicted with the comic familiarity of Alexandrian poetry) amusingly recalls Lucretius' invocation to the goddess at the beginning of the *De Rerum Natura*—'En rerum naturae prisca parens, en elementorum origo initialis, en orbis totius alma Venus...!'[3] The signposting phrases *rerum naturae* and *alma Venus*, and the Lucretian words *elementorum* and *origo* demonstrate the borrowing.

Later, when Psyche's wicked sisters tell her that her unseen husband is a snake, their description of it, 'immanem colubrum multinodis voluminibus serpentem, veneno noxio colla sanguinantem, hiantemque ingluvie profunda' is a pastiche of several Virgilian portrayals of snakes.[4] Then, when Cupid flies

---

[1] *Met.* 10.2.7: *Aen.* 4.65 f.

[2] For the beginning of the story, 'erant in quadam civitate rex et regina' (whose daughter Psyche is then described), cf. Xen. Eph. ἦν ἐν Ἐφέσῳ ἀνὴρ τῶν τὰ πρῶτα ἐκεῖ δυναμένων, Λυκομήδης ὄνομα... (Lycomedes' son's appearance is then recounted). The description of Psyche, and the reactions she evokes (the προσκύνησις of citizens and strangers who take her for Venus) is undoubtedly adapted from Chariton's description of Callirhoe, who is venerated as Aphrodite (cf. 1.1.2, 1.14.1, 2.3.6, etc.); cf. also Xenophon's Anthia, similarly mistaken for Artemis (1.2.7).

[3] *Met.* 4.30.1. Professor D. A. West draws attention to the dactylic rhythm here.

[4] *Georgics* 4.458: 'immanem ante pedes hydrum.' *Aen.* 2.206 ff.: 'iubae / sanguineae...immensa volumine terga'; *Georgics* 3.430 f.: 'atram / improbus ingluviem...'.

away in anger at being observed by Psyche, the account of
Psyche's restless longing to be with him is inspired by the
Phaedrus, where Plato describes how the soul itches to be
united with God.[1] There follows a short rustic scene in which
Pan gives kindly advice to Psyche; here Apuleius creates the
appropriate atmosphere by using the language of pastoral.[2]

For a scene on Mount Olympus, where Venus requests from
Jupiter the loan of his messenger Mercury, Apuleius duly
introduces the flavour of Homeric epic. Jupiter's reply is
indicated in the words: 'nec rennuit Iovis caerulum supercilium'—an extraordinary phrase even in Apuleius' baroque
Latinity until we recall that it amusingly and precisely translates
the phrase of the *Iliad* which indicates Zeus' answer to Thetis.[3]

But perhaps the most sustained literary evocation is the
exploitation of the sixth book of the *Aeneid* for the description
of Psyche's journey to Hades. Here is a section of Apuleius'
narrative in which Psyche is advised about her journey:

inibi spiraculum Ditis et per portas hiantes monstratur iter invium...sed
non hactenus vacua debebis per illas tenebras incedere, sed offas polentae
mulso concretas ambabus gestare manibus...nec mora, cum ad flumen
mortuum venies, cui praefectus Charon protenus expetens portorium sic
ad ripam ulteriorem sutili cumba deducit commeantes...huic squalido
seni dabis nauli nomine de stipibus quas feres alteram...canis namque
praegrandis...servat vacuam Ditis domum.[4]

[1] Plato (248 c) describes how the soul which is filled with forgetfulness
and evil is weighed down, loses its wings, and crashes to earth; so
Psyche 'tandem fessa delabitur solo' (5.24.1). In the *Phaedrus*, the
initiate, 'when he sees a divine face or physical appearance which is a
good imitation of beauty, first trembles...and then as he gazes
reverences it as a god'; compare Psyche's reactions on beholding
Cupid for the first time (5.22 f.). Plato describes how the soul 'in its
madness cannot sleep at night, and during the day it cannot be still,
but runs with longing to wherever it thinks it will set eyes on the
possessor of beauty' (251 E). This is closely parallel to such passages
as 5.28.1. On all this, see ch. 7.

[2] Note, for example, that Pan is seated 'iuxta supercilium amnis', and
compare *Georgics* 1.108. Close to the bank are 'tondentes capellae';
cf. *Ecl.* 10.7. Pan describes himself as *upilio*—cf. *Ecl.* 10.19.

[3] κυανέῃσιν ἐπ᾽ ὀφρύσι νεῦσε Κρονίων (*Il.* 1.528).

[4] *Met.* 6.18.2 ff., 19.3.

This description is virtually a mosaic of Virgilian phrases—
'saevi spiracula Ditis / monstrantur', 'medicatis frugibus offam',
'cumba / sutilis', 'terribili squalore Charon', 'ripae ulterioris',
'perque domos Ditis vacuas'.[1] A little earlier in Apuleius,
other Virgilian expressions are incorporated in the phrase
'Stygias...paludes et rauca Cocyti fluenta';[2] and one may
further note Virgilian motifs, as for example the old man who
begs entry to the boat, as Palinurus does in Virgil.[3]

These are some of the more striking examples of such
literary evocation in *Cupid and Psyche*, drawn from a wide
range of Greek and Roman authors; the exemplification could
be multiplied.[4] Apuleius' technique, it will be observed, is more
allusive than Petronius', with less direct quotation of an extended kind; he prefers to incorporate the reminiscences in
his narrative, and to adapt them to his strikingly personal
style.[5]

Like Petronius, Apuleius in recounting his narrative sometimes burlesques the presentation of the rhetorical historians
like Sallust and Livy. The deliberate connexion with the genre
is established by his use of the word *historia*.[6] The episode in

[1] *Aen.* 7.568 f., 6.420 f., 413 f., 299, 314, 269.

[2] *Met.* 6.13.4: *Aen.* 6.369, 327.

[3] *Met.* 6.18.8 and *Aen.* 6.337 ff. Note also the prominence of Cerberus
at 6.19.3, and cf. *Aen.* 6.417 f. At 6.10.6 we read 'terrae omniparentis
agiles alumnae'; cf. *Aen.* 6.595 'Terrae omniparentis alumnum'. I am
grateful to Mr J. R. G. Wright for assistance in the compilation of
these reminiscences.

[4] See the useful edition of P. Grimal (Paris 1963), where many such
reminiscences are noted. And similar results could be obtained by
scrutiny e.g. of the Charite story.

[5] Apuleius' more complex evocation is well illustrated at 3.1.1, where
he combines two Homeric images of the dawn. 'Commodum puni-
cantibus phaleris Aurora roseum quatiens lacertum caelum inequita-
bat.' Dawn is here in her chariot, and the image of her 'rosy fingers'
is replaced; she 'shakes her rosy arm' as charioteer. Cf. *Aen.* 7.26,
6.535. In English literature Fielding is especially fond of parodying
such epic formulae.

[6] 8.1.4: 'referam vobis a capite quae gesta sunt quaeque possint merito
doctiores...in historiae specimen chartis involvere.'

the robbers' lair is an outstanding example. When Lucius and the robbers arrive at the cave, the narrative is halted to allow the insertion of a description of the locale, which is introduced by the traditional formula. 'Res ac tempus ipsum locorum speluncaeque illius, quam latrones inhabitabant, descriptionem exponere flagitat.'[1] The bandits hold a consultation; it is adorned with the characteristic phraseology of the *genus deliberativum* as employed by the historians.[2] When the robbers are overcome, and the relieving soldiers escort the kidnapped Charite back to her home, there is a description of how the entire city turns out to meet her. The technique is a stock practice in rhetorical historiography. 'Tota civitas ad votivum conspectum effunditur. procurrunt parentes adfines clientes alumni famuli....'[3] At a later point of the narrative, Apuleius signals the impending calamities of an estate-owner, who loses his three sons and then kills himself, by depicting a series of exotic prodigies, just as an historian like Livy does before the disasters of Trasimene and Cannae.[4]

There is parody too of the procedure and characteristic speech of the law-court, as in the exploitation of the 'spoof' trial at the Festival of Laughter. The trial-scene is already a stock episode in both the ideal and the comic romance, as the stories of Chariton and Petronius demonstrate.[5] The public crier commands prosecutor and defendant to speak, and the

[1] 4.6.1. For this formulaic introduction of the ἔκφρασις (on which, see J. F. D'Alton, *Roman Literary Theory and Criticism* (London 1931) 507 f.), cf. Sallust, *B.J.* 17.1: 'res postulare videtur Africae situm paucis exponere.' For similar phrases, see Caesar *B.G.* 6.11, Sall. *B.J.* 95.2 (quoted by E. Mensching, *H* (1967), 457). A similar formulation is found in Apuleius at 9.32.1, the description of the market-gardener's routine.

[2] E.g., 6.31.2: 'tunc unus, omnium sedato tumultu, placido sermone sic orsus est.' Then the reaction to the speech: 'non pedibus sed totis animis latrones in eius vadunt sententiam.' Compare Livy 9.8.13, etc.

[3] 7.13.1. So, e.g., Livy 31.14.12 writes: 'civitas omnis obviam effusa cum coniugibus ac liberis, sacerdotes cum insignibus suis...ac di prope ipsi...'.

[4] 9.33–4; cf. Livy 21.62, 22.1.8 ff.

[5] Char. 5.6 ff.; Petr. fr. 8 Müller.

water-clock is set. The speech of the prosecutor is precisely in the recommended pattern of *exordium, narratio, probatio, conclusio*. His *exordium* duly recounts the importance of the topic, the obligation of his audience, and his own disinterestedness (*principium a re ipsa, ab auditoribus, a propria persona*); his *narratio* recounts the facts, and his *probatio* establishes them; and the *conclusio* properly exhorts the jury to bring in a verdict of guilty. Before replying, Lucius the defendant bursts into tears—a stock ploy in trial scenes as described in dramatic historiography. And his speech, a candid confession of technical guilt, is duly structured with *exordium, narratio* and *conclusio*.[1]

Nor is the judicial type of speech the sole one parodied. It is clear, for example, that the climax of the robber's saga of Thrasyleon with its sententious rhetoric echoes the banal formula of the epideictic utterance—'sic etiam Thrasyleon nobis perivit, sed a gloria non peribit.'[2] Elsewhere such parody again undercuts the serious strain of the narrative. After the sadistic boy has been torn to pieces by a bear, his mother angrily addresses Lucius in the tones of a prosecuting counsel: 'Nam pro deum fidem, quadrupes nequissime, licet precariam vocis usuram sumeres, cui tandem vel ineptissimo persuadere possis atrocitatem istam culpa tua carere, cum propugnare pedibus et arcere morsibus misello puero potueris? an ipsum quidem saepius incursare calcibus potuisti, moriturum vero defendere alacritate simili nequisti?'[3] Inevitably an English version fails to echo the Ciceronian techniques of *apostrophe* and *interrogatio*, antithesis and *isocolon*, alliteration and *homoioteleuton*, and the jocular force may escape those who fail to read the original.

In retelling the story of Lucius, Apuleius constantly com-

---

[1] Prosecutor's *exordium*, 3.3.2–4; *narratio*, 3.3.5 f.; *probatio*, 3.3.7 f., including a splendid *sententia* ('providentia deum, quae nihil impunitum nocentibus permittit'); *conclusio*, 3.3.9 f. On the divisions, see Arist. *Rhet.* 2.26; Quint. 3.9. Lucius' speech is at 3.4.3 ff. For the tears, cf. Livy 40.8 ff., the trial of Demetrius before his father Philip.
[2] 4.21.6: see P. Vallette in the Budé edition.
[3] 7.27.5.

pares his characters to well-known figures of mythology and literature. The witch Meroë in Aristomenes' story anticipates public prosecution 'like the famous Medea'. The miserly host Milo urges Lucius to regard his lodging as Theseus did the hospitality of Hecale after he had fought the bull of Marathon; here one observes how Apuleius exploits the mythological type to reflect ironically or grotesquely on his characters, for Milo is notorious for his meanness.[1] Photis amusingly compares Lucius, in his battle with the inflated wine-skins, to the cattle-slaying Ajax, a comic reference capped by Lucius when he calls himself a Hercules slaying a three-headed Cerberus or Geryon.[2] Some allusions are taken over from the original story. When Lucius the ass tries to escape from the robber's cave, the old woman guarding him tries to hold him back δίκην Δίρκης, an allusion which Apuleius explains with the fuller phrase 'non tauro sed asino dependentem Dircen aniculam'.[3] Or again, compare the description of the ass-turned-gallant in the *Onos*, ὁ τῆς Πασιφάης μοιχός, with Apuleius' description of the matron as 'ad instar asinariae Pasiphaae'.[4] Some of Apuleius' allusions take the learned Alexandrian form avoided by Petronius. So, when the story-teller Thelyphron compares himself in his tribulations to Pentheus and Orpheus, he writes: 'sic in modum superbi iuvenis Aoni vel Musici vatis Piplei laceratus...'.[5] The learned formulation demonstrates the sophistication demanded by the author of his audience, who are expected to be as familiar with the plastic arts as with literature; they are to recognise in his description of a pose of Photis, for

[1] 1.10.2: 1.23.6. The Theseus reference may be a reminiscence of Callimachus' *Hecale*. Junghanns, 19 n. 22, comments: 'Mythologische Vergleiche liebt Apul., besonders als wirksame Szenenabschlüsse. Sie stehen oft in gewolltem Kontrast zum Ethos der betreffenden Situation.'

[2] The point being that there were three skins; 3.18.6 f., 3.19.1 f.

[3] *Onos* 23; *Met.* 6.27.5. On Dirce's punishment (torn apart by a bull) see Ps. Apollod. 3.5.5.

[4] *Onos* 51; *Met.* 10.19.3 and cf. 10.22.4.

[5] *Met.* 2.26.8. See also the far-fetched comparison to Althaea at 7.28.4.

example, an evocation of representations of *Venus pudica* described by Apuleius in another work.[1]

For this readership at once learned and Roman, Apuleius makes interesting modifications of metaphor to the Greek novel. In the Greek version, the love-encounter between Lucius and Milo's comely slave-girl is described through the metaphor of wrestling. The girl's name is Palaestra, and Lucius bids himself strip for this 'wrestling-ground'.[2] Apuleius translates the metaphor to the sphere of warfare. The Augustan poets, especially Ovid and Propertius, are fond of adapting military images to the language of love; and Apuleius, having changed the girl's name to Photis, takes over this favourite Roman motif. 'Fortiter proeliare...nec enim tibi cedam nec terga vortam...grassare naviter et occide moriturus. hodierna pugna non habet missionem.'[3]

Another specifically Roman strand in the texture of the novel is the introduction of legal motifs for humorous effect. Apuleius was himself a trained lawyer, and since the Roman higher education was geared pre-eminently to the fostering of eloquence, written and spoken, he could assume an appreciative awareness of these jocose legal touches in his sophisticated audience. Like Petronius, Apuleius is not troubled about the inconsistencies involved when Greek characters show themselves thoroughly Roman in their legal references.[4] Moreover, even the deities in the *Cupid and Psyche* episode show a shrewd

---

[1] 2.17.1: 'in speciem Veneris...glabellum feminal rosea palmula... obumbrans'. Cf. *Apol.* 33.7: '...quodam libro meo legit: inter-feminium tegat et femoris obiectu et palmae velamento.' (Cf. 34.3.)

[2] *Onos* 5: ἄγε δὴ σύ...ἐπὶ τὴν θεράπαιναν τὴν Παλαίστραν ἤδη ἀποδύου ... and cf. 10.

[3] 2.17.3. M. Bernhard, *Der Stil des Apuleius*, 197, lists other passages with such military metaphors.

[4] So in the Thelyphron story (2.24.3) an inventory of the corpse's features is included to stipulate the contract. See also the episode of the auction of Lucius, where the auctioneer tries to sell the ass as a hard-working Cappadocian rather than as a Roman citizen, for to sell a citizen is against 'the Cornelian law' (probably a 'nom de fan-taisie'; cf. Vallette *ad loc.*) (8.24.4).

awareness of their rights in Roman law; the legal threats of
Venus are one of the consistently comic motifs which Apuleius
has himself introduced into the story. She threatens to disinherit her son Cupid, and to adopt instead one of her slaves;[1]
she maintains that his marriage with Psyche was illegal, 'in
villa sine testibus et patre non consentiente'.[2] The other deities
likewise profess themselves bound by the Roman legal statutes.
Juno, for example, will not allow Psyche to linger in her shrine
because she is regarded as the runaway slave of Venus, and the
law forbade the harbouring of slaves against a master's will.[3]
Even the king of the gods himself hints that he finds it embarrassing to transgress the *lex Iulia de adulteriis*.[4]

Equally sophisticated is the incorporation of procedural and
even sacral formulae in the narrative of sexual encounter. When
Apuleius takes over from his Greek source the soliloquy of
Lucius at the point where the hero decides to seek a knowledge
of magic through prior intimacy with the slave-girl Photis, the
Latin version strikes a note of high comedy with such phrases.
In proposing to himself the encounter with Photis, Lucius uses
the phrase of good augury adopted by Roman state officials
on graver occasions, 'quod bonum felix et faustum'. In
approving his own proposal, he employs the formula of
senatorial voting, 'pedibus in sententiam meam vado'; and in
the initial confrontation with the girl he says that she has
declared war on him 'sine fetiali officio'.[5]

The description of Lucius' first actions after becoming an
ass is invested with similar humour. He retires to the stables,

---

[1] 5.29.5. This was perfectly possible in Roman law; on this see F. Norden, *Apuleius von Madaura und das römische Privatrecht* (Leipzig
1912), 74.

[2] On the passage (6.9.6), see Grimal *ad loc.* Venus adds that the child
of the marriage will be likewise illegal.

[3] 6.4.5. Cf. *Dig.* 11.4.1, where the rescript from Marcus Aurelius and
Commodus no longer permits the twenty days' grace previously
allowed for turning in runaway slaves apprehended on one's estate.
See Appendix 2.

[4] 6.22.4. There is a lot of this kind of legal joking in Fielding's novels,
e.g. in *Joseph Andrews* and *Jonathan Wild*, as well as in Smollett.

[5] 2.6.8, 7.1, 16.5.

hoping for 'hospitium ac loca lautia' from his horse—the technical term for hospitality given to distinguished public visitors at Rome. His fellow-beasts he describes as *collegae*. And after enduring hardship from the robbers, he thinks of applying for a medical discharge from service![1]

It is appropriate to consider at this point the general question of the Latinity of the *Metamorphoses*[2] against the background of this sophistication of texture in the ancient romance. Unlike the simple and elegant Latin of Petronius, reflecting the best colloquial usage of the educated classes of his day, Apuleius' studied artificiality is a conscious experiment to adapt the presentation to the theme. It should be noted that the style is utterly different from that of the *Apology*, where Cicero is the model, and from that of the philosophical works, where there is no attempt to write with élan or colour.[3] This deliberate variation of styles should alone dispose of the theory of a 'tumor Africus', which sought to align Apuleius with Fronto and with the Christian writers Minucius Felix and Tertullian as heirs to an ebullient regional Latinity.[4] Second-century Carthage was the cultural centre of the Roman civilisation, and the provincialisms are marginal.[5] The alleged 'tumor Africus' is in fact a 'tumor Romanus' already in evidence in the time of Petronius and reflecting Asianic influences on the central current of Roman writing.[6]

---

[1] 3.26.5 (and again at 9.11.2: cf. Livy 28.39.19, 30.17.14, etc.); 3.27.1; 4.4.5, 'mereri causariam missionem' (cf. *Dig.* 3.2.2).

[2] M. Bernhard, *Der Stil des Apuleius*, is the best general guide; it incorporates Norden's important contribution in *Die antike Kunstprosa*, 2.588 ff.

[3] Besides Norden, see P. Médan, *La latinité d'Apulée*, in the avant-propos.

[4] See Norden's classic demolition; also (earlier) Kroll, *RhM* (1897), 569 ff. There are good comments in Purser's edition of *Cupid and Psyche*, lxx ff.

[5] So Bernhard, 3: 'höchstens...lassen sich einige afrikanische Provinzialismen in der Sprache jener Autoren nachweisen'.

[6] Encolpius in Petronius' novel complains: 'nuper ventosa istaec et enormis loquacitas Athenas ex Asia commigravit...' (2.7) and sees this as the bane of Roman schools of rhetoric.

This Asiatic influence at the height of the Second Sophistic is especially powerful in Greek oratory and in those subjects for formal recitation so popular in the 'Isocratean' tradition of pedagogy.[1] But it also exercises a magnetic effect on the writers of ideal fiction, whose learned excursuses affect the manner of the epideictic lecture. Repeatedly these descriptive passages incorporate double or triple or quadruple clauses, all more or less of the same length (*isocolon*) and all ending with the same syllable (*homoioteleuton*). Achilles Tatius, for example, describes a formal garden with the words: ἔθαλλον οἱ κλάδοι . . . αἱ γείτονες τῶν πετάλων περιπλοκαί, τῶν φύλλων περιβολαί, τῶν καρπῶν συμπλοκαί . . . or an Egyptian ox like this: τὸν αὐχένα παχύς, τὸν νῶτον πλατύς, τὴν γαστέρα πολύς.[2] Longus prefers the double rhyme to the triple. So Cupid has πτερά ἐκ τῶν ὤμων ἔχοντι, βέλη σμικρὰ ἅμα τοξαρίῳ φέροντι . . ., and images of nymphs are described as follows:

χεῖρες εἰς ὤμους γυμναί, κόμαι μέχρι τῶν αὐχένων λελυμέναι, ჳῶμα περὶ τὴν ἰξύν, μειδίαμα περὶ τὴν ὀφρύν.[3]

It will be remembered that the hero of Apuleius' romance is a Greek who in the amusing introduction comically excuses himself for his unschooled Latin in a passage of remarkable rhythmical dexterity.[4] Under the pretext of the Greek narrator,

[1] Purser well mentions Philostratus' descriptions of statuary and compares Apul. *Met.* 2.4.

[2] 1.15.2, 2.15.3.

[3] 1.7.2, 1.4.2. Castiglioni well analyses the similar passage in 2.34: ἀλλὰ παρθένος καλὴ καὶ τὴν φωνὴν μουσική. αἶγας ἔνεμεν, Νύμφαις συνέπαιζεν. See also 4.12.2–3, 4.14.1–2.

[4] It is instructive to look at Oudendorp's edition of Apuleius (Leiden 1786) to see how Scaliger and others arranged these introductory comments in verses, e.g.:

at ego tibi sermone isto Milesio
varias fabellas conseram, atque aures tuas
lepido susurro benivolas permulceam;
modo si papyrum Aegyptiam tu argutia, etc.

Which only proves the truth of Quintilian's observation, 'nihil, quod est prosa scriptum, non redigi possit in quaedam versiculorum genera' (9.4.52).

Apuleius introduces into Latin the rhythms and rhymes which are commonplace in Greek epideictic compositions; and since the realisation of this aim is much easier in Greek, where nouns, adjectives, participles more readily rhyme, Apuleius' imitations in Latin[1] are at once more ingenious and more bizarre, and repeatedly wring from the bemused reader precisely that ironical applause which Apuleius sought to elicit. The *Florida* shows that he practised these techniques in other compositions besides fiction.[2]

These Gorgianic techniques, which exploit for ancillary purposes alliteration and assonance, clearly exercise an important influence over Apuleius' exotic diction, which is the other main feature of his colourful style. It has frequently been noted, for example, that in the splendid tricolon

> mulieres candido splendentes amicimine / vario laetantes gestamine / verno florentes coronamine

coronamen appears nowhere else in Latin, and *amicimen* only in Apuleius, who appears to be introducing neologisms to achieve his rhythmical balance.[3] Such Gorgianic aims are of course only one strand in the complex skein of factors which affect his diction. The element of parody in pompous declamation, the effect of *naïveté* in simple tales demand considerable variation in tone and in language; then there is the passion for archaising introduced by Fronto and taken up enthusiastically by Marcus Aurelius, so that in Apuleius' day Sallust and Cato have become favourite authors.[4] In general, Apuleius takes a Joycean joy in experimenting with words, and employs not only

---

[1] Bernhard, 7: 'Der Roman ist durchaus in griechischem Geist geschrieben.'   [2] See e.g. *Flor.* 18.3 f., 16.9.

[3] 11.9.2; see Bernhard, 140, for other examples of neologisms to aid Gorgianic balance (3.18.1, 6.2.5, 10.21.2, etc.). Such tricola with a rhyming effect are recommended in the *Ad Herennium*, 4.19.26.

[4] D'Alton, *Roman Literary Theory and Criticism*, 348 ff.; F. Portaluppi, *Marco Cornelio Fronto* (Turin 1961), 21 ff.; L. Callebat, *REL* (1964), 364 ff., emphasising the influence of Sisenna as a 'Milesian' writer, and citing characteristic Apuleian archaisms condemned earlier by Quintilian; B. C. Dietrich, *GR* (1966), 189 ff.

archaisms and neologisms, but also well-known words with strange senses to shock and to amuse; the Latin has to be studied with almost the same desperate concentration as *Finnegan's Wake*. Cupid is *inhumanus*—not 'savage' but 'divine'; the voices of the unseen servants in Cupid's palace are *informes*—not 'ugly' but 'disembodied'. Psyche's virginity is *interfectus*, not 'killed' but 'penetrated'. He is constantly punning, as in 'savia suavia', 'atra atria'.[1] These random examples (every page tells the story) suffice to demonstrate how the style contributes to the entertainment.

In summary, then, Petronius and Apuleius continue the tradition of Greek comic fiction in telling their exotic stories in a bookish manner. For Petronius the exploitation of themes from epic and satire allows him to underline the dual nature of the *Satyricon*, the synthesis of the Greek picaresque and the Roman satirical elements. Further, within the individual episodes he comically burlesques the presentation of historians and the tone of epic, and he introduces all manner of literary allusions. Throughout, his main purpose is to amuse his sophisticated readers, and the only writers against whom he directs ridicule are the humdrum versifiers of his own age. Apuleius' narrative is not so consistently structured after literary models as is Petronius', but after the manner of the Greek ideal romance he regularly adds atmosphere to a scene by the evocation of the appropriate literary master, and in this he draws upon a broader choice of Greek authors than does Petronius. The literary evocation in Apuleius has not the uniformly comic aim of Petronius; in some scenes it has such a humorous purpose, but in others it intensifies the dramatic and indeed tragic mood. Apuleius' Roman version of a Greek story reveals that it is directed at a Roman literary audience not only by the Latin literary reminiscences but also by the introduction of amusing legal and procedural references; and his use of language itself is a constant contribution to the intellectual entertainment.

[1] I take these examples from Purser for the most part. His account of similar Euphuism in Lyly is well worth reading (xc ff.).

4

THE 'SATYRICON'

Of all kinds of satire, there is none so entertaining and universally improving as that which is introduced, as it were, occasionally in the course of an interesting story. SMOLLETT, Preface to *Roderick Random*

When no moral, no lesson, no instruction is conveyed to the reader, where the whole design of the composition is no more than to make us laugh, the writer comes very near to the character of a buffoon.

FIELDING, *The Covent Garden Journal*, No. 10
(Tuesday 4 February 1752)

Thus far the *Satyricon* has been presented in its derivatively literary aspects. But these provide no more than a framework and a conventional mode of narrative. Petronius develops the picaresque tradition for a Roman audience by the involvement of his hero in situations closely familiar to readers of educated taste. These themes are underscored by the evocation of amusing parallel situations in earlier literature, but they are also issues of lively contemporary interest, and accordingly they should be viewed, at least summarily, against the backcloth of Neronian society.

The *Satyricon* was written between the years 63 and 66.[1] Its author, Titus Petronius Niger, was of a *gens* which had emerged from the obscurity of its Republican history to a prominent role in the political life of the Julio-Claudians.[2] With his money

---

[1] See Appendix 1.
[2] Though the Petronii could boast occasional ancestors of Republican distinction (one had been a senatorial *legatus* in 156 (Pol. 32.26.5) and another participated in Caesar's assassination (App. *B.C.* 5.4.15)), it is only with the Augustan age that they proliferate in public life. C. Petronius was prefect of Egypt 29–22 B.C., and his grandsons included the consul suffectus for A.D. 25 and the cos. suff. for A.D. 19 (*CIL* 1.766: *PIR*[1], 198: Hanslik, *RE* 19.1199 ff.). It is possible to distinguish six branches of the Petronii in the early empire. The most prominent are the Petronii Turpiliani (one was consul in 61 and

and influential family-connexions, he might have been expected to seek from the outset a distinguished public career. This is why Tacitus in the famous character-sketch[1] makes so much of his ostentatious idleness, castigating his sense of values but clearly fascinated by the style with which he pursued his interests. Petronius had spent his early manhood in 'celebrated sloth'. It was not 'gluttony or wild spending' which made him a byword, but the manner of his 'fastidious luxury';[2] and his cynical candour and indifference to personal danger conferred on him an immunity which was doubtless also ensured by his scorn for political advancement.

Subsequently, however, he did embark on a political career. Perhaps his praetorship and the subsequent governorship of Bithynia fell in the later years of Claudius.[3] Under Nero he became consul suffectus in 62 or 63,[4] and the date is significant. 62 was the year of the death of Burrus, an event which broke the dominance of Seneca.[5] The place of these moderate and principled advisers was seized by a group of *deteriores* aspiring to court power.[6] Tigellinus, the dominant praetorian prefect appointed in 62, was 'closer to the ear of the emperor, and a participant in his secret debaucheries'.[7] Vibius Crispus and Eprius Marcellus, both branded by the tradition as able administrators who prostituted their talents to timeserving and personal advancement, reached the consulship in that same year. These are the dubious associates of Petronius in his

governor of Britain), the Petronii Turcones, and the Petronii Umbrini. The cos. suff. of A.D. 19, P. Petronius, governed Syria 39–42 and was an intimate of the emperor Claudius (Sen. *Apocol.* 14.2). I am grateful to Dr T. J. Cadoux and Mr R. G. Lewis for this and more detailed information on the *gens*, which would perhaps be otiose in this context.

[1] *Ann.* 16.18.
[2] 'Hunc ignavia ad famam protulerat, habebatur non ganeo et profligator sed erudito luxu.'
[3] There is of course no evidence for this suggestion.
[4] See Rose, *Latomus* (1961), 821 ff.
[5] Tac. *Ann.* 14.52.1: 'mors Burri infregit Senecae potentiam...'.
[6] '...et Nero ad deteriores inclinabat.'
[7] *Ann.* 14.51.6.

rise to prominence.[1] It is wholly in keeping with all that we know of Petronius that he should have eschewed any prospect of political association with the worthy Stoic Seneca, and have attained prominence only with Seneca's discomfiture.[2]

By 63 Petronius had supplanted Seneca as the central cultural figure in the palace. For three years Nero leaned on him as his tutor in refinement (*arbiter elegantiae*) until Tigellinus was able successfully to awake the emperor's suspicions of him. Petronius' weak spot was his friendship with a leader in the Pisonian conspiracy, Flavius Scaevinus, whom Tacitus scornfully depicts as another Neronian degenerate.[3] Petronius appears to have believed that he could persuade Nero of his innocence, for he set out to join him in Campania. But he was halted at Cumae, where he died by his own hand in the early summer of 66. In death as in life he was the studied antonym of Seneca, whiling away his last hours in frivolous poetic composition, and compiling for Nero's benefit a clinical account of the emperor's sexual diversions with named members of both sexes.

As Tacitus presents him, Petronius is the complete cynic, his panache in life and death a meretricious gloss over a selfish career untouched by moral principle. For three years he was Nero's intimate. He observed the hounding of the nobility which culminated in the conspiracy of 65. He retained his position through the great fire and the persecution of the Christians in 64. He encouraged the extravagances which led to the depreciation of the currency.[4] The *Satyricon* is the fruit of these years at court, when Petronius was the trusted confi-

---

[1] So R. Syme, *Tacitus*, 743.

[2] It is probable that Seneca was antipathetic to P. Petronius, who in the *Apocolocyntosis* is lampooned as 'homo Claudiana lingua disertus' (14.2). Family tensions may have exacerbated personal antipathies.

[3] 'Dissoluta luxu mens, et proinde vita somno languida' (*Ann.* 15.49.5).

[4] Plutarch, *De disc. adul. et am.* 60 D–E: 'That form of flattery is dangerous ὅταν τοὺς ἀσώτους καὶ πολυτελεῖς εἰς μακρολογίαν καὶ ῥυπαρίαν ὀνειδίζουσιν ὥσπερ Νέρωνα Τίτος Πετρώνιος.' For the extravagance and its outcome, see e.g. E. T. Salmon, *History of the Roman World*, ch. IV §6.

dant of Nero. The ambivalence of his attitudes towards the emperor is revealed by his documentation at death of the emperor's sexual aberrations. The *Satyricon* is to be visualised as an entertainment for Petronius' friends in which the narrative is enlivened by comic allusions to the life of the court and of the city. In this sense the description 'novel of escape' has a strikingly apposite connotation. Nero may not have fiddled as Rome burned, but Petronius wrote his *Satyricon*.

The suggestion has frequently been advanced that the novel was a court-entertainment. Just as earlier Seneca's plays, more suitable for recitation than for acting,[1] may have been declaimed to a literary circle centred on the court, so the *Satyricon* may have been designed as a hilarious successor, and read in instalments to an audience of intimates.[2] This hypothesis goes far to explain some of the characteristic features of the novel. The literary structuring presupposes a highly literate audience: the parodies of Seneca and Lucan are addressed to those who have already heard their works declaimed by their authors. And in reading the various episodes, we become aware that much of the humour has a local reference. Yet the hypothesis of a court-entertainment must be advanced with caution. Above all, in the Trimalchio episode there are many details of characterisation comically taken over from Nero's own appearance and habits which the emperor could hardly have failed to recognise.[3] Nero himself can scarcely have attended such readings. He was not the man to accept ridicule with a smile. We are told, for example (the story is doubtless apocryphal), that when Lucan in a public privy declaimed a half-line of Nero's poetry in apt description of his activities, those present took to their heels.[4] It is more prudent to assume that the circle for whom Petronius wrote was a restricted audience of trusted intimates.

[1] W. Beare, *The Roman Stage*, Appendix P.
[2] G. Boissier's suggestion in *L'Opposition sous les Césars* (Paris 1875), ch. 5, has been taken up by most critics.   [3] Below, pp. 137 ff.
[4] Suetonius' life of Lucan retails the *magna consessorum fuga* when the poet quoted the Neronian phrase 'sub terris tonuisse putes'.

It has recently been suggested that Petronius' whole purpose in writing the *Satyricon* was to provide as pretext for his poetic and literary experimentation a vehicle which would not provoke the jealousy of the emperor.[1] The tradition is certainly unanimous that 'Nero's pride in his talents as a poet made it difficult for him to brook known or respected rivals.'[2] There is even a report that the emperor appropriated the impromptu efforts of promising versifiers, filling out his own mediocre compositions with theirs.[3] One of the allegations made against Seneca in 62 was that 'he was composing verses more often, now that Nero had come to love the pursuit'; and Lucan was actually forbidden to publish, a veto which followed upon an earlier incident in which the emperor walked out of his *recitatio* to diminish the poet's popular acclaim.[4] The elder Pliny's prudent decision to devote the years 66 to 68 to grammatical publication rather than to history is a further indication of the repressive climate attending literary studies.[5] Yet the thesis that the *Satyricon* is a mere 'container' for literary, philosophical, and artistic expression, 'a strong shield against the suspicion that he was engaged in anything other than tomfoolery', is wholly unconvincing. First, because the poetic efforts and the literary discussions are not a serious and original contribution. Secondly, because all that we know of the author encourages us to believe that the *Satyricon* as it is—sophisticated and literary, disreputable and amusing—is his

[1] Perry, *The Ancient Romances*, 205.

[2] D'Alton, *Roman Literary Theory and Criticism*, 452.

[3] *Ann.* 14.16.1 (A.D. 59). The charge is rejected by Suetonius, *Nero* 52.

[4] Tac, *Ann.* 14.52.3: '[Senecam] carmina crebrius factitare postquam Neroni amor eorum venisset.' The implication is that Seneca was trying to outshine Nero. The veto on Lucan's publication is reported at *Ann.* 15.49.3 (A.D. 65). For the walk-out, see Suet. *Vita Lucani*, where the motive is recorded 'nulla nisi refrigerandi sui causa'; but Lucan's case is complicated by the poet's offensive reaction, which included a *famosum carmen* against Nero and his friends, and this was doubtless the cause of the ban on publication.

[5] See Pliny, *Ep.* 3.5.5: 'sub Nerone novissimis annis, cum omne studiorum genus paulo liberius et erectius periculosum servitus fecisset.'

monumentum aere perennius. And thirdly it may be noted that Nero's repression extended only to rivals of some political eminence, or to those who made their intransigence explicit. There is no suggestion that the unpolitical Persius was discouraged from writing, and Petronius himself makes it clear that composition of verses is the national vice.[1] The novelist himself, a privileged intimate, hardly falls into the category of a Seneca and a Lucan in this respect.

Petronius gave his novel a title of characteristic cleverness and ambivalence, denoting its derivative connexion with its two predecessors, Greek comic fiction and Roman satire. As an episodic narrative of comic adventure within the Greek tradition it bears the Greek title 'Σατυρικῶν libri', 'a story of lascivious behaviour'. The Greek word bears the additional sense of 'derisive', and the adjective is so aptly descriptive of the book that Petronius may well have intended this additional overtone. Then there is a punning pointer towards Roman satire. True, the adjective *satiricus* is not found in extant Latin before the fourth century, and the Greek and Latin words are unconnected. But the philological distinction is not in question; rather, would the title *Satyricon* have immediately registered in a Roman ear the association with *satura?* There can be little doubt that it would. Petronius intended his title to convey to the alert reader that his book was a derisive account of lascivious behaviour, infused with satirical elements.[2]

[1] Persius of course died in 62, the year in which Seneca was attacked for his verses. Eumolpus calls versification the harbour for those who find litigation too arduous. 118.2: 'sic forensibus ministeriis exercitati frequenter ad carminis tranquillitatem tamquam ad portum refugerunt, credentes facilius poema extrui posse quam controversiam sententiolis vibrantibus pictam.'

[2] In Greek literature, regional epics like Rhianos' *Messeniaka* (on which see Otis, *Virgil*, 17) and doubtless some early romances (cf. Heliodorus' *Aithiopika*) with local names gave Aristides the notion of calling his sexy stories *Milesiaka*. Other titles described the type of story, for example *Poimenika* (see Courtney, *Philol.* (1962), 86 ff.), and Petronius' title is in this tradition. For Satyricon as a Greek genitive plural, see Henricksson, *Griechische Büchertitel* (Helsinki 1956), 74 ff.; others (e.g. Van Rooy, 154) improbably argue for a

Much ingenuity has been expended on the speculative question of the original length and scope of the novel. The chief profit derivable from such studies is a realisation of the frailty of the evidence. The manuscript indications suggest that the extant parts of the novel belong to Books XIV–XVI, but this information is late and conflicting.[1] The *Satyricon* would certainly have been by ancient standards of fiction a monster work if the surviving portions had been preceded by a narrative five times as long. Since the book was already in a fragmentary state in the Carolingian age, these allusions to XIV–XVI should be regarded with reserve.[2] Surer evidence of the earlier extent of the novel is obtained by consultation of the fragments and references in the surviving parts of the book. We may infer that it began with Encolpius in his native habitat, betrothed to a girl called Doris, probably at Marseilles.[3] He is warned in a dream or by an oracle to journey overseas:

neuter singular. For the ambivalence of the title, harking back to satire, see Kroll, *RE* 19, 1201; Van Rooy, 155. Those who argue against this, like Perry, 191 f., put weight on the philological distinction which is not in dispute.

[1] The fifteenth-century *codex Traguriensis* calls the extant sections up to 137.9, and excluding the *Cena*, 'fragmenta ex libro XV et XVI'; Poggio refers to the *Cena* as 'XV liber' (*Ep.* 1.7, ed. De Tonellis (Florence 1832)); an unknown interpolator in Fulgentius' *Mythologiae* (3.8) states that the episode preceding the *Cena* is from XIV; and a note on the *codex Harleianus* ascribes ch. 89 to Bk. XV. Many are tempted to resolve the inconsistency by ascribing the incidents before the *Cena* to XIV, the *Cena* to XV, and the subsequent adventures to XVI; Sullivan, *The Satyricon*, 35, divides: Bk. XIV, 12–26.6; Bk. XV, 1–11, 26.7–99; Bk. XVI, 100–end. K. Müller, *Praef.* 30 f., suggests: XIV, 1–26.6; XV, 26.7–78; XVI– , 79–141 (more than one book).

[2] Collignon, ch. 1, suggests that we have barely one-sixth of the whole; Heinze, *H* (1889), 495, registers a protest, for no other ancient fiction is written on that scale. One suggested solution is that the numbers 14–16 represent *scenes* not books (the extant sections take place in three locales, the city in the Naples area, the ship, and Croton), and that the previous thirteen could have been shorter (so Sinko, *Eos* (1935), 385 ff., whose arguments are developed by Marmorale).

[3] For Doris, see 126.18. The evidence for Marseilles is not secure. Sid. Apoll. *Carm.* 23.155 ff. (Petr. fr. 4 Müller) calls Petronius 'Mas-

linque tuas sedes, alienaque litora quaere
⟨o⟩ iuvenis; maior rerum tibi nascitur ordo.
ne succumbe malis; te noverit ultimus Ister...[1]

In his early travels, Encolpius encounters Lichas and Tryphaena, whom he is to confront again aboard ship. He becomes an intimate friend of Lichas and his wife Hedyle ('Sweetie'), and the intimacy with Hedyle goes too far, ending with a brawl with Lichas 'in the portico of Hercules'. It is tempting to set this episode in Monaco.[2] Encolpius has a sexual encounter also with Tryphaena, from whose service he spirits away the comely slave Giton.[3] We may infer that these incidents occur in the same town because Lichas and Tryphaena are friends, and in a third episode there Encolpius is indicted, probably for abducting Giton. He is prosecuted by a *Cerberus forensis* called

siliensium...colonum / Hellespontiaco parem Priapo', a description which suggests that Sidonius is identifying Petronius with Encolpius, just as Apuleius is identified with his hero. Then in fr. 1 Müller (Serv. *ad Aen.* 3.57), a Massilian rite is described by which a poor man is selected and fed for a year before being pushed off a cliff to avert a pestilence. Could Encolpius have been chosen as scapegoat, and have fled to avoid this fate? (For a development of the suggestion, see Sullivan, 41 f.) The theory is at any rate no more bizarre than that of Cichorius (*Röm. Stud.* (1922), 438 ff.) that the hero was in trouble for impersonating a statue of Priapus during a ladies' orgiastic outing, a bold interpretation of fr. 4.

[1] Fr. 37 Bücheler (44 Ernout). K. Müller rejects the verses as spurious, but the Virgilian references are in keeping with the parodying manner of Petronius, and the oracular utterance at the outset is a convention in the love-romance which Petronius may be burlesquing; see e.g. Xen. Eph. 1.6.2, and compare Apuleius, *Met.* 4.33.

[2] The friendship with Lichas and Hedyle, *Sat.* 107.1, 107.11, 105.9, 107.5, etc. Seduction of Hedyle, and assault on Lichas, 106.2. The site of the assault, *in Herculis porticu*, could by a slight emendation become *in Herculis portu* (Monaco, which derives from the epithet of Hercules, *monoikos*). The town had been recently famed in Lucan's epic (1.405 ff.) and would be *en route* from Marseilles to Italy. The usual theory for the locale is Baiae; see Sullivan, 43. (Tryphaena later (ch. 104) tells of a dream in which the statue of Neptune at a shrine in Baiae speaks to her).

[3] Encolpius lover of Tryphaena, 113.8; Giton her slave, 105.5 ff.

Euscius (?Paleface),[1] and after a public outburst against the immorality of Tryphaena the hero decides to anticipate condemnation by flight. In his departure he leaves for dead the man at whose house he was detained; this was perhaps the Lycurgus (Harshlaw) who handled Encolpius with severity, and whose house was plundered by the hero and his friends.[2]

Encolpius and Giton move on to the bay of Naples, at some point in Gaul or Italy striking an acquaintance with Ascyltus, who accompanies them. They are together involved in a peeping-Tom episode in which they observe Quartilla celebrating the Priapic rites. During this episode Ascyltus loses his shirt in a desolate spot, suspicion for the theft of which falls on Encolpius.[3]

Though reconstruction is speculative, it will be clear that all these references can be embraced in half-a-dozen episodes, taking place in one or other of two towns, perhaps Marseilles and Monaco, if we exclude the Quartilla affair which immediately precedes the first extant scene. It is true that one or two further incidents can be posited; for example, there may have been an affair with a certain Albucia, whose name had a local Roman significance as a lady of easy virtue.[4] But this limited evidence, admittedly in itself inconclusive, hardly indicates that as many as thirteen books of adventures preceded the first extant episode.

The scene is now set in an unnamed city on the bay of Naples for the series of eight incidents which commence with the discussion with Agamemnon at his school of rhetoric. The town has been variously identified, but more probably Petronius has deliberately refrained from siting these events in an

---

[1] Fr. 8 Müller.

[2] Outburst against Tryphaena, 106.4; murder of host, 81.3; Lycurgus, 117.3 (this fragment is probably wrongly placed in the text). This conjunction of events is of course highly speculative. See Ciaffi, *La Struttura*, 17; Sullivan, 43 ff.

[3] The peeping-Tom episode, 17.6–9; the shirt, 13.4, 12.5.

[4] Albucia, fr. 6 Müller. In *Ann.* 6.47.2, Tacitus tells how Albucilla, 'multorum amoribus famosa', achieved fame at the close of Tiberius' reign by implicating prominent senatorials on a charge of *maiestas*.

identifiable Italian city.[1] This *Graeca urbs* which is a Roman colony with a decaying harbour is a composite creation. So too after the journey by ship the final four episodes are set in no existent city but in one with the symbolic name of Croton. For by the first century Croton was a ghost city, attempts to re-vitalise the town which was formerly a byword of luxurious life having failed.[2]

Did the *Satyricon* come to a close with the events at Croton? The final extant scene, in which Eumolpus apparently on his death-bed decrees that the legacy-hunters should devour his intestines before obtaining a wholly imaginary legacy of ten million sesterces, could have provided an appropriately bizarre conclusion, followed by the conventional departure by ship of the hero from that predatory city. But there is the alternative possibility of a whole new round of adventures; those who attach weight to the references to Books XIV–XVI will be attracted by the notion that the comic *Odyssey* may have filled out twenty-four books, ending with a homecoming. These alternatives are most fruitfully weighed by an exposition of the central thread of the novel, which strongly supports the thesis that the Croton episodes are the climax and culmination of the book.

The pervasive motif of the *Satyricon* is of a hero beset by the anger of Priapus; Encolpius is thus the mimic equivalent of Odysseus and Aeneas. Priapus' anger constantly looms over the Italian adventures. It is his shrine which the heroes profane by their spying; it is he who is responsible for delivering them into the hands of Lichas aboard ship.[3] To him at Croton

---

[1] For the various candidates (Naples, Cumae, Puteoli, Misenum, Formiae, Minturno, etc.) see the discussion of Marmorale, 117 ff., whose view, taken over from Paratore, I adopt here. (Compare Cervantes' similar vagueness at the beginning of *Don Quixote*.) Sullivan, 46 ff., argues forcefully but inconclusively for Puteoli.

[2] Below, p. 104. It may be noted that T. S. Eliot's *The Waste Land* (§v) seems deliberately to evoke a ghost city, and, after the shipwreck episode in §IV, we may assume that Petronius has inspired this sequence.

[3] 16 ff., esp. 17.8; 104.1.

Encolpius addresses a grotesque *deprecatio*; to him the hero attributes his persecution:

> Iunonem Pelias sensit, tulit inscius arma
> Telephus, et regnum Neptuni pavit Ulixes.
> Me quoque per terras, per cani Nereos aequor
> Hellespontiaci sequitur gravis ira Priapi.[1]

Priapus, then, has a hand in every major misadventure—the humiliation by Quartilla, the capture by Lichas, the loss of virility with Circe.

Beneath this divine economy of Priapus' anger, the unifying theme is the attachment of Encolpius to Giton. It is hard to believe that the liaison has no reference to Priapus' anger. If Virgil is the chief model for the burlesque, there will be an interrelation between the divine and the human levels of action. It is true that the role of Encolpius as thief is repeatedly mentioned, and Priapus exercised a protective power against thieves.[2] But Priapus has also a generative function, and Encolpius' infatuation with the comely slave leads him to despise heterosexual associations. The pattern in the earlier sections of the novel, it may be suggested, is a series of heterosexual amours with Albucia, Hedyle, and Tryphaena, which are then wholly abjured through the hero's passion for Giton. At any rate there is no doubt about Encolpius' subsequent revulsion from women. In the brothel-scene he rushes out, dumb with horror. In the Quartilla episode he fails to respond to the lady's advances.[3] Throughout the subsequent episodes all the emphasis is on his longing for Giton—jealousy and despair when his rivals try to win the slave or temporarily prevail, ecstasy in reunion, anger when Tryphaena reclaims him. Only when he sets eyes on Circe[4] does his flagging interest in women revive, and here Priapus renders him impotent.

---

[1] The *deprecatio*, 133.2; the soliloquy, 139.2 ff.

[2] The Priapea ascribed to Virgil, especially the third, emphasise this power. See H. W. Prescott, *The Development of Virgil's Art* (N.Y. 1963), 36 ff.   [3] 6 ff.; 16 ff.

[4] Her comment, 'habes tu quidem fratrem...sed quid prohibet et sororem adoptare?' indicates the preceding pattern of the story (127.2).

The central pattern, then, is of Encolpius' renunciation of women in favour of an exclusive attachment to Giton which is punished by the angry Priapus. Encolpius is finally brought to a realisation of his sickness,[1] and though recourse to the Priapic priestess Oenothea brings no relief, he is finally healed by the intervention of a kindly deity.

The course of the homosexual relationship is traced by burlesquing the characteristic action of the Greek love-romance. Bliss alternates with the pain of separation, and with moral and physical dangers. So, after the *Cena*, the ecstasy of intimacy with Giton is described by Encolpius in lyrical verses, but soon afterwards Ascyltus bears off the loved one. After the affectionate reconciliation, they are faced with other hazards from the jealous rivals Ascyltus and Eumolpus. Then on the ship a storm threatens to separate them; they embrace in what they believe is death, lashing themselves together as a symbolic gesture. As in the love-romances, the motif of cruel Fortune is continually introduced to accentuate the theme of true love never running smooth. So when Lichas is discovered to be the captain of the ship they have boarded, Encolpius cries: 'aliquando, inquam, totum me, Fortuna, vicisti.' In the shipwreck, he laments: 'The gods have granted our union only in death, but cruel Fortune does not allow even this.' So too at Croton Encolpius is apprehensive of Fortune's continuing spite.[2]

Another striking parallel with the love-romance is the constant emphasis on the religious element, but with ironical undertones. In the Greek stories the problems of the lovers are conventionally solved through the beneficent aid of a deity, and the divine providence is continually stressed. So too in Petronius; the gods' presence and intervention are ironically

---

[1] 128.5: 'quasi quodam visu in horrorem perductus interrogare animum meum coepi an *vera* voluptate fraudatus essem.' There is a philosophical joke here, the true nature of pleasure being a stock topic, here resolved into a choice between girls and boys.

[2] 101.1; 114.8 ('crudelis Fortuna'); 125.2. Amongst others Sullivan, 93 ff., is sceptical of the thesis that Petronius parodies the love-romance.

stressed in several scenes.[1] And, after the encounter with Circe, when Encolpius is cured of his sexual enervation he gives thanks to Mercury. 'There are greater gods [than Priapus] who have restored my health, for Mercury, the customary escort of souls to and from the world of the dead, has by his kindness restored to me what an angry hand had amputated.'[2] What Aphrodite achieves in Chariton's novel, Isis in Xenophon's, and Pan in Longus', is performed by Mercury the god of thieves in the *Satyricon*. Croton is indeed the climax of the story, and by a comic and ironical paradox the outcome is not the guarantee of a happy life together for the lovers, but the deliverance of Encolpius from his obsessive attachment and the recovery of his heterosexual appetite.

This thesis, that the *Satyricon* is in its main lines a burlesque of the ideals and motifs of the Greek love-romance, casts a revealing light on the attitude of mind and the purpose of the author. The book is a satirical entertainment, a derisive commentary not only on the authors of such pietistic fiction but also on the prevalent religious and moral attitudes which such fiction reflects. To express this ethos in the traditionally Roman terms, it is the canons of *pietas* and *virtus*, *dignitas* and *pudicitia* which the amoral hero subverts. Under his cynical guidance the reader is taken on what purports to be a conducted tour of the Greek city-life of Gaul and Italy, but which is essentially a review of the Roman contemporary scene. Though the hero and his friends are Greeks,[3] their attitudes and preoccupations are wholly Roman. The inconsistency did not trouble Petronius, whose aim was ephemeral entertainment, not a closely articu-

---

[1] E.g. 17.5, 98.6, 104.1, 106.3. Parody of prayers is observable at 17.9, 127.3; cf. H. Kleinknecht, *Die Gebetsparodie in der Antike*, 189.

[2] 140.12. Mercury ὁ ψυχοπομπός (Homer, *Od.* 24.1 ff.; Virg. *Aen.* 4.242 ff.) is appropriately designated as deliverer because he has both a fertilising function (Farnell, *Cults of the Greek States* v (Oxford 1909), 12 ff.) and, as Hermes Dolios, the patron guidance of thieves, which makes him the ideal saint for a picaresque hero (Farnell, v, 19 ff., 23). There is a striking parallel in the *carmina Priapeia* 37.8 ff.; so Cèbe, 280.

[3] See P. Veyne, *REL* (1964), 301 ff.

lated work of art; and the Romanising of the characters and situations lends the novel a greater immediacy and realism.

The tone, then, is uniformly ironical, and the depiction of the characters and situations encountered by the hero is satirically orientated. But the activities and attitudes of Encolpius and Giton themselves are not objects of consistent satire. They represent wandering scholars at large in the world, and their reactions are invariably and exaggeratedly scholastic; but this comedy of rhetorical foibles is affectionately presented. In other words the satirical element in the novel is not integral or sustained; no moral judgment is passed on the hero, and in many episodes the satirical intention is wholly absent. The thesis that Petronius wrote the entire *Satyricon* 'to show the repulsiveness of the manner of life, and the danger and guilt it brings', that the work is 'interesting and amusing, but it is at the same time vile and shocking—and it was intended to be both' cannot be sustained.[1] So far from conveying moral censure, the author recounts the hero's adventures in a lively, not to say titillating, manner. To adduce the argument that Encolpius is like Trimalchio—a satirical portrayal which has no need of explicit criticism—precisely reveals the frailty of the thesis. For Trimalchio's character is carefully and consistently drawn to present the damning portrait, whereas Encolpius' attitudes are much more fugitive and ambivalent.[2]

[1] This is the thesis of G. Highet, *TAPA* (1941), 176 ff. Highet suggests that Petronius led Nero's excursions into the night-life of the city (cf. Tac. *Ann.* 16.18) and that the *Satyricon* is a 'gigantic imaginative record' of them. On this interpretation the novel preaches Epicurean *tranquillitas* by portraying its grim opposite. But the Tacitean character-sketch hardly suggests that Petronius was an austere son of the Garden; nor would a true Epicurean have indulged in these alleged expeditions. For a detailed thesis that Petronius writes not *qua* moralist but *qua* artist, see Sullivan 106 ff.

[2] In fact, Trimalchio is directly criticised as at 73.2, 'putidissimam eius iactationem'; 78.5, 'ebrietate turpissima', etc. There is much justice in Sullivan's thesis that Encolpius is to be viewed as narrator rather than realistic hero.

Encolpius ('?Darling Boy' or 'Incrutch'?)[1] is essentially the rootless student whose education in eloquence equips him to react in the appropriately mannered way to every situation which confronts him. Even in his exposé of the fatuities of the Roman rhetorical education, he reveals himself the true product of it. In his encounters with Ascyltus and Eumolpus, in his intimate dialogue with Giton, and in his soliloquies, he is constantly striking scholastic attitudes and mouthing scholastic utterances.[2] Petronius seems constantly to make the point that Roman education breeds the actor. Yet even within this hypocritical exterior Encolpius has as many *personae* as there are situations. Simple soul and man of the world, sadist and soft-hearted sentimentalist, parasitic flatterer and ingenuous guest,[3] he is the chameleon of the I-narrator who sees the complexities within himself but only the consistent traits in others. The self-contradictions are of course explicable in part by the comic pose of the anti-hero as simpleton; deceived by Trimalchio's jokes, credulously aghast at tales of witches and werewolves, terrified by the arrival of authority, he is faithful to the convention of self-mockery with which the Milesian story-teller leads the laughter against himself.

Moreover, since the novel exploits the foibles of contemporary society, it was virtually impossible for Petronius wholly to exclude his own attitudes from the character of the I-narrator. Total identification between the youthful Greek goliard and the senior Roman consular would of course be an absurd view; contrary to some overheated imaginings, Petronius was no knockabout frequenter of taverns and brothels. 'Habebatur non ganeo et profligator...sed erudito luxu' implies the clinical detachment of the scholarly cynic. Yet total dissocia-

---

[1] Cf. E. Maass, *RhM* (1925), 447; I owe this reference to Dr E. K. Borthwick.

[2] The later detailed analysis will exemplify this, but the soliloquy at 100.1 ff., and the conversation with Giton at 91.2 ff. are particularly striking cases.

[3] Simple soul, 7.4, 18.2, 19.3, etc.; but not deceived, 17.2, etc. Sadistic, 96.4; softhearted, 115.12 ff. Parasitic flatterer, 39 ff., 47 f., 56; ingenuous guest, 41.5, etc.

tion from his hero was impossible, and some scenes bear a
striking similarity to Petronius' own situation. One thinks at
once of the *Cena* as a parable of the author's own life at court,
with the ambivalence of Encolpius towards Trimalchio reflecting Petronius' own relationship with Nero. And more
generally, the Epicurean sentiments of Encolpius harmonise
with Petronius' attitudes as they emerge from the Tacitean
character-sketch and from his own poems.

But Petronius' main intention in this characterisation of
Encolpius is the comic projection of the wanderer, the anti-
hero in the real world posturing as an Odysseus or an Aeneas.
The ideal romance represents the projection of the epic poem;
and the comic romance, which burlesques the action of the
ideal romance, moulds its central character into a travesty of
the epic hero. The consistently ludicrous and ineffectual pretensions, and the absence of the firm lines of characterisation
which would mark him out as a stock figure, suggest that he is
not a butt of satire but a comic character through whose eyes
the reader is to contemplate the persons and the attitudes
satirically represented.

The same judgment is true of Giton ('Neighbour' in a
sexual sense), the *infidus Achates* to Encolpius' Aeneas. He too,
as a recent study perceptively demonstrates, is the vagrant
scholar of 'intensively literary' style, whose almost every
utterance is no ordinary conversation but 'extracts from
declamations' of an artificial kind.[1] The sententious generalisation, the apposite literary parallel, the exotic language of the
schools fall constantly from his lips, and his sentences slip into
the approved rhythms of the orator. His 'spurious emotions
and false drama...have in him become indistinguishable from
genuine emotions and real drama'.[2] Here, as with all his
characters, Petronius is suggesting that sincerity is at a pre-
mium; life is a studied pose.

The ambivalence of Giton is of course the hinge of the
novel. The curly-haired effeminate ('crispus mollis formosus')
is constantly proclaiming his fidelity, and equally constantly

---

[1] P. George, *Arion* (1966), 338 ff. [2] George, 341.

playing the opportunist, encouraging Ascyltus or Eumolpus
or Tryphaena to incite Enclopius' jealousy.[1] But the wantonness is not satirically depicted, and the characterisation is
affectionately drawn. The whole relationship between Encolpius and Giton is a comedy of manners without satirical intent.

Ascyltus too is associated with this central comedy, and
again there is no satirical aim in the portrayal beyond the pretentious manner of speech. For Ascyltus too is a student of
rhetoric whose derision for the rhetor's profession[2] cannot
eradicate his own declamatory tendencies. His affected speech
contrasts hilariously with his uninhibited manners; his name
('Unwearied') is the index to his character, for he is the honest-
to-goodness profligate, 'adulescens omni libidine impurus',
whose prodigious parts signal his absorbing interest in life.[3]
His role in the book is the pursuit of Giton and the provocation
of Encolpius; his appearances herald bawdy laughter or
violence, as he roars maliciously at finding the hero tucked up
with Giton, or laughs intemperately at the feeble jokes of
Trimalchio.[4] Again here there is no intention on Petronius'
part of an extended satirical portrait; with Giton and Encolpius, Ascyltus represents the attitude of the amoral vagrant
scholar through whose eyes we behold the world of Agamemnon, Quartilla, and Trimalchio.

The first extant scene finds Ascyltus and Encolpius at the
school of rhetoric run by 'the brothers Atridae', Agamemnon
and Menelaus. Their presence is motivated not by the dis-
interested pursuit of learning, but by the hope of cadging a
dinner.[5] Encolpius is delivering an impassioned denunciation
of the whole system of education in such schools. The rhetor
Agamemnon ('lord of the host') agrees with the general indictment, but shifts the blame from the teachers to the pupils
and their parents; finally he expresses his own educational ideal
in verses.

---

[1] Protestations of fidelity, 91.8, 94.9, 114.11; wantonness, 80, 96 f., 113.
[2] 10.1: Agamemnon's utterances are 'bits of broken glass and dream
explications'.   [3] 91.2, 79.9, 81.4, 92.9.   [4] 11.2, 57.1.
[5] 10.2: '...ut foris cenares poetam laudasti.'

Petronius here comically exploits an obsessive preoccupation with Roman higher education and its faults which dominates the cultural discussions of the early empire; long lists of the pundits who pronounced on the question can be compiled.[1] And Petronius was especially concerned to satirise the tendency to relate the decline of eloquence to the decline of morality at Rome. Tacitus' later extended discussion reflects a number of earlier views, amongst them a well-known letter of the younger Seneca which may well have been the immediate provocation for Petronius' scoffing treatment.[2] The whole of this first scene is to be interpreted as an amusing exposition not merely of the fatuities of the school of rhetoric and its irrelevance to the needs of Roman society, but also of the all-too-familiar Roman tendency to ascribe the cultural crisis, and every other crisis, to the moral degeneration of the community.

Encolpius' criticism of the subjects and the modes of declamation is reasonable, and may well represent Petronius' own judgment; but this is not the main point. When he looks for the cause of decline, and harks back to Sophocles and Euripides, Pindar and the lyric poets, Plato and Demosthenes, Thucydides and Hyperides, he is mouthing a threadbare, cliché-ridden appeal to 'the world's greatest'. And the highly rhetorical nature of the style, with its studied antithesis, chiasmus, *anaphora, congeries verborum,* and profusion of *sententiae,* shows that Petronius is making sport here by ironically inserting a declamation against declamation:

qui inter haec nutriuntur, non magis sapere possunt quam bene olere qui in culina habitant. pace vestra liceat dixisse, primi omnium eloquentiam perdidistis. levibus enim atque inanibus sonis ludibria quaedam excitando effecistis ut corpus orationis enervaretur et caderet. nondum iuvenes declamationibus continebantur, cum Sophocles aut Euripides

---

[1] See H. Bornecque, *Les déclamations et les déclamateurs* (Lille 1902), ch. 6; S. F. Bonner, *Roman Declamation,* ch. 4: Sullivan, 163 n. 1. English readers will be reminded of the 'disputation on schools' in *Joseph Andrews,* Bk. 3 ch. 5.

[2] Tac. *Dial.,* esp. 34 f.: earlier, Seneca, *Contr.* 1 *pr.* 7, etc. The letter of Seneca, *Ep.* 114, esp. 2 ff., is usefully introduced by Summers's learned note in his edition.

invenerunt verba quibus deberent loqui. nondum umbraticus doctor ingenia deleverat, cum Pindarus novemque lyrici Homericis versibus canere timuerunt...

It is clear that the medium is the message here.[1]

In his reply, Agamemnon reveals himself all too damningly as the compliant teacher who gives his pupils what they demand and not what they need. He justifies his attitude because he will be out of a job if he follows his convictions. 'The teacher of rhetoric has to bait his hook like a fisherman. Unless he dangles the bait which he knows the little fish want, he'll wait on the rock without hope of a catch.'[2] And in another revealing image he compares the teacher to the flatterer, cadging dinners from the rich; it is surely no coincidence that he himself assumes precisely this role of flattering parasite at Trimalchio's table.[3]

There are likewise undertones of irony in the verses which Agamemnon recites as pedagogical advice for those who wish to attain high station. Here the traditional moral arguments are set down in iambics. For Petronius' contemporaries the comic point is that the hackneyed, heavy moralising comes from the hypocritical timeserver:

If any man seeks achievement in a difficult art, and sets his mind to an exalted task, he should first refine his character by the proved regimen of frugal living. He should disregard the harsh palace with its haughty air, and avoid the humbling dinners of incontinent hosts. He should not drown his fervid genius in wine, in the company of ne'erdowells, nor sit a hired claqueur before the stage, cheering the actor's gaping grin.[4]

The parody of the schoolmaster's moral advice has its comic effect enhanced by the fact that Agamemnon shows no inclination to follow his own advice in this ode to *frugalitas*, when he

[1] 2.1 ff. Cf. George, 350 f. Sullivan, 161 ff., would like to take it all more seriously.   [2] 3.3 f.

[3] 3.3: '...sicut adulatores cum cenas divitum captant nihil prius meditantur quam id quod putant gratissimum auditoribus fore.' At 52.7 Agamemnon laughs loudest because he knows 'quibus meritis revocaretur ad cenam'. That the rhetorician as parasite was probably a stock satirical butt is indicated by Lucian's *The Dependent Scholar*.

[4] 5.1 ff.

accepts the invitations of Trimalchio. And it may well be that there is a further level of irony intended here. Underlying the derisive portrayal of Agamemnon *chez* Trimalchio there is the author's personal situation in the cultural life of the Neronian court. His friends must have relished this injunction 'to disregard the harsh and haughty palace', to avoid drinking bouts, and to refrain from attending the stage-performances in which Nero was so enthusiastic a protagonist.

The rest of Agamemnon's advice is in hexameters, the change of metre signifying the progression from moral to literary precepts. Again the suggestions are conventional. The student should read Homer, the Socratic dialogues and Demosthenes, and then the Roman tragedians,[1] Roman epic, and Cicero. The hoary precepts are duly wrapped in tinsel-paper. 'Athenians or Spartans' is rendered in this highflown couplet:

> sed sive armigerae rident Tritonidis arces
> seu Lacedaemonio tellus habitata colono...

and the rest of his language is similarly ornamental, 'a tide of words' as Encolpius calls it.[2]

The humour of this first scene, then, derives from its comic exploitation of the anguished debates on the decline of eloquence. Encolpius' critique echoes the prevalent line of criticism of the rhetorical school, and in the manner and form of the declamation which the school prescribed. Agamemnon's verses enjoin as an ideal a life of secluded sobriety risibly at odds with the practice of both narrator and author, and a programme of reading, couched in flowery language, which every pedagogue approved. Agamemnon is the typical teacher of the age, complaisant to the whims of students yet earnestly proposing a solution to the educational crisis on well-worn lines. His own manner of life brands his programme as hypocrisy.

Deliberately juxtaposed with this critical discussion of

---

[1] It is probable that 'fortuna...celeri distincta meatu' is a description of tragedy, which the Romans considered superior to their comic drama (cf. Quint. 10.1.97 ff.) [2] 6.1.

Roman education is a series of diversely comic episodes—the synthesis of *satura* and σατυρικά. Encolpius loses his way to his lodgings and asks a harridan greengrocer 'rogo, mater, numquid scis ubi habitem?' Surprisingly she professes an ability to satisfy this Irish request; the ingenuous hero follows her, believing she is a goddess.[1] The joke is perhaps a literary one. As Aeneas was directed to Carthage by his mother Venus, so this *mater* leads the way for Encolpius—to a local brothel. There Encolpius finds Ascyltus escaping from the clutches of *his* kind guide, a respected *pater familias*.

Together they return to their lodging, where Giton waits, complaining of an attempted assault by Ascyltus. The two rivals measure up to each other for a battle—of rhetoric! Here is Ascyltus' studied riposte to Encolpius' insults:

> non taces, gladiator obscene, quem meridiana harena dimisit?
> non taces, nocturne percussor, qui ne tum quidem cum fortiter
> faceres cum pura muliere pugnasti?
> cuius eadem ratione in viridario frater fui
> qua nunc in deversorio puer est.[2]

No translation can possibly indicate the scholastic nature of this exchange, yet the language is the pointer to the artificial nature of the controversy. The tone has already been indicated by Giton's reporting of Ascyltus' threat to his honour. 'Gladium strinxit, et "si Lucretia es" inquit "Tarquinium invenisti".'[3] It is all a charade, and talk of earthy realism in such scenes is very wide of the mark. So too, when Ascyltus breaks up the cosy intimacy of Encolpius and Giton, and begins to lay about Encolpius with a strap and the words 'sic dividere cum fratre nolito', the phraseology suggests a literary joke. 'This is what you get for not sharing with your brother'—Ascyltus

---

[1] 7.2: 'divinam ego putabam...'. Prof. D. A. West points to Hor. *Od.* 3.27.10, *Sat.* 1.9.30 to suggest that *divinam* merely denotes a sixth sense here.

[2] 9.8. The antitheses are studied and stunning. non taces/non taces; gladiator/percussor; meridiana/nocturne (for the reading meridiana, *CR* (1967), 137); obscene/ne...quidem...cum pura muliere; viridario/deversorio (note the isocolon). I am grateful to Prof. D. A. West for assistance here.   [3] 9.5.

becomes a *Remus redivivus*, taking a comic revenge on Romulus.[1]

There follows a comic episode in a market. The two students try to sell a cloak which they have stolen, but the prospective buyers prove to be not only owners of the garment but also possessors of Ascyltus' grimy shirt with his gold coins sewn in it. The scene develops farcically when the law-enforcement officers try to bring the dispute to law, but finally Ascyltus gets away with his shirt. Strikingly enough, there is in the *Metamorphoses* of Apuleius an adventure in the market-place, in which an official interferes with the hero's purchase;[2] it is clear that the market-place anecdote is a favourite Milesian type in which the narrator recounts his discomfiture.

The episode in itself is amusing, but again the main comic element lies in the scholastic tone. Though Ascyltus' shirt is 'torn and filthy', Encolpius insists that they recover it by legal processes; Ascyltus on the contrary has no enthusiasm for the law as arbiter of justice, and to make his point more forcefully he declaims some elegiac verses on the venality of equestrian jurymen. It has been suggested that here Petronius parodies the increasing tendency to employ elegy for the purpose of moralising,[3] but beyond such literary joking these verses convey in the Menippean manner a general message which is of course ironically intended. Just as in the opening scene the moralising exhortation rings oddly from the hypocritical rhetor, so here the moral indignation of Ascyltus, as he condemns the corruption of the courts, is expressed with the passionate vehemence of a thief caught red-handed.

This series of low episodes is rounded off with a scabrous sequence in Encolpius' lodging. Quartilla, the priestess of

---

[1] 11.4. Ernout, Sullivan and others seem to me to mistranslate here. It will be remembered that in Livy's account Romulus cries: 'sic deinde quicunque alius transiliet moenia mea' (1.7.2). This use of *sic deinde* is deliberately intended as 'an archaic-sounding formula' (Ogilvie). In the present passage the use of *nolito* accentuates the archaic flavour of *sic*.

[2] *Met.* 1.24 f., a story apparently inserted by Apuleius himself.

[3] Cahen, 45 f.

Priapus whom the students have previously spied upon, sits weeping on Encolpius' couch, and finally tells them that by witnessing her Priapic ritual they have committed an *inexpiabile scelus* which has brought on herself a severe chill. She has been ordered in a dream to seek her remedy from the heroes, and to swear them to silence. When Encolpius innocently agrees to lend assistance, Quartilla indicates her requirements in some enigmatic verses. She and her maids then explode in 'mimic laughter', and explain more explicitly. The students are to appease the god by undergoing the Priapic *secreta*. Though the text is fragmentary here, the hero is clearly reluctant. After his humiliation at the hands of Quartilla, he has next to endure the attentions of a *cinaedus*. Finally, after a mimic interlude in which two Syrians try to steal the silver tableware, Quartilla stages the 'marriage' between her child-maid Pannychis and Giton.

This episode and others show an obsessive preoccupation with scopophilia which casts a revealing light on the author.[1] But though the conception of Petronius obtaining vicarious satisfaction as literary voyeur harmonises well enough with the Tacitean portrait, it ought to be emphasised that the Milesian tradition throws up many such unabashed and titillating descriptions—for example in *Lucius or the Ass.*[2] Moreover, these squalid perversions are not in themselves the sole focus of the comedy. There are elements of local Roman reference more meaningful to Petronius' circle than to us. Quartilla's name, like the name of every major character in the *Satyricon*, must be a comic index to her character, but to us her identity remains fugitive. She is clearly Roman not Greek. Her role as priestess of Priapus in the area of Cumae is presumably a comic evocation of the Virgilian Sibyl; the hero's first duty after landing on Italian soil is to visit the Priapic shrine, just as Aeneas repairs to the temple of Apollo. But the Petronian priestess is observed by Encolpius and his friends illicitly;

---

[1] Unlike me, some may find a Freudian analysis enlightening. See J. P. Sullivan, *Critical Essays*, 78 ff.; *The Satyricon*, ch. 7.
[2] Below, ch. 6.

'*imprudentes* enim, ut adhuc puto, admisistis inexpiabile scelus'.[1]
The echo of Ovid's lament in exile is striking:

> cur *imprudenti* cognita culpa mihi?
> inscius Actaeon vidit sine veste Dianam...[2]

The Ovidian reference suddenly makes the priestess of Priapus
a latter-day Julia.[3] Now in A.D. 62 Nero's wife Octavia, already
relegated to Campania, was exiled to Pandateria on a charge of
adultery, and Tacitus records how this punishment reminded
contemporaries of earlier exiles of royal ladies on such scandalous charges.[4] Quartilla's name may well be a punning
reference to Octavia. However appalling the possibility of this
is as an index to Petronius' cynicism, the fact must nonetheless
be faced that Petronius' intimacy with the emperor begins at
the time of the enforced death of his innocent empress.

This speculative hypothesis does not demand that the
characterisation of Quartilla be visualised as even a caricature
of Octavia. We shall presently see that the portrayal of
Trimalchio incorporates certain traits of Nero, but emphatically does not represent him in the round; so too there may
well be in the Quartilla episode certain reminiscences of
Octavia.[5] But having bestowed on his promiscuous priestess a
name punningly recalling the recent *cause célèbre*, Petronius
could have built up the portrait quite independently.

Quartilla is in fact initially a female counterpart to Encolpius, Giton and Ascyltus—a scholastic figure who utters an
eloquent *supplicatio*, and who then declaims some elegant verses

---

[1] 17.6. cf. *Aen.* 6.258: 'procul, o procul este, profani' / conclamat vates,
'totoque absistite luco...'.

[2] *Tristia* 2.104 f.

[3] It will be recalled that Ovid's *error* may have been to have indiscreetly
observed some peccadillo of the younger Julia; see J. C. Thibault, *The
Mystery of Ovid's Exile* (Berkeley, 1964); Wilkinson, *Ovid Recalled*,
299 f.   [4] *Ann.* 14.63.2.

[5] It is of course impossible to decide how seriously Petronius took the
evidence of Octavia's alleged misconduct with Eucairus, Anicetus,
and others. There is at 17.8 a horrifyingly apposite comment.
Quartilla begs Encolpius not to reveal her secret. 'maior enim in
praecordiis dolor saevit, qui me *usque ad necessitatem mortis* deducit...'

which generalise the situation to be enacted. But soon the elegant respectability melts away to reveal the bawdy woman of wealth, the predatory huntress whose secrets 'scarce a thousand men have shared'.[1] Through Quartilla Petronius projects a derisive attack on religious attitudes and cults. 'Our part of the world' she remarks 'is so crowded with the presence of deities that you can more easily find a god than a man.'[2] The implications of her meaning become later only too apparent. So also in boasting of her own precocious infancy she swears *by Juno* that she never remembers having been a virgin.[3] The anti-religious sentiment is characteristic of popular Epicureanism, and the whole religious flavour of the episode is introduced to accentuate the shamelessness of the 'remedy' demanded by the priestess.

The mock marriage between Giton and Pannychis, which rounds off the Quartilla episode, may also have a topical reference. Emphasis is laid on the formal accessories for the 'wedding'. The little girl wears a marriage-veil; the attendant is present with the marriage-torches; the women present form a long line; and the bridal chamber is adorned 'incesta veste'.[4] It is impossible not to be struck with the similarity to Nero's 'marriage' to Pythagoras in 64. 'Inditum imperatori flammeum, visi auspices, dos et genialis torus et faces nuptiales, cuncta denique spectata quae etiam in femina nox operit.' Even the voyeurs in Petronius have their counterparts here. As so often the Tacitean narrative of Nero's reign may open up a new dimension of Petronius' satirical purpose.[5]

[1] 17.9—the 'libidinous and aggressive female' (Sullivan, 119), so popular in ancient literature. For *secreta* in the sexual sense, see Juv. 3.113, etc.

[2] 17.5.

[3] 25.4.

[4] 26.1. It has been suggested by Rosenblüth that this scene is based on a mime of Laberius.

[5] Tac. *Ann.* 15.37.9. For the troublesome question of whether the Quartilla-scene should precede the Agamemnon-scene, and for a rearrangement of the Quartilla fragments, see Sullivan, 45 ff. (with bibliography).

The next episode is the *Cena Trimalchionis*, the satirical centre-piece of the *Satyricon*. Just as the story of Cupid and Psyche is developed on a more ambitious scale than any other episode in the *Metamorphoses* of Apuleius, so Petronius depicts Trimalchio in more loving detail than any other of his characters. The whole technique of character-creation, which is so difficult to observe elsewhere because of the fragmentary nature of the text, can here be reconstructed; accordingly this long episode deserves more detailed analysis.[1]

After this static scene set in the Roman satirical tradition, Petronius again sets in motion the plot of his Greek adventure-story to achieve the alternation of *satura* and σατυρικά. The next sequence chronicles the bliss of Encolpius' union with Giton, and the subsequent desolation of the hero when the slave deserts him for Ascyltus. After three days' solitary sulking, Encolpius sallies forth to seek revenge, but he is comically deflated by a passing soldier.

We have already seen how the whole of this episode ironically portrays the hero in epic roles—first as Achilles moping by the seashore and then as an *Aeneas furibundus* stalking the enemy in the streets of the town.[2] As elsewhere in the novel where Petronius focusses our attention on the picaresque characters with this literary treatment, he introduces also the mimic element.[3] So, as Encolpius in his jealousy bids Ascyltus pack his bags and go, his friend strikes a characteristically exaggerated attitude, threatening to split Giton down the middle in fair division. 'at ille gladium parricidali manu strinxit et "non frueris" inquit "hac praeda super quam solus incumbis".' Encolpius duly faces up to him and Giton predictably employs the apposite literary reference in begging them not to fight over him.[4]

Encolpius' bitter mood after his desertion is expressed in

---

[1] Ch. 5.   [2] Above, pp. 36 f.

[3] For the verses declaimed here ('grex agit in scaena mimum...') and for a general survey of the mimic element, see above, pp. 24 ff.

[4] 80.3: 'ne Thebanum par humilis taberna spectaret'.

some savage verses which generalise on the specious nature of friendship.

> nomen amicitiae sic, quatenus expedit, haeret...
> cum fortuna manet, vultum servatis, amici,
> cum cecidit, turpi vertitis ora fuga...[1]

The references to fortune's fall and to squalid flight have little reference to Encolpius' situation. It is tempting to see in these verses a Petronian reflexion on the hazards of political prominence in the later years of Nero.

After a brief lacuna in the text, we find Encolpius in a picture-gallery—the hero has resumed the role of earnest student. The description of the pictures, we may presume, is a burlesque of a similar technique in the Greek ideal romance, itself a development from the example of Homeric epic, where the motifs on the shield of Achilles inaugurate a tradition of descriptions of works of art eagerly taken up by later poets. Virgil constantly uses this device of pictorial representation to symbolise the situation of the hero.[2] In the Greek romances it is a commonplace to describe the story as a development of a pictorial theme; for example, the proem to Longus' *Daphnis and Chloe* states that the tale is motivated by a picture, and Achilles Tatius' novel commences with a description of Europa and the bull to demonstrate his theme that Eros rules over land and sea. So in Petronius the pictures at which the hero gazes all have the homosexual theme which is the central feature of the novel. Ganymede is en route for heaven, Hylas rejects the nymph's love, Apollo mourns for Hyacinth. Encolpius has come to the

---

[1] 80.9.

[2] The famous Homeric artistic digression is at *Il.* 18.478 ff. The Alexandrians advanced the technique by linking the representation with the poetic theme; Callimachus' *Hecale* is an example taken up by Catullus in poem 64. There are many examples in the *Aeneid*, beginning with the reliefs on Dido's new temple in the first book; at 6.14 ff., for example, the pictorial theme of Daedalus' exile from Crete on the gates of the Cumaean temple symbolises Aeneas' own finished journey. See V. Pöschl, *The Art of Virgil*, 149 ff., and in general R. D. Williams on *Aen.* 5.254 ff.

gallery miserable at Giton's betrayal, and he is comforted by the thought that even the gods are afflicted by similar emotions. Inevitably, as he describes the pictures he strikes the scholastic pose of other scenes, 'disputing with the winds'.[1]

Against this background Eumolpus ('Bon chanteur') makes his first appearance. As has been earlier suggested, Petronius here presents a satirical portrayal of a type frequently lampooned in Roman satire,[2] but in more affectionate detail. In appearance an elderly dedicated genius ('exercitati vultus et qui videretur nescio quid magnum promittere'), Eumolpus is in fact the manic poetaster with a perpetual chip on his shoulder about the exigent status of the creative writer,[3] and with time to spare for comely boys. He is a further exemplar of Petronius' cynical exposition that no man is as good as he seems. That impressive air of distinction cloaks a shallow poetic talent; the bubble of high seriousness and moral concern ('Anyone who takes up arms against all vices', he laments 'and starts to tread the straight path, is the butt of hatred because of superior manners')[4] is pricked by the revelation of his duplicity and wanton behaviour at Pergamum. In this first appearance of Eumolpus Petronius carefully indicates his future role. By a few characterising strokes which demonstrate Eumolpus' similarity to the would-be poets of Roman satire, he prepares us for a character who will spout verses or speeches at the drop of a hat;[5] and by the insertion of the anecdote about the youth of Pergamum, he signals Eumolpus' future role as the new rival

---

[1] 83.7: 'dum cum ventis litigo...'.

[2] Above, ch. 3.

[3] The theme, a stock one in Roman satire (compare Juvenal *Sat.* 7) is introduced at the outset when Eumolpus declaims hexameters on the subject (83.9 f.): 'sola pruinosis horret facundia pannis / atque inopi lingua desertas invocat artes.'

[4] 84 ff. P. Faider, *Etudes sur Sénèque* (Ghent 1921), 21, suggests that there is ridicule of Seneca (*Ep.* 76.4) here.

[5] So for example he is asked to compose abusive verses for Bargates the landlord to sling at his wife (96); he writes an epitaph for Lichas (115.20); in the shipwreck, *in vicinia mortis*, he is polishing his verses, a second Virgil (115.3 ff.). He also defends Encolpius in the mock trial (107).

of Encolpius for the affections of Giton. We may suspect that amongst Nero's literary and philosophical intimates Petronius found a living model for certain touches in this portrait. 'There were some' writes Tacitus 'who were keen to have their lugubrious faces prominent in the entertainments at court'[1]—he is referring to the literary and philosophical poseurs of the day. As with Trimalchio and Quartilla, so with Eumolpus we may presume a synthesis of the literary and the observed in the creation of this comic character.

For Eumolpus is undoubtedly a character derisively drawn. Over and over again his addiction to versification is branded as foolishness or madness. His composing is 'a disease', his lines 'inept', his wit 'tiresome'; he is 'a lunatic', a 'mooing poet'.[2] He lives in an unreal world, where every event is a mere pretext for a poem or declamation, or is visualised in purely literary terms. So on the ship, when the heroes realise that the captain is their enemy Lichas, Eumolpus formulates a plan of escape with the words: 'Imagine we have entered the Cyclops' cave.'[3] When he declaims in public he is pelted with stones, but this does not deter him, for verses are his food and life.[4] Even in the shipwreck, when the rest of the travellers have abandoned ship, he is found 'pouring verses on to a massive parchment', and when he is rescued, he is enraged at the interruption.[5]

Everything that Eumolpus declaims must be interpreted within this comic and scathing characterisation. The scholars who insist on regarding the long poems as serious compositions, who believe that the *Halosis Troiae* is Petronius' model for tragic writing and the *De Bello Civili* his ideal for epic, can hardly maintain that such an interpretation squares with Petronius' portrait of the versifier. These are deliberately mediocre compositions which reflect Eumolpus' mediocre talents.[6]

---

[1] *Ann.* 14.16.3. Cf. Suet. *De Gramm.* 23.
[2] 90.3: 'isto morbo'. 110.1: 'plura...et ineptiora.' 109.8: 'frigidissima urbanitate'. 115.5: 'phrenetico...poetam mugientem.'
[3] 101.7.   [4] 90.6.
[5] 115.2 ff.   [6] Above, ch. 3.

So too Eumolpus' sententious lament on the decline of the arts is the utterance of a shallow and hypocritical poseur. 'It was love of money that brought about the change. In early times, when virtue unadorned was still sufficient, the noble arts flourished...'[1] This is a moralising cliché similar to that pronounced by Agamemnon, and when the nostalgia for the distant days of moral rectitude is here put into the mouth of a self-confessed lecher we must assume that the purpose of the author is ironical. Eumolpus exemplifies the days of noble research with Democritus, who 'squeezed out the juices of every plant, and devoted his life to experiments to ensure that the properties of stones and shrubs became known'; with Eudoxus, 'who grew old on the peak of the highest mountain to catch the motions of the stars and the sky'; and with Chrysippus who 'cleansed his mind thrice with hellebore to prevent his ideas drying up'. Even in an English translation the sententiousness of these exemplars is apparent, but more important these attributions are risibly eccentric.[2] So too with his comments on the plastic arts. Lysippus 'died through poverty as he concentrated on the lines of a single statue', and Myron 'almost reproduced the souls of men and animals in bronze'. These judgments are the exact opposite of what the expert art-historian pronounced.[3] This comically inaccurate survey of the

---

[1] 88.2. Sullivan, 206, well compares Sen. *Ep.* 115.10 ff., and Petronius may be parodying Seneca here.

[2] Democritus was certainly not renowned as a dedicated physiologist and geologist. Eudoxus, so far from being a solitary, joined Plato at the Academy, and was later prominent in the political life of Cnidus. And Chrysippus needed no hellebore to aid *inventio*; he was notorious for his book-making, writing no fewer than seventy-five works (D. L. 7.180). There was in fact a standard joke that Chrysippus took hellebore as a cure for madness—three times! See Lucian's *Vera Historia* 2.18 and especially *Vitarum Auctio*, 23. There may have been similar jokes directed against Democritus; cf. Hor. *Ep.* 1.12.12: 'miramur, si Democriti pecus edit agellos/cultaque, dum peregre est animus sine corpore velox.' Also Cic. *Fin.* 5.87, and Zeller, *Pre-Socratic Philosophy*, 2.213.

[3] The elder Pliny's compendium is useful here. He emphasises that Lysippus, so far from being a slow worker, was said to have made

philosophical and artistic geniuses of the past is then followed
by an inflated condemnation of the morality and the ignorance
of the Neronian age: 'at nos, vino scortisque demersi, ne
paratas quidem artes audemus cognoscere, sed accusatores
antiquitatis vitia tantum docemus et discimus.'

The Petronian irony is already evident, but Eumolpus piles
on the agony, rebuking his contemporaries for failing to thank
the gods for their scholarly attainments. They do not even pray
for a *mens sana in corpore sano*, but solely for money however
unscrupulously obtained. This is the cause of the decline of art.
We are back with Petronius' favourite Aunt Sally, the theory
of the coincidence of a healthy culture with a healthy morality,
and the nostalgia for the days when the Romans were *religiosis-
sumi mortales*. The lament that the Romans do not pray for the
right things, a proper disposition and good health, is the
repetition of a refrain familiar in Roman satire. It is likely that
Petronius makes fun of it here, as also in the *Cena Trimalchionis*,
because Seneca had recently pronounced on the subject.[1]

After this moralising declamation, and after the extempore
recitation of the *Halosis Troiae* which earns Eumolpus a
fusillade of stones and the rebuke of Encolpius, the central
theme of the homosexual relationship is resumed. Encolpius
meets a penitent Giton at the baths, and they return to the
lodging for a reconciliation. Eumolpus, whom they had
deserted declaiming a poem in the baths, turns up and at once
announces himself a rival for Giton's affections. Encouraged
by Giton's amiability, he locks Encolpius in and bears off

1,500 pieces of statuary, a remarkable number considering their
quality; and so far from dying through *inopia* ('poverty', not 'starvation' as Sullivan and others) his heir found 1,500 gold pieces stored
away, one from each payment (*N.H.* 34.37). Of Myron, Pliny says
precisely that he did *not* succeed in expressing the sensations of the
mind; 'corporum tenus curiosus, animi sensus non expressisse'
(34.58).

[1] For the satirical theme, see Juv. 10.356 with Friedländer's note. Cf. in
the *Cena*, 61.1, 44.17 f. Seneca, *Ep.* 10.4, writes: 'roga bonam mentem, bonam valetudinem animi, deinde tunc corporis...'.

Giton. The hero is just hanging himself when the others burst
back in; Giton is so overcome at the sight that he attempts to
cut his throat. The din rouses the resident supervisor of the
house, and a general mêlée ensues in which Encolpius locks out
Eumolpus, and witnesses with pleasure through a hole in the
door the drubbing administered to the poet. Eumolpus is saved
by the arrival of the superintendent Bargates, an admirer of his
eloquence. A herald next appears announcing a reward offered
by Ascyltus for the discovery of Giton; the boy hides himself
under a mattress, but his sneezing betrays him to the returning
Eumolpus. The poet is prevailed upon not to claim the reward,
and the three comrades evade Ascyltus and embark on a ship
for Tarentum.

Here, as earlier in the love-liaison, the whole episode is
enacted as mimic entertainment with literary overtones. After
Eumolpus has reported on his comic confrontation with
Ascyltus at the baths, and has routinely declaimed some verses
on the Roman passion for exotic fare—this echo of Trimalchio's poem is perhaps a comic commentary on Encolpius'
modest board—the scene is set for the melodrama. Giton's
encouragement of Eumolpus' attentions evokes a comically
literary proposal.[1] Encolpius follows his hoary routine of hot
jealousy, bidding his rival depart. The subsequent staging, in
which Encolpius stands with his head in the noose while Giton
addresses him with a lover's reproach, draws a razor across his
throat, and collapses, is sheer farce. The razor is a training
model, the death a *mimica mors*, the whole scene a 'fabula inter
amantes'. So too the subsequent brawl in which Eumolpus is
struck by an earthenware jug, chases the aggressor with a
wooden candlestick, and incurs the attacks of cooks and
drunken lodgers, is slapstick pure and simple.

The final stage of the episode continues this mimic fun when
Ascyltus enters looking for Giton, and the slave 'outdoes

[1] 94.1: 'O felicem matrem tuam, quae te talem peperit; macte virtute
esto. raram fecit mixturam cum sapientia forma. itaque...amatorem
invenisti.' Compare Apollo's congratulations to Iulus in the *Aeneid*,
9.641 ('macte nova virtute, puer...'), and 9.296 ff.

Ulysses' with his stratagem of strapping himself under the mattress. So after Ascyltus' departure, when Eumolpus detects him there, Giton is 'a Ulysses whom even a hungry Cyclops could have spared'. These literary references are of the banal kind appropriate to the narrative equivalent of the low stage. Yet the presence of Eumolpus the crazed litterateur ensures the continuation of a more sophisticated level of entertainment, and the episode is amusingly rounded off by Encolpius' precious plea for reconciliation: 'The snows cleave longer to the rough and uncultivated country, whereas the land made obedient and sleek with the plough loses its light covering of frost at once. It is the same with anger, which clings to the barbaric mind but melts away from the cultivated.'[1]

After a short gap in the story, we find Encolpius communing with himself aboard ship. As he tries to sleep, he hears the voice of his former adversaries Lichas ('Cruel') and Tryphaena ('Luxuria') in conversation on the deck above. Giton and he are paralysed with fright, and Eumolpus tries to reassure them. They discuss various hilarious suggestions for escape, and finally decide that the lovers should shave their heads and eyebrows and travel as Eumolpus' slaves. Unfortunately a seasick traveller notices the haircutting operation, which he stigmatises as impious. Simultaneously Lichas and Tryphaena are dreaming that Encolpius and Giton are aboard. When the inauspicious tonsure is reported to them, and the 'slaves' are awarded forty lashes each, Giton's squeals reveal his identity to Tryphaena's maids, and Lichas recognises Encolpius by his distinctive parts. He attributes the detection to divine providence, and proposes execution. Eumolpus puts forward a *deprecatio* on their behalf, but Lichas as prosecuting counsel demolishes his arguments. There ensues a pitched battle which is followed by an armistice. At the meal which follows, Eumolpus first declaims some lines on hair and hairlessness, and then tells the story of the Widow of Ephesus,

---

[1] 99.3; perhaps another joke against Seneca, who deals at length with the cultivation of the mind to exorcise anger (*De Ira, passim*).

which pleases all the company except the puritanical Lichas. Meanwhile Giton is provoking Encolpius to jealousy by charming his former mistress Tryphaena.

This episode on board ship contains in microcosm all the essential features of the Petronian comic romance. The main attention is on the heroes, who continue the mimic foolery[1] by which they confront their theatrical misfortunes, so familiar as the crises redolent of the love-romances. Fortune, or the influence of the malign Priapus, casts them into the clutches of their enemies; the threat of execution leads to a mock trial, in which the speeches of defendant and prosecutor recall similar scenes in the novels of Chariton and others. The various types of action are described in the appropriate literary styles.[2] And the characters reintroduced here, Lichas and Tryphaena, are depicted as *superstitiosi mortales*, so that the Roman satirical element is also represented.

This characterisation of Lichas and Tryphaena allows Petronius again to indulge his anti-religious scepticism. Though utterly different in their sexual *mores*—Lichas is the stern Puritan and Tryphaena the cosmopolitan hedonist—they are jointly portrayed as sharing the same superstitious outlook. We first find them exchanging accounts of their dreams:

'Priapus seemed to say to me in sleep: "The Encolpius you seek has been brought aboard your ship by me."' At this Tryphaena shivered. 'You'd think we had slept in the same bed, for a statue of Neptune in a shrine at Baiae seemed to tell me: "You'll find Giton on Lichas' ship."'

They hasten to search the ship in case they appear to disregard these manifestations.[3] When Lichas hears that some impious men have cut their hair on his ship—an act permissible only when a storm arises,[4] and which may therefore precipitate such disaster—he orders them forty lashes. And when Encolpius

---

[1] 106.1: 'mimicis artibus'.

[2] See ch. 3.

[3] 104.1 ff. Eumolpus' praise of Epicurus here at once seeks to deter Lichas from searching the ship and indicates the philosophical allegiance of the heroes.

[4] Cf. Ovid, *Fasti* 3.327 ff.

and Giton are unmasked as a result, Lichas sees this as proof that
'the immortal gods take thought for human affairs, for having
led the guilty men all unknowing to our ship, they advised us of
their action in identical dreams'. This *superstitiosa oratio*[1] induces Tryphaena to agree to the proposed execution of Giton.
Again, when a storm blows up, Lichas' first thought is to urge
Encolpius to replace the stolen garment and rattle of Isis to its
place of honour on the ship.[2] It is in keeping with Petronius'
sardonic scepticism that Lichas, in spite of his punctilious observance, should be drowned whilst the unjust survive.[3] Lichas
is portrayed as the man who justifies his cruelty through fear of
divine retribution—'non sum crudelis, sed vereor ne quod
remisero patiar'—and when Eumolpus early in the scene
protests that Lichas is no Hannibal, the comic point is that
Hannibal is proverbially the personification of the cruelty
which Lichas exhibits.[4]

The whole episode is studded with the exaggeratedly
rhetorical declamations which set the tone of the novel as a
whole. When Encolpius communes with himself on the
rivalry of Eumolpus, his thoughts are a series of school
clichés: 'Which of nature's finest gifts are not the property of
all? The sun shines on all men. The moon even guides the
beasts to their food. What can be said to be lovelier than water?
Yet it flows for the use of all. . . '[5] So too when Encolpius begs
the aid of Eumolpus, he adopts the posture and the language of
the *supplicatio*; and the whole of the subsequent consultation is
a sort of debating competition in which each man makes his
proposal or demolishes the others' with a profusion of *sententiae*,
literary *topoi*, and the figures and rhythms of oratorical
language.

Towards the close of the episode, when relations are more

---

[1] 106.4.   [2] 114.4 f.

[3] It should however be remembered that in the literary structuring
Lichas plays Orontes (or perhaps more appropriately Palinurus, since
his body is cast ashore).

[4] 106.3; 101.4.

[5] It is possible, as Sullivan, 194 ff., suggests, that there is a skit on
Seneca (*Ep.* 73.6 ff.) here.

affable, Eumolpus tells the story of the Widow of Ephesus. Just as his previous story of the *ephebus* of Pergamum was apposite to the situation, pointing forward to Eumolpus' own role as admirer of Giton, so this Milesian story suitably harmonises with the characters on the ship. On the one hand, the story of the *furor* of the Widow reminds Lichas of his wife's involvement with Encolpius, and on the other it signals Tryphaena's role in the book as *mulier libidinosa*.[1]

A storm now gets up. Encolpius and Giton are helped from the wreck by some fishermen, and they rescue Eumolpus. The three comrades spend the night in a fisherman's cottage. The next day Lichas' body is washed ashore; Encolpius pronounces an encomium, and Eumolpus composes an epitaph. They then explore the terrain.

It has already been demonstrated how this section of the heroes' adventures is closely modelled on the storm and landing near Carthage in the first book of the *Aeneid*.[2] Within this literary structuring, the burlesque of the love-romance is continued, for there is an affecting scene between the principals as they bitterly contemplate the malignity of fortune. As elsewhere, the declamatory tone conveys the desired effect of a crude melodrama.

Encolpius. Hoc a diis meruimus ut nos sola morte coniungerent. sed non crudelis fortuna concedit. ecce iam ratem fluctus evertet, ecce iam amplexus amantium iratum dividet mare...

Giton [*lashing them together with a cord*]. si nihil aliud, certe diutius iuncta nos mors feret, vel si voluerit mare misericors ad idem litus expellere, aut praeteriens aliquis tralaticia humanitate lapidabit, aut quod ultimum est iratis etiam fluctibus, imprudens harena componet.

So too on the following day, when Encolpius delivers his soliloquy over the corpse of Lichas, it is a complete misreading of the tone to assume that Petronius 'is putting forth his best artistic efforts', and to build on such passages the thesis that there is in Petronius 'a sadness akin to tragedy in the

---

[1] 113.7. For an analysis of the Tale, see above, pp. 11 ff.
[2] Above, pp. 37 f.

contemplation of humanity in the large'.[1] The entire scene is yet another declamatory performance, the entire purpose ironical. This is obvious not only from the pun with which the floating body is greeted ('en homo quemadmodum natat') but also from the shower of sententious clichés and the blatant incorporation of all the rhetorical figures in the handbook. Nor is Encolpius content with the banal commonplaces inspired by the savagery of the sea; he extends his survey to the hackneyed theme of the uncertainty of life in other spheres.[2]

Once more Petronius introduces here into his mannered narrative the authentic note of Roman satire. On their way to Croton the heroes meet with the foreman of an estate, who warns them of the *mores* prevailing in the town. By an ironical inversion of the prevailing Roman snobbery, he implies that the traders are the *honesti*, and that the idle upper class is the scum. This condemnation reads like a catalogue of stock satirical motifs.

In this city literary studies have no prestige, and eloquence no standing. The simple life and decent morals win no praise and therefore no reward. Just realise that every man you clap eyes on belongs to one of two groups, the money-hunters and the hunted. In Croton no one brings up children, for this disqualifies him from dinners and public entertainments; he gets none of the perks, and lives unknown as a social leper. But those who have never married and have no close relatives not only reach the top, but are regarded as the only men of true courage and integrity. You are approaching a town that is a plague-ridden expanse, dotted with nothing but corpses being pecked to pieces, and the crows at work pecking them.

Here we may assume that this 'series of incoherent complaints'[3] from such an unlikely spokesman is a comic echo of the stock Varronian laments of the degradation of first-century Rome.

[1] So Perry, *The Ancient Romances*, 200.
[2] So rightly Cèbe, *La caricature*, 265: 'le morceau n'est, de bout en bout, qu'un travestissement comique.' So the hazards of soldier and civilian, traveller, glutton and abstemious man are recounted (one may suspect that a phrase balancing the traveller has fallen out—perhaps a phrase like ⟨*ille pedibus*⟩ *properans* should replace *properantem* at 115.16). Some scholars draw attention to the many echoes of Seneca in this chain of crashing clichés. See, e.g., Faider, 18, and Sullivan, 196 ff.
[3] 116.6 ff. (Nettleship's unhappy description of Juvenal's first satire).

And an essential part of the joke is the fact that Croton was physically in Petronius' day a city of the past; the corpses and the crows are a symbolic representation of the village which was once the centre of luxurious life.[1]

The trio now proceed to Croton under the guise of a ship-wrecked millionaire and his slaves, for the foreman's warning enables them to prepare a trap for the legacy-hunters. *En route* to the city, Eumolpus discourses on the nature of true poetry, and by implication criticises the epic poem of Lucan.

The mimic framework is prominent here. The hypocritical opportunist Eumolpus declares that he would have liked 'a bigger stage, more refined costumes, and more elegant luggage to win greater credence for our deceit', and asks: 'Why don't we lead on the mime? Pretend I'm your master, if you like the plan.'[2] The 'slaves' go through an extravagant swearing-in ceremony, and Eumolpus for his part is bidden to rehearse his graveyard cough to entice the fortune-hunters. And 'to make the play complete' he is to address his 'slaves' by the wrong names to demonstrate the size of his retinue.

The journey is conventionally lightened by an entertainment, consisting of Eumolpus' reflexions on the nature of true poetry followed by a recital of his poem on the Civil War. The poem should be assessed within the derisive characterisation of its declaimer.[3] Likewise the discussion on the nature of poetry is not a serious or original contribution. It is difficult for us to realise how cliché-ridden the debate on the ideal content and style of epic had become. The dispute was as old as the fifth century, when Choerilus wrote his *Persika*: it had been a staple topic at Alexandria: it was a vexed issue between neoterics and conservatives in first-century Rome. After Virgil the traditionalists multiplied; in the Neronian age Persius reveals his

---

[1] Livy 24.3 describes how the site was abandoned in 215; the population was transferred to Locri. The Romans established a colony on the site in 194 (Livy 34.45.4), and it remained a place of passage to Greece (Cic. *Att.* 9.19); but it never regained its importance. For the archaeological surveys, see J. Bérard, *Bibliographie topographique des principales cités grecques de l'Italie méridionale* (Paris 1941), 48 ff.

[2] 117.2 and 4.   [3] Above, p. 95.

disgust with the swarm of second-rate imitators.[1] Eumolpus'
utterances should be read not as a vehement condemnation by
Petronius himself of Lucan as the new Choerilus, but as the
sort of comment which shored up the writing of every pompous and traditionalist litterateur. This does not divorce
Eumolpus' criticism of Lucan of all justification. But the
comedy of the situation is this. Eumolpus' theorising prepares
us for a poem utterly different in tone from Lucan's, yet when
he declaims it the phraseology, the rhythms, the extravagant
spread ('ingenti volubilitate verborum')[2] inevitably identify
the poem as a Lucanesque performance.[3]

The next scene is all but lost. Arriving at Croton the heroes
fall in with the legacy-hunters who vie in heaping gifts on
Eumolpus. All that remains of this satire-inspired scene is a
fragment of dialogue between Eumolpus and Encolpius.
Enough survives of Encolpius' contribution to reveal yet again
the declamatory tone whose artificiality deprives the episode
of all realism.

The climax of the novel follows. The maid Chrysis approaches Encolpius on behalf of her mistress Circe. Circe
joins him, and at once the hero is enslaved. But when he tries
to consummate the affair he finds himself impotent. Circe
takes umbrage at this failure, and the hero crystallises his discomfiture in verses. There is an exchange of letters. Encolpius
makes diligent preparation for a second meeting, but in spite of
magical treatment from the aged crone Proselenus ('Older
than the moon') he remains enfeebled. Circe orders him to be
beaten and thrown out. Returning to his lodging, he expresses
reproaches in verse to his parts, and prays to Priapus for help.
Proselenus takes him to the priestess of Priapus, Oenothea
('Wine-goddess'). During the magical rites he kills one of the
geese sacred to Priapus; and eventually he flees from the old

---

[1] The useful analysis of Otis, *Virgil*, ch. 2, may be consulted with
profit. For Persius' condemnation, see *Sat.* 5, later to be echoed in
Juvenal's first satire.   [2] 124.2.

[3] Above, pp. 48 ff. Sullivan (165 ff.) takes the criticism as serious and
Petronius' own.

women's attentions. Finally his disability is healed not by Priapus but by Mercury, the patron of picaresque thieves and the god who brings souls back to earth.

This is at once the most extensively scabrous and the most literary episode in the *Satyricon*. Significantly enough, the theme of the high-born lady seeking sexual satisfaction from a slave was enacted in the mime;[1] Petronius' narrative is permeated with a mimic unreality. But the performance is emphatically literary, and he 'distances' the sexual crudities with a wide range of parody and evocation, and with the extensive deployment of the verse form. As we have seen, the adventure is enclosed within the regular epic framework; the hero adopts the name Polyaenus to confront Circe.[2] And Mercury is the healing god, just as it was this god who provided Odysseus with moly to resist the charms of Circe. The progress of the love-affair follows the pattern of a notorious Ovidian poem; the exchange of letters, we may presume, is a burlesque of a literary exercise practised in the schools of rhetoric;[3] and the rebuke of Encolpius to his parts comically cites Virgil. Moreover, the meeting with Oenothea evokes other Ovidian poems.[4] Encolpius indeed assumes a highly Ovidian *persona* in this episode, even to the point of defending his lubricious narrative.[5]

It should be noted that Circe upon her entrance bears a striking resemblance to the typical heroine of the Greek love-romance.[6] Like the girls in Chariton, Xenophon, and other novelists, Circe is endowed with a divine beauty. She is 'more perfect than any statue', quite beyond description; her eyes outshine the stars, her lips resemble those of Praxiteles' Artemis, her smile is like the full moon emerging from a cloud.

---

[1] Above, p. 26.   [2] Above, p. 38.

[3] For the Ovidian poem, above, p. 42; on the letters, we may infer burlesque from the prominence of the letter-form in Augustan poetry (as in Ovid's *Heroides*, Propertius 4.3; cf. the advice of Ovid at *A.A.* 1.437, 3.619, etc.) and from the discussions of later rhetoricians like Theon. See Wilkinson, *Ovid Recalled*, 86; Cahen, 46 (who thinks the letters parody the love elegy—but they are in prose).

[4] Above, p. 42.   [5] See the elegiacs in 132.15.

[6] So Courtney, *Philol.* (1962), 99.

Like the suitors of the love-romances, Encolpius addresses her
with a prayer appropriate to a goddess: 'Per formam tuam te
rogo, ne fastidias hominem peregrinum inter cultores admit-
tere. invenies religiosum si te adorari permiseris. ac ne me
iudices ad hoc templum Amoris gratis accedere, dono tibi
fratrem meum.'[1] And later Circe retires to the shrine of Venus.[2]

It seems certain that Petronius intends his nymphomaniac
Circe to be viewed as a grotesque reflexion of the innocent
heroines of earlier Greek romances. There is associated with
this parody an implicit mockery of religious ritual—Encolpius'
offering is Giton!—which continues throughout the scene.[3]
Especially notable is the killing of the sacred goose and the
appalled reaction of the priestess; this must surely be a comic
reference to the punctiliously observed tradition of tending
the sacred geese on the Capitol.[4]

As has earlier been suggested, the restoration of Encolpius'
virility, and his thanks to Mercury which echoes the conventional prayer of gratitude in the love-romance, mark the climax
of the novel. Priapus' persecution of the thieving homosexual
is abandoned, and the enervation ceases. Here the text becomes
fragmentary, with no further mention of either Circe or Giton;
but it is clear that Encolpius is cured of his obsessive attachment to Giton alone, perhaps through an affair with Circe's
maid Chrysis.[5]

It is tempting to believe that the novel ends shortly after the
last extant scene—another stage-set with Eumolpus apparently
on his death-bed, surrounded by the legacy-hunters. One of
them, the matron Philomela ('inter primas honesta' in this city
of debauchery), had already left her son and daughter to
Eumolpus' tender affections whilst on a pretended visit to her
religious duties. At that stage, Eumolpus was simulating gout

[1] 127.3.
[2] Chariton's Callirhoe has the beauty of Aphrodite (1.1.2, 2.3.6, etc.),
and Xenophon's Anthia is mistaken for Artemis (1.2.7).
[3] See Kleinknecht, 189; Cèbe, 280 ff.
[4] For the continuation of the custom in Petronius' day, see Pliny, *N.H.*
10.51.
[5] 139.4, where Chrysis expresses her passion for Encolpius.

and general infirmity;[1] the death-bed scene is presumably another exotic device engineered by Eumolpus, this time to rid himself of the embarrassment of the legacy-hunters. Having freed his 'slaves', he demands that those who wish to become his heirs should promise to devour a portion of his corpse in public. Warming to his bizarre theme of cannibalism, he adorns his death-bed oration with *exempla* from Roman history. The comic effect of these citations of the behaviour of the Saguntines, Petelians and Numantians is enhanced by Eumolpus' rhetorical disregard for historical accuracy.[2] He clearly hopes that his demand will cause the *captatores* to melt away before they discover that he is an impostor. But the ruse fails,[3] and we may assume that the heroes finally make their escape from Croton by some elaborate subterfuge, or in a welter of mimic violence.

Though the *captatores* are a stock literary motif of satire, and though the episode is set in a ghost town, the theme was closely relevant to similarly scandalous practices in Neronian Rome.[4] The Roman conception of *amicitia* demanded the customary acknowledgment of such friendship by formal mention in one's will; the technique of the *captator* was therefore to haunt a sick person's company till recognised as an *amicus*. There are hair-raising stories of how relentlessly this aim was achieved.[5] Eumolpus in this scene is being pressed to include his new *amici* in an amended will, and Petronius has doubtless some contemporary rhetorician in mind when he

---

[1] 140.6.

[2] The accounts of these sieges recorded by Livy (21.7 ff.; 23.30; *epit.* 59) make no mention of such cannibalism. For cannibalism at Saguntum as a sensationalist theme in the schools of rhetoric, see Friedländer on Juv. 15.114, with references.

[3] One of the *captatores* at least, Gorgias, agrees to carry out the stipulation (141.5).

[4] The younger Pliny's description of Rome at *Ep.* 2.20.12 ('in qua iam pridem non minora praemia, immo maiora, nequitia et improbitas quam pudor et virtus habent') strikingly echoes the sentiment of the *vilicus* in Petronius 116.

[5] See Pliny, *Ep.* 2.20.2 ff., 5.5.2, with Sherwin-White's notes.

gives the name Gorgias to one of the most shameless of Eumolpus' pursuers.[1]

Such, then, is the action of the *Satyricon*, and Petronius' purely comic intention is evident throughout. The portrayal of the author as an early-day Dr Johnson, brooding over the sensual follies of the age, is wholly misguided.[2] The novel is essentially a *jeu d'esprit* in which all the major figures—Encolpius, Giton, Ascyltus, Eumolpus—are mannered scholars who confront a series of hazards, physical and moral, with the exaggerated rhetoric of their trade and with the studied postures of the mimic stage. In spite of their Greek names, they are really Romans in a Roman world. And though Petronius presents his main characters as play-actors in a series of crude melodramas often inspired by the motifs of the love-romance, the backcloth is authentically Roman. The subordinate characters too are recognisably types of the age, and their portraits incorporate the attitudes and mannerisms of living figures. To this extent the *Satyricon* marks an advance in realistic fiction; and an attentive reading of Tacitus' account of Nero's reign brings surprising illumination to individual episodes.

The suggestion that the novel is a coherent satire with a basis in austere Epicureanism has already been ruled out, since this conflicts with both the psychology of the author and with the characterisation of the hero. In fact the satirical element subserves the comic purpose, as the Trimalchio episode perfectly illustrates. But there is a strong case for maintaining that the novel reflects the ethos of popular Epicureanism, the debased version popular in first-century Rome. In this vulgarisation, Epicurus' respect for religious worship disappears, and the emphasis is on scepticism, with a particularly sardonic

---

[1] There had been, for example, a celebrated case in A.D. 61, when a grandson of Asinius Pollio was implicated in a scandal of a forged will (Tac. *Ann.* 14.40).

[2] I think of such treatments as Arrowsmith's in *Arion* (1966), 310, where the theme of the *Satyricon* is visualised as 'the death which *luxuria* brings', and where the critic claims a 'deliberate symbolic intent beneath the comic realism'.

attitude towards superstitious practices. The ethical teachings of the master are more permissively interpreted. The concept of *ataraxia* is given a slanted connotation, implying retirement to enjoy *voluptas*. These are the Epicurean attitudes prominent both in Tacitus' character-sketch and in Petronius' verses.[1]

Encolpius' progress through the sleazy Greek cities can hardly be adduced to justify any rational philosophy of life. His career of theft, sacrilege, murder, seduction and sadism, constantly attended by comic humiliations, is a mere extravaganza. But Petronius does project a popular Epicurean outlook in his satirical portrait of superstitious attitudes, above all in the characterisation of Lichas and Tryphaena. This popular Epicureanism is one influential strand in Petronius' sardonic comedy; it takes its place with his contempt for tasteless ostentation and his derisive eye for the pretentiousness of mediocre intellectuals. This trinity of values—contempt for the hypocrisy of religion, of learning, of wealth—could have provided the cutting edge for a coherent satire on Neronian society. But Petronius' view of the world is too cynical for this. Life is for him a bizarre comedy in which no man's motives are above suspicion—least of all the narrator's.

So the corrupt narrator presents us with a series of vignettes, the blisters of his corrupt society—the hypocritical rhetor, the vulgar nouveau-riche, the manic versifier, the superstitious travellers, the calculating *captatores*, the nymphomaniac matron. In this parade Trimalchio, the paradigm of rusticity and vulgar wealth, is accorded the central position. His is the only character study in the novel which can be examined in its awful completeness. Poised between the Hellenistic and the Roman worlds, an Asiatic slave turned Italian millionaire, he happily consummates the marriage between Greek comic fiction and Roman satire, and deserves the accolade of the richest comic figure in antiquity. How did Petronius build up this splendid characterisation? A detailed study of Trimalchio will help to cast light on Petronius' character-studies elsewhere.

[1] So Raith. Note especially fr. 27 Müller, where Petronius' theology contrasts with Lucr. 5.1161 ff.

5

'CENA TRIMALCHIONIS'

I declare here once for all I describe not men, but manners; not an individual, but a species. Perhaps it will be answered, Are not the characters then taken from life? To which I answer in the affirmative; nay, I believe I might aver that I have writ little more than I have seen.

FIELDING, *Joseph Andrews*, Bk 3, ch. 1

An episode centring on the dinner-table was an appropriate centrepiece for Petronius' synthesis of Greek fiction with Roman satire, for the dinner-party, the traditional occasion for social relaxation, was already established in both Greek and Latin literature as the backcloth for recreative fiction. Plato and Xenophon in their Symposia had exploited the concourse of friends at table as a setting for philosophical discussion, and these dialogues have their imitative Roman counterparts.[1] For other writers it is the testing-ground of social behaviour, as frequently in Theophrastus' *Characters*; Athenaeus' *Deipnosophists* provides a rich store for the whole literature of the dinner-table, with quotations from specialists ranging from the fare itself to the parasites who eat it. The Greek diatribe castigates the luxury and excess which characterise the tables of many.[2]

For the Roman satirists the topic of the dinner is even more staple and stylised; handled by Ennius and taken up by Lucilius, it is exploited by Horace, Varro and Juvenal. The theme was congenial to the puritanical Roman spirit reacting against luxurious fare, and the earlier literature of the dinner-

[1] E.g. in the Convivia of Maecenas and Asconius Pedianus; see L. R. Shero, *CP* (1923), 126 ff. For Habinnas' drunken entry into the Cena as an evocation of Alcibiades' arrival in Plato's *Symposium*, see Averil Cameron, *CQ* (1969), 367 ff. and above, p. 40 n. 1.

[2] On such literary gourmets as Archestratus, see Rudd, 204 ff. The sixth book of the *Deipnosophists* is rich in parasites. For the diatribe, see Oltramare (above, p. 19 n. 1).

table allowed the later satirists the opportunity for creative imitation and evocation. In the stylised presentation, the host characteristically appears as a boorish figure condescending to his intellectually superior guests and humiliating his freedmen by serving them with inferior stuff.[1] There is censure of ostentatious display in furnishings and table-ware, of effeminate attendants, of voluptuous entertainment.

Trimalchio's Feast stands recognisably within this Roman satirical tradition. It would be otiose to claim that Petronius owes a direct debt to Lucilius,[2] and the correspondences with Varro are of a general rather than a particular kind.[3] But the connexions with Horace's *Cena Nasidieni,* itself evoking its Lucilian precursor, are demonstrably conscious and close.[4]

Thus the type represented by Trimalchio which Petronius

---

[1] With Juv. *Sat.* 5 and Mart. 3.60 compare Pliny *Ep.* 2.6 and Macaulay on the life of the English domestic chaplain (*History of England,* ch. 3): 'It was permitted to dine with the family; but he was expected to content himself with the plainest fare. He might fill himself with the corned beef and carrots; but as soon as the tarts and cheese-cakes made their appearance, he quitted his seat and stood aloof till he was summoned to return thanks for the repast, from a great deal of which he had been excluded.'

[2] The auctioneer Granius, who plays host in a satire of Lucilius, does not appear to have cut such a ridiculous figure as Trimalchio; cf. Shero, *CP* (1923), 126 ff. But the comments on the human condition, and the verses uttered by Trimalchio about iniquitous fortune (55.1 ff.) may hark back to fr. 489 f. (Warmington), on the interpretation of which see Tyrrell, *Hermathena* (1876), 365.

[3] In Varro's *Peri Edesmatōn* (Gell. 6.16.2 ff.) the 'several kinds of fare which gluttons seek on land and sea' are detailed; compare Trimalchio's verses at *Sat.* 55, where Petronius' comic irony makes the luxurious host condemn exotic fare. Varro's *Nescis Quid Vesper Serus Vehat* (Gell. 13.11.1 ff.) details the apposite number of guests for a dinner ('nam multos esse non convenit, quod turba plerumque est turbulenta') who should be neither 'loquaces' nor 'muti'. The lord of the feast should be 'non tam lautus quam sine sordibus'. Trimalchio's dinner contravenes all these precepts. There are at least fourteen guests (making Sedgwick's diagram at ch. 31 of his useful edition a fantasy), many of them comically *loquaces* and others *muti*; and Trimalchio is of course *lautissimus* throughout.

[4] Above, ch. 3.

selects for the central satirical creation of the *Satyricon* is described with the deliberate evocation of the themes of the boorish host in Roman satire. It is at the dinner-table that the full horror of the self-made magnate is revealed. Trimalchio, the former Asian slave turned nouveau-riche, who has made a quick fortune out of transport and usury, is a new phenomenon of Italian bourgeois society from which the traditionalist Roman recoils. As an ex-governor of Bithynia, Petronius could picture with the mind's eye the infant Trimalchio in his native habitat. As an ex-consul, he was all too aware of how the more intelligent of such *liberti* had supplanted the traditional ruling-class in positions of imperial responsibility in the Rome of the 50s. The fastidious *arbiter elegantiae* chose to concentrate his attack on such resented immigrants by depicting the social solecisms of the more ignorant and pretentious amongst them, a type in evidence both at Rome and in Campania.

The stuff of the dinner is important chiefly as providing a framework for the derisive portrait of the host. The introduction of the various courses structures the narrative to allow the salient facets of the characterisation to be repeatedly emphasised. In depicting these leading traits, Petronius regularly alternates between the techniques of the *descriptive* and the *ipse dixit*; the commentary of the narrator Encolpius is interwoven with the revealing words and actions of Trimalchio himself. And in several scenes the character of the host is reflected in the language and attitudes of his boon-companions at table.[1] This synthesis of the judgments of narrator with the postures of the host and the testimonials of his guests enables Petronius repeatedly to accentuate the same general vices but from different viewpoints and in different situations.

The main lines of the character of Trimalchio are indicated in the first memorable scenes on the exercise-ground and in the

[1] These are the stock techniques of characterisation exploited by the Roman historians, as I. Bruns pointed out long ago in his *Die Persönlichkeit in der Geschichtsschreibung der Alten* (Berlin 1898). To this extent the suggestion that Petronius is an innovator here (so Auerbach, *Mimesis* (English edn. Princeton 1953) ch. 2) should be qualified.

bath, before the guests assemble in the dining-room.[1] In this descriptive sequence there is a brief prefiguration of the host's more risible characteristics. His morbidity and preoccupation with death are at once established by mention of the clock in the dining-room and the trumpeter announcing 'quantum de vita perdiderit'. The vulgarity of the host is reflected in his passion for dazzling colours—his shirt is crimson, the balls bright green, his cloak scarlet, his doorman clad in green with a cherry-coloured belt. His boorishness is seen in his public use of the chamber-pot, and equally in his private enjoyment of music *en route* from the baths. His prodigality is illustrated in his refusal to use a ball once it has touched the ground; and his masseurs not only drink Falernian but throw it around. There is the luxury of his establishment as reflected by the towels 'of the softest wool', the chamber-pot of silver, the golden bird-cage and the silver peadish. Above all, his ambivalence towards his monstrous ménage is at once indicated—at one moment the playmate of affectionate slaves, at another the stern taskmaster ('Quisquis servus sine dominico iussu foras exierit, accipiet plagas centum'). This capriciousness is one of the traditional marks of the arrogant host, as we shall presently see.[2]

These characteristics merge into a rounded portrayal of the ignorant and vulgar buffoon who is also the arrogant master (Trimalchio means 'the lord *par excellence*'). His ignorance is reflected not only in the lack of literary discrimination but also in his superstitious interpretation of the real world, which degenerates after heavy drinking into a smothering morbidity. His buffoonery is illustrated by the constant succession of practical jokes in course after course, by his passion for execrable puns, and by his horseplay with his favourite Croesus and with his slaves. His arrogance is reflected in his condescension to his guests, in his attitude to his slaves, and in his proprietorial claim to vast tracts of the country of his adoption.

[1] The same technique was noted in the first appearance of Eumolpus; see above, pp. 94 f.

[2] All these references are contained in 26.7–28.9.

And above all the vulgarity of the nouveau-riche is revealed in the oppressive abundance of the food, in the décor of the villa, in the uneducated friends and shrewish wife, and in his pretentious and ignorant conversation.

The meal itself reflects the host's vulgarity by its very prodigality:

gustatio: olives, dormice, sausages, damsons, pomegranates, figpeckers (31)
ferculum primum: hare, fowl, sow's udders (36)
ferculum secundum: boar with dates and grapes (40)
ferculum tertium: pork (47)
?*ferculum quartum*: veal (59.7)
matteae (savouries): whole fowls and goose's eggs (65.1)
epideipnis: pastry thrushes stuffed with raisins, nuts, quinces; pork-
    shapes (69.6)

That this meal would have been regarded by elegant diners as gluttonous can be inferred not only from a comparison with the dinners recommended by other Roman writers but also by the comments of the narrator during the course of the meal. Horace's amusing account of being lectured by the gourmet Catius suggests that the ideal meal had three courses—a *hors d'œuvre* of eggs, cabbage, mushrooms and sea-food, a main course of Umbrian boar or venison or hare and fowl, and savouries of prawns, snails and sausages followed by apples and grapes.[1] Pliny's ideal meal is still simpler; he remonstrates with a friend for failing to share a dinner which is wholly vegetarian, suggesting like Horace before him that one can eat elegantly without expensive fish or meat.[2] It is against this standard that Trimalchio's offerings should be assessed; his board is of the dimensions of Nasidienus', where boar is followed by fowl, fowl by lamprey, lamprey by crane and hare, then by blackbirds and pigeons—at which point the guests flee![3] Such gargantuan fare must have been a commonplace at

---

[1] Sat. 2.4; see Rudd, 206 ff. The 'fecundae leporis armos' may have inspired Petronius' 'leporem pinnis subornatum ut Pegasus videretur', which is likewise served with fowl.

[2] Hor. *Ep.* 1.5.2: 'nec modica cenare times holus omne patella.' Pliny *Ep.* 1.15 offers lettuce, snails, eggs, olives, beet, gourds, onions, and 'alia mille non minus lauta'.   [3] Hor. *Sat.* 2.8.

the banquets of the wealthy; Augustus, a modest eater, sometimes served six courses, and Elagabalus gave a notorious
dinner with twenty-two.[1]

But it was the mark of the solicitous host to realise that
'multos morbos multa fercula fecerunt',[2] and Trimalchio's
meal causes his guests first discomfort, then disgust, and
finally panic. Encolpius assumes that the boar-course has
brought the main business of eating to an end, not realising that
the guests were still toiling up-hill 'in medio lautitiarum clivo'.[3]
The very thought of the savouries, in which whole fowls were
served 'instead of thrushes', makes the narrator wince.[4] At the
epideipnis, the sight of the pork-shapes is an affront;[5] and when
Trimalchio suggests a visit to the bath to enable the guests to
resume their eating subsequently, Encolpius whispers to his
friend 'Si videro balneum, statim exspirabo.'[6] So like the guests
at Nasidienus' table they decide to flee. If Trimalchio's dinner
was not an orgy, it was certainly a monumental exhibition of
the prodigal gluttony which is the mark of the vulgar host.[7]

Just as the food comprises courses individually acceptable
at a Roman gourmet's table, and is intolerable only by its
weight and interminability, so too Trimalchio claims to serve
only the best wine—'Falernian of Opimian vintage, a hundred
years old'. Argument has raged on whether this reference to
the vintage of 121 B.C. is purposely absurd; but the point of the
joke is surely the bottling in glass jars. Trimalchio's claim to be
serving a vintage Falernian is readily contradicted by its con-

---

[1] Suet. *Aug.* 74: *SHA Heliog.* 30.

[2] Sen. *Ep.* 95.18; for dinner-references in general, see Mayor's note at
Juv. 1.94.

[3] 47.8. The dish holding the previous course took four slaves to remove
the lid (36.1).

[4] 65.1: 'etiam recordatio me offendit'. Thrushes were the gourmet's
choice, as Persius 6.24 suggests.

[5] 69.7: 'ferculum longe monstrosius...'.

[6] 72.6; compare Juvenal's lively picture at 1.142 ff.

[7] I press the obvious point in view of Bagnani's disposition to regard
the meal as a normal Roman repast (in *Essays presented to Gilbert
Norwood*, ed. M. White (Toronto 1952), 218 ff.).

tainers.[1] The wine is pressed on the guests in embarrassing quantity. 'Pisces natare oportet.' And for those who do not care for Falernian, Trimalchio is willing to provide another, like Nasidienus offering to replace the Caecuban! The immoderate drinking has its inevitable results; the room begins to swim before Encolpius' eyes, and the host becomes first sportive and later utterly maudlin.

So far as the house is concerned, Petronius does not suggest a *domus* architecturally more pretentious than the normal run at Pompeii or Herculaneum. The enlargement of a smaller dwelling, it has 'four dining-rooms, twenty bed-chambers, two marble porticoes, and upstairs a store-room, my own bedroom, a sitting-room for this viper Fortunata; there's a good office for the doorman, and the visitors' wing takes the guests...*et multa alia sunt*.'[2] The house sounds much smaller than the Villa dei Misteri, for example,[3] and architecturally less ambitious than Pliny's Laurentian villa.[4] The only apparent peculiarity is the portico from the front door, leading through the curtained-off atrium to the main dining-room. The bath ('angustum scilicet et cisternae frigidariae simile') is curiously primitive by elegant first-century standards, recalling the 'balneolum angustum, tenebricosum ex consuetudine antiqua' of Scipio Africanus, as described in a letter of Seneca.[5] It is possible that Trimalchio envisages himself as a latter-day

---

[1] 34.6. The wine of 121 B.C. would obviously be undrinkable nearly two hundred years later; but since Martial mentions wine of Opimian vintage being drunk still later, the term may well be standard for a venerable vintage. Glass was not used commercially till the early empire; see Pliny *N.H.* 36.194 f. It looks as if Trimalchio, who never buys his wine (48.2), is affixing approved labels on new bottles. The phrase 'diligenter gypsatae' suggests that the fraud is apparent to Encolpius, who would know that vintage-labels were unusual and that Opimian Falernian was unknown at such an early date (cf. P. Bicknell, *AJP* (1968), 347 ff.).   [2] 77.4 f.

[3] See G. Bagnani, 'The house of Trimalchio', *AJP* (1954), 16 ff., who computes fifty rooms in Trimalchio's house as compared with ninety in the Villa dei Misteri at about A.D. 79. See Maiuri's commentary on the *Cena, ad loc.*   [4] Pliny, *Ep.* 2.17.

[5] *Ep.* 86.4. The passage may have been picked up by Petronius.

Scipio, preserving his bathroom as a genuine antique; incidentally he ensures a decent privacy. 'He said that there was nothing better than bathing out of the crush, and that the room had previously been a bakehouse.'[1]

It is the murals and the furnishings which reflect the vulgar man. The depiction at the entrance of the dog on a chain with the subscription 'Cave canem' was clearly inspired by house-decoration which Petronius had observed and considered as hardly the essence of elegance.[2] This vulgar dog-mural harmonises with the chattering magpie over the entrance, another feature popular with the less discerning householder of the Neronian age.[3] The colonnade inside the front door is adorned with scenes from the early life of Trimalchio; the absence of autobiographical motifs in excavated Campanian houses enhances our appreciation of Trimalchio's boundless egotism.[4] Other public rooms within, we are told, are adorned with scenes from 'the *Iliad*, the *Odyssey*, and Laenas' gladiatorial show'—again the comic philistinism of this juxtaposition is emphasised by the absence of scenes from the contemporary arena in Campanian dwellings.[5] The dining-room has an entrance decorated with the *fasces*, the symbol of *imperium*, with the subscription 'Cinnamus the steward dedicates this to C. Pompeius Trimalchio, *sevir Augustalis*.'[6]

[1] 73.2. For the dream bath of the late first century, see Mart. 6.42 and Statius *Silv.* 1.5; Martial criticises the notoriously dark and small private baths; cf. 2.14.11, 1.59.3. (Petronius of course chose to begin the *Cena* episode at the public baths, and the small bath at the house may be so depicted to account for the magnate's visiting a public bath. Or, as Prof. D. A. West suggests, the fact that his ostentation does not extend to the private parts of the house may also reflect his vulgarity.)

[2] 29.1. There are two examples of the *cave canem* motif on floor-mosaics at Pompeii; see Maiuri, *ad loc.*

[3] Friedländer quotes Pliny *N.H.* 10.78 on the Neronian craze for magpies 'quae longa insignes cauda variae appellantur'.

[4] The structural value of this device depicting Trimalchio's previous history should be noted; it is a clever refinement in Petronius' techniques of characterisation.   [5] 29.9.

[6] 30.1 f. So the petty religious priesthood for freedmen is exalted to the eminence of a high magistracy.

Even the most trivial social engagements are commemorated on tablets, as if to immortalise every movement of the great man; 'III et pridie Kalendas Ianuarias Gaius noster foras cenat.'[1]

So too with the furniture, especially the table-ware; Trimalchio's possessions are expensive but in revolting taste. His huge collection of silver goblets is adorned with scenes from mythology and gladiatorial heroes.[2] The olives for the *hors d'œuvre* are served in sacks hitched to a statue of a donkey (Corinthian, of course), and the silver trays above bear Trimalchio's name and their weight![3] The dish bearing the first main course has four figures of Marsyas, one at each corner, their skins spraying gravy into a moat in which fish are floating.[4] Add to these tasteless features the covers pulled over the couches, displaying hunting motifs appropriate to the boar-course, and the false panels in the dining-room ceiling which allow the theatrical descent of a tray bearing gifts for the diners,[5] and the portrait of the house and furniture is damningly complete.

It is the further mark of the man of low taste to have no regard for the value of his possessions. A silver dish accidentally dropped is swept up with the scourings, and Trimalchio affects complete nonchalance when his crystal glasses are shattered in a fight between the dogs.[6] The costliest silver is used for the meanest utensils like the chamber-pot and the dish for the foot-ointment.[7] And in the second dining-room, where a new feast is prepared after the bath, a new set of dinnerware set on solid silver tables reveals the limitless range of his wealth.[8]

The vulgarity of the host is further demonstrated in the description of his wife and friends. By their origins and occupations, by their range of interests and their picturesquely low speech, Petronius adds yet another dimension to this aspect of the characterisation of the host. Fortunata's rig-out is superbly vulgar—light green waistband, cherry-coloured petticoat,

[1] 30.3.
[2] 52.1 ff.
[3] 31.9 f.
[4] 36.3.
[5] 40.1; 60.1.
[6] 34.3; 64.10.
[7] 27.3; 70.8.
[8] 73.5.

anklets and white slippers tricked with gold. Her 'great fat arms' (*crassissimis lacertis*) are covered with jewelry of stunning weight.[1] An ex-slave purchased by Trimalchio, and therefore risen from nothing ('You wouldn't have taken bread from her hand'), she has become the managing genius behind the scenes.[2] Throughout she is portrayed as the tactful wife and dutiful *mater familias*, preventing her husband with a flattering word from dancing the cordax, soft and sympathetic when he is hurt by a tumbling acrobat, storing away the silver and feeding the slaves before she takes her own meal.[3] But her mask as controller of domestic harmony slips a little as the meal progresses. First Habinnas with characteristic refinement throws her over a couch so that her petticoat flies up. Next she shows signs of wanting to dance (Trimalchio claims that she is an expert at the cordax), and at the climax she expresses pungent resentment at her husband's attentions to a comely slave.[4] Subsequently Trimalchio deals her the same capricious treatment accorded to his whole ménage. Having just proclaimed her his heiress and praised her to the skies, he throws a goblet at her head, and reminds her of her debt to him in no uncertain terms.[5]

In addition to the 'refined' guests Agamemnon, Encolpius and Ascyltus, there are at least eleven(!) of Trimalchio's earthy friends at the dinner, and most of them paint revealing self-portraits in their contributions to the table-gossip. Hermeros, who has most to say, is a Trimalchio in miniature. A slave for forty years, he has worked his way up, invested his money in land and expensive plate, and now has a household of twenty slaves; like Trimalchio he has been invested with the priesthood open to freedmen in the provincial city.[6] He tells Encolpius the history of two others at table: Diogenes, who 'used

---

[1] 67.4 ff.
[2] 74.13; 37.2 ff., where Hermeros further characterises her as shrewd and able to hold her own in argument.
[3] 52.10; 54.2; 67.2.   [4] 67.13; 70.10; 74.9.
[5] 74.9 ff.
[6] 57.1 ff. He is a *sevir Augustalis*.

to carry logs on his shoulders' but now possesses eight hundred thousand sesterces and is buying a detached house; and Proculus, who made a million but lost it, and now 'can't call his hair his own'; he had been an undertaker who lived it up, and is even now putting a brave front on bankruptcy.[1] Of the other guests, Phileros has likewise risen from street-vendor ('modo modo collo suo circumferebat onera venalia') to small-town lawyer; Echion is a rag-merchant; Niceros is an ex-slave; Plocamus a former stage entertainer; and Habinnas is a stone-mason who has also been exalted with the priesthood of Augustus.[2]

The topics discussed by these unlettered *liberti* are an index to their host's own interests in life. Petronius has devoted a whole scene exclusively to this town-gossip. Trimalchio leaves the table to relieve himself, and there follows an elaborately patterned conversation to which five of the freedmen contribute. First Dama (a stock name for a slave in Horace) utters a few banalities on the weather and on his own inebriation. After this introduction, Seleucus (whose name deliberately suggests a Syrian provenance) reveals himself as local worthy and sententious Jeremiah; he exploits the topic of Chrysanthus' funeral, which he has just attended, to pronounce on the frailty of man's estate as evidenced by the misfortunes of the dead man. His contribution is balanced by that of the next speaker Phileros, whose more optimistic outlook emphasises that the dead man had no real grumble with his fortune. The fourth contributor, Ganymede (the name typifies the handsome slave-boy), moves away from the trivial discussion of personalities to topics of more serious import—the price of bread and the size of loaves! He is the arch-moraliser, pining for the good old days of his youth, when the town officials were kept under control and when popular piety ensured prosperity. This pronouncement too is balanced by the opposing opinion; Ganymede's pessimistic fusillade arouses Echion (like Phileros

---

[1] 38.7 ff., 38.11 ff.

[2] Phileros, 43.1 ff., 46.8; Echion, 45.1; Plocamus, 64.2; Habinnas, 65.5.

a Greek name) to count the town's blessings, and especially the imminence of a juicy gladiatorial show. These, then, are the large concerns of Trimalchio's circle—the weather, the recent funeral, the local acquaintances, the price of bread, the gladiatorial contests. And Habinnas later adds the equally momentous topics of the menu at a friend's table, and wives as an expensive commodity.[1]

Petronius makes the implicit contrast between these guests and Agamemnon's party explicit on several occasions. Echion notices Agamemnon looking down his nose. 'You don't belong to our class, and so you laugh at the conversation of common folk. We know that you're a crazy litterateur.' And referring to his son's prospects, he extols the rewards of legal knowledge as against literary studies ('nam litteris satis inquinatus est'), in preference to which he has recommended to his son a steady profession as 'barber, auctioneer, or at any rate barrister'. His attitude is echoed by Hermeros' attack on Ascyltus and Giton: 'You'll soon realise that your father wasted his money, even if you do know rhetoric.'[2] Niceros prefaces his werewolf story by acknowledging his fear that the scholarly pedants will laugh at him; it is clear that the introduction of these Milesian stories of magic by himself, and later by Trimalchio, is a further demonstration of the gulf between the host's credulous and superstitious boon-companions and the ironical and agnostic scholars.[3]

This gulf is also indicated by the racy but rude Latinity of the group of freedmen. To some extent the language provides a criterion of their varying levels of cultivation; the Latin of the lawyer Phileros and that of Ganymede diverge less from educated usage than does that of Dama, Seleucus and Echion. Dama uses the forms 'balneus', 'vinus', 'calda', and such outlandish expressions as 'staminatas' and 'matus', all in five

[1] 41.9–46; 65.9–67.10.   [2] 46.7; 58.8.

[3] 61.4. The rationalising attitude of scholars like Encolpius is reflected in Pliny's sceptical comment (*N.H.* 8.80): 'homines in lupos verti rursusque restitui sibi falsum esse confidenter existimare debemus...'. See M. Schuster, *WS* (1929), 149 ff.

lines. Seleucus is not so illiterate, but amongst his solecisms we notice 'neminem nihil boni facere oportet', as well as the picturesquely vulgar Graecism 'frigori laecasin dico'. Echion the rag-man is another Dama. 'Medius caelus', 'munus excellente', 'amphitheater', 'vinciturum', 'tu qui potes loquere non loquis', 'pauperorum', 'thesaurum' are a mere selection of his vulgar usages.[1]

In general, the vulgar language of the freedmen, including that of the host himself, provides one of the richest comic veins in the *Cena*. The technique was not unfamiliar in Old Greek Comedy or in Roman drama, but the juxtaposition of the rude with the cultivated guests makes Petronius' exploitation particularly effective. The first extended example of this *lingua vulgaris*, the conversation of Hermeros with Encolpius, in which Trimalchio's wife and friends are described, may serve for a brief analysis of the nature of the language. The sentences are short and staccato. Graecisms abound, as is natural in the common speech of the Naples area: 'Trimalchionis topanta est', 'adeo saplutus est', 'familia vero babae babae', 'phantasia non homo'. Diminutives too are common: 'obiter et vernaculae...meliusculae a Graecis fient.' As in the speech of Dama and Echion, colloquial forms like 'lacte' and 'sucossi' appear.[2] But it is in the graphic turns of phrase that the main humorous possibilities of this vulgar quotation lie. 'Everything is produced on his estates; look for cock's milk and you'll find it.' 'Trimalchio's farms are so big it takes a kite to fly over them.' His wife is 'a magpie of the couch', and 'if she tells Trimalchio it's dark at midday, he'll believe her.'[3]

All these elements are observable also in Trimalchio's

[1] 41.10–12; 42.7 and 2; 45.3, 4, 6, 10; 46.1, 8. The forms of vulgar Latin are studied in V. Väänänen, *Introduction au Latin Vulgaire* (Paris 1963), ch. 4. W. Süss, *De eo quem dicunt*, etc., claims more subtle differences; Dama shows 'simplicity' in brief utterance, Phileros 'verbose obscurity', Hermeros 'agitated confusion' making him inarticulate, Echion a 'falsa urbanitas'.

[2] Chs. 37–8. K. Müller excises the second *s* of *sucossi*.

[3] 38.1; 37.8, 7, 5. Hermeros' later outburst (57–8) is still richer in this pithy colloquialism.

language, especially when his anger at Fortunata makes him forget his pose of cultivated scholar:

quid enim? ambubaia non meminit se de machina? in⟨de⟩ illam sustuli, hominem inter homines feci. at inflat se tamquam rana et in sinum suum non spuit, codex non mulier. sed hic qui in pergula natus est aedes non somniatur...rogo, Habinna, sic peculium tuum fruniscaris; si quid perperam feci, in faciem meam inspue. puerum basiavi frugalissimum non propter formam sed quia frugi est...sed Fortunata vetat. ita tibi videtur, fulcipedia? suadeo bonum tuum concoquas, milva, et me non facias ringentem, amasiuncula; alioquin experieris cerebrum meum.[1]

Finally, Trimalchio's vulgarity and buffoonery are consistently reflected in his passion for parlour-tricks, weak jokes and excruciating puns. Here the lines of satirical portrayal are softened, and a perceptibly affectionate note is sounded by the author. Trimalchio begins to amuse us more than to disgust us, and this because his wealth and petty power have not wholly eroded his ingenuous capacity for innocent pleasure.[2] Every course has its element of comic surprise. In the *gustatio*, the wooden hen has laid 'peahen's eggs', which in fact prove to be figpeckers in seasoned yolks. The substantial first course is concealed by frugal fare displayed on a trick lid. The boar is accompanied by hunting-dogs, and thrushes fly out of the carved carcase. The guests are asked to select their pig for the pork course, and there is a charade between Trimalchio and his cook who pretends that he has omitted to gut the pig. The confectionery when touched emits saffron juice. The *epideipnis* consists of 'goose', 'fowl', 'fish', 'poultry'—all of which are made of pork; and the oysters and mussels are served after a mimic squabble between two litigants, who smash their pitchers against each other to allow the seafish to pour out.

These rustic pleasures are punctuated by equally rustic puns. The carver's name is Carver. The slave Dionysus is told 'Liber esto'. Before the dessert (*secundae mensae*), clean tables are

---

[1] 74.13 f., 75.3–6.

[2] Note especially his love of acrobats and trumpeters: 53.12: 'reliqua [animalia] acroamata tricas meras esse.' As the doctor in *Joseph Andrews* remarks, men discover themselves 'in nothing more than in the choice of their amusements' (Bk. 3 ch. 7).

brought in, to be greeted predictably by the exclamation of the host 'Poteram quidem hoc fericulo esse contentus; secundas enim mensas habetis.' Trimalchio's eggs are 'boned chickens'. His wife's bracelets and anklets are 'women's bonds'. And the departing-gifts consist of innumerable packages labelled with infantile puns; Ascyltus throws his hands into the air to greet each sally with exaggerated hilarity.[1] This draws the ire of Hermeros; one feels that in this attack by the self-made man on the parasitic scholars there is more than a hint of the author's latent sympathy towards Hermeros. This is fatal to Petronius' satirical intention, which is frequently undercut by distracting the reader from Trimalchio to the inadequacies of the narrator and his friends; by comparison with their attitudes, the host's foibles appear candid and innocent, and begin to evoke a wry affection.

Trimalchio's role as vulgar and boorish host is thus reflected in his food and furnishings, in the interests and manner of speech of his circle, and in his fund of tricks and quips. But unlike his friends, he has pretensions to learning, and this is the second main strand in the characterisation. On the portico at the entrance, Trimalchio is depicted as under the guidance of Mercury and Minerva—the god to ensure his success in the hard world of commerce, the goddess to lend him qualities of effortless learning and aesthetic discrimination. Trimalchio waits till the first course is removed before regaling his guests with a series of intellectual treats, but then they must all buckle down to serious stuff: 'oportet etiam inter cenandum philologiam nosse.'[2] Astrology, literature, philosophy, mythology—all their arcane lore is at his fingertips.

So in his illiterate Latin he first unfolds his encyclopaedic knowledge of the signs of the zodiac. 'Twelve gods dwell in this heaven, so it changes into twelve shapes. At one time it becomes a ram, so whoever is born under Aries has many flocks, a lot of wool, a hard head, a shameless face, a sharp

---

[1] 36.5 ff.; 41.7; 65.2; 67.7; 56.7 ff.; 68.2. Habinnas likewise jokes in this way (66.6).   [2] 39.3.

horn. Many schoolmasters and cavillers are born under this sign.' He proceeds solemnly to work through the other eleven signs, offering similarly risible interpretations of their influence. Some of the connexions are in fact too witty and ingenious to reflect Trimalchio's ignorance, and it is clear that Petronius reveals more of himself here than of his character. 'Under Sagittarius are born the crosseyed, who look at the vegetables and lift the bacon...; under Aquarius, inn-keepers and gourds; under Pisces, cooks and rhetoricians.'[1] There is so much of Petronius' own sophistication here that the satirical purpose again is blunted, but the comment of the narrator shows that we are meant to laugh at Trimalchio rather than with him. For the guests 'swear that Hipparchus and Aratus were not in the same league as Trimalchio'.[2]

Subsequently in his scholarly conversation with Agamemnon, Trimalchio boasts of his libraries, adjudicates brusquely on the *controversia* set earlier in the day for Agamemnon's pupils, and asks: 'Do you recall the twelve labours of Hercules, or the story of how the Cyclops twisted off Ulysses' thumb with the pincers? I used to read these things in Homer when I was a boy—and as for the Sibyl of Cumae, I saw her with my own eyes...'[3] So again his explanation of the origin of Corinthian ware gets a little confused: 'When Troy was captured, that crafty old scoundrel Hannibal heaped all the bronze, gold and silver statues on a pyre and set fire to it... That's how Corinthian ware began.'[4] He boasts of the mytho-

[1] 39.11 ff. Babylonian and Egyptian representations show Sagittarius as a centaur with two heads looking opposite ways. Rhetoricians are under Pisces because they fish for pupils; cf. earlier at *Sat.* 3.4. On the astrological explanations in general, see de Vreese, *Petron 39 und die Astrologie* (Amsterdam 1927); S. Eriksson, *Wochentagsgötter, Mond, und Tierkreis* (Stockholm 1956), ch. 2 ('Die Astrologie bei Petron'). Eriksson's contribution is especially valuable as demonstrating Petronius' attacks on the exegeses of astrologers.

[2] 40.1.

[3] 48.7 f. Trimalchio appears to assume that the Sibyl of Cumae is described in Homer.

[4] As Saguntum and Troy are confused here (50.5), so at 59.4 the Trojan and Second Punic Wars are again conflated.

logical themes on his goblets—'Cassandra killing her children, with the boys lying there so vividly dead you'd think they were alive', and 'Daedalus enclosing Niobe in the Trojan horse'.[1]

The egregious errors are only part of the point. Petronius makes much play also with Trimalchio's baffling changes of conversational direction. A little later the host again turns to Agamemnon. 'Master, what difference do you find between Cicero and Publilius? I think the one is more eloquent, the other more sincere.' (There follows an amusing imitation of Publilius Syrus' mimic style,[2] in which the humour is not wholly literary. The message, characteristic of Varronian satire, that exotic foods and jewelry are vain, is declaimed by the host apparently in blissful ignorance that *fabula de se narratur*!) Trimalchio then passes abruptly to the question of the most difficult professions; and after a paralysingly weak joke he turns equally abruptly to the most difficult assignments in the animal world, so that he can perpetrate a cliché or two on the thankless role of oxen and sheep, and on the bee as the symbol of the bitter-sweet. The inability to sustain a topic for more than two sentences has added comedy in that the pronouncements are directed to a practising rhetorician.[3]

Again and again Trimalchio exposes his comic ignorance of literature. This is his version of the theme of Troy. 'Diomede and Ganymede were brothers; their sister was Helen. Agamemnon bore her off and offered a stag to Diana in her place. So now Homer is telling how the Trojans and the Tarentines are at war. Agamemnon of course won, and gave his daughter Iphigeneia as wife to Achilles. So Ajax goes mad, and he will now develop the story.' This is the prelude to the appearance of the carver, who cuts up some veal with crazed gestures.[4]

---

[1] 52.1–2. Note how instantly recognisable the howlers are—Cassandra confused with Medea, and Niobe in the horse with Pasiphaë in the cow.

[2] 55.5 ff. Marmorale, *ad loc.*: 'un pezzo di bravura nello stile di Publilio.' Note besides the sentiment the alliterative proverb in the first line (shades of Hannibal at Capua!) and the patterned alliteration later; the compound adjectives in l. 6 and the rhetorical questions at the end are also characteristic. See Sullivan, 192 f.

[3] 56.1 ff.   [4] 59.3 ff.

Trimalchio also fancies himself as a poet, and in unforgettable lines consigns to immortality two incidents at the dinner. First the diversion with a skeleton causes him to reflect on the mortality of man in the incongruous mixture of a hexameter followed by an elegiac couplet. When he is struck by a falling acrobat, after 'a brief but anguished meditation' he recites a similarly bizarre triplet:

> quod non expectes ex transverso fit
> et supra nos Fortuna negotia curat,
> quare da nobis vina Falerna, puer.

Scholars have devoted similarly anguished meditation to the completion of the hexameters in the first two lines, on the assumption that words have fallen out; it would however be thoroughly in character with the poetic tiro to have a first line deficient at the end, and a second at the beginning.[1]

The third notable line of characterisation is Trimalchio as arrogant master. As 'the lord *par excellence*', he organizes his whole establishment as an imperial court in miniature. We shall presently see that in his dress and habits he evokes the presence of the emperor Nero and the better-known foibles of his predecessors Augustus and Claudius. Not that Trimalchio represents Nero or any other emperor in any extended sense; but one purpose of these similarities is to strengthen the impression of Trimalchio in the role of posturing *princeps*.

For Trimalchio's retinue of slaves is as large as an emperor's. Hermeros' establishment of twenty—'viginti ventres pasco et canem'[2]—will be the norm for the small-town notable by which Trimalchio's retinue can be measured. His slaves are so

---

[1] 34.10, 55.3. It is a common experience in the early stages of verse-composition to write hexameters with five feet. It is said of two eminent contemporaries in classical studies that on commencing verses together they foreshadowed their future roles in scholarship; one put seven feet in his hexameter, the other five. (Mr E. J. Kenney comments that hexameters with seven feet are not uncommon in *CLE*, and that a recent metrical inscription from Chester has lines with $6\frac{1}{2}$ feet!)

[2] 57.6.

numerous that he orders them in companies. 'What company are you in?' he asks the harassed cook, and when he replies 'The fortieth', the master retorts 'See that you put before us a well-prepared dish, or I'll order your demotion to the company of messengers.'[1] The implication is that the total complement of slaves runs into thousands. 'Familia vero babae babae, non mehercules puto decimam partem esse quae dominum suum noverit.'[2] The great majority, still awaiting their privilege of clapping eyes on the master, work on the vast country estates such as that of Cumae, where on a single day the birth of thirty boys and forty girls is recorded, and where his private police force of aediles operates.[3]

Even at the *domus* where the *Cena* is enacted the establishment is so huge that they work in shifts;[4] the house as described would be wholly inadequate for this teeming mob. At the higher level there is an *atriensis*, a *procurator*, a *dispensator* with a private slave, and an *ostiarius*. There is a plurality of doctors.[5] The musicians include a trumpeter to sound the hours, and a slave who plays the pipes privately to his master. There is a company of bemedalled runners. Trimalchio has no fewer than three masseurs, and other slaves to tend the feet of the guests. Amongst the crowd of waiters there are long-haired Alexandrians providing iced water for washing the hands, two Ethiopians with wine in skins for the same purpose, and an Egyptian serving bread. There is a *supellecticarius*, two carvers, a cook, two 'torturers', fowlers with limed reeds, a threshold-watcher,[6] a *nomenclator*; there is a troop of entertainers, including a strong man, an acrobat, and a company of Homeristae. Even if we assume that some of these double up in their duties, the establishment is as big as an army.

Trimalchio's treatment of his slaves characterises him as the capricious master—'interdiu severa, nunc hilaria'.[7] At one moment he calls his slaves *putidissimi*, and keeps them at a

---

[1] 47.12. (At 70.1 ff. he shows that he knows him well!)
[2] 37.9.   [3] 53.2, 53.9.
[4] 74.6.   [5] 54.2.
[6] 30.5: 'qui supra hoc officium erat positus'.   [7] 64.13.

distance.[1] One is cuffed for picking up a fallen cup; another is told 'cito te ipsum caede' when he drops a goblet; others have to beg the guests to save them from punishment.[2] At another time, Trimalchio suddenly frees a slave, or gives the cook a drink on a silver tray, and presents him with a new set of carvers.[3] And in the final scene, after earlier dispensing wine to all the slaves ('Those who refuse get it poured over their heads'), he invites them to share the couches. Daedalus the cook sings, and then offers to lay a wager with his master on the coming chariot-races. Finally, Trimalchio delivers a sententious speech on the equality of mankind: 'Amici, et servi homines sunt et aeque unum lactem biberunt...' (Petronius, himself hardly an early-day Wilberforce, here parodies the earnest moral pronouncements of philosophers like Seneca, who à propos of slaves writes: 'Vis tu cogitare istum quem servum tuum vocas ex eisdem seminibus ortum eodem frui caelo, aeque spirare, aeque vivere, aeque mori...')[4] In short, Trimalchio ludicrously combines in himself the roles of harsh autocrat and gentle philosophic master.

Over these slaves, and over his huge country retinue, Trimalchio governs with the trappings and the justice of the imperial court. Half-way through the meal Trimalchio's lawyer recites Trimalchio's Gazette, 'tamquam acta urbis', for 26 July. The formula of the court-circular is reproduced in this pretentious attempt to impress the dinner-guests,[5] with the stock entries of births, corn-stocks, executions, fires, aediles' edicts and judicial decisions.[6] The slave Mithridates has been

---

[1] 34.5.   [2] 34.2; 52.4; 30.7, 54.3.   [3] 41.7, 50.1, 70.3.

[4] Sen. *Ep.* 47.10. For Petronius' own caprice in his respect, cf. Tac. *Ann.* 16.19: 'servorum alios largitione, quosdam verberibus adfecit.'

[5] 53.1–10. Rose, *CP* (1967), 259, notes that if there had really been a daily bulletin, Trimalchio would not have been ignorant of the purchase of the Pompeian gardens; but it is doubtful if Petronius intended this inconsistency.

[6] On the *acta urbis*, see G. Boissier, *Tacitus and other Roman Studies* (London 1906), 197 ff. The fire which began 'ex aedibus Nastae vilici' may covertly refer to the second outbreak of 64, which began in the Aemilian property of Tigellinus (Tac. *Ann.* 15.40.3).

crucified for 'blaspheming against the genius of our Gaius'; Trimalchio has allowed himself to be excluded from the wills of his foresters.[1] This is only one of several features of the dinner which characterise Trimalchio as *princeps*. Later the representation of the host is set with a group of gods' statues to be kissed in obeisance by the guests, just as later in Bithynia Pliny makes the Christians venerate Trajan's statue to gain acquittal.[2] It may be suspected that when the guests rise to recite the formula 'Augusto patri patriae feliciter', they do so with sidelong glances at their host.[3] The cook confesses that he has been left to Trimalchio *testamento Pansae*—just as it was the contemporary custom to include the emperor in one's bequests.[4] And in the hierarchy of the retinue, the *dispensator* has a personal slave and speaks of a *cliens* of his, just as in the imperial house it was known for more important slaves to have their own attendants.[5]

So too Trimalchio's acres extend almost as far as the imperial holdings. 'All the food that makes your mouth water' says this owner of huge *latifundia*, 'is produced on an estate I haven't yet seen. They tell me it's bounded by the towns of Tarentum and Tarracina.[6] At the moment I'm trying to join Sicily to my estates, so that if I take a fancy to go to Africa I shall be travelling through my own territory.' This significant criticism of Trimalchio as landowner on an imperial scale suggests that Petronius could well have mounted his satirical attack at a wholly different level. Elsewhere he documents with surprising detail the rise of Trimalchio and the source of his wealth, thereby reminding us that as a former politician he has considerable awareness of the changing economic and social conditions of Italy.[7] But he prefers to enclose this criticism of

[1] 53.9.
[2] 60.9; for the custom in the eastern provinces, Pliny *Ep.* 10.96.5.
[3] 60.7.   [4] 47.12.
[5] 30.10; for a similar instance, see Dessau, 1659.
[6] Which is the equivalent of saying that Lord X's grouse-moors stretch from Aberdeen to Oban.
[7] 48.2–3; 75.10 ff.

Trimalchio as a new Italian phenomenon within the traditional framework of the arrogant lord and master.

Superstition and morbidity are the fourth main strand in Trimalchio's make-up; Petronius had doubtless observed how large a part these tendencies play in the lives of many self-made men. Trimalchio wears stars on his ring to avert the evil eye. All who cross his threshold must put their right foot over first. His dinner-service contains a serving plate embossed with the signs of the zodiac.[1] When he hears a cock crow, he orders wine to be sprinkled under the table and on the lamp, and transfers his ring to his right hand.[2] He explains how, after he had made his fortune, he gained the help of Serapa, a Greek astrologer 'who advises the gods'. The gems of arcane lore and prescience quoted by Trimalchio as evidence of Serapa's powers include these: 'You are unlucky in your friends. Nobody ever pays you back as you deserve. You nurture a viper in your bosom.' Trimalchio has been so shaken by this uncanny insight that he firmly believes Serapa's assurance that he has thirty years four months two days to live.[3]

Towards the end of the *Cena* drink transforms this superstitious view of life into a morbid preoccupation with death. Trimalchio orders his will to be brought, and declaims every line to a chorus of lamentation. He has already ordered the design of his tombstone, but he takes Habinnas through all the detail of its size and ornamentation, concluding with its proposed inscription: 'Gaius Pompeius Trimalchio Maecenatianus rests here. The sevirate was bestowed on him in his absence. He could have been a member of every Roman club, but refused. God-fearing, brave and faithful, he rose from nothing and left thirty million. He never heard a philosopher lecture.'[4]

The maudlin infection spreads from Trimalchio's copious tears to the whole retinue. Repressed momentarily by the general exodus to the bath, this mimic performance breaks out

[1] 32.3; 30.5; 35.
[2] 74.1. On the cockcrow and its meaning, see Cic. *Pis.* 67 with Nisbet's note; Pliny *N.H.* 10.49.   [3] 76.10 ff.   [4] 71.5 ff.

again in the final scene, when Trimalchio orders his funeral-bier and laying-out clothes to be brought in. Then, having invited all and sundry to his anniversary feast, he lies on the death-couch and bids the trumpeters: 'Fingite me mortuum esse. dicite aliquid belli.' So the enthusiastic rendering of the Last Post rounds off the episode on the note with which it had commenced, with the trumpeters recalling to mind the musician who sounded the lost hours, and the skeleton dancing on the table.[1]

Where did Petronius derive his inspiration for this portrait of the vulgar host and overweening master with literary preten-sions and a superstitious and morbid outlook? It has been suggested that Trimalchio had a model in life; apparently the evidence for the existence of Petronii at Herculaneum is to be harnessed to support this view of Trimalchio as an historical figure. He is a former slave of Petronius' own family. 'Behind Trimalchio lurks a real family freedman... Petronius finds his old family dependant terribly vulgar and in certain ways almost disgusting, but he cannot help rather liking him.' To this suggestion of a model from life we can say neither yea nor nay; the evidence is wholly inadequate.[2] What must be said is that Trimalchio is much more than a photograph of a single person. He is a rich creation in which the author achieves a synthesis between the traditional portrayal of the boorish, arrogant master and the contemporary freedman of substantial wealth—that is, between the vulgar man in Theophrastus and Horace, and the vulgar man of Petronius' own observation; in short, Trimalchio is a combination of the literary and the observed.

Petronius naturally looks to Theophrastus for some of the detailed touches in his characterisation of the host at table who is a garrulous boor, because the *Characters* enjoyed a great

---

[1] 78.5 ff.; 26.9; 34.8 f. (The skeleton is sometimes used for magic; see Apuleius, *Apol.* 63.6.)

[2] In this thesis of G. Bagnani, *Phoenix* (1954), 77 ff., it is slightly alarming to find how a speculative hypothesis is gradually transmuted into certainty, and Trimalchio into an historical figure.

vogue in antiquity as a terrible warning on how not to behave in civilised company. The parallels between Trimalchio and the several characters of Theophrastus are many and suggestive. The boor in Theophrastus summons his dog in front of his guests, lays hold of its muzzle, and exclaims: 'This is the guardian of my home and household'; Trimalchio requests that Scylax be brought in, and echoes these very words, 'praesidium domus familiaeque'.[1] The boor, according to Theophrastus, sings in his bath; and Trimalchio, 'invitatus balnei sono'—enticed by the acoustics—'diduxit usque ad cameram os ebrium, et coepit Menecratis cantica lacerare'.[2] The shameless man in Theophrastus is capable even of dancing the cordax when drunk; Trimalchio begins the dance, 'erectis supra frontem manibus', before Fortunata dissuades him.[3] The garrulous man in Theophrastus praises his wife before strangers; so Fortunata is lauded by her husband.[4] The disgusting man in Theophrastus recounts how he managed to cure his constipation; and Trimalchio proudly reveals how, when his doctors were at a loss, he cured himself with pomegranate rind and pine-wood dipped in vinegar.[5] Theophrastus condemns the man who recounts course by course what he had for dinner —and by doing precisely this, Habinnas the intimate of the host stigmatises the manners of Trimalchio's circle.[6] So too Ganymede, in his lament for the good old days and his comments on the price of bread, indulges in that garrulity which

---

[1] *Char.* 4.10: [ὁ ἄγροικος] τὸν κύνα προσκαλεσάμενος καὶ ἐπιλαβόμενος τοῦ ῥύγχους εἰπεῖν· οὗτος φυλάττει τὸ χωρίον καὶ τὴν οἰκίαν. In Petronius *Sat.* 64.7, the dog-joke is developed further, because Scylax, which means 'pup' in Greek, is 'ingentis formae...canis catena vinctus'.

[2] *Char.* 4.13: καὶ ἐν βαλανείῳ δὲ ἆσαι... *Sat.* 73.3.

[3] *Char.* 6.3: [ὁ ἀπονενοημένος] δυνατὸς καὶ ὀρχεῖσθαι νήφων τὸν κόρδακα ... *Sat.* 52.9.

[4] *Char.* 3.2 (ὁ ἀδολέσχης); *Sat.* 67.2, 52.8.

[5] *Char.* 20.6 (ὁ ἀηδής); *Sat.* 47.2: 'multis iam diebus venter mihi non respondit. nec medici se inveniunt. profuit mihi tamen malicorium et taeda ex aceto.'

[6] *Char.* 3.3:...ὦν εἶχεν ἐπὶ τῷ δείπνῳ τὰ καθ' ἕκαστα διεξελθεῖν. *Sat.* 66.1 ff.

Theophrastus deprecates.[1] Possibly Petronius has derived these amusing examples of social lapses not from Theophrastus directly, but from a collection of excerpts; but the literary inspiration here is beyond all doubt.[2]

The tenth book of Philodemus' *Peri Kakiōn* provides other illuminating parallels, this time to demonstrate the traditional vices of the arrogant master. Trimalchio's pretended ignorance of the identity of slaves is an example of a trait castigated by Philodemus.[3] So too is the vacillation between the extremes of aloofness and familiarity.[4] Trimalchio's pose as a man of profound knowledge, with his explanations of astrological lore and his magisterial comments on literature and history, reflects a trait repeatedly condemned by Philodemus;[5] and—strikingly —the same can be said of Trimalchio's scorn of philosophers in the splendid auto-epitaph.[6] In general, Philodemus' treatise appears to have been directed precisely against the type of ignorant, overbearing host who does not hesitate to take the place of honour at the table; Petronius' portrait is lovingly assembled in this image.[7]

[1] *Char.* 3.3: λέγειν ὡς πολλῷ πονηρότεροί εἰσιν οἱ νῦν ἄνθρωποι τῶν ἀρχαίων, καὶ ὡς ἄξιοι γεγόνασιν οἱ πυροί. In *Sat.* 44, the price has gone up.

[2] On these parallels, see Collignon, 312 (I would contest his suggestion that they are 'très vagues et lointains' (315)); M. Rosenblüth, *Beiträge zur Quellenkunde von Petrons Satiren* (diss. Kiel 1909), 56 ff.; Sullivan, 138 f. (like Collignon, sceptical, and perhaps underestimating the diffusion and popularity of Theophrastus). For the possibility of excerpts of Theophrastus having been consulted, see O. Raith, ch. 2.

[3] Phil. col. 17.1–4: παῖδα πριάμενος...καλεῖν δὲ παῖδα καὶ μηθὲν ἄλλο ... *Sat.* 47.11.

[4] Phil. col. 7.12–17: θαυμάσιον μὲν οὖν φαίνετ' εἰ δοκοῦσι τότε μὲν ὑπερήφανοι, τότε δὲ ταπεινοί... *Sat.* 34.5 and 70.11.

[5] *Sat.* 39.4 ff., 48.4 ff., 50.4 ff., 52.1 ff., etc.; Phil. col. 4.27–31, 18.11–18 and 35–7.

[6] *Sat.* 71.12: 'nec umquam philosophum audivit'. Phil. col. 4.22–6: καὶ τῶν φιλοσόφων δὲ καθυπερηφανεῖ...

[7] Trimalchio sits in the *locus primus* (31.8); cf. Phil. col. 15.5–8. O. Raith, from whom I take these parallels, cites them to argue for an 'epikureische Charakterologie', since Philodemus was an Epicu-

These parallels reveal that the main lines of Trimalchio's character—garrulous boor, haughty master, pretender to cultural knowledge—harmonise closely with the Hellenistic social criticism represented by Theophrastus and Philodemus; and it is worth adding that the other main facet of Trimalchio, his superstition, reflects Theophrastus' preoccupation with *deisidaimonia*.[1] When with these traditional details are fused the several characterising touches derived from Horace's Nasidienus,[2] it is clear that Trimalchio is the incarnation of all that is distasteful and disreputable in the traditional portrayal of the offensive host. But Petronius' invention is not to be undervalued; he has synthesised this literary material with a depiction of the characteristic phenomenon of his age, the nouveau-riche freedman.

The reader of Seneca's letters, which are the most valuable individual index to the manners of Neronian society, repeatedly gasps with surprise at encountering Trimalchio-like figures abroad in first-century Rome; and the situations in which they are depicted demonstrate that Petronius' portrait is not a mere literary caricature. There is Calvisius Sabinus, the epitome of the weathy *libertinus*; 'et patrimonium habebat libertini et ingenium; nunquam vidi hominem beatum indecentius.' Like Trimalchio, Sabinus aspires to be a litterateur, and like him cannot remember such recondite names as Ulysses and Priam.[3] There is another *libertus* of whom we read: 'habet domum pulchram: multum serit, multum foenerat'—the combination of land-cultivation and usury as a source of wealth being precisely Trimalchio's.[4] In another letter we read: 'An estate embracing a nation is too small for one master. How far will you extend your ploughed fields? You are not satisfied to

rean. But the philosophical connexion seems nebulous; the range of influences suggests a literary rather than a philosophical preoccupation.

[1] *Char.* 16, but without detailed correspondences.

[2] Above, ch. 3.

[3] *Ep.* 27.5. Bagnani, *Phoenix* (1954), 77 ff., believes he is an *ingenuus*, but the argument is inconclusive. Sullivan, 129 ff., rightly quotes this letter *in extenso*.   [4] *Ep.* 41.7; *Sat.* 48.2 ff., 76.9.

enclose the limits of your farms even within the confines of provinces... You have insufficient unless you have surrounded seas with your estates, unless your steward rules beyond the Adriatic, Ionian and Aegean seas, and unless the island homes of great chieftains are reckoned the cheapest of possessions.' The parallel with Trimalchio's megalomaniac plans is striking.[1]

In other letters Seneca condemns various foibles of contemporary life practised by Trimalchio. One thinks at once of Pacuvius, who according to Seneca 'celebrated his own death with wine and the notorious funeral feast; he was carried from dinner into his chamber to the applause of his catamites and the cry to music: βεβίωται, βεβίωται.' It seems impossible that the close of Trimalchio's banquet was not inspired by this celebrated exemplar.[2] One thinks too of Seneca's condemnation of the master who keeps a slave, as Trimalchio keeps Carpus, solely for carving; and of the man whose devotion to exercise impels him to keep as trainers 'homines inter oleum et vinum occupati', like Trimalchio's masseurs who swill and spill his Falernian.[3] Seneca remarks on dining-rooms in which the ceiling-panels are on swivels—and a memorable feature of Trimalchio's dinner is the descent of gifts from the ceiling, 'diductis lacunaribus'.[4] These striking parallels (the list is by no means exhaustive)[5] show that many of the detailed touches in the characterisation of Trimalchio are attributable to Petronius' observation of contemporary manners, especially amongst wealthy freedmen.

Other striking sources of comic detail in Trimalchio's

[1] Sen. *Ep.* 89.20 (cf. 90.39); Petr. 48.
[2] Sen. *Ep.* 12.8. Note also a similar example at *Brev. Vit.* 2.20.3. I owe this reference to Mr Martin Smith.
[3] The carver, Sen. *Ep.* 47.6: 'infelix, qui huic uni rei vivit, ut altilia decenter secet'; Petr. 36.5 ff. Masseurs, Sen. *Ep.* 15.3, Petr. 28.3.
[4] Sen. *Ep.* 90.15; Petr. 60.
[5] Sullivan, 135 f., draws attention to Seneca's portrait of Maecenas in *Ep.* 114, and Trimalchio's appearance is certainly similar. Hence the *agnomen* of Trimalchio, Maecenatianus (71.12) may have allusive point. For a further example, Seneca like Theophrastus complains of the man 'cui vox sua in balneo placet' (56.2) and Trimalchio is such a performer.

portrayal are the appearance and appurtenances of the emperor Nero; the correspondences which can be established with Suetonius' life of the emperor seem too close and numerous to be coincidence. Trimalchio wears a golden bracelet on his right arm, as Nero did. The emperor often appeared in public with a napkin round his neck, as Trimalchio does at the commencement of dinner.[1] Nero kept his first shaving-hairs in a golden casket; Trimalchio has a 'pyxis aurea non pusilla, in qua barbam ipsius conditam esse dicebant'.[2] In their slave-retinues, both Nero and Trimalchio have bemedalled runners (*cursores phalerati*), and both have a slave called Carpus.[3] In the course of the *Cena*, a singing acrobat falls from a ladder and bruises Trimalchio; a not dissimilar incident occurred to Nero in the arena, when 'Icarus' fell and bespattered him with his blood.[4]

It is important not to draw the wrong conclusions from these and other less cogent correspondences.[5] Trimalchio is not a fictional representation of Nero.[6] In his main lines he is

[1] Bracelet, Suet. *Nero* 6.4, Petr. 32.4; napkin, Suet. *Nero* 51, Petr. 32.2 ('laticlaviam...mappam').

[2] Suet. *Nero* 12.4; Petr. 29.8.

[3] Runners, Suet. *Nero* 30, Petr. 28.4 (*cursores* were of course a regular feature of the retinues of rich men; cf. Sen. *Ep.* 123.7). Carpus a Neronian favourite, see P. Grimal, *RPh* (1941), 19 f.

[4] Suet. *Nero* 12. 2; Petr. 54.1.

[5] Conveniently assembled in H. Crum, *CW* (1952). 161; for earlier bibliography, see Rose, *Arion* (1966), 298 n. 2. The striking parallel between Trimalchio's ceiling-panels and those in the Golden House should not be pressed for chronological reasons, despite Tac. *Ann.* 15.52.2 (see Furneaux's note). Likewise the correspondence between Sporus (Suet. *Nero* 28.1) and Croesus.

[6] The comment of Voltaire is worth reproducing. 'Quel rapport d'un vieux financier grossier et ridicule et de sa vieille femme, qui n'est qu'une bourgeoise impertinente qui fait mal au cœur, avec un jeune empereur et son épouse, la jeune Octavie ou la jeune Popée? Quel rapport des débauches et des larcins de quelques écoliers fripons avec les plaisirs du maître du monde?' Collignon, *Pétrone en France* (Paris 1905), 96 ff., in quoting this and other passages, describes Voltaire as almost the sole great eighteenth-century writer in France who takes a keen interest in the Petronian question.

an upstart old ignoramus who has made his way in the world by trade. Yet the comic detail of Nero's appearance and habits is incorporated to cause merriment to contemporaries close to the court. I conclude that Nero could hardly have been present at a recitation of the *Cena*.[1]

It is likely that Petronius in these jocose allusions was simultaneously guying Nero and building up Trimalchio in his role of quasi-emperor. The second motive may have been at work also in his exploitation of well-known foibles of earlier emperors, especially Claudius and Augustus Claudius is said to have contemplated an edict permitting guests to break wind and to belch at table; Trimalchio urges the same licence.[2] Augustus and Trimalchio share a passion for astrology and superstitious observance. Augustus made much of being born under Capricorn, Trimalchio of being born under Cancer. Augustus would not transact business on the nones, and Trimalchio keeps careful record of *dies incommodi*.[3] Augustus used to come in late for dinner, and after his guests had commenced—a trick which Trimalchio exploits to good effect. And most striking of all, the *apophoreta* at Augustus' dinners were often of a mean character—'nothing but hair-cloth, sponges, pokers, tongs and such like under labels hard to work out because of their double meaning'; Trimalchio's gifts of 'passeres et muscarium', 'muraena et littera' and the rest are precisely of this kind.[4]

Trimalchio is thus at once not only the recognisable heir to the role of Theophrastus' boor, Philodemus' arrogant master, and Horace's vulgar host, but also a type familiar on the stage of Neronian social life, loathed by those with a pretence to breeding and cultural accomplishment. Encolpius and his friends stamp each example of ill-breeding with the seal of ironical approval. Trimalchio's triumphant progress from the baths leaves them 'admiratione saturi', the first sight of the

[1] Above, p. 70.　　　　[2] Suet. *Claud.* 32; *Sat.* 47.4.
[3] Suet. *Aug.* 94.12, Petr. 39.8; *Aug.* 92.2, Petr. 30.4.
[4] Suet. *Aug.* 74, Petr. 32.1; *Aug.* 75, Petr. 56.8 ff.

house and dining-room finds them 'his repleti voluptatibus'. Every course, every accompanying surprise, every witticism of the host is labelled *lautitiae* or *elegantiae*, or is greeted with exaggerated applause.[1]

The extended study of this single character allows the reader to speculate that the other subordinate characters of the *Satyricon* may likewise be complex creations. True, the *Cena* episode as centrepiece is the longest of the episodes, and no other character receives so much loving attention from the author as does Trimalchio. But all of them—Agamemnon, Quartilla, Eumolpus, Tryphaena and Lichas, the fortune-hunters at Croton—are recognisable as types attacked in Roman satire, and all simultaneously represent facets of contemporary society under attack from Petronius. None of them has survived in the round, as Petronius described them; if the full novel had survived, we might see in them also more fully the synthesis of the traditional and the contemporary, of the literary and the observed.

[1] 28.6, 30.5, 32.1, 34.8, 70.7, 27.4, 31.8, 34.5, 60.1, 35.1, 40.1, 50.1, 55.1, 57.1, 58.1, 65.6.

6

THE 'METAMORPHOSES'

Therefore is it that you must open the book, and seriously consider of the matter treated in it, then you shall find that it containeth things of far higher value than the box did promise; that is to say, that the subject thereof is not so foolish as by the title, at the first sight, it would appear to be.

And put the case that in the literal sense you meet with matters that are light and ludicrous, and suitable enough to their inscriptions; yet must you not stop there, as at the melody of the charming syrens; but endeavour to interpret that in a sublimer sense, which, possibly, you might think was spoken in the jollity of heart...for in the perusal of this treatise, you shall find another kind of taste, and a doctrine of a more profound and abstruse consideration, which will disclose unto you the most glorious and dreadful mysteries.

RABELAIS, *Gargantua and Pantagruel*
Prologue to the First Book

A century elapsed between the *Satyricon* and the *Metamorphoses*. Apuleius of Madaura, it can be assumed with fair certainty, wrote his romance after returning to permanent domicile in the Roman province of Africa. Indefatigable traveller, precocious litterateur, popular philosopher interpreting Plato for Roman readers, professional advocate as the polish of his *Apology* demonstrates—he is a non-political Cicero in the changed conditions of second-century western society. He had returned to Carthage a celebrity. Indicted on a capital charge of magic at Sabrata in 158/9, he had routed that accusation of having exploited the black art to win the hand of the wealthy widow Pudentilla. His defence on the one hand vindicated the sincerity of his philosophical commitment to Platonism and his Roman religious orthodoxy, and on the other established his predominance as learned orator in the Ciceronian tradition, steeped in the classics of Greece and Rome. The *Florida*, a collection of his occasional speeches and literary set-pieces, is an index to his subsequent activities at Carthage in the 160s. He has learnt his lesson at Sabrata, and is determined to foreclose his wanderings, which had taken him to Greece and the Aegean islands, to Rome and Tripolitania. At Carthage, as the resident darling of the Roman establishment, he is the incumbent of the chief priesthood, the declaimer of nicely turned valedictories to retiring proconsuls, the recipient of public statues erected in his honour.[1]

At first sight such detail of the background of the *Metamorphoses* and the personality of the author seems largely irrelevant to the study of Lucius' adventures. The book is after all a romance rather than a novel; unlike Petronius' *Satyricon*, at no point apparently does it come to grips with the author's real world. The theme of how the hero is transformed into an ass with a human mind, his ingenious plans continually limited by the donkey's capacity for action, has been taken over from an earlier Greek version; and though the site of his metamorphosis to an ass is localised at Thessalian Hypata, and his reformation to human shape at Corinth, the situations and the characters are almost as stylised as those in Grimm's *Fairy Tales*. Study of daily life in second-century Carthage or Greece would be an unrewarding introduction to the *Metamorphoses*.

Yet Apuleius' romance is much more than a jocose Latin rendering of a timeless Greek story. The *Metamorphoses* does indeed proclaim itself at the outset a work of comic entertainment and nothing more. But the reader who can put down the book still satisfied by the artless description of the first chapter has ignored the patterning of anecdotes and adventures which culminate in the dramatic climax of religious conversion to Isis. The story in Apuleius' version is also a fable. Its moral is that full knowledge of reality is gained not by magic but by the contemplation of divinity in the other, more real world, and that true happiness is to be sought not in sensuality but in the gratuitous love of the godhead. The vital prerequisite for measuring the sincerity of this testament is study of the psychology of the author; in seeking this, much can be gleaned

---

[1] On the date of the *Metamorphoses* and a survey of the biographical detail, see Appendix 2.

from Apuleius' other writings to satisfy us that the moral is seriously intended.

It can rightly be objected that the romance is not closely articulated throughout to press home this moral, and in particular that the progress of Lucius-turned-ass through a world of violence and sadism, of deaths by magic and deceit by errant wives, is recounted with such lubricious zest that the serious purport of the book virtually disappears from view until the message rings out like a thunderclap in the final pages. There is in fact a central ambivalence in the romance, a tension between Milesian ribaldry and Platonist mysticism, which reflects the complexity of the author's personality. Rabelais and perhaps Joyce suggest themselves as apposite parallels in other societies of believers. *The Golden Ass*[1] in this sense contrives to be simultaneously entertainment and fable. Criticism of the romance has been to some degree vitiated by regarding these as exclusive alternatives, whereas a round appreciation demands that both purposes be taken into account, with the necessary corollary that the book accordingly lacks the homogeneity of a closely articulated work of art.

The final book introduces a further complexity. As entertainment, the romance comprises the adventures of a human donkey, and reaches its logical close when Lucius is reformed into human shape; so the Greek original, after restoring Lucius to manhood, quickly closes the story by dispatching him home.[2] Considered as fable, Apuleius' version demands the religious climax of the merciful intervention of Isis and of Lucius' confession of the true path to universal knowledge. But the author is not content to indicate this and then to end the tale; he draws out the story for a further book with extended detail of religious

---

[1] I use the name as variation from the correct *Metamorphoses*. St Augustine (*C.D.* 18.18) reveals that this was the name by which it was known. 'aureus' is a colloquial usage for 'splendid' (cf. Pliny *Ep.* 2.20.1), so Apuleius' romance is 'the prince of ass-stories'.

[2] The ending is achieved with a crude *deus ex machina* effect. Not only does the governor before whom the reformation to man is enacted prove to be a friend of Lucius' parents, but by a coincidence Lucius' brother also turns up at the same time with money.

practice at the shrines of Isis. The episode seems unduly protracted and out of scale, and one wonders whether this last
act had been initially a part of the author's intention.[1] In
short, this extraordinary romance becomes finally not only
entertainment and fable simultaneously, but also religious
apologia. Apuleius' motives have been variously interpreted
here according to individual assessments of the purpose of the
romance as a whole; but perhaps insufficient attention has been
given to the hectic religious climate of Africa against which the
romance was composed.

For those who are satisfied to interpret *The Golden Ass*
solely as entertainment, it is enough to study his art as story-
teller against the compendious *Lucius or the Ass*, for such
comparison throws a flood of light on his aims and techniques
of narration. But for those open to the suggestion that the
romance is patterned as a fable, it is rewarding to analyse the
nature of Apuleius' proclaimed beliefs as *philosophus Madaurensis* and of the contemporary reconciliation between Platonism
and the Isiac faith. And finally the confessional element in the
final book, if taken seriously as religious apologia, demands a
prior awareness of the syncretism by which the worship of
Isis had become acceptable to this Roman priest, and of the
special African circumstances which may have prompted this
extraordinary denouement to the romance.

The apologists for the view of *The Golden Ass* as entertainment
begin from the solid bases that this was traditionally the sole
purpose of the comic romance,[2] and that Apuleius formulates
his aim unambiguously at the outset. 'at ego tibi sermone isto

---

[1] For discussion, see Wittmann, 8 ff. I draw attention in *Phoenix*
(1968), 148 f., to the strange number of eleven books in the *Metamorphoses*. Chariton's and Achilles Tatius' romances have eight,
Heliodorus' and Xenophon's ten. There is a close interconnexion
between Bk. 11 and *Cupid and Psyche*, which led me to speculate that
Apuleius may initially have planned a work in eight books and later
decided to incorporate these two further episodes.

[2] See the programmatic statement of Lucian above, pp. 3 f. For a useful
treatment, see E. Cocchia, *Romanzo e Realtà*, ch. 7.

Milesio varias fabulas conseram auresque tuas benivolas lepido susurro permulceam. . .fabulam Graecanicam incipimus. lector intende; laetaberis.'[1] The whole work on this interpretation is no more than a loose connexion of exciting and romantic and comic incidents which are adorned with apposite anecdotes. Apuleius' originality lies on the one hand in the insertion of numerous *fabulae* at suitable points to augment the chronicle of Lucius' wanderings, and on the other in the part comic, part romantic development of the adventures of the hero recorded in the Greek story which he followed.

At this level the novel may be visualised as a *jeu d'esprit* describing how Lucius is turned into an ass, and in servitude attends on a series of masters, some vicious—the robbers, the sadistic boy, the catamite priests, the baker's wife—and some more kindly, especially the nurseryman and the rich Corinthian Thiasus. This range of experiences, so similar to the fortunes of the hero in the Spanish picaresque novel, is to be found in outline in the compendious version of the original Greek story, but Apuleius' originality is revealed especially in the attention he devotes to the characters. Milo, Photis, Byrrhena, Pamphile, the main persons Lucius encounters before his metamorphosis, are all endowed with a fuller portrait than they have in the Greek story. So too the various masters of Lucius the ass are described in more characterising detail. The cruelty of the boy, the obscene hypocrisy of the priests, the depravity of the baker's wife all receive more loving attention than in Apuleius' source.

This originality can be observed by systematic comparison with *Lucius or the Ass*, which is traditionally ascribed to Lucian. It is clear that this is an abbreviated version of a Greek comic romance probably called the *Metamorphoses*, and that Apuleius' story develops that fuller version.[2] The author of it

---

[1] *Met.* 1.1.1 and 6.

[2] For a discussion of the evidence of Photius and a modern bibliography, see Vallette's Budé edition of the *Metamorphoses* I, vi ff., A. Lesky, *H* (1941), 43 ff., and Perry, *The Ancient Romances*, ch. 6. *Lucius or the Ass* can now be conveniently consulted in M. D.

is uncertain, but arguments from the traditional attribution and from stylistic features make Lucian an attractive candidate.[1] We are likewise uncertain of the length of the Greek original, but the most systematic investigation persuasively suggests that *Lucius or the Ass* is 'at most only five pages shorter than the original'.[2] Precision here is clearly impossible; but the important fact is that *Lucius or the Ass* is a uniformly comic and ironical story in which Apuleius' extended anecdotes of a more serious and romantic kind can have had no place. It is overwhelmingly probable that the original contained only the narrative of Lucius' own adventures, and careful comparison of Apuleius' novel with *Lucius or the Ass* reveals the kind of circumstantial detail which the Greek abbreviator has excised.[3]

Since *Lucius or the Ass* is in essence the original *Metamorphoses*, the schematic comparison with *The Golden Ass* set out on p. 147 will demonstrate how Apuleius has systematically elaborated on the original.

This outline reveals quite clearly the structural principles of *The Golden Ass*. *Cupid and Psyche*, an inserted *conte* some two books long, stands at the centre of the narrative, a 'story within a story' with a theme deliberately aligned to the main adventure.[4] The narrative around this central story divides into three parts. The events leading to the transformation are recounted

McLeod's Loeb edition of Lucian, vol. VIII. For the prevalence of the metamorphosis-story in folk-lore (including the remedy of roses), see Stith Thompson, *Motif-Index of Folk-Literature* (Copenhagen 1955–8), II, D 132.1.

[1] See Perry, 221 ff.; Lesky, 43 n. 1.

[2] Junghanns, 118: 'Nach meinen Feststellungen ist der Ὄνος in ganzen höchstens ca. fünf Teubnerseiten kürzer als die Vorlage.' For doubts, see Lesky with earlier bibliography.

[3] McLeod in his Loeb edition draws attention to the half-dozen most blatant examples signalled by earlier scholars of 'unskilful epitomising', which indicate the type of abbreviation achieved. A persuasive general argument for the view of the original *Metamorphoses* as a short story without extended ἐκφράσεις is of course the fact that no extant comic romance in Greek comes remotely near to the length of Apuleius', whereas Petronius may have blazed the trail for Apuleius himself. [4] Below, ch. 7.

THEMATIC COMPARISON OF 'LUCIUS OR THE ASS' AND 'THE GOLDEN ASS'

(Italicised matter indicates an addition or development by Apuleius)

APULEIUS		ONOS	
Book	Theme	Section	Theme
1	*Aristomenes and Socrates*		
	Hypata; house of Milo	1–3	Hypata; house of Hipparchus
2	Byrrhena; Photis	3–11 *init.*	Abroea; Palaestra
	Thelyphron		
3	*The spoof trial*		
	Metamorphosis and departure	11–17 *init.*	Metamorphosis and departure
4	Journey to robbers' cave	17–23 *init.*	Journey to robbers' cave
	Three robbers' stories		
	⎧ *Cupid and Psyche i* ⎫		
5	⎨ *Cupid and Psyche ii* ⎬		
6	⎩ *Cupid and Psyche iii* ⎭		
	Escape and recapture	23–6 *init.*	Escape and recapture
7	*Tlepolemus rescues Charite (and Lucius)*	26–33	Rescue of girl (and Lucius)
	Privations at farm		Privations at farm
8	*Death of Charite*		
	Further adventures (the priests)	34–9	Further adventures (the priests)
	Three incidents		
9	Adventures with priests, baker, market-gardener	40–5	Adventures with priests, baker, market-gardener
	Four anecdotes of adultery		
	Baker's magical death		
	Death of estate-owner and sons		
10	*Stepmother and stepson*	46–53	
	Lucius' soft life with cooks' master		Lucius' soft life with cooks' master
	Condemned woman's history		
	The day of the show (*Corinth*)		The day of the show (Thessalonica)
11	*Metamorphosis to man through Isis; self-dedication and ritual*	54–6	Metamorphosis to man at games; appeal to governor; rejection by 'Pasiphaë'; return home

in three books, the adventures of Lucius-turned-donkey extend over five, and the final book, which like *Cupid and Psyche* is wholly independent of the Greek original, recounts the hero's resumption of human shape and his subsequent devotion to Isis.

Except in the two episodes of Psyche and of Lucius' conversion, Apuleius has systematically incorporated into each book a section of the original story, which he supplements with contrasting anecdotes or episodes. For example, in the first book the amusing detail of Lucius' arrival at the house of his miserly host is contrasted with the inserted story of the dramatic death of Socrates by magic; in the second, the narrative of social and sexual encounter with Byrrhena and Photis respectively is juxtaposed with another chilling story of magic likewise inserted, the mutilation of Thelyphron. Conversely in the third book, where the magical episode of the metamorphosis of Lucius is taken over from the source, Apuleius has inserted the comic sequence of the Festival of Laughter. Thus in each of the three books there is a characteristic convergence of the magical and the ironically amusing.

This *variatio* continues in the second main section, but here the contrast is chiefly between the romantic and the comic. *Cupid and Psyche* strikes a note wholly different from Lucius' experiences with the robbers amongst which it is set. Subsequently in the seventh book the rescue of Charite has been romantically developed by Apuleius to be placed against Lucius' privations at the farm. In the eighth book Apuleius' original version of Charite's death, diverging notably from *Lucius or the Ass*, is a tragic episode providing a telling contrast with the subsequent comic adventures of Lucius with the bogus priests. After this book the content becomes more fragmented and anecdotal; Apuleius follows his source closely, and in Book Nine has to include Lucius' adventures under three owners. As commentary on these experiences he introduces half-a-dozen new scenes, four of them on the theme of adultery and two introducing further magical motifs. But in spite of this proliferation of anecdotes, Apuleius still seeks a contrast in each book between the magical or romantic or tragic on the one hand, and the ironically amusing on the other, and the tenth book illustrates the balance admirably. Beginning with a potentially tragic story on the Phaedra theme, it passes to the comic detail of Lucius' life with the cooks and then with their master; there follows the insertion of another tragic episode, which is set against the jocular account of the games at which Lucius is the star performer. The final book, the third main section which recounts the strange adventures of *Lucius reformatus*, contains no such division between the dramatic and the comic. Constructed wholly independently of the comic Greek original, it maintains a serious and indeed lyrical tone throughout.

After the self-depreciatory introduction—the Greek narrator strikes an appropriately sophisticated note of humour by apologising for his rough Latinity[1]—Lucius describes how, as he was giving his horse a break ('a walking breakfast') on the way to Hypata, he fell in with Aristomenes and a sceptical companion; Aristomenes is pressed to while away the journey with a personal experience which he swears is true.[2] It is the story of his encounter with his old friend Socrates at Hypata, and of Socrates' helplessness in the clutches of the witch Meroë. Aristomenes' plan had been to deliver him, but unavailingly, because the supernatural intelligence of the witch guides her and her companion to visit the two friends at dead of night, to drain Socrates' blood and remove his heart, blocking the wound with a sponge. Aristomenes believes him dead, tries to bolt for it, and, when this fails, to hang himself. But the rope breaks and he falls on Socrates, who proves to be very much alive. They depart elatedly, but Socrates dies as soon as he

[1] Above, pp. 64 f.
[2] For these conventions in the Milesian Tale, above, pp. 11, 15. The names Aristomenes and Socrates are ironically chosen (see Helm, in his Preface to the *Florida*; B. Brotherton, *CP* (1934), 36 ff.). Aristomenes is the 'bonus consiliator' (cf. 1.12.7); Socrates is feebly subject to Meroë (the Ethiopian name indicates her barbaric nature). Her aide Panthia suggests Penthea (1.13.2 'quin igitur hunc...bacchatim discerpimus...?').

stops at a stream for a drink. Aristomenes has been compelled to retire in fear to Aetolia. The credulous Lucius lends vehement credence to the story, and expresses thanks for the *festivitas lepidae fabulae*.[1]

The story is told with the dramatic verve and humour— and with the indifference to loose ends—so characteristic of Apuleius. As at several points later, he has combined two different anecdotes without resolving the inconsistencies; the scene in which Aristomenes addresses his bed pathetically and tries vainly to hang himself suitably introduces comic relief of a mimic type as entr'acte between the two macabre acts of the main story, but thereby introduces also fatal inconsequentialities.[2] And the very fact that Aristomenes, who claims to have moved hearth and home to Aetolia through fear of the world of Hypata, is happily approaching that city as he tells his story, makes a mockery of his protestations of fear. Apuleius is in fact more concerned with the creation of atmosphere than with the meticulous construction of a consistent story; the reader is to be made aware that Hypata is the centre of Thessalian magic where the supernatural is an everyday occurrence, so that Lucius' metamorphosis is foreshadowed.

Having thus depicted the nature of Hypata, Apuleius now develops the account in the Greek source of Lucius' arrival at his host's house. Everything is here subordinated to the characterisation of Milo. In *Lucius or the Ass* the host (whose name is Hipparchus) is fond of money and lives modestly, but the house is quite tolerable (ἀνεκτόν) and the guest-chamber

---

[1] 1.20.5. On Apuleius' narrative-art here, see Junghanns, 123. Lesky's suggestion that this story goes back to the Greek original has won little acceptance—and rightly.

[2] See Perry, 259 ff. (and *CP* (1929), 394 ff.). Why didn't Aristomenes make sure that Socrates was dead before trying to escape? Why does the janitor refuse to let him leave? Why does Aristomenes address his bed? The whole of this intermediate scene is a burlesque of a lover's attempted suicide (cf. Petronius 94.8 ff.) incorporated into the main story. Note also that the invocation to the bed (1.16.2: 'iam iam grabbatule...') parodies a prayer; H. Kleinknecht, *Die Gebetsparodie*, 202 f.

pleasant (κάλλιστον οἰκημάτιον). The dinner served is not at all
frugal, and the wine is good (τὸ δὲ δεῖπνον οὐ σφόδρα λιτόν· ὁ
δὲ οἶνος ἡδὺς καὶ παλαιὸς ἦν). Apuleius' version by contrast
makes Milo a skinflint hypocrite. A dialogue between an inn-
keeper and Lucius is first inserted to make this abundantly clear;
the house is out of town, Milo's appearance 'habitu mendicantis',
but in fact he is 'ampliter nummatus et longe opulentus, verum
extremae avaritiae et sordis infimae infamis homo'.[1] The
dining-room is so tiny that Milo's wife has to give the guest her
place, and the host feeds Lucius only on words.[2] This single
aim of thoughtful comedy in the characterisation of Milo
dominates the entire episode. Though Pamphile his wife is
later to emerge as a fearsome witch, she is here the submissive
spouse; Photis the slave-girl is soon to assume surpassing
attractions, but here is a colourless maid.[3] The hero himself is
admittedly characterised; but this portrait of the boy of good
family with good clothes and good manners only serves to
emphasise by contrast the niggardly reception of the host.[4]

The reception at Milo's house is punctuated by a comic
episode in the market. On his way to the public bath—Milo's
house is too small to boast its own—Lucius buys some fish for
his supper, doubtless anticipating frugal fare at his host's.[5] He
meets Pythias, an old friend of his Athenian student-days, who
is now superintending the market, and who is so scandalised at
the price of the fish that he makes the vendor stamp on it—
leaving the hero 'without his money and his dinner'.[6] The
theme of comic humiliation in the market is doubtless a stock
Milesian motif;[7] and though it is true that Apuleius himself

---

[1] 1.21.7 and 5.
[2] Dining-room, 1.22.6–7; the meal, 'evasi aliquando rancidi senis
loquax et famelicum convivium, somno non cibo gravatus, cenatus
solis fabulis...'.　　　[3] Pamphile, 1.23.1, 22.7; Photis 22.2, 26.1.
[4] 23.1 ff., 26.1. On this scene, see Junghanns, 16 ff.
[5] So this scene is an insertion by Apuleius, since in the Greek version
the host is not so characterised, and Lucius dines with him.
[6] 25.6. The name Pythias ironically recalls Πυθώ (Helm).
[7] Above, p. 88. It may also have connexions with Roman satire and the
mime; Junghanns, 126.

met a student at Oea whom he had known at Athens, and was accused of showing too much interest in strange fish, the circumstances were so different in life that an autobiographical interpretation is here unhelpful.[1]

The two contrasting themes of the second book are love and magic, the love-liaison with Photis being inserted between two visits to the house of Byrrhena, a friend of Lucius' mother whom the hero chances to meet. The first visit follows closely the version of the Greek source, though the wealth of Byrrhena and her lavishly appointed home are given greater prominence than that of Abroea in the Greek tale to contrast with the niggardly establishment of Milo. Like Abroea in *Lucius or the Ass*, Byrrhena warns the hero of the dangers of residing with Pamphile, who is a witch. This is enough to send him scurrying back to his lodging, and to determine to seek acquaintance with the witch's powers by suborning the slave-girl to assist him.

In the Greek version, the girl is called Palaestra,[2] and the whole encounter is described clinically as a sexual exercise, with Palaestra playing the role of ἐρωτοδιδάσκαλος or *magistra amoris*.[3] Though Apuleius reproduces the *doubles entendres* of the source in Lucius' dialogue with Photis in the kitchen, he develops the encounter more romantically. Whereas Palaestra is no more than a gratifying means to an end, Apuleius' Photis enchants the hero with her physical attractions and especially her hair, which inspires a disquisition worthy of a sophistic love-romance.[4] The meanness of Milo is now forgotten and no longer emphasised; the horrific potential of Pamphile is still ignored. In this book the romanticised Photis takes the spotlight. Though he incorporates realistic sexual description with

---

[1] On the fish, *Apol*. 29 ff.: on Pontianus his friend, *Apol*. 72. For the autobiographical interpretation, see Hicter, *Ant. Class.* (1944) 95 ff., (1945), 61 ff.

[2] Above, p. 61.   [3] *Onos* 8 ff.

[4] 2.8.2 ff. Compare, for example, Achilles Tatius' praise of the mouth as the fairest part of the body (2.8). Though such excursuses may be prominent in the literature of the Second Sophistic, fiction is the likeliest inspiration for Apuleius here. Apuleius himself had flowing hair (see *Apol*. 4), and Lucius' enthusiasm reflects his author's.

the imagery of war replacing that of wrestling, Apuleius dispenses with the *initiamentum amoris* and abbreviates the gross technicalities of the source, emphasising instead the beauty of Photis and the romantic feelings she induces in Lucius.[1]

The second visit to Byrrhena's house, prompted by an invitation to a formal dinner-party, does not appear in *Lucius or the Ass*, and it is reasonable to assume that the whole episode is inserted by Apuleius.[2] The purpose is to provide a backcloth for Thelyphron's story of the hazards of confronting a witch at Hypata. Like the anecdote of Aristomenes, it is described in phrases which emphasise its role as entertainment, and which undercut the serious impact;[3] Thelyphron's studied pose in commencing the tale, and the laughter which follows his account of how he lost his nose and ears, likewise convey an atmosphere of levity.[4] The story itself, an ingenious conflation by Apuleius of two separate anecdotes, has as its purpose the further demonstration that Hypata is a place where strange things happen, and throughout the narrative Apuleius introduces touches evoking the earlier story of Aristomenes. So Thelyphron is warned of the dangers of challenging witches; he is told that they can turn him into bird or dog or fly, just as Socrates had cautioned Aristomenes earlier.[5] But like Aristomenes he is the self-confident hero who cheerfully exposes himself to their magical power. As in the earlier anecdote, all seems well when morning comes, with corpse and keeper alike apparently unharmed. But Thelyphron's false security, like Aristomenes', is soon shattered by the unexpected outcome.

The Thelyphron story resembles that of Aristomenes also in its minor inconsistencies arising from the interweaving of

[1] 2.16 f.
[2] Perry, 273 ff., believes that this visit was in the original. He complains about the transition in *Onos* 10–12 from the affair with Palaestra to the metamorphosis as 'noticeably abrupt and poorly motivated'. But Palaestra is approached in order to win acquaintance with the witch's magic.
[3] 'More tuae urbanitatis...lepidi sermonis tui...comitate' (2.20.7).
[4] 'Porrigit dexteram et ad instar oratorum conformat articulum' (2.21.2). The laughter, 31.1.　　　[5] 2.22.3, 1.9.1 ff.

the different anecdotes. The first story Apuleius exploits described how a man deputed to guard a corpse fell asleep, and awoke to find the corpse robbed of nose and ears, in return for which he had to forfeit his own as stipulated in the contract. To this tale Apuleius subjoins the story of how a husband's corpse was resurrected to condemn his widow as a murderess. The stories are connected by amending the first so that the witches take Thelyphron's nose and ears *by mistake*; then, when the corpse is raised to life, the dead man attests his veracity by revealing that Thelyphron's nose and ears are wax substitutes. But what point in this new version has the stipulation of a contract for guarding the dead man's specified features? Why did the witches trouble to cover up the mutilation? Why was Thelyphron buffeted by the widow's servants for a mere slip of the tongue? And most disconcerting of all, how can the widow of the first part of the story, who is a model of *pietas*, suddenly become the worthless wife of the second part? These loose ends, as in the Aristomenes episode, demonstrate that Apuleius anticipates from his readers not a sustained and critical analysis, but applause for improvised spontaneity. Many of his readers would presumably be familiar with the two anecdotes which he has grafted ingeniously but precariously into one.[1]

After the dinner-party at Byrrhena's, Lucius returns to his lodging having drunk too well, to encounter at Milo's gate three 'robbers'. They are in fact animated wine-skins, and Photis is later to explain how her mistress' magic had unwittingly drawn them to the house. The obvious inference again here is that Apuleius has himself introduced this ending to the second book to develop the farcical trial at the Festival of Laughter;[2] the motif of the 'murder' of animal parts sub-

[1] For greater detail, see B. J. de Jonge (*Comm. ad Met.* 2), Praef.; Perry, 264 ff., and *CP* (1920), 231 ff. I see no need to posit three original stories, as Perry does. Brotherton (*CP* (1934), 36 ff.) challenges Perry's thesis, and believes it 'a well-constructed story'. This goes too far.

[2] It is true, as Perry 278 says, that the encounter with the skins was 'an unforeseeable accident' which the organizers of the mock trial could

stituted for human bodies may have been suggested to him by similar episodes in the love-romances.[1] The language with which Apuleius describes the 'slaughter' amusingly indicates to the attentive reader the true nature of the 'victims'; 'quoad ... vastis et crebris *perforati* vulneribus *spiritus efflaverint.*'[2]

The trial-scene, as has already been suggested,[3] is a sophisticatedly comic set-piece in which Apuleius constructs the speeches according to the *genus iudiciale.* Such judicial scenes are a feature regular in the ideal romances, even in the 'presophistic' such as Chariton's; and Petronius' novel shows that they had been previously exploited in comic fiction. Within this literary framework the ignorance of Lucius is the central comic feature. Having awakened all a-tremble and having been led round the city, he undergoes the entire ritual of a criminal trial before being forced to expose the 'corpses' and his own role as laughing-stock.[4] Milo escorts him home as he sobs in humiliation; the magistrates visit him to apologise, and promise that the god Risus will henceforward take Lucius under his wing—an ironical guarantee for one soon to experience a comic transformation. And Apuleius jocularly adds an autobiographical touch, for the people of Hypata offer to set up a statue for Lucius after the trial, just as the citizens of Oea had done when Apuleius was acquitted on his capital charge.[5]

After the episode of the mock trial follows Photis' tearful explanation of how the skins had been summoned by Pam-

hardly have counted on. But it is a *non sequitur* to claim that *therefore* Apuleius has inserted the Risus Festival into this incident of the skins claimed by Perry to be in the source. Why could he not have introduced both, with his lofty indifference to such inconsistencies?

[1] Compare the episode of the sheep's stomach in Achilles Tatius 3.15.
[2] 2.32.6.
[3] Above, pp. 58 f. Some scholars argue for a lacuna in *Onos* 11, which indicates to them that this whole episode was in the original; but see p. 154 n. 2 and Paratore, *La novella*[2], 144 ff.   [4] 3.1–3.9.7.
[5] 3.11.5; Augustine, *Ep.* 138.19. For the occasion of the Risus Festival, see D. S. Robertson, 'A Greek Carnival', *JHS* (1919), 110 ff., comparing the Roman Hilaria (Macrob. *Sat.* 1.21.10). Junghanns, 132, is sceptical: 'Selbstverständlich ist der Hypatenser Geloskult nur eine literarische Fiktion...'

phile. This allows Apuleius to build up a horrific picture of Pamphile, hitherto the colourless spouse but now the main characterisation in this book. She is described at work in her witch's office which is littered with human bodily parts; she utters incantations and burns hair to draw to her the Boeotian youth whom she wishes to ensnare.[1] There is no trace of this scene in *Lucius or the Ass*; Apuleius has here drawn on his own resources to shape the portrait of the witch, as he did with Milo in the first book and Photis in the second.

The metamorphosis-scene itself is a faithful version of the Greek original, but Apuleius introduces characteristic elaboration of a psychological and a comic kind. Lucius' stupefaction on observing Pamphile turn into an owl and fly out ('exterminatus animi attonitus in amentiam vigilans somniabar') and his apprehensions on what may befall him as a bird are the prominent psychological motifs in the narrative of the preliminaries.[2] Then, in the account of the transformation itself, Apuleius' bent for ironical humour finds its most splendid opportunity. Anticipating his birdlike form with movements of his arms—'iamque alternis conatibus libratis bracchiis in avem similis gestiebam'—Lucius finds to his consternation that he is sprouting the bristles, hooves and tail of an ass.[3] This comically ironical elaboration continues when Lucius-turned-ass retires to the stables for the night to await from Photis the roses which will restore him to human form. Repelled by his own horse ('*praeclarus* vector meus')[4] as in *Lucius or the Ass*, the hero is in Apuleius also beaten by his own ostler, enduring the irony of his first ill-treatment at the hands of his own dependants.

So too in the following scenes we find Apuleius constantly adding or amending details in the interests of a better story. In

---

[1] 3.15.7 ff., 17.3 ff.   [2] 22.2, 23.3 ff.   [3] 24.3 f.

[4] Apuleius is fond of the ironical adjective. So his friend in the market, Pythias, is *prudens*, the widow in Thelyphron's story *egregia*, the bandit who is fond of the stick is *benignus*, Psyche's sisters are *egregiae*, the baker's wife is *pudica*, and so on (1.25.6, 2.29.6, 6.30.6, 5.9.1, 9.22.3).

Lucius or the Ass, the hero is prevented from eating roses the next morning because the robbers muzzle him to stop him breakfasting *en route*; *The Golden Ass* presents a subtler, more psychological reason—Lucius fears that the robbers will kill him if he resumes human shape openly.[1] When the party halts at a village at midday, the beasts are given barley in the Greek version, but Apuleius puts them out to pasture, which enables Lucius more naturally to discover the vegetable garden and the deceptive rose-bays.[2] This refining process continues in the subsequent account of the beating sustained for kicking the gardener; in *Lucius or the Ass* he is beaten 'till the pain made me excrete all the vegetables', whereas in *The Golden Ass* he ends the beating by directing excrement and foul odour at his persecutors.[3]

Apuleius' account of the events at the bandits' hide-out is likewise close to the version of the Greek story, but here Apuleius inserts a series of apposite *fabulae*. First, what the Greek version calls 'a long conversation' between the robbers is translated into the narration of three desperate exploits which depict the violence and lawlessness rampant amongst Lucius' new masters.[4] Secondly, the insertion of the story of Cupid and Psyche, a *conte* relevant to the role of Charite separated from her bridegroom, necessitates a slight change from the framework of the original. In *Lucius or the Ass*, the hero goes with the bandits on an expedition, but in Apuleius he stays behind,[5] and so during the bandits' absence overhears not only the old

---

[1] *Onos* 17; *Met.* 3.29.7.   [2] *Onos* 17; *Met.* 4.1.4 ff.

[3] *Onos* 18; *Met.* 4.3.10—perhaps 'refining' is not the *mot juste*.

[4] *Onos* 21; *Met.* 4.9–21. On Apuleius' fondness for trinities of stories, see Junghanns, 156 ff. Lesky, 57, believes that there was a corresponding narrative in the original.

[5] In *Lucius or the Ass*, after Charite's arrival the bandits depart to despoil a traveller, *taking Lucius*; on returning they go again with the horse, *leaving the lame Lucius behind*. In Apuleius they first go *without Lucius* (and *Cupid and Psyche* is then recounted after Charite's account of her abduction); they return and take *both horse and Lucius*; but his malingering makes them decide *to leave him* and kill him later, thus allowing him a chance of escape and a compelling reason to do so.

woman's tale of Cupid and Psyche but also the girl's account of her kidnapping and dream, characteristic motifs of the ideal romance.

The bandits' exploits are recounted with typical Apuleian ambivalence, their serious purport as an index to the rapacious violence encompassing Lucius being undercut by a note of ironical and affectionate mockery which converts their operations into something approaching farce. The first is the story of the raid on Thebes led by Lamachus; 'inter inclitos reges ac duces proeliorum tanti viri memoria celebrabitur.' The name and the exaggerated encomium recall the fifth-century general who perished in another famous expedition.[1] The attack on the house of Chryseros results in the bandit's arm becoming humiliatingly stuck in the door; his comrades hack it off and bear off 'the rest of Lamachus' ('ceterum Lamachum'). When he at last runs himself through, his comrades commit his body 'to the sea'—almost as if he had become that earlier-day Lamachus at Syracuse, and not a bandit at inland Thebes![2] The second story recounts the even more ignominious end of Alcimus on the same raid. He is duped and pushed from a window by an old woman, a fate reflecting the irony of his name ('Strong'). The third story, the most extended, tells how Thrasyleon ('Lionheart') volunteers to impersonate a bear to penetrate a residence of a magistrate Demochares ('People-pleaser') who is in need of bears for a forthcoming show. Thrasyleon duly performs his job as insider, opens the doors for his comrades (who carry off the loot to deserted tombs, 'the houses of the most trustworthy'), but is then attacked by dogs and dispatched by spears—a timely warning to men who wear the guise of animals! The sententious tribute to Thrasyleon at the end of this story ('sic etiam Thrasyleon nobis perivit, sed a gloria non peribit'), like that to Lamachus earlier, is an indication of the mock-serious tone in which Apuleius recounts these harrowing adventures.

[1] 4.8.7 f.
[2] Thuc. 6.103. This is a typically Apuleian loose end, the careless adaptation of a story set in another locale.

After the long tale of Cupid and Psyche follows the attempted escape of Lucius and Charite. By comparison with *Lucius or the Ass*, much greater attention is paid to the character of Charite ('Grace'), whom Apuleius depicts in the image of heroines of the Greek love-romances. This literary evocation has already been mentioned in connexion with her tale of abduction and of her dream, motifs familiar from the ideal romance; and now as Charite rides away on Lucius she invokes the gods' help and a relaxation of Fortune's spite in a prayer which might have been uttered by a Callirhoe or an Anthia.[1] So too when the bandits recapture her and discuss her fate, Apuleius' development of their debate strikingly echoes a scene in Xenophon's novel after Anthia has killed a pirate who sought to ravish her. In Xenophon's version, one pirate suggests crucifixion, another that Anthia should be lowered into a trench with two dogs; in Apuleius likewise two of the proposals for Charite are crucifixion and exposure to animals.[2]

Within the framework of Charite's romantic portrait Apuleius also develops the comic potentialities of the escape and recapture. Throughout the whole of the adventures of Lucius-turned-ass, the situation of a human intelligence contemplating action impracticable for an ass's body inspires a riot of ass-jokes and puns, some taken over from the source[3] but some clearly original. So Lucius condemns his own preoccupation with finding a place of refuge after escape; he tells himself that this a 'a most asinine' problem for a donkey to ponder, since any traveller will gladly adopt him.[4] The ass with human sensibilities feels so romantic with Charite on his back

[1] 6.28.3. The prayer is mentioned in *Lucius or the Ass*, but developed by Apuleius.

[2] Xen. 4.6.2 ff.; *Met.* 6.31. It is of course possible that the author of the Greek *Metamorphoses* adapted the scene from Xenophon, and that Apuleius has developed this version of his source.

[3] Most obviously the Roman citizen's appeal to Caesar, of which the donkey can pronounce only the *O* and not the *Caesar* (*Onos* 16; *Met.* 3.29.3). Apuleius exploits it again, 7.3.3, 8.29.5.

[4] 6.26.9. For variations on the joke, 7.3.4, 7.13.3, 10.13.7, 10.33.4, etc.

that he pretends to scratch himself to kiss 'her lovely feet'.[1]
Our author frequently exploits dramatic irony by making
subsidiary characters remark on the quasi-human qualities of
Lucius; or they wish that he were human, as does the traveller
who needs a witness to attest his innocence.[2] Charite promises
him that if they gain their freedom she will confer on him not
only food and leisure but also a commemorative plaque, so that
historians will celebrate him together with the ram of Phrixus,
the dolphin of Arion, and the bull of Europa; 'If indeed
Jupiter lowed in the shape of an ox, it is possible that in this
ass of mine is concealed a human or a divine form.'[3]

Shortly after being recaptured by the bandits, the prisoners
are liberated by the arrival of a relieving force. Apuleius has so
transformed the story here that we may say he has virtually re-
written it. In *Lucius or the Ass* the girl and the donkey are recaptured well into the night, and back at the hideout the
bandits while away the remaining hours of darkness planning
the girl's fate. Then at dawn a force of soldiers arrives, accompanied by the girl's fiancé; 'he was the one who revealed
the robbers' lodging.'[4] The soldiers imprison the robbers and
hand them to the governor. Some compression is manifest
here, for no indication is given of how the bridegroom found
the hideout; and perhaps the original Greek version contained
his impersonation of a brigand and his subsequent escape to
summon the military.

In *The Golden Ass*, a brigand arrives from Hypata at the
robbers' lair at daybreak after the recapture of Lucius and
Charite. He recounts that Lucius is being held responsible for
the pillaging of Milo's house. This brigand urges a recruiting
campaign to fill out the depleted ranks of the bandits, and he
himself brings in 'Haemus', who claims he is a famed Thracian

---

[1] 6.28.2.   [2] 7.25.8.

[3] 6.29.5. So again at 8.25.1 the auctioneer says: '...ut in asini corio
modestum hominem inhabitare credas.'

[4] *Onos* 26. Lesky, 59 ff., in his discussion of this passage assumes that
Apuleius derives his version from the Greek original; this seems to me
untenable. See Paratore, *La novella*[2], 135.

bandit and who stands a head higher than the rest.[1] 'Haemus' is elected robber-chief after he has recounted his exploits—which are in fact the story of Plotina. He proposes that they keep Charite alive to consign her to a brothel; she has already recognised him as her fiancé Tlepolemus. He drugs the bandits as they feast, delivers Charite home, and returns with a posse of citizens to finish off the bandits by slaughtering them.

Apuleius has in fact introduced an extra day into the time-scale, and as always the insertion leaves loose ends trailing. How could the bona fide bandit (clearly a gang-member, since he knows the hideout) have introduced 'Haemus'? Was he an accomplice of Tlepolemus? Then how did they meet? And what happened to him subsequently?[2] Apuleius hardly cares. His aim has been to introduce Tlepolemus as a heroic figure who copes with the bandits single-handed[3] in order to intensify the romantic atmosphere of this scene, and in the course of it the lovers are able covertly to display their affection to each other, much to the disgust of Lucius.[4]

Haemus' previous adventures, which he tells ostensibly to convince the robbers of his standing and fame as a leading Thracian bandit, turn out in fact to be the romantic story of Plotina; Apuleius' evident purpose in inserting this story is to adumbrate the virtues of Charite. For this is the account of a wife's courage and integrity, glossing the similar behaviour of the imprisoned girl. Here Apuleius' romanticism contrasts markedly with the cynicism of a Petronius—and indeed with his own later quartet of unfaithful wives. Plotina is 'rara fidei atque singularis pudicitiae femina' who 'spurns with contempt

[1] There is of course here a jocose play on Mt Haemus, a high range in Thrace.

[2] So again when 'Haemus' recounts his adventures in Thrace he tells the bandits that he escaped the Roman military by dressing as a woman and passing through the enemy lines on an ass. Apuleius has already forgotten that 'Haemus' is as high as a mountain and would have made an impossibly singular woman (7.8.1; 7.5.2).

[3] Contrast Onos 26: ἔτυχεν δὲ καὶ ὁ τὴν κόρην μεμνηστευμένος σὺν αὐτοῖς ἐλθών, suggesting a much less central role for Tlepolemus.

[4] Until he realises who 'Haemus' is (7.11.4 ff.).

city luxuries' to be with her husband in exile. This 'sanctissima et unicae fidei femina' pertinaciously persuades the Roman authorities to hunt down the robbers who had plundered her possessions at Actium. Apuleius emphasises throughout aspects of the story wholly irrelevant to the *persona* of 'Haemus'; Plotina's *fides, frugalitas, pudicitia* hardly impinge on the reputation 'Haemus' wins as bandit. 'Haemus' (and Apuleius) tell the story with an eye on Charite, and here Apuleius takes a more idealistic view of human nature under the stimulus of the ideal romance.[1]

After this freely composed version of Tlepolemus' rescue of Charite, Apuleius in the rest of the seventh book follows his source closely for Lucius' privations at the farm. The accounts of the labours in the mill, of the hostile reception from the horses out of doors, of the manifold cruelty of the sadistic boy are all substantially the version of *Lucius or the Ass*. The climax to these hardships seems however to have been introduced by Apuleius. In the Greek story the farmhands decide to castrate Lucius because the sadistic boy lyingly accuses him of pursuing young boys and girls with amorous intent, and Lucius escapes this sentence when his masters decide to escape on the death of their lord.[2] In Apuleius, after the plan of castration is approved, a further expedition for wood under the supervision of the sadistic boy culminates in the appearance of a bear; Lucius deserts the youth, running 'from the monstrous bear and the boy worse than the bear'. He is gratefully adopted by a passing traveller, but they encounter the farmhands, who hale the traveller back and accuse him of murdering the boy, whose limbs are scattered about the hillside. The book closes with a verbal and a physical attack on Lucius by the dead boy's mother; the donkey is in the dock, the mother the prosecuting advocate, and Apuleius' intention is the jocose exploitation of the conventions of the judicial speech in a wholly inapposite setting. The whole story of the boy's death contains characteristically Apuleian improbability of detail—what countryman would ever have accused the human traveller of the

---

[1] 7.6.2 ff. For further detail, Junghanns, 156 ff.   [2] *Onos* 33 f.

mangling committed by a bear?—but also his inimitable creation of atmosphere in depicting the savagery of man and nature.[1]

In the first half of the eighth book Apuleius departs radically from the theme of Charite's accidental drowning recorded by the source. In its place he composes a story of romantic chastity with a tragic ending. After *Cupid and Psyche* this is the most extended of Apuleius' romantic anecdotes, and as in other stories he has combined two main themes to create a novel synthesis.

The villain of the piece, Thrasyllus ('Overbold'), a combination of Sextus Tarquinius and Catiline, forms the foul scheme of insinuating himself into the friendship of Tlepolemus and Charite to murder the husband and win the wife. The two men go hunting for goats and encounter a boar; Thrasyllus deliberately brings down Tlepolemus' horse and murders him after the boar has gravely wounded him. He then offers consolation to a grief-wracked Charite, who is spending all her time near the corpse; he persuades her to show greater interest in life, and finally proposes marriage. She is shocked, suspects the plot, and has her suspicions confirmed in a dream by her husband. She dissimulates, and entices Thrasyllus to a secret assignment. After drugging him, she declaims a bitter valedictory, blinds him and then commits suicide at her husband's tomb. Thrasyllus condemns himself to starvation in the vault.

Apuleius has again achieved a striking synthesis here of two stories well known to his contemporaries. The first is the Atys motif—Atys, newly married, is unwittingly slain by his comrade in a boar-hunt, and the friend Adrastus commits suicide at his tomb; this theme is popular in Greek love-fiction.[2] Intermingled with the hunting story is another popular theme, the vengeance of the chaste widow. Plutarch records some striking historical examples, of which the story of Camma is closest to the Apuleian anecdote. Camma, wife of Sinatus, is loved by another tetrarch Sinorix, who kills Sinatus and woos

[1] 7.24.3 ff.
[2] The original story, Herodotus 1.34 ff.; cf. Achilles Tatius 2.34.

the widow, admitting to the murder as proof of his love. Camma agrees to the marriage, but poisons Sinorix and then herself at the betrothal.[1]

Within this synthesis of the two main stories other famed literary forbears are evoked in individual touches. The blinding and the self-immolation in the beloved's tomb are reminiscent of the great Sophoclean tragedies. The literary forbear of Thrasyllus—noble, rich and famous, but 'luxuriae popinalis, scortisque et diurnis potationibus exercitatus', a comrade of brigands, stained with human blood[2]—is clearly Sallust's Catiline, and that of Charite Virgil's Dido.[3] But in addition a deliberate contrast seems to be made with the ethos of Petronius' Widow of Ephesus. Like the Widow, Charite spends her time in her husband's vault, 'inedia misera et incuria squalida, tenebris imis abscondita'.[4] Thrasyllus is cast in the role of the persuasive soldier, providing food to restore her appetite for food and sex; but in contrast to the cynical outcome of the Petronian anecdote, Charite remains constant to her husband's memory.

After this long insertion, Apuleius now resumes the story of Lucius' wanderings as told by the Greek source, but with some elaboration. The Greek version records that 'after three days' the party reached Beroea in Macedonia, where Lucius is sold to a catamite priest. In Apuleius the subsequent adventures of Lucius with the priests are substantially as in the original; but the narrative of the three-day journey to the town, which Apuleius does not specify as Beroea,[5] is amplified by an inserted adventure or anecdote for each day. Since he is fond of groups of three stories,[6] we may infer that all these are introduced by him. On the first day the party is warned and forearmed for an

[1] Plutarch, *Mul. Virt.* 20; *Amatorius* 22. The historical story has much in common with other such stories of *pudicitia* and *fides* like that of Lucretia in the first book of Livy.

[2] 8.1.5.

[3] Sall. *Cat.* 5 and 14 f.; Charite and Dido, above, pp. 53 f.

[4] 8.7.5. On the Widow, above, pp. 11 ff.

[5] Presumably because he transfers the scene of Lucius' resumption of human form from Thessalonica to Corinth.   [6] Above, p. 157 n. 4.

attack by wolves, but instead they are set on by farmhands and dogs. On the second day they enter a pleasant grove, which is in fact haunted by a supernatural dragon; though warned by a goatherd, they are deceived and one of their number devoured. The third day finds them at a village, where Lucius hears the account of the slave who deserted his mate for another woman. When the *contubernalis* killed their child and herself, their master tied the sinning slave to a tree smeared with honey to be devoured by ants. With these three inserted incidents Apuleius depicts the range of hazards confronting Lucius and those with whom he associates. First they anticipate the hostility of nature, but are attacked not by wolves but by men; next they are lulled into security by the deceiving face of nature, only to be the target of demonic forces; and finally the ants are a lesson that nature herself can be an enemy. Lucius' travels take him through a hostile world of spirits, nature and men.

In his comic narrative of Lucius' life with the eunuch-priests, Apuleius intensifies the scathing portrayal of the source. Again and again he insists on the spurious nature of the religious activities of these priests of Atargatis—'simulabat sauciam vecordiam', 'conficto mendacio', 'fictae vaticinationis mendacio'[1]—and on their effeminacy. Their leader's name Philebus[2] is taken over from the source; the followers are *cinaedi*, or *puellae*, their voices effeminate, their practices unnatural.[3] And as always the comic effects of the Greek version are developed further, as in the wisecracks of the auctioneer who sells Lucius, and the witty comment describing Lucius' role as bearer of both statue and collected food—'ut...et horreum simul et templum incederem'.[4]

The first chapters of the ninth book continue the saga of Lucius' adventures with the priests, in which the version of the source is augmented by a *fabula*. The second and most extensive section of the book describes his tribulations at the baker's

[1] 8.27.6, 28.1, 29.2.   [2] 'The Rev. Love-Boyes' (McLeod).
[3] 8.24.2, 26.1, 26.2, 29.
[4] The auctioneer, compare 8.24 with *Onos* 35; the addition, 28.6.

mill, in which eighteen out of twenty-one chapters are anecdotal elaborations by Apuleius. The last chapters describe
Lucius' life with the nurseryman, seven out of the eleven being
devoted to an additional episode inserted by Apuleius.

The final adventures with the priests bring Lucius into the
house of a rich landowner, whose cook in *Lucius or the Ass*
discovers that 'some dogs' have stolen 'the ham of a wild ass'
which he was to serve for dinner. He is about to hang himself,
when his wife suggests saving the situation by slaughtering
Lucius. The ass escapes by rushing into the dining-room 'to
get locked up'; but when instead weapons are brought to
slaughter him, he rushes into a bedroom, where he is then
locked in for safety. Some compression of detail is probable
here, for no indication is given of how this incident ended.[1]
Curiously, in Apuleius' version (where the meat stolen is
transformed into venison for Roman consumption, and more
credibly borne off by 'a hunting dog'),[2] Lucius' irruption into
the dining-room results *in his being locked up*, and it is a later
report of a rabid dog abroad, thought to have infected the ass,
that leads to the decision to kill him, as a result of which he
bursts into the bedroom and is incarcerated there. The 'rabid
dog' motif looks like an Apuleian elaboration, for it leads to a
characteristic inconsistency; how could the ass have broken
out of his dining-room prison into the bedroom? Moreover the
'rabid dog' theme is exploited for the concoction of some
amusing names of victims—Myrtilus the muleteer, Hephaestio
the cook, Hypnophilus the chamberlain, Apollonius the doctor[3]—in keeping with Apuleius' regular technique of investing
his characters with apposite labels.

After Lucius has proved that he is as sane as any donkey, the
priests proceed with him to a village. Comparison with the

---

[1] See Junghanns, 94 ff. The bedroom is that of the priests, who have a
vested interest in keeping Lucius alive. Possibly in the original they
offered him water as in Apuleius to see if he were *sanus* after his
dining-room capers.   [2] 8.31.1.
[3] 9.2.3. Myrtilus was Oenomaus' charioteer, suborned by Pelops to kill his
master (Hyg. 84.4). Hypnofilum is Castiglioni's emendation of
Hypotafium.

Greek version reveals here a most instructive divergence in Apuleius' narrative technique. The Greek records how the priests stole from the village-shrine a golden chalice, and how the villagers pursued the priests and imprisoned them. In Apuleius the arrest takes place without prior indication of the reason—'et ecce nobis *repente* de tergo manipulus armati supercurrit equitis'[1]—and only then does the reader learn of the earlier theft. The priests are committed to 'the Tullianum'; this exploitation of the mention of the Roman subterranean gaol ('in the Bridewell') is a reminder that Apuleius writes for a Roman audience.

In this final journey with the priests is inserted the *lepida fabula* of the cuckolded husband and the lover in the jar; the pretext is that Lucius heard it in the village. This Milesian tale is told with the comic irony and cynicism of the genre. The husband, returning home unexpectedly and finding the doors barred, praises his wife's chaste ways ('uxoris laudata continentia'); the wife, having concealed the lover, rounds on her husband for his indolence, contrasting her own diligence with the idleness of the adulteress next door. He replies that he has found a buyer for the jar in which the lover is concealed; she quick-wittedly pretends that the adulterer also is a purchaser, and offering a higher price. The adulterer plays up, emerging from the jar in pretended ignorance of the husband's identity— 'Quin tu, quicumque es, homuncio'—and demanding a lamp to examine the inside of the jar. The unsuspecting husband insists that he clean the inside for the prospective buyer, and when he disappears from view the impudent couple take advantage of his prolonged sojourn within the jar. And the ironical sequence is rounded off by the husband's being forced to carry the jar to the adulterer's lodging.[2]

---

[1] *Onos* 41; *Met.* 9.9.3. The technique is common in Roman historiography; see Walsh, *Livy*, 203.

[2] 9.7. Graves's amusing translation makes rather more of the episode than the Latin justifies; there are no *doubles entendres* in the wife's instruction to her husband on where to direct his attention. Boccaccio (*Decameron* 5.10) exploits this anecdote.

After the imprisonment of the priests, Lucius is sold to a baker. The donkey's privations in the mill are an extremely short episode in *Lucius or the Ass*, with no mention of the baker's wife. But in Apuleius this unfaithful and sadistic spouse is set at the centre of the adventure.[1] Her deceit of her husband is told in three stages, interspersed by two parallel anecdotes of deceiving wives, and when the baker discovers her guilt and dismisses her, she encompasses his death by magic.[2]

The first act artistically sets the scene with the description of the wife and her victimisation of Lucius, which makes him eager to ascertain her guilty secret. With his big ears he can overhear the confidences which pass between her and her old retainer. It is this ancient hag who tells as entr'acte the anecdote of a fellow-townswoman Arete and her cuckolded husband Barbarus, the slave Myrmex and the gallant Philesitherus.[3] This tale is a suitable gloss on the conduct of the baker's wife, though her own paramour is 'puer admodum...adhuc adulteros ipse delectans', who, when the baker unexpectedly returns, 'pales and trembles with fear'.[4] The husband now enjoys the repast prepared for the lover.

A second entr'acte follows; as the first was recounted by the old crone, so this second is told by the baker as the young gallant lies hidden in the flour-bin. It is yet another story of a cuckolded husband, his friend the fuller. The wife of the fuller is conventionally at the outset of the Milesian tale 'alioquin servati pudoris ut videbatur femina', but she is harbouring a lover when the two men arrive for dinner. She hides him in a sulphur-cage, where his repeated sneezing betrays him. This story too is an apt illustration of the theme of the baker's wife,

---

[1] 'Every possible vice was embraced in that most wicked of women; her heart had become the receptacle of every foulness, like some filthy privy. *saeva scaeva, viriosa ebriosa, pervicax pertinax, in rapinis turpibus avara, in sumptis foedis profusa, inimica fidei, hostis pudicitiae.*' (9.14.3 f.).

[2] *Onos* 42; *Met.* 9.11–31.

[3] For an analysis of the story, above, pp. 13 f. On this sequence of adulteries see Paratore, *La novella*[2], 190 ff.

[4] 9.23.2.

but it is awkwardly set in the context of a dinner-party with an invited guest, when such a wifely indiscretion would be improbable.

Apuleius now returns to the final act of the story of the baker's wife. In the course of the dinner, Lucius gains spectacular revenge on his cruel mistress by treading on the concealed gallant's fingers and causing him to betray himself. This denouement happily draws together end and beginning, and the baker's comment unites the three parallel stories under the single moral of the frailty of female *pudicitia*. 'Non sum *barbarus*, nec *sulpuris* te letali *fumo* necabo';[1] instead, he submits the youth to the humiliation of sexual assault and whipping, and the *adulterorum omnium fortissimus* runs off with his tail between his legs. The baker expels his wife from the house, a fate anticipated in the flight of the fuller's wife.

The saga of the baker now takes a disconcerting change of course. As in the early books, an interconnexion is suggested between sexual appetite and magical practices. The lascivious wife applies to a witch for marital rehabilitation or revenge. The shade of a murderess visits the baker, who is subsequently found strung up; and his daughter comes from a neighbouring village having already been forewarned of his death in a dream. That this introduction of magical motifs has been made by Apuleius is sufficiently clear from *Lucius or the Ass*, where the baker is hale and hearty when he sells Lucius to his next owner.[2]

A similar introduction of a magic motif is observable in the final episode of this ninth book, Lucius' life with the nursery-man. In the Greek story, the donkey's mixed fortunes of light duties but poor food and no shelter are followed by an adventure in which the market-gardener repels a soldier's attempt to requisition Lucius by striking him senseless; he then hides

---

[1] The fuller did not actually kill his wife's visitor—another 'loose end' demonstrating Apuleius' indifference to inconsistencies of detail; see Vallette, *ad loc.* Or is the phrase *letali fumo necabo* loosely used?

[2] *Onos* 43: λεπτὸς οὖν πάνυ γίνομαι καὶ ἀσθενὴς τῷ σώματι, ὥστε ἔγνω με ὁ δεσπότης πωλῆσαι...

Lucius and himself in the neighbouring town, but Lucius gives the game away by peeping through a window.[1] This version is taken over by Apuleius, but with an extended dramatic insertion. The nurseryman is visited by a wealthy neighbour who invites him to his estate. After their arrival a series of astonishing prodigies presages disaster; we are to see here the influence of the love-romance but still more the exploitation of Roman historians like Livy, whose lists of prodigies are frequently juxtaposed with the great disasters which they foretell.[2] In Apuleius the birth of a fully-formed chicken, the spring of blood welling beneath the table, the wine boiling in the cellar are followed by the tragic narrative of the murder of the estate-owner's sons, who die defending the rights of a poor husbandman against a tyrannical neighbour.

The tenth book opens with Lucius in the charge of the soldier who has claimed him. In *Lucius or the Ass* he at once sells him to a wealthy Thessalonican's cook, who lodges with his brother the baker. This represents an interlude of well-being in Lucius' privations; whenever the brothers go out, he eats the leftovers which they had brought for their supper from the master's table. They finally discover the thief, and their master is so delighted with the gourmet-ass that he feeds him on delicacies and wine in his own dining-room; then he buys him, and has him trained by a freedman to dine at table and to perform sophisticated tricks. He takes Lucius home to Thessalonica, where the ass becomes a by-word. Among the sightseers is a wealthy foreign lady, who pays handsomely for the ass's sexual services; on discovering this, the master decides on a novel attraction for his forthcoming show—Lucius' copulation with a condemned female criminal. The ass is wheeled into the arena on a great couch to a table laden with dainties and

---

[1] *Onos* 43 ff. (Lucius is πάντα περίεργος, continuing the curiosity motif). In Apuleius, 9.42.4, an attempt is made to combine two donkey-proverbs but unsuccessfully (Perry, 256 f.).

[2] In the love-romances I think of such passages as Longus 1.7, Achilles Tatius 2.11 f.; but the kind of prodigy Apuleius lists is very Roman. For the conjunction of Livian prodigy-lists with historical disasters, see my discussion in *Livy*, 63.

attended by waiters. Suddenly he notices a man carrying rose-petals, bounds over and eats them, and becomes a man. Rushing over to the governor of the province, he explains his situation and identity; the governor opportunely is a friend of Lucius' parents and releases him. By a remarkable coincidence, Lucius' brother then arrives with money for the journey home; as an ironical close to the story, the human Lucius visits his Pasiphaë, but finds her contemptuous of his human parts. The story is brought to its conclusion rapidly and circumstantially.

Apuleius structures his version of events before Lucius' recovery of human shape into four parts, in which he introduces two extended stories of a serious nature to alternate with two amusing episodes derived from his Greek source. To introduce the first of these dramatic stories he modifies the Greek outline; the soldier takes Lucius to be lodged with a decurion in a city near by, and the 'accursed and wicked crime' which he now relates is said to have been committed in that city. It is the story of a stepmother's destructive passion for her stepson, and Apuleius prepares us for the tragic fate of a Hippolytus: 'iam ergo, lector optime, scito te tragoediam non fabulam legere, et a socco ad coturnum ascendere'.[1] This programmatic statement, however, which is in general a significant indication of Apuleius' aim of a synthesis of the comic and the tragic, is not carried through to the end of the story, which ends happily. Our author seems hardly to have known how his story was going to end when he launched it, and this gives us the clearest picture of the rapidity with which he assembles different stories into an uneasy unity.

At the outset the lady is recognisably a Phaedra, the step-mother struggling unavailingly in the grip of sexual passion, and the psychological portrayal of the lovesick woman owes something to Virgil's Dido.[2] When she finally steels herself to announce her infatuation to her stepson, he is horrified but dissimulates, and seeks advice from an old tutor ('compertae gravitatis educatorem senem').[3] It looks as if in the first of the

---

[1] 10.2.4. On this *novella*, see Paratore, 195 ff.
[2] Above, pp.54 f.   [3] 10.4.3.

stories exploited by Apuleius this tutor was the source by which the father learned the truth after his innocent son's death, but in Apuleius this Hippolytus does not die, and the old tutor plays no further part in the story. When the stepmother's passion is unrequited and her love turns to hatred, she prepares poison for her stepson which is mistakenly drunk by her own son. At this point, as Apuleius joins the first story to the second, there is a perceptible shift in the characterisation of the stepmother.[1] From being a sensitive woman whose passion drives her to unpremeditated spite, she becomes a heartless fiend who thinks nothing of her son's death or her husband's grief—'malitiae novercalis exemplar unicum'.[2] She accuses the stepson of murder. When the unhappy father demands the execution of this son, an old apothecary at the trial breaks the evidence of her slave by revealing that he had furnished the 'poison' which was in fact a mere soporific. Though the stepmother is exiled and the slave crucified, the ending is happy, for the father 'post orbitatis periculum, adulescentium duorum pater repente factus est'.[3] The ingenious conjunction of the two themes is revealed above all by the substitution of the apothecary for the tutor for establishing the stepson's innocence and to provide the story with a happy ending.

Apuleius now reverts to the adventures of Lucius to embark on the comic history of the ass as a social attraction, and his development of the comic situations is shown, for example, in the amusing dialogue between the slave brothers when Lucius eats their food and they suspect each other of thieving.[4] But the main lines of the original are retained, except that the master Thiasus ('Revel') returns not to Thessalonica but to Corinth, and takes Lucius back there. This prepares the ground for the Isiac detail in the final book, the choice of locale presumably having been made because Apuleius was better acquainted with the religious life at Corinth, where he himself may have been initiated. The decision of Thiasus to

---

[1] Compare the widow in the Thelyphron story.
[2] 10.5.3.   [3] 10.12.5.   [4] 10.14.4–7.

couple Lucius with a condemned woman at his show is the point at which Apuleius introduces his second serious anecdote, which purports to be the previous history of this female criminal.[1]

This tale is compounded of three disparate elements crudely strung together. The first part describes how a jealous wife cruelly kills a supposed rival for her husband's affections who in fact turns out to be his sister. In the second part, with that abrupt inconsistency of character so familiar in Apuleius' synthetic stories, she changes from jealous spouse to shrewish wife dominated by greed.[2] She poisons her husband, then seeks to cover herself by poisoning also the doctor who provided the potion. But he reveals the situation to his wife before dying, and the third section of the story is virtually a reduplication of the second, with the avaricious wife now poisoning her own daughter and simultaneously the doctor's wife who prescribed the drug. As the doctor had time to tell his wife, so she manages to reveal all to the magistrate, and the murderess is condemned. This is the worst managed of Apuleius' patchwork stories, badly articulated and full of improbabilities;[3] in his desire to make the crime fit the punishment, he makes the lady a mass murderess in a society of simpletons.

For the last section of the tenth book, Apuleius returns to the history of Lucius and his prospective part in the games. But before describing the main attraction, he inserts a charming description of a mimic prelude. After a pyrrhic dance, a mime is mounted describing how 'Goddesses three to Ida went'; Paris' award of the prize to Venus is jocularly interpreted as the beginning of bribery in judicial cases—one of Apuleius' many legal quips. The point of the Mount Ida scene is of course to presage the great love-encounter; instead of Helen and Paris,

---

[1] 10.23–28. On this story, S. Hammer, *Eos* (1923/4), 6 ff.

[2] The theme of jealousy, 10.24.2: 'coepit puellam velut aemulam tori succubamque primo suspicari, dehinc detestari, dehinc...insidiari'. The faithless wife, 25.2: 'iam pridem nomen uxoris cum fide perdiderat'.

[3] Why doesn't the doctor's wife expose the murderess? Is it remotely likely that she would be interested only in being paid for the poison? Why doesn't she suspect a similar design on herself? And so on.

the spectators are to witness in comic anticlimax an ass and a murderess. As in the Greek story, Lucius seeks escape, but not by eating roses to resume human shape. Instead he bolts to Cenchreae and sleeps on the shore there.

For those who visualise *The Golden Ass* solely as entertainment, the eleventh book extends the range of weird and improbable adventures into the realm of cult-initiation and hectic religiosity. Our author, it might be claimed, exploits an area of experience which was quickening the attention of more and more contemporaries in the later second century, but traditionally this type of topic was not taken seriously by Greek and Roman writers.[1] Those expounding this explanation readily concede Apuleius' interest in religious mysticism, but visualise him as having exploited it purely to beguile his readers. One scholar describes him as 'a juggler', 'keeping his best trick for the climax of the performance'; another slightly refines the argument by depicting him as a ringmaster making a personal appearance, and ending on a serious note as if in apology for the prevailing levity of the earlier books.[2]

On this level of interpretation it is worth noting that the religious climax of deliverance by Isis and of acknowledgment of her saving power echoes the characteristic denouement of the ideal love-romance. These love-stories, like that of Ninus, originate in the romantic treatment of local legends which usually have religious associations, and in their early development the romances are closely associated with Egypt, where earlier demotic stories offer suggestive parallels.[3] The traditional religious element develops into a conventional climax in which the lovers in the various stories are united by the intervention of a kindly deity. In Chariton it is Aphrodite, in Longus it is Pan, and in Xenophon of Ephesus, whose romance

[1] See Reitzenstein, *Hellenistische Wundererzählungen*, 34.

[2] F. Norwood, *Phoenix* (1956), 5; Perry, 243. Haight, *Apuleius and his Influence*, 57, also rejects any fable or allegory, and believes the religious element is a reflexion of contemporary life.

[3] See, in general, Lavagnini, *Le origini del romanzo greco*; J. W. B. Barns, *Mitteil. aus d. Papyrussamml. d. Ost-Nat. Bibl.* (1956), 29 ff.

was conceivably known to Apuleius, it is Isis whom Anthia and Habrocames address in reverent thanksgiving: 'We acknowledge thanks for our safety to you, greatest goddess; it is through you, whom we honour above all, that we have regained each other.' Elsewhere in this novel there is emphasis on Isis' role as protector of chastity and lover of purity, themes likewise prominent in the last book of Apuleius' romance.[1]

This is not to suggest that the scale of Apuleius' apologia for Isis is remotely paralleled in Xenophon. The extended prayer of Lucius for pardon, the appearance and appurtenances of the goddess, her answer emphasising the universality of her sway, the annual feast of the *navigium Isidis*, the emphasis in her cult on chastity and mystical contemplation—all this suggests that Apuleius has personal stimuli leading him to devote a whole book to the theme of Isis. Yet it may legitimately be claimed that the religious climax in general, and the choice of Isis as *dea sospitatrix* in particular, are inspired by the Greek love-romance, and that he exploited an Isiac aretalogy in developing his portrait of the saviour goddess.[2]

This conclusion leads into what is by far the most significant feature of Apuleius' originality as story-teller. Throughout the *Metamorphoses* it is clear that he is experimenting with a synthesis of comic, romantic, ghoulish, and tragic episodes never previously essayed in Greek or Roman extant fiction; and an important quarry was the love-romance, as is revealed by the incorporation of characteristic themes and techniques of presentation. These elements are especially relevant to the *conte* of Cupid and Psyche, but are also observable in the episodes in which Charite and Photis are prominent.[3] Scholars

---

[1] Xen. 5.13.4: σοί, ὦ μεγίστη θεά, τὴν ὑπὲρ τῆς σωτηρίας ἡμῶν χάριν οἴδαμεν. διά σε, ὦ πάντων ἡμῖν τιμιωτάτη, ἑαυτοὺς ἀπειλήφαμεν. Cf. also Xen. 3.11; 4.3.4.

[2] On Apuleius' debt to an Isiac aretalogy or litany, see Appendix 3.

[3] Some of these elements I have adverted to in the course of this chapter. The clearest example of a direct debt is at the outset of *Cupid and Psyche*, where Psyche is modelled on Chariton's Callirhoe, and the story begins with echoes of Xenophon. See below, 200; Perry, 261; Paratore, *La novella*[2], 31 ff.

now date the novels of Chariton and Xenophon considerably earlier than Apuleius, and it is possible that Achilles Tatius' and even Longus' romance predated the *Metamorphoses*.[1] To express his aim in formal terms, Apuleius has attempted to unite the two hitherto disparate streams of Greek fiction into a new pattern of romance, in which he simultaneously seeks to achieve the ironical comedy of a Lucian and the edification of a Chariton.

The Golden Ass is, however, more than a delightful if slapdash entertainment: it is also a fable.[2] The germ of the fable is discernible in *Lucius or the Ass*, where the hero's περιεργία (*curiositas*) is stigmatised as the cause of his humiliating metamorphosis. 'What untimely curiosity was mine!' smiles the ass before his troubles begin; and the final sentence of the story hails with relief his escape 'from the curiosity of an ass'.[3] But the author is not concerned to present this curiosity as a transgression or sin, nor to draw a moral in any emphatic way; the Greek story is an ironical exploration of the consequences of a human weakness, but told to entertain rather than to improve.

Apuleius, however, draws the moral seriously and explicitly. In his final book, composed wholly independently of the Greek source, he describes the resumption by Lucius of his human shape and the commentary passed by the priest of Isis on Lucius' strange experiences. He has been delivered from the hands of blind Fortune into the custody of Fortune with eyes, who is Isis; 'freed from his former hardships by the providence of great Isis, Lucius now joyfully triumphs over his Fortune.' Birth, rank, and learning, adds the priest, had not saved Lucius from himself; 'sed lubrico virentis aetatulae, ad serviles delap-

---

[1] See O. Weinreich, 'Der griechische Liebesroman' in *Heliodor, die Abenteuer der schönen Chariklea* (Hamburg 1962), 233 ff.; Perry, 350. I am grateful to Prof. Bryan Reardon for helpful information on this subject.

[2] In this section I am especially indebted to H. Riefstahl, *Der Roman des Apuleius* (Frankfurt 1938), whose work has not in Britain or North America received the recognition it merits.

[3] *Onos* 15, 56.

sus voluptates curiositatis improsperae sinistrum praemium reportasti.'[1] This sequence in the priest's analysis is important as the key to the fable. Lucius had renounced the ties of hearth and home to embark on a course of slavish sensuality, and a connexion is implied between his sexual obsession ('serviles voluptates') and his obsession with magic ('curiositas improspera'); the second follows upon the first. In the priest's judgment, Lucius' sufferings as an ass are a punishment for involving himself in base sensuality and magic. *The Golden Ass* is thus 'the story of a soul which fell, and which suffered by reason of that fall, and which the merciful hand of Isis raised up and saved.'[2]

The first three books document the fall, illustrating how 'nec...natales ac ne dignitas quidem, vel ipsa...usquam doctrina profuit'.[3] In the grip of his twin obsessions, Lucius refuses to recognise the warnings which repeatedly come his way. Brushing aside the cautions of friends, the demands of his social status, and the lessons taught by philosophy and literature, he rushes headlong into sexual slavery and involvement with magic. The story of Aristomenes posts the first warning. Socrates is an exemplar of the man who, forgetful of his family, binds himself by sexual ties to a witch. As he himself records his experiences, Socrates insists that his consenting to share the bed of Meroë was the start of his sufferings; and his friend Aristomenes tells him he deserved all he got for preferring the enjoyment of an old harlot to his home and children.[4] The sexual association is the prelude to subjection by magic, just as Lucius too is to seek his experience of magic by way of Photis' bed. The anecdote of Aristomenes is a warning, disregarded by the hero, to dissociate himself from entanglements of casual sex and magic.

---

[1] 11.15.1 ff.

[2] A.-J. Festugière, *Personal Religion amongst the Greeks*, ch. 5.

[3] The priest's words, 11.15.1.

[4] 'Ab unico congressu annosam et pestilentem consuetudinem contraho...'; 'tu dignus es extrema sustinere...qui voluptatem Veneriam et scortum scorteum Lari et liberis praetulisti' (1.7.9, 8.1).

In the second book the warning is reinforced. In the atrium of his mother's friend Byrrhena the hero sees some splendid statuary. Apuleius' description of it should not be regarded as padding characteristic of the Second Sophistic, an excursus on an *objet d'art* included for its own sake. The scene is functional. The group depicts Actaeon spying on the goddess Diana *curioso optutu*, and being turned into a stag; it is a warning against prying which a man of literary education ought to have heeded. Lucius is to become a second Actaeon whose *curiositas* turned him into an ass.[1]

Byrrhena makes the implicit warning explicit. Pointing to Diana, she begs him 'per hanc deam' to beware of Pamphile. Once she has bound good-looking boys *with the fetters of love*, she controls them utterly and can transform them to any shape. Byrrhena describes Pamphile in almost precisely the same terms as Aristomenes used in describing Meroë.[2] Lucius is now trebly warned, but his *curiositas* impels him to rush with mad haste to satisfy his *cruciabile desiderium* for magic by forming a love-association with Photis. The slave-girl adds a fourth warning in a sentence of studied ambiguity; 'cave ne nimia mellis dulcedine diutinam bilis amaritudinem contrahas'.[3] This is not intended to express mere post-sexual melancholy, for the honey is the *serviles voluptates*, the bitterness the *sinistrum praemium curiositatis improsperae*. Yet another warning follows at dinner, when the flickering lamp presages a storm, and Lucius is made (a splendidly ironical touch) to defend this prophecy of the unpropitious future against the scepticism of Milo.[4] The whole point of Lucius' vehement defence of the Stoic doctrine of cosmic harmony, by which disorder in the macrocosm is revealed in the microcosm, is to establish him as the philosopher who fails to foresee the dangers to which he exposes himself. Lucius is another Diophanes, whose story is amusingly told by

[1] 2.4. [2] Compare 2.5.4 ff. with 1.8.4 ff., 1.9.1 ff.
[3] 'Curiosus...festinus...vecors animi...amenti similis' (2.6.1–4); 'cruciabile desiderium', 2.2.1. Warning, 2.10.2.
[4] 2.11.5 (for the meaning of the flickering lamp, cf. Aristophanes *Wasps* 262; Virgil *Georgics* 1.391; Pliny *N.H.* 18.357).

Milo at dinner; the prophetic Chaldean fails to look further than his own nose, just as Lucius fails to see the implications of his beliefs for his own conduct.[1]

Later, when Lucius is at Byrrhena's dinner-party, he is asked how he likes Hypata, and his answer reveals his ignorance of his situation in all its irony. He is enthusiastic about living there because he believes himself freer than ever before, whereas in fact he is in the toils of slavish love; and on the very night when he expresses fear of the dark abodes of magic, he does his best to search it out.[2] Apuleius yet again draws attention to his hero's twin weaknesses, sensuality and curiosity.

The story of Thelyphron which follows again reflects on Lucius' situation. Thelyphron was a young visitor to Thessaly who scoffed at the malevolent power of magic, and brashly undertook the job of guarding a corpse through overconfidence in his human endowments. The loss of his ears and nose is yet another warning to Lucius, likewise a naïve visitor to Thessaly, not to measure his puny human powers against the world of the occult. And the demonstration of superhuman attributes by the priest of Isis (Zachlas, whose name means 'peritia Aegyptiaca') shows Lucius where the true religion lies.[3]

Finally there is the lesson of the wineskins and the highly significant pattern of events in the third book. First Lucius refuses an invitation to a dinner-party at Byrrhena's; in a message to this *parens*[4] he pleads a prior promise to Milo, a

---

[1] 2.13.3 ff. Diophanes ('Divine manifestation') and Cerdo ('Gain') have the symbolic names to which Apuleius is so partial. Despite the doubts of Bürger (*De Lucio Patrensi*, 32), and Hammer, *Eos* (1925), 68, I believe with Junghanns and de Jonge (*Comm. ad Met.* 2, 2) that Apuleius has inserted this story.

[2] 2.20.1.

[3] On Zachlas, see M. Souter, *JTS* (1936), 80. On the story in general, see Hicter, *Apulée*, 65 ff.

[4] 3.12.3. The word is deliberately employed. Scholars get obsessed with the minimal difficulty that Lucius addresses the messenger of Byrrhena with words appropriate to the lady herself. But the slave is of course to repeat the message. Much more interesting is the significance of *parens* by which Apuleius contrives to suggest Lucius' rejection of his kinsfolk.

gesture symbolising his preference for Photis against the claims
of friends and kin. This rejection becomes explicit in his subsequent confidences with Photis. After she has told him that
his humiliation at the Festival of Laughter was the result of
Pamphile's magical practices, his reactions are described in a
key passage which yet again combines his twin faults. 'Show
me your mistress when she essays some deed of her supernatural art. Let me watch when she invokes the gods, or at any
rate when she changes her shape. For I am aflame with desire
to observe magic with my own eyes.' Then, juxtaposed with
this confession of heightened *curiositas*, follows the admission
of enslavement to the charms of Photis. 'Previously I spurned
the embraces of matrons, but you keep me your willing slave.
So now I do not desire home or hearth; this night with you I
count above all that.'[1]

In these first three books, then, Apuleius depicts a hero of
good breeding and education who is given warning after
warning not to dissociate himself from kin and friends, not to
enslave himself to sex, above all not to indulge his curiosity for
magic. It is important to note that Lucius' *curiositas* is in
Apuleius of a different order from his περιεργία in the original
Greek story. *The Golden Ass* depicts Lucius as a man in love
with knowledge who believes that through magic he will
command a cosmic wisdom. Repeatedly he attacks those who
throw doubt on the efficacy of magical arts or on prophetic
interpretation of natural phenomena. In *Lucius or the Ass* the
hero's approach to magic satisfies a desire for amusing or
bizarre experiences so as 'to observe something unusual (παρά-
δοξον)—'a man flying or one turned to stone'; in Apuleius
it begins much more as an intellectual quest by one firmly con-
vinced that magic is the key to knowledge of the other world.
It is this attitude which the fable condemns.[2]

---

[1] 3.19.4 ff.

[2] Attacks on sceptics, 1.3.1 ff., 2.11.6 ff. (cf. Junghanns, 122 n. 3); the
Greek passage, *Onos* 4. See in general S. Lancel, *Rev. hist. rel.* (1961),
25 ff.; H. J. Mette, *Festschr. Bruno Snell* (München 1956), 227 ff.;
A. Labhardt, *Mus. Helv.* (1960), 206 ff.

The second part of the story, Books 4–10, describes the penalty incurred by Lucius for his sins. A human being enclosed in the most bestial of bodies, he lives a rootless, pointless existence amongst the mass of unregenerate mankind. With the bandits he shares a life of cruelty and violence. Delivered from them by Charite and Tlepolemus, he is promised rewards appropriate to his status—unstinted food and coupling. But the promise of freedom is seen to be illusion, and he is the victim of privations in the mill and at the hands of a sadistic boy. As elsewhere through the book, these hardships are inflicted by Fortune,[1] whose cosmic role is indicated by the priest of Isis in the final book.[2] Fortune symbolises the cruel, arbitrary and irrational course of events imposed on those bounded by the preoccupations of the material world, and deliverance from her comes only when Lucius raises his eyes to acknowledge the true reality.

After the mill and the boy follows the nightmare journey in which Lucius and his masters are exposed to the violence of both men and magic; every situation is potentially hostile, never more so than when all seems secure. Fortune continues her savagery by consigning Lucius to the eunuch-priests, whose spurious religion and impure life represent another facet of the unregenerate world, making men 'debiles vel aegroti' instead of 'sui meliores'.[3]

At the next stage of his adventures, where Lucius recounts several stories of cuckolded husbands, Apuleius is depicting the facet of obsessive sexual lust. The central figure here, the baker's wife, combines in her wicked person the adulterous *libido* and the recourse to magic which are the two chief marks of unregenerate mankind. The tenth book again emphasises the hazards of sexual relationships; the infatuated step-mother, the criminal who poisoned her husband and daughter are

---

[1] 7.16.1: 'novis Fortuna saeva tradidit cruciatibus.' 17.1: 'Fortuna meis cruciatibus insatiabilis aliam mihi denuo pestem instruxit.' 25.3: 'illa Fortuna meis casibus pervicax.' So earlier, 7.2.4 f., 7.3.1.

[2] 11.15; above, p. 176.

[3] Fortune, 8.24.1; the effect of the priests, 8.27.6.

followed by the vignette of the judgment of Paris, who destroyed his whole nation 'lucro libidinis'.[1] Lucius has to turn away from this world to seek deliverance by prayer from 'the queen of heaven'.[2]

It is worth re-emphasising that Apuleius does not closely articulate his condemnation of the various aspects of this unregenerate world; only in the final book is the contrast explicitly made between the life of the uninitiated and that of the reborn. He is content to let the Greek story be its own commentary, for the story in itself aptly describes the rootless wanderer ripe for conversion; but the added adventures and anecdotes are frequently patterned to emphasise the destructive forces aroused by *libido* and by the magic arts.[3]

To understand this moral which Apuleius seeks to inculcate, it is necessary to visualise his philosophical and religious view of the world. He was regarded by his contemporaries, and more important by himself, as first and foremost a Platonist. It is beside the point that he is nowadays regarded as an indifferent practitioner; everything he writes bears the stamp of his Neoplatonist outlook, and *The Golden Ass* is pre-eminently a fable which synthesises Platonist philosophy with Isiac religion.

A vital document for this reconciliation of Neoplatonism and the Isiac beliefs is the *De Iside* of Plutarch, whom Lucius claims as an elder relative; and this connexion may have been made by Apuleius to stress the similarity in spiritual outlook and ideology.[4] Plutarch stresses that the Isiac dogma is to be

---

[1] 10.33.1.

[2] 11.2.1. W. E. Stephenson, *Arion* (1964), 87 ff., labels this preoccupation of Apuleius 'the laughable basis of purely physical attraction', and 'the perversion and misery of sex without spiritual sanction'.

[3] In this patterning, the romantic stories play a contrasting role. See Highet, *The Anatomy of Satire*, 182: 'The loveliness of the Cupid and Psyche story and other scenes is intended to enhance the cruel satiric contrast of ideal and real, soul and body, virtue and vice... which is the basic theme of the book.'

[4] *Met.* 1.2.1. It is worth noting that Plutarch wrote a short treatise *De Curiositate* (*Mor.* 515 B–523 B), condemning in general terms the vice which is the cause of Lucius' (and Psyche's) discomfiture.

interpreted ὁσίως καὶ φιλοσόφως, that nothing in Isiac ritual is ἄλογον or superstitious. Osiris is the νοῦς or λόγος of the soul, and all that is ordered and healthy in the material universe is 'the emanation and image of Osiris'; Isis is 'the female principle in nature' who innately loves the first and most supreme of all things.[1] Against these deities of order and reason stands Typhon, the irrational and disordered element who is responsible for all abnormalities in creation, whether manifest in stars, weather, or earthly creatures. Typhon is the cause of existence of *stupid creatures like the ass*.[2] The respect and reverence shown by Plutarch for the Egyptian religion is shared by Apuleius;[3] and it is notable how in *The Golden Ass* his veneration for Egyptian priests contrasts markedly with his scorn for *superstitiosi*.[4] Thus the whole existence of Lucius-turned-ass can be visualised as symbolic of a life controlled by Isis' mortal enemy, and his deliverance as a liberation from Typhon. In Platonist terms, Lucius passes from the animal life of coupling and guzzling (βοσκημάτων δίκην)[5] to the higher contemplation of the true reality.

Just as Lucius' life as ass has this symbolic significance, so his earlier behaviour as man is reprehensible in Platonist and Isiac eyes. In the *Apology*, Apuleius dilates on the two forms of love. There are two Venuses, one for beasts and the common herd of men, one for the few. The first 'binds in her embrace the *enslaved* bodies of animals, broken by her harsh and boundless power'; the second is 'the heavenly Venus who affects her votaries with no incitements or enticements to base living, for her love is not pretty and wanton but unadorned and serious, recommending virtues by beauty of character to those who love her.'[6] *The Golden Ass* is the story of how

---

[1] 355D, 371A–B, 372E.

[2] 371C: διὸ καὶ τῶν μὲν ἡμέρων ζῴων ἀπονέμουσιν αὐτῷ τὸ ἀμαθέστατον, ὄνον. Cf. also 362F, the ass who resembles Typhon.

Cf. *Flor.* 15.14 f. (Pythagoras taught by Egyptian priests); *Flor.* 6.1: 'Aegyptios eruditos'. *Apol.* 56.2: 'sanctissimis Aegyptiorum sacerdotibus'.

[4] Contrast 2.28 with 9.14.5.

[5] Plato *Rep.* 586A.   [6] *Apol.* 12.

Lucius under the guidance of his Isiac mentor learns to renounce the first Venus for the second.

Secondly, Apuleius firmly believes that magicians exist and wield supernatural powers, as his *De Deo Socratis* clearly shows. In the Isiac view all manifestations of natural disorder such as witches achieve[1] are the work of Typhon; in the Platonist philosopher's theory, they are to be attributed to the demons dwelling between earth and heaven.[2] The entire argument of Apuleius' *Apology* is developed to prove the world of difference between practice of magic and initiation into religious mysteries; the first is to be strenuously avoided, the second is a commendable procedure for a man of religious fervour who desires to know the truth.[3] In this sense the final fortunes of Lucius can be seen to be closely connected with Apuleius' own religious career; and when Lucius the Corinthian becomes *Madaurensis* in the final book,[4] this is to make the autobiographical connexion with his hero more explicit.

All that we can piece together of the psychology of the author supports the assumption that Apuleius' romance is seriously intended as a fable in which the sins of Lucius, obsession with sexual lust and obsession with magic, are punished by his relegation to the world of the depraved majority, enclosed within the beast of Typhon. He is delivered from his life of helpless futility only after he commits himself to the protection of Isis.

---

[1] See e.g. *Met.* 1.8.4.

[2] *Apol.* 43.2: *De Deo Socratis* 6: Augustine, *C.D.* 8.14.

[3] *Apol.* 55: '...multiiuga sacra et plurimos ritus et varias caerimonias *studio veri et officio erga deos* didici.' For extended studies of the significance of Apuleius' eleventh book as an account of his religious practice, the reader can consult the books of Festugière, Nock, and Angus (see bibliography). I list more specialised studies in *Phoenix* (1968), 144 n. 8. To these, add P. Roussel, *REG* (1929), 137 ff.; R. Harder, *Abh. Preuss. Akad.*, phil.-hist. Kl. (1943), no. 14: D. Müller, *Abh. Sächs. Akad.* (1961), Heft 1: Festugière, *HThR* (1949), 209. (I owe these references to Mr Stephen Ryle.)

[4] 11.27.9: for this as signature or σφραγίς, Paratore, *La novella*², 65.

It is at first sight an extraordinary fact that the man who holds the highest Roman priesthood at Carthage should devote the final book of the *Metamorphoses* to the glorification of the Egyptian goddess. But Apuleius, so Roman in his literary and oratorical interests, is wholly un-Roman in his religious outlook. The *Apology* offers extraordinary insights into his private devotional practices. He is for ever dropping into shrines for meditation. He carries a statue of Mercury—significantly he had in commissioning it been wholly indifferent about its identity, leaving this minor matter to the sculptor!—amongst his books for private worship, offering incense and sacrificing before it on festal days. He has a particular veneration for Aesculapius.[1] The picture emerges of the Neoplatonist vividly conscious of the existence of the other world, and worshipping the truest reality under the conventional Roman labels for deity.

Apuleius' indifference to the labels attached to the reality he worships reflects syncretist tendencies in the second century generally, and the *Metamorphoses* itself proves how Isis is readily equated with Cybele, Minerva, Venus, Diana, Proserpina, Ceres, Juno, Bellona, Hecate, Nemesis.[2] This redeeming goddess who saves Lucius is in Plutarch's words τὸ τῆς φύσεως θῆλυ, or in the words of Plato τιθήνη καὶ πανδεχής, the all-embracing nursing-mother.[3] By Apuleius' time Isis is no longer accorded in Roman Africa that intolerance earlier extended by Roman officials to eastern deities. Tertullian, writing in 197, provides explicit proof that Isis has been accepted into the Roman pantheon.[4]

The evidence persuasively suggests that a man of Apuleius' religious inclinations—initiate of mystery-religions, mystic,

---

[1] Frequents shrines, *Apol.* 56.3 ff.; statue, 63.3; Aesculapius, *Flor.* 18.38 ff.

[2] *Met.* 11.5.2 ff.

[3] Plut. 372E: Plato *Tim.* 49A, 51A.

[4] Tert. *Apol.* 6: 'Serapidem et Isidem et Arpocratem cum suo cynocephalo Capitolio prohibitos inferri...his vos restitutis summam maiestatem contulistis.'

Neoplatonist—conceived his final book in a spirit of serious apologia. Here a vital local factor must be taken into account. If it is conceded that *The Golden Ass* was composed when Apuleius was in Africa, and that the final book is a serious confession of religious commitment, the explosion of Christianity there in the later part of the century must have exercised its effect. The extent of the inroads made by the new religion is reflected in Tertullian's boast: 'We came but yesterday, but we have thronged all your cities and islands, villages and townships, councils and very armies, tribes and guilds, palace and senate and forum. We have left you only your temples; *paene omnium civitatium paene omnes Christianos*...'[1] This dramatic growth of Christianity, at which the Roman authorities showed their concern with the first martyrdoms in 180, may well have been influential in firing Apuleius to his glorification of Isis. In the words of an eminent student of ancient religions: 'Genuine conversion to paganism will appear...only when Christianity had become so powerful that its rival was, so to speak, made an entity by opposition and contrast.'[2] If the climax of *The Golden Ass* is visualised against the contemporary Christian advances and propaganda, it swings sharply into focus as commitment to pagan personal religion composed under the stimulus of hostile taunts and opposing claims.[3]

A comic romance is certainly a bizarre framework for such a personal confession conceived in polemical terms. One speculative suggestion may be advanced to account for this adaptation of the ass-story. Tertullian tells us that in Africa it was widely believed that Christians worshipped an ass's head,[4] and relates an extraordinary story of how a condemned mercenary tried to save his life in the amphitheatre by de-

[1] *Apol.* 37.
[2] A. D. Nock, *Conversion*, 14. He is writing about Apuleius.
[3] For the rivalry between the Isiac and the Christian faiths, and the similarity of many of their practices, see R. E. Witt, *Proc. Camb. Phil. Soc.* (1966), 48 ff.
[4] Tertullian explains this as a distortion of the Tacitean excursus on Jewish religion (*Hist.* 5.3 ff.), illustrating the common confusion between Jews and Christians in Roman minds.

picting the Christian god as an ass wearing a toga and carrying a book.[1] African Christians in the late second century were known as *asinarii*, and the story of how Lucius-turned-ass found his help and salvation in Isis may well have had a pregnant local significance. Isis bids Lucius: 'pessimae mihique iam dudum detestabilis beluae istius corio te protinus exue',[2] and this is rightly interpreted as Isis' deliverance of Lucius from the beast of Typhon, but in Africa it could bear the additional interpretation of deliverance from Christian superstition. Apuleius' own hostility to Christian beliefs and ritual may well be reflected in his characterisation of the baker's wife, whose religious practices certainly correspond to Roman popular misconceptions of Christianity;[3] and his decision to adapt the comic story of Lucius to present Isis as the goal for those searching for universal truth reflects his personal involvement in the ideological struggle. Lucius the Corinthian suddenly in the last book becomes a Madauran; Apuleius is identifying himself with his hero, and translating the ideological confession to that African province transformed by the inroads made by Christianity.

It is tempting to speculate on Apuleius' possible encounters with Christian testimonies. It would be surprising if no whiff of the controversies had come the way of a man of his philosophical interests, fluent equally in Greek as in Latin, and resident for many years in Athens. Moreover, about the time of and shortly after his residence in Rome, a series of Christian apologies was being published there in Greek; he may have heard of such documents as *The Shepherd* of Hermas or the apologies of Justin and Marcianus Aristides, the last of which contains a scathing attack on Isis.[4] But Apuleius is no

---

[1] *Apol.* 16.

[2] 11.6.2.

[3] *Met.* 9.14.5, 15.4 f. Lightfoot long ago suggested (*The Apostolic Fathers* 2.1, 532) that the reference could equally be to Jewish belief, but in the context of late second-century Africa, the Christians are a likelier target. See L. Herrmann, *Latomus* (1953), 188 ff., well comparing the language with Tac. *Ann.* 15.44.

[4] Aristides *Apol.* 12.3.

Celsus,[1] and more probably his encounter was primarily with the Christian witness in Africa, with its uncompromising rejection of Athenian culture and Roman religion, in both of which Apuleius had a stake.

Examination of his *apologia Isidis* in the eleventh book certainly suggests a rebuttal of Christian charges and claims. The emphasis on Isis' *numen unicum multiformi specie*, and on her providential and compassionate care, calls to mind Christians' jibes about polytheism and the detached life of Roman deities, and the Christian insistence on one God.[2] Like the Christian God, Isis demands of her followers the consecration of their entire lives, 'adusque terminos ultimi spiritus'; 'this is an original touch, practically unknown amongst the ancients, which can only be compared with a religious vocation amongst Christians.'[3] She also demands sexual chastity, and such emphasis is laid on this requirement that one wonders if the Christians' distinctive claim to this virtue is being challenged.[4] Whatever substance is allowed to these suggestions, there can be no doubt that the eleventh book contains propaganda elements. The emphasis on the great number of initiates of every rank and age finds an echo in Tertullian's claims for Christianity; the claim that the religion of Isis is hallowed by antiquity may be polemically directed against an upstart Christianity.[5] The explanation of the ritual in unprecedented detail suggests an apologetic or proselytising purpose, perhaps prompted by Christian attempts to remove vulgar misapprehensions by accounts of their liturgy.[6] Lucius' conversion is certainly presented as a lesson to all 'irreligious' bystanders:

[1] On Celsus' *True Discourse* as a probable answer to Justin's *Apology*, see now H. Chadwick, *Early Christian Thought and the Classical Tradition* (Oxford 1966), 22 ff.

[2] E.g. in Tertullian *Apol.* 13, 17 ff.

[3] *Met.* 11.6.5; Festugière, 80.

[4] 11.6.7, 19.3, 23.3. For Christian emphasis on sexual chastity, Hermas 29.1 ff., Justin 1 *Apol.* 15, Tert. *Apol.* 9, etc.

[5] 11.10.1: 'viri feminaeque omnis dignitatis et omnis aetatis' (cf. Tert. *Apol.* 1); 11.5.5: 'aeterna...religio.'

[6] So Justin 1 *Apol.* 61–8, etc.

'Videant irreligiosi, videant et errorem suum recognoscant.' Tertullian makes it clear that the label of *irreligiosi* was being pinned on the Christians in the Africa of Apuleius' day.[1]

The Golden Ass is a complex creation, masking behind its comic exterior an artful but sincere evangelism. At many points of the romance, Milesian exuberance, bookish humour, and the virtuosity of the story-teller dominate Apuleius' more serious purposes, and his fidelity to the main lines of his original story further restricts his ability to maintain throughout a clearly articulated fable. Yet the intention to develop the story as a fable can hardly be denied, and the lyrical tone of the final book reflects Apuleius' engaged standpoint as he appends a religious confession to the moral of the tale.[2] We must accordingly be satisfied to regard *The Golden Ass* as an ambivalent creation. Planted in the tradition of the comic romance whose aim is solely τέρψις or pleasure, the jocose chronicle of Lucius' adventures is patterned into a trinity of fall, suffering and salvation to present a serious and indeed religious message. The centrepiece, the story of Cupid and Psyche, projects the ambivalence into the realms of mythology and folk-lore. We must now examine the story within a story to demonstrate its purpose, which is closely related to the theme of Lucius' character and wanderings.

---

[1] 11.15.4. For Christians as *irreligiosi*, see Tert. *Apol.* 24, where Tertullian seeks to make the title rebound; cf. Justin 1 *Apol.* 6. It is worth noting that *error* is used by Christian writers to denote misguided belief; see *TLL* v 2, *s.v.*

[2] John Ferguson, *GR* (1961), 61 ff., well compares Chesterton's *The Man Who Was Thursday* as a fantastic romance ending with 'a moment of true profundity'.

7

'CUPID AND PSYCHE'

Bien certainement, Psyché n'a été admise dans les *Métamorphoses* que pour divertir le lecteur. Prenons l'épisode pour ce qu'il est, un joli conte encadré dans un roman.

P. MONCEAUX, Apulée, 143

L'histoire d'Amour et Psyché est une 'odyssée' de l'âme humaine, elle n'est pas une 'nouvelle' qui n'aurait d'autre fin que le plaisir de conter.

P. GRIMAL, Le conte d'Amour et Psyché, 19

At the centre of the *Metamorphoses*, extending over the space of two books, is set the story of Cupid and Psyche, for which Apuleius is best known and most gratefully recalled. He has himself introduced this tale, at once simple and sophisticated, into the framework of the original *Metamorphoses*, rather incongruously allotting its telling to the aged crone deputed to the task of bandits' housekeeper. In seeking to lull the wasting distress of Charite, whom the bandits hope to ransom for a high price, the old woman tells her the story of Psyche; for Psyche similarly suffered separation from her bridegroom, but her privations were finally forgotten in the joy of reunion with her beloved.

Cupid and Psyche is not, however, a tale told merely to underscore the situation of Charite. It is the centrepiece of the whole *Metamorphoses*, and the adventures of Psyche are deliberately shaped to stress the connexion between the maiden's error, suffering, and redemption and the similar experiences of Lucius. Apuleius has here adopted the Alexandrian technique exploited by Callimachus in his *Hecale* and taken over by Catullus in his sixty-fourth poem; *Cupid and Psyche* is a story within a story, and designed to illuminate the larger whole. It is in fact the projection of Lucius' pilgrimage into the world of myth, where the message is clearer for being universalised. Not that every situation and every character in the tale of Psyche has a correspondence in the *Metamorphoses* as a whole; for just as the story of Lucius is not an Apuleian creation, being taken over in substantial measure from the Greek *Metamorphoses*, so the adventures of Psyche are not the author's invention, but the adaptation of a traditional story pressed into service to illuminate in allegorical terms the nature of Lucius' spiritual odyssey. Thus the correspondences between Psyche and Lucius cannot be consistent and particularised, but Apuleius makes the connexion explicit with the sequence of adventures and the delineation of similarities of character.

It is natural but unfortunate that *Cupid and Psyche* should be so often studied and edited in isolation from the rest of the *Metamorphoses*. Natural, because it is apparently a self-contained story, and unlike the saga of Lucius of a wholly edifying kind; unfortunate, because the understanding of its point depends on an understanding of the purpose of the *Metamorphoses* as a whole.[1]

We have seen how *The Golden Ass*, with the Rabelaisian ambivalence of its author, presents itself simultaneously as entertainment and fable. A similar ambivalence characterises the story within the story, and critics' reactions have demonstrated this, for students of the *conte* are divided between those who regard it as a pleasant story told for its own sake and those who insist that it has a symbolic or allegorical purport.[2] In fact it is a two-sided creation—at once a sophisticated, part-frivolous literary composition and simultaneously an extension of that Platonist–Isiac message which rings out so clearly from the final adventures of Lucius.

The previous chapter showed Lucius in his role of modest, credulous youth who believes that he can unlock the door to reality by magical experience, which he seeks by way of sexual infatuation. Expressed conceptually, his is the history of

---

[1] I emphasise this obvious point because so many essays (e.g. Grimal's Introduction to his edition) ignore the connexion.

[2] See the quotations prefacing this chapter. The mantle of Purser and Helm, who take up the standpoint of Monceaux, has now passed to Perry.

simplicitas seeking to satisfy *curiositas* and suborned by the slavery of carnal desire; and the penalty of this culpable *curiositas* is the protracted suffering of the wanderer, from which through anguished prayer he is finally redeemed by the gratuitous grace of Isis. The final book recounts the religious initiation necessary for regeneration and the life of the elect. The general lines of Lucius' character and career are reflected in the history of Psyche. She too is the epitome of *simplicitas*;[1] she too is brought low by her *curiositas*.[2] Like Lucius, she is repeatedly warned of the dangers of such *sacrilega curiositas*, and of the 'great evil' which will be its outcome.[3] But in her simplicity she cannot resist the temptations to which she is exposed, and her curiosity in snatching a forbidden glimpse of her sleeping husband results in Cupid's sad departure. Like Lucius, she wanders forlornly through the world. As he commits himself to Isis to undergo a period of trial, so Psyche surrenders herself to Venus, by whom she is made to discharge stern tasks. The fourth and last of these involves a journey to Persephone in Hades, just as Lucius in his ceremony of initiation undergoes a type of voluntary death, 'treading the threshold of Persephone'.[4] After successfully performing these tasks, Psyche is united with Cupid in the company of the gods, and the fruit of their union is *voluptas*; this union reflects that special relationship of Lucius with Isis which after initiation is represented as apotheosis, and which brings Lucius *inexplicabilis voluptas*.[5] In this sense Apuleius has made the histories of Lucius and of Psyche converge.

[1] 5.11.5, 15.4, 18.4, 19.5, 24.3; 6.15.3. Lucius's *simplicitas*, 1. 3–4, 3.1 ff.
[2] The *curiositas* motif is emphasised at 5.23.1, 6.19.7, 20.5, 21.4.
[3] 5.6.6, 19.3.   [4] 11.21.7, 23.7.
[5] The child previously promised was male (5.11.6). The change in the story, introducing an allegorical element with a female child Voluptas, may well have been made to harmonise with Lucius' *inexplicabilis voluptas* (11.24.5). In this sense I would agree with H. J. Mette, *Festschr. Bruno Snell* (München 1956), 232, who believes that the child Voluptas represents the true ἡδονή, opposed to *serviles voluptates*. Purser, 123, is sceptical about such judgments: 'Cupid did not necessarily know the future in every respect. Parents always assume

To achieve his aim of the exploitation of a universal story to cast a clearer light on the nature of Lucius' pilgrimage, Apuleius had available to him, in folk-lore and in literary mythology, various histories of errant maidens. We may now turn to the contentious question of the earlier development of the *Cupid and Psyche* theme; this will permit the advancing of some suggestions, inevitably speculative, about the shaping of Apuleius' original contribution.

The basic elements of the plot of Apuleius' story can almost all be paralleled in one or other of the widespread versions of a basic folk-tale.[1] These variations on the basic theme are found as far apart as the eastern Mediterranean and Scandinavia, mainland Europe and Africa, Asia and Indonesia. A selection of motifs from various sources could present a pattern remarkably close to the story in Apuleius. An enchanted suitor with supernatural powers forces a father to promise him his daughter in marriage. The suitor is reputed to have the form of a snake or other monster, but the girl is not allowed to set eyes on her new husband. Though forbidden to look on him, she seeks to do so at night by means of a candle, but wakes him with the dripping wax; he departs in anger, in some versions in the form of a bird. The heroine searches forlornly for her husband. Arriving at the house of a witch where her husband is in thrall, she is given impossible tasks to perform in a short time, or tasks which though apparently harmless are in fact mortally dangerous. She is assisted successfully to complete these tasks, usually by supernatural assistance from her husband. One of these tasks is a visit to a second witch, usually the sister of the first, from whom she is commanded to bring back a box. (Some variants depict this culminating test as a visit to the realm of the dead, but these are Scandinavian ver-

that their first-born will be a boy; and when the sex is unknown it is allowable to use the masculine.'
[1] The most recent study of the folk-traditions is J. Ö. Swahn's *The Tale of Cupid and Psyche* (Lund 1955). This part of my essay owes much to Swahn and Friedländer. I am grateful to Mr J. R. G. Wright for helpful discussion.

sions, and one must accordingly be cautious of assuming that Psyche's journey to Hell has been taken over from the folk-tale.) She brings back the box, but on opening it against instructions finds baneful creatures inside. Ultimately, however, she achieves reunion with her husband to live happily ever after.[1]

Cupid and Psyche is clearly an artistic development of a tale with this pattern. Of particular interest is the North African version of the story,[2] which has prompted some scholars to suggest that Apuleius has created his literary work of art directly from an oral tale heard on his native heath. Others draw attention to eastern versions, like the strikingly similar Indian tale of Tulisa, and that of Purūravas and Urvásī.[3] Such tales as these provide the starting-point for one scholar's thesis that Apuleius' story is descended from an Iranian sacral myth, in which the heroine, symbol of the human soul, is a goddess-figure, and the enchanted suitor likewise has a divine *persona*. Egypt is posited as an intermediary by which this sacral myth was diffused through the Hellenistic world, and the Zauberpapyri are cited as evidence for the suggestion.[4]

[1] This composite version approximates to Swahn's 'Sub-Type A'. Swahn's evidence, 259, suggests that the visit to the underworld was introduced in Denmark. One must accordingly allow for the possibility that Apuleius has himself introduced the theme of κατάβασις; but obviously Swahn's inference cannot be conclusive.

[2] Cf. E. Dermenghem, *Contes Kabyles* (Algiers 1945), 11, and 'Le mythe de Psyché dans le folklore nord-africain', *Rev. Afr.* (1945), 40 ff.; L. Frobenius, *Volksmärchen der Kabylen* II, 281 ff., on which see O. Weinreich, 'Eros und Psyche bei den Kabylen', *Arch. f. Religionswiss.* (1930), 88 ff. (now in Binder/Merkelbach, 293 ff.).

[3] For Tulisa, see T. Benfey, *Pantschatantra* II (Leipzig 1859), 255, on which see F. Liebrecht's essay 'Amor und Psyche' in *Zur Volkskunde* (Heilbronn 1879), 239 ff. (now in Binder/Merkelbach, 44 ff.). For the second story, see R. Reitzenstein, 'Noch einmal Eros und Psyche', *Arch. f. Religionswiss.* (1930), 42 ff. (Binder/Merkelbach, 235 ff.).

[4] The thesis of an original sacral myth reproduced in a debased version by Apuleius was propounded by Reitzenstein. Psyche's name 'ist uns jetzt als griechische Deutung und Bezeichnung einer orientalischen Gottheit erklärt', and so far as Eros is concerned, 'mit dem Gott ist

Whatever the validity of the theory of the Iranian sacred myth, its impact on the Apuleian composition would be so nebulous and indirect as to have no more than an academic interest. It is much more in keeping with the psychology of the author to assume that he has adapted a story which he has heard or read, and to attribute the 'sacral' elements of his version, which are absent from the folk-tale, to the introduction of the figures of Eros and Psyche. In other words, Apuleius has grafted on to the folk-tale a story of a love-encounter between Eros and Psyche which derives from a Platonist myth and which becomes popular in the Hellenistic age.

It must be stressed that there is no evidence to prove that Eros and Psyche had already been absorbed into the folk-tale before the time of Apuleius. But there was certainly in existence *a* story of the love of Cupid and Psyche, inspired by the *Phaedrus* of Plato and with basic affinities to the folk-tale. The literary evidence is however tantalisingly fragmentary. Eros, the wanton, cruel boy who inflames with passion both gods and men, is of course ubiquitous in postures and situations incidentally described in Apuleius.[1] But Psyche is more fugitive. There are certainly poems which imaginatively depict Cupid in love, suffering the torments he inflicts on others. In one of them Crinagoras writes:

πέπονθας οἷ' ἔρεξας· ἐσθλὸν ἡ δίκη

and another imagines Eros' outraged words in his lovesick plight.[2] But most striking of all is a poem of Meleager describing how his soul (psyche) suffers the onset of Eros:

die Erzählung von Anfang an verbunden'. (*Das Märchen von Amor und Psyche* (Leipzig 1912), 20 ff., now in Binder/Merkelbach, 87 ff.)

[1] So, e.g., Eros in the service of Venus, *A.P.* 9.325: λάτρις ἐϋστεφάνου Κύπριδος ἁβρὸς Ἔρως. Also 9.157, etc. Eros asleep without quiver and bow, *A.P.* 16.210. Eros threatening Zeus, *A.P.* 16.200 (Moschus), etc.

[2] The poems on Eros bound are at *A.P.* 16.195 ff. Crinagoras' poem (his floruit is the Augustan age; Geffken, *RE* 11.2.1859 ff.) is at 16.199. In another poem (*A.P.* 9.449, subtitled τίνας ἂν εἴποι λόγους Ἔρως ἐρῶν) we read: τίς πυρὶ πῦρ ἐδάμασσε; τίς ἔσβεσε λαμπάδι πυρσόν;/...καινὸς Ἔρως κατ' Ἔρωτος ἐμῷ μένει ἰσοφαρίζει.

ψυχὴ δυσδάκρυτε, τί σοι τὸ πεπανθὲν Ἔρωτος
τραῦμα διὰ σπλάγχων αὖθις ἀναφλέγεται;
μή, μή, πρός σε Διός, μή, πρὸς Διός, ὦ φιλάβουλε,
κινήσῃς τέφρῃ πῦρ ὑπολαμπόμενον.
αὐτίκα γάρ, λήθαργε κακῶν, πάλιν εἰ σε φυγοῦσαν
λήψετ' Ἔρως, εὑρὼν δραπέτιν αἰκίσεται.[1]

It is possible to argue that this is a highly personal poem in which Meleager addresses his inner self (ψυχή), and to visualise it simultaneously as evocative of the Platonist myth, an expression of the cruel reality of that idealised cosmic vision. In a much later poem written long after Apuleius, Marianus Scholasticus offers a completely philosophical interpretation of the relationship between Eros and the soul. Eros has no wings or torch, no bow or arrows; he proclaims himself no son of promiscuous Aphrodite (Κύπρις πάνδημος). Then he continues:

ἀλλ' ἐγὼ ἐς καθαρὴν μερόπων φρένα πυρσὸν ἀνάπτω
εὐμαθίης, ψυχὴν δ' οὐρανὸν εἰσανάγω.

Though this poem cannot be cited in evidence for the Hellenistic period, the ideas and the language are directly derived from Plato's *Symposium*, and it might have been written at any time during the revival of Platonism.[2]

These poems do not in themselves justify the *a priori* assumption that a developed story of Cupid and Psyche existed before Apuleius. The indications of Hellenistic statuary are accordingly all the more welcome. On Alexandrian table-ware predating Apuleius, the figures of Cupid and a maiden are identifiable in various postures. It is perhaps significant that none of these corresponds to any incident in the Apuleian story.[3] But Cupid's love for a maiden was certainly exercising the artists as well as the poets of the Hellenistic age.

[1] *A.P.* 12.80.
[2] *A.P.* 16.201. Marianus writes in the sixth century, but the language is that of *Symp.* 180E, 181A.
[3] I follow Reitzenstein, 'Eros und Psyche in der Ägyptisch-Griechischen Kleinkunst', *Sitzb. Heidelb. Akad.* (1914), 3 ff. (Binder/Merkelbach

Since the subject of Cupid's love-affair was celebrated in both poetry and art, it is possible that it was treated also in a Greek love-romance.[1] It should be noted, however, that no extant romance has an Olympian god as hero, and, if Greek fiction was Apuleius' quarry, it is more probable that he found the story as a brief excursus like those in the novels of Longus and Achilles Tatius. These Greek writers love to hymn the powers of Eros, whom they introduce into *amoena diverticula*;[2] and like Apuleius they tend to describe him in the familiar, disrespectful imagery of Alexandrian poetry, whilst simultaneously acknowledging him in his cosmic role. Most critics envisage as a Greek source an already developed version of the story which Apuleius has merely had to adapt for his particular purposes. It should be stressed, however, that such evidence as exists tells against this view. It is much more in keeping with Apuleius' handling of the *novella* elsewhere in the *Metamorphoses* to assume that he has himself attempted a synthesis of the folk-tale with the Hellenistic theme of Cupid's love for Psyche.

One other ancient writer is known to have treated the theme of Cupid and Psyche. He is an Athenian, Aristofontes, of whom nothing further is known. Fulgentius, writing about A.D. 500, details his contribution as follows: 'sed quia haec saturantius et Apuleius pene duorum continentia librorum tantam falsitatum congeriem enarravit, et Aristofontes Atheneus

159 ff.), where Weber is quoted as maintaining that five of the pieces are datable before Apuleius. There is a full discussion of the monumental evidence in Beck's edition of *Cupid and Psyche* (Groningen 1902), xiii ff.

[1] Many scholars posit an earlier literary version in Greek of *Cupid and Psyche*, amongst them Rohde (pointing to Aristofontes, but see this page); Reitzenstein, *Das Märchen*, 9; Purser, 52 ff.; Helm, *NJb* (1914), 209; Paratore, *La novella*[2], 327.

[2] Note, for example, in Longus 2.3 ff. the story of Philetas, who tells how Eros appeared in his garden λευκὸς ὥσπερ γάλα καὶ ξανθὸς ὥσπερ πῦρ, and informs Philetas that he is 'older than Saturn and all that is'. He has wings on his shoulders, and between the wings a bow with darts. Cf. also Achilles Tatius, 1.1.13.

in libris qui disarestia nuncupantur hanc fabulam inormi verborum circuitu discere cupientibus prodidit...' The order in
which Fulgentius cites the two accounts known to him, and
his emphasis on the length of Aristofontes' account, suggests
that Apuleius came first; it would be rash to posit Aristofontes
as a possible source for our story.[1]

Considered as a story, *Cupid and Psyche* has been well described as 'a folk-tale with mythological additions'.[2] It will be
convenient to visualise its action in five divisions, summarised
as follows:

ACT ONE   *Ira Veneris* 4.28.1–35.4

Scene 1: Divine Honours to Psyche 28.1–29.4
    2: Venus commissions Cupid 29.5–31.7
    3: Psyche's father consults the oracle 32.1–33.5
    4: Psyche exposed on the rock 34.1–35.4

ACT TWO *Amor Cupidinis* 5.1.1–24.5

Scene 1: The enchanted palace 5.1.1–4.5
    2: Cupid's warnings 4.6–6.10
    3: The sisters' envy 7.1–11.2
    4: Cupid's warnings repeated 11.3–13.6
    5: The sisters' envy renewed 14.1–21.2
    6: Detection and flight of Cupid 21.3–25.4

ACT THREE *Psyche errans* 5.25.1–6.8.3

Scene 1: Kindly advice of Pan 5.25.1–25.6
    2: Death of the sisters 26.1–27.5
    3: Venus informed 28.1–31.7
    4: Psyche at the shrines 6.1.1–5.4
    5: Venus commissions Mercury 6.1–8.3

ACT FOUR *Psyche apud Venerem* 6.8.4–21.2

Scene 1: Hostile reception 8.4–9.6
    2: First trial: sorting of grain 10.1–11.3
    3: Second trial: golden wool 11.4–13.2
    4: Third trial: water from the hilltop 13.2–15.6
    5: Fourth trial: visit to Hades 16.1–21.2

[1] Fulgentius, *Mitol.* 3.6 (ed. Helm, Leipzig 1898). Paratore, 325 f.,
well remarks that the scale of Aristofontes' treatment suggests that
he should be set amongst later allegorisers.   [2] Swahn, 377.

ACT FIVE   *Felix coniugium*   6.21.3–24.4

Scene 1: Cupid rescues Psyche   21.3–4
    2: Cupid visits Jupiter   22.1–5
    3: Divine assembly   23.1–5
    4: Marriage-feast   24.1–4

This outline tells its own fascinating story of the problems of unification of *Märchen* and mannered story. Initially (Act I) Cupid has his customary literary role, 'flammis et sagittis armatus', but in Act II the wanton child is to become the sober, apprehensive, devoted husband. This schizoid character persists to the final scene, demonstrating the gulf between the conceptions of the hero in literary tradition and in folk-tale.[1] Once Cupid is established in the folk-tale role, however, the main lines of the traditional tale require little adaptation in the account of marriage and separation (Act II). The events of the third act have likewise a basis in the folk-tale, though it is clear how extensively the story is developed here under the stimulus of both Platonist ideas and literary evocation. Similarly Act IV, once Venus has assumed the role of the traditional witch, can follow the pattern of the folk-tale, though with considerable literary ornamentation. The final section (Act V) can be seen to have a starting-point in the folk-tale, but the last three scenes are wholly extraneous to it, rounding off the *conte* with an Alexandrian burlesque of revelry on Olympus. If we view the total structure, it is astonishing how clearly the bones of the folk-story show through the literary and philophising covering. It has been lent an extraneous literary beginning and its Alexandrian end, but the three central acts stand revealed as artistic development of the popular tale.

A particularly striking feature in the literary development of Psyche's earthly pilgrimage is the introduction of characteristic motifs of the Greek love-romance. The start of Act I closely echoes the opening scenes in Chariton and in Xenophon, and

[1] Cupid in his literary guise, *Met.* 4.30.4. For the motifs, see Theocr. 23.4, *A.P.* 9.449, etc. The sober, devoted Cupid may of course reflect not only the ethos of the folk-tale but also the Platonist conception of Eros.

the consultation of the oracle is likewise paralleled in Xenophon. In Act II the description of Cupid's palace recalls
similar set-pieces in the novels. The visits by the pious heroine
to shrines, in the wanderings described in Act III, evoke
similar accounts in the Greek romances.[1] One may almost
speak of *Cupid and Psyche* as a folk-tale shaped to the character
of a Callirhoe or an Anthia, for Psyche is just such a heroine of
fidelity and piety, but disconcertingly moving between two
worlds.

Apuleius' story opens with what is usually described as the
exordium of a folk-tale, but it should not be forgotten how
often the formula ('erant in quadam civitate rex et regina') is
appropriated by the love-romance and the mannered story in
other writers.[2] The emphasis on Psyche's beauty so remarkably
echoes the phraseology of Chariton that this can hardly be
accidental. In both, the fame of the heroine's radiant presence
causes men to flock to her from far and near, and they show
obeisance as if she were Venus herself.[3] This motif of the
divine maiden is then exploited to explain Venus' resentment;
the goddess's worship in Cyprus, Asia and Greece is neglected
because of the admiration accorded to a human girl, and she
determines to humiliate this presumptuous rival.[4]

The scene now changes, in conscious imitation of the regular
narrative-technique in epic, from earthly to divine realms. We
are at once in a different world of Greek mythology portrayed
in Alexandrian burlesque. Venus is presented uttering a

[1] I draw attention to these similarities in more detail later. See in general
Schaller, *De fabula Apuleiana* (diss. Leipzig 1911), 67; Helm, *NJb*
(1914), 190 ff. (Binder/Merkelbach, 204 ff.); Paratore, 356 ff.
[2] Above, p. 55 n. 2. Helm well compares Herod. 1.6, Xen. *Anab.* 3.1.4.
I have benefited here and later from Helm's learning; cf. also J. Dieze,
Philol. (1900), 136 ff.
[3] Above, p. 55 n. 2.
[4] Venus is thus cast in the role of the folk-tale queen whose hitherto
peerless beauty is excelled by that of the simple maiden like Snow-
white. But of course the motif is well-known in literature. Cf. Prop.
2.28.9: 'num sibi collatam doluit Venus?'

comically indignant soliloquy, shaking her head and grinding her teeth. She repeats to herself phrases of Lucretius' glowing eulogy in the exordium of the *De Rerum Natura*,[1] resolves to take revenge, and summons her son. He appears in his regular role, for at this point he must show his Hellenistic *persona* of mischievous ne'er-do-well[2] to justify his choice for the mission. He is instructed to fire Psyche with love for the most ignoble creature he can find.[3] Having made these arrangements, Venus now retires to the sea attended by her baroque train; the point of her retirement to the ocean is that she must be ignorant of the subsequent action.[4] She has previously surveyed terrestrial events in anger; in the ocean she will be blessedly ignorant of her son Cupid's change of heart from *procax puer* to *sollicitus maritus*.

Apuleius now translates us back to earth, and from Alexandrian sophistication to the folk-tale. We should not be so beguiled as to fail to observe an inconsistency in the plot here, which may be attributable precisely to the transition from mythology to folk-tradition. Cupid simply fails to carry out his mission. He does not, as we might have anticipated, become enamoured with Psyche whilst arranging Venus' revenge. The train of events by which Psyche becomes his wife develops without direct supernatural intervention. It is because Psyche's beauty is too great for any suitor to aspire to that her father becomes troubled about her future ('suspectatis caelestibus

[1] Above, p. 55. The striking parallel with *Met.* 11.5.1 must also be intended as one of the many pointers to a connexion between Psyche and Lucius.
[2] Cf. Apoll. Rhod. 3.129 ff., Ovid *Met.* 5.365 ff., etc. The description in Apuleius is at 4.30.4 f.: 'malis suis moribus, contempta disciplina publica...omnium matrimonia corrumpens...nihil prorsus boni facit'.
[3] So, in Xenophon's novel, Manto plans to give Anthia to a slave, αἰπόλῳ τινι ἀγροίκῳ (2.9).
[4] I prefer this pragmatic explanation of the journey to the mystical view of the sea as 'symbolisant la matière, où est enfermée l'âme... Venus, "âme du monde", réside dans l'océan, "lieu du devenir"' (Grimal). The sea as Venus' provenance is the natural place for her to retire to.

odiis') and consults the oracle of Apollo at Miletus.[1] The oracle, it is true, bids the king expose his daughter on a rock for an immortal suitor, 'saevum atque ferum vipereumque malum', so that Apollo may be said to carry out Cupid's design;[2] but the author has failed to make this sequence of events explicit, and gives the impression of hastily bridging a gap between mythology and folk-tale. The oracle-motif itself, by which Psyche is surrendered to her fate, is of course a favourite device of literary mythology, and Callimachus' story of Cydippe, whose father consults Apollo at Delphi, is strikingly similar; the theme is also prominent in the love-romance.[3] Likewise Psyche's noble valedictory, as she departs to her marriage with death, is a rhetorical utterance in the Greek literary tradition, recalling to our minds the bravery of an Antigone and similar declamations in the love-romances.[4]

The second act begins with Psyche's being wafted down from the rock—on which, Andromeda-like, she is exposed—into

[1] Miletus is chosen because Apuleius has proclaimed his initial intention of writing 'sermone...Milesio' (1.1). Thus Apuleius himself is the *Milesiae conditor* (32.6), not Sisenna as Reitzenstein improbably suggested. Note that the action is set here as elsewhere (4.29.3, 6.18.1) vaguely in the Aegean area.

[2] Merkelbach lays too much weight on Apuleius' Isiac preoccupations when he assumes here that Apollo is Horos and Eros is Harpocrates, so that Apollo and Eros are identical (*Roman und Mysterium*, 8 ff.).

[3] Callim. *Ait.* 3, fr. 75 Pfeiffer, ll. 20 f. Compare also the history of Io (above, pp. 52 f.). In the Greek novels see especially Xen. 1.6, where the parents consult the oracle at Colophon and get a reply in hexameters. As a result οἱ πατέρες αὐτῶν ἦσαν ἐν ἀμηχανίᾳ καὶ τὸ δεινὸν ὅ τι ἦν πάνυ ἠπόρουν—compare *Met.* 4.33.3. The oracular utterance, which so obviously denotes Cupid as husband that doubts must be entertained about the king's I.Q., is full of literary echoes. For the snake-motif, cf. Sappho's γλυκύπικρον ἀμάχανον ὄρπετον (L–P, 130); for *saevum atque ferum*, Bion fr. 9 Gow; *A.P.* 12.48.1, 12.144.1 (Meleager).

[4] Antigone's famous ὦ τύμβος, ὦ νυμφεῖον speech (891 ff.) handles the same imagery of marriage with death; for other references see Purser's note at 4.34. It appears in Achilles Tatius 3.7 and 1.13.2. For the rhetorical form of the speech, see O. Schissel, *H* (1941), 106 ff.

the enchanted demesne of Cupid's palace. The Zephyr or west wind performs this service. This is so clearly a basic folk-lore theme that it is surprising that no trace of it has been found in the numerous collected versions of our tale.[1] Though the description of the idyllic grove and royal palace evokes the mannered accounts of gardens and mansions in the love-romances, the whole passage, with its stress on the absence of guards and barred doors and on the service of disembodied spirits, suggests a source in traditional folk-lore.[2] Hence whilst it is possible to point to such literary parallels as the house of Menelaus in Homer, or the palace of Helios in Ovid,[3] Apuleius is here fairly certainly drawing on an extended tale whose roots are deep in popular tradition.

Cupid now enters in his new role of devoted suitor, and in a description as brief as it is delicate, consummates the marriage. 'Iamque aderat ignobilis maritus et torum inscenderat, et uxorem sibi Psyche fecerat, et ante lucis exortum propere discesserat. statim voces cubiculo praestolatae novam nuptam interfectae virginitatis curant.' The paratactic clauses, the

[1] Swahn, 373 ff., can find only one parallel—the story 'Ermenegilda e Cupido' in Pitre, *Novelle popolari toscane*[2] (1941), 143, which probably draws on Apuleius. Such stories as Grimm 99, where the north wind conveys the youngest brother, suggest its provenance in folk-lore. Those who argue for an Alexandrian source point to Catullus 66.52 ff. The thesis of Merkelbach that the *mitis aura* of 4.35.4 is related to 11.23.7 ('per omnia vectus elementa') and to the flying-machines used in the mystery-cults (Livy 39.13.13) seems to me far-fetched. But doubtless Apuleius was aware that the winds are often visualised as vehicles of the soul or psyche; see Grimal, *ad loc.*

[2] 5.1. For an obviously independent description of an enchanted demesne and palace, see Andreas Capellanus' treatment of the Arthur legend in *De Amore* 2.8. For typical ἐκφράσεις in the romance, see Achilles Tatius 1.15 (the garden in the house of Clitophon, who describes the power of Eros over nature); Longus 4.2 f. Grimal well compares Apuleius' own description of Persian palace-architecture in the *De mundo*. The lay-out (5.1.6 f.) corresponds to the general features of the Roman *domus*.

[3] *Od.* 4.43 ff. (θεῖον δόμον), 71 ff.; Ovid *Met.* 2.1 ff.

pluperfect tenses relegating the action to the past, the hint of archaism conspire to achieve this appropriate restraint.[1]

This scene sets the stage for the second act, in which the action is skilfully developed by alternation of prominence to Cupid with Psyche and to the jealous sisters. Both motifs stressed here, the warnings of the husband and the jealousy of the sisters, were presumably part of the folk-tale, but the artistic alternation by which their interplay develops to the climax may well be Apuleius' own contribution. First we are briefly told that the sisters hear of their parents' grief and solicitously hasten to be at their side.[2] Then the attention focusses on Cupid, who solemnly warns his wife that if she hears their lamentations she is not to heed them; otherwise it will mean suffering for him and certain death for her. But Psyche in her longing to renew the ties of kinship constrains him to allow her to offer hospitality to her sisters. His assent is given with further warnings never to be persuaded to pry into his identity, for such *sacrilega curiositas* will be her undoing.

The sisters' arrival through the Zephyr's help is next described. But their joy in reunion with Psyche soon turns to jealousy, and they ask with curiosity ('curiose') about her husband; she spins a story of his being a young man out hunting, and sends them home with gifts. Their envy swells ('gliscentis invidiae felle fraglantes'), and is charted in a splendidly amusing dialogue in which they contrast their sister's blessings with their own marital misery. One has for husband an old man 'balder than an onion, without the virility of a stripling'; the other complains of a mate 'knotted and bent with rheumatics', to whom she is not so much a wife as an

---

[1] 5.4.3 f. The use of *ignobilis* for *ignotus*, and the use of *interficere* in its literal sense contribute to the archaic flavour.

[2] As so often, Apuleius has no concern for consistency in characterisation. The sisters are later callous and calculating; here they are as pious as can be (5.4.6). It is the sight of Psyche's possessions that unhinges their minds. Apuleius does not subscribe to Juvenal's dictum 'nemo repente fuit turpissimus'.

exhausted nurse.¹ They resolve to conceal from their relatives all knowledge of Psyche's fortune, and to return later to plot her downfall.

The departure of the sisters brings Cupid once more into focus. He now elaborates on his warning to Psyche in more urgent terms. Fortune, which had previously merely threatened, has now begun to skirmish and will soon close;² in other words, the unscrupulous sisters will soon press her to unveil his identity. She has conceived a child who will be divine if she maintains their secret. As before, he renews the warning as the sisters approach, intensifying the military metaphor.³ She begs him by his fragrant locks, smooth cheeks and fevered breast to allow her to embrace her sisters again, and she will henceforth be content to accept him as her light in darkness without beholding his face.⁴

The sisters duly arrive, feign pleasure at Psyche's pregnancy,⁵ and innocently enquire about her husband. The naïve bride now depicts him as a middle-aged businessman, forgetting her earlier description of the youthful hunter. The sisters realise that she has a divine husband, and consumed with jealousy they set their snare. The following day they tell her that her consort is a monstrous snake—in a description with

¹ 5.9.8, 10.1 f. Note the characteristic inconsistency here when compared with 4.32.3.
² 5.5.2: 'exitiale tibi periculum minatur fortuna saevior...'; 11.3: 'velitatur fortuna eminus...'. The *fortuna*-motif, as we have seen, is pervasive in Greek and Roman fiction, but in Apuleius has a consciously theological significance; above, pp. 176, 181.
³ 5.12.4: '...sanguis inimicus iam sumpsit arma et castra commovit et aciem direxit et classicum personavit...'.
⁴ Her words, 'nil officiunt mihi nec ipsae nocturnae tenebrae; teneo te, meum lumen' have probably here a symbolic sense, in accord with the Platonist–Isiac interpretation. See below and, for a detailed exposition of the meaning of the passage, S. Lancel, *Rev. hist. rel.* (1961), 41 ff.
⁵ Apuleius practises dramatic irony for sportive purposes here. The sisters say that if the child 'matches its parents' beauty, a Cupid will surely be born' (5.14.5). A similar effect is achieved at 5.6.7, where Psyche professes such love for her husband that she ranks him 'higher than Cupid'.

pronouncedly Virgilian overtones;[1] here, then, is the common folk-motif of the prince-turned-serpent who resumes his human shape as long as he remains invisible. Poor Psyche ('utpote simplex et animi tenella') believes every word and craves their advice. They tell her that her path to salvation is to sever the snake's head once he is asleep, and that they will then arrange for her a human marriage.

The final scene and climax of the second act now follows. Psyche is depicted as the prey of conflicting emotions. 'Festinat differt, audet trepidat, diffidit irascitur, et, quod est ultimum, in eodem corpore odit bestiam diligit maritum.' It is the psychological portrayal of the irresolute heroine so notably painted in Euripides' *Medea* and in Seneca's drama, and so frequently imitated in the Greek romances.[2] Finally she steels herself to approach the sleeping figure with lamp and razor. But the beast she sees is 'the mildest of all beasts and the sweetest; *ipsum illum Cupidinem formonsum deum formonse cubantem...videt capitis aurei genialem caesariem ambrosia temulentam, cervices lacteas genasque purpureas pererrantes crinium globos decoriter impeditos...*' The detailed physical description here and in what follows depicts the Hellenistic Cupid with wings, bow, quiver and arrows, but his character remains the serious, rational husband of the folk-tale, gently rebuking his wife before sorrowfully departing. The love which grips Psyche on beholding her husband[3] reflects that totality of attachment so memorably described in the *Phaedrus*. It has frequently been suggested, and reasonably so, that Plato has directly inspired the action at this point of the story, when Psyche clutches Cupid's leg as he flies away, and is borne with him some distance before falling wearily to the ground. For in

---

[1] Above, p. 55.

[2] 5.21.4; cf. Eur. *Med.* 1042 ff., Sen. *Med.* 893 ff. For such psychological portrayals in the love-romances, cf. Achilles Tatius' picture of Leucippe, caught by her mother receiving Clitophon by night (2.25); or Xen. 2.5, the picture of Manto when she receives a letter from Habrocomes rejecting her approaches.

[3] For the importance of the eyes in love, cf. Achilles Tatius 1.4.4, Heliodorus 3.7 f. (Rohde, 132 ff.).

the *Phaedrus*, when the soul is 'filled with forgetfulness and wickedness, it grows heavy, and the weight robs it of its wings, and it falls to the ground'.[1] But though these literary and philosophical influences are prominent, it ought not to be forgotten how prominently the breaking of the taboo—by stealing a forbidden glimpse of the husband—figures in different versions of the folk-tale. The prohibition against seeing the husband by light, her contravention of this instruction, his disappearance wounded are all motifs of the folk-tale, and such detail as the lamp's being endowed with its own capacity for action is likewise characteristic of such a source.[2] The whole of this second act is essentially folk-tale.

The third act describes Psyche's wanderings in search of Cupid; the strong similarity to the mythological wanderings of Io has already been detailed.[3] Io contemplates suicide from a cliff; Psyche goes further, but the river-waters, themselves victims of Cupid's fire,[4] wash her safely to the bank. There she encounters Pan in a charming rustic setting, described in the motifs and language of Greek and Roman pastoral.[5] He plays Prometheus to her Io, encouraging her to endure in the certainty of future reconciliation with Cupid.

In her wanderings, Psyche now chances successively on the two cities where her sisters dwell. There is a minor inconsistency

---

[1] *Met.* 5.24.1: *Phaedr.* 248c: ...λήθης δὲ καὶ κακίας πλησθεῖσα βαρυν-θῇ, βαρυθεῖσα δὲ πτερορρυήσῃ τε καὶ ἐπὶ τὴν γῆν πέσῃ... For this Platonist influence, see Jahn, *Archäol. Beiträge* (1847), 121 ff.; G. Heinrici, *Preuss. Jahrb.* (1897), 407 ff. (Binder/Merkelbach, 75 ff.); P. Scazzoso, *Le Metamorfosi di Apuleio* (Milan 1951); R. Thibau, 'Les Métamorphoses d'Apulée et la théorie platonicienne de l'Eros', *Studia Philosophica Gandensia* (1965), 89 ff.

[2] 5.23.4. See Swahn's list of common motifs at this point of the story. It should however be noted that the lamp as personified witness of, or hindrance to, love is not uncommon in Hellenistic poetry; see *A.P.* 5.7 (Asclepiades), 5.8 (Meleager).

[3] Above, pp. 52 f. For the suggested connexion of Io with Isis, below, p. 221 n. 4. [4] Another common literary motif; see Grimal *ad loc.*

[5] Pan is embracing Echo as at Moschus 6; for the theme in statuary, cf. Callistratus 1.4. For the language, above, p. 56.

in the story here, perhaps suggesting that Apuleius has inserted this episode for his own purposes. The sisters were previously described as dwelling beyond the sea,[1] whereas Psyche is wandering on foot when she stumbles on each of their homes in turn. This introduction of the demise of the sisters on the one hand lends an appropriate note of morality to the story, and on the other has a symbolic import in the context of Psyche's pilgrimage. The sisters represent the earthly attachments which are the cause of her fall from grace, and which she must now slough off. This symbolic addition to the story is betrayed not only by the inconsistency of circumstantial detail already mentioned, but also by the central anomaly in Psyche's behaviour; for the *simplex puella* shows a yearning for revenge and a hitherto unknown craftiness in raising the hopes of her sisters that Cupid wishes to marry them,[2] and they presume too often on the Zephyr's readiness to act as their flying-machine.

With Psyche at this significant point in her pilgrimage—her renunciation of worldly connexions—Apuleius leaves her to transport the reader, again epic-wise, to the realms of the gods. Cupid lies seriously wounded in his mother's chamber, though earlier he had flown off effortlessly enough[3] in escaping the attentions of his bride. It is tempting to ascribe this further inconsistency once more to Apuleius' symbolic preoccupations. The physical wound of Cupid, a mere drop of burning oil on the shoulder, symbolises the pain of separation from Psyche; this is the 'gravis vulneris dolor' which prostrates him.[4] The news of his sickness is conveyed to his mother, sporting in happy ignorance in the ocean, by her informant the tern; this motif of the bird-informer is common both in folk-tales and in mythology, and it seems probable that Apuleius has happily introduced the tern, so comfortable in this diving role, into the

[1] 5.21.2.
[2] Paratore calls this vendetta 'un vero assurdo psicologico' (359).
[3] 5.24.5: 'pinnis in altum se proripuit.'
[4] Every word or phrase in the description of Cupid's sickness, 'adustum ...gravi vulneris dolore maerentem dubium salutis iacere' (5.28.3) is deliberately ambivalent, suggesting both physical and emotional suffering.

part played by other birds in similar mythological situations.[1] Venus demands more detail, and on being informed that her son is Psyche's lover, she is consumed with anger. In effect the burlesque of Venus is now resumed. She abuses her son like a fishwife, she petulantly threatens to disinherit him;[2] then, 'vultu tumido' and 'truci supercilio' she cuts off Ceres and Juno for defending the Cupid they fear, and storms back to the ocean.

In this literary episode worked into the story, with its conspicuous evocation of a similar scene in Apollonius Rhodius' epic,[3] Cupid is strangely silent, as if to underplay the incongruity of his resumed Alexandrian role; the comically vindictive Venus is at the centre. But this scene is not burlesque for its own sake. It has the functional purpose of prefiguring the neutral attitudes of Ceres and Juno in the next scene, and of preparing the reader for Venus' hostile confrontation with Psyche in the following act. Apuleius achieves a high degree of artistry in his interlocking of the earthly and the Olympian episodes at this stage of the story.

For Psyche meanwhile decides that she will search for Cupid in a shrine she descries on a hill. It is clearly Ceres' temple, for heaps of corn and barley are in evidence as offerings there, together with agricultural tools which Psyche, as befits a pious heroine, arranges more tidily. (Apuleius' debt to the love-romance is suggested here, for visits to deities' shrines are like-

---

[1] On the *gavia* as tern, not sea-mew, see W. G. Arnott, 'Notes on *gavia* and *mergus* in Latin literature', *CQ* (1964), 249 ff., esp. 261 n. 6. Compare the crow as informant of Minerva, Ovid *Met.* 2.531 ff. (Purser) and the hawk as tell-tale at Ps. Apollod. *Bibl.* 2.1.3. The *gavia* is chosen here because of Venus' location, and perhaps also because her name in Greek (λάρος) suggests the chatterbox; it is used of Cleon by Aristophanes. I am grateful to Mr J. R. G. Wright for assistance here.

[2] 5.29.2 and 5 f. As elsewhere in the *Metamorphoses*, there are jocose references to Roman legal procedure. Venus threatens to adopt a slave (perfectly possible in Roman law; see F. Norden, *Ap. und das röm. Privatrecht* (Leipzig 1912), 74). She carefully explains that his wings, flames, bow, etc. were not bequeathed by his father, so that he has no prescriptive right to them.

[3] Ap. Rhod. 3.36 ff., 90 ff.

wise a feature of the Greek novels, and there is a particularly
striking parallel at the beginning of *Daphnis and Chloe*, where
the Nymph's cave in which Chloe was found is festooned with
pails, pipes and reeds, the offerings of former shepherds.)
Ceres appears and informs Psyche that Venus is searching for
her. The girl pleads to be allowed sanctuary for a few days till
Venus' anger is softened, but Ceres pleads that she cannot
break faith with her relative. A similar outcome befalls Psyche
when she makes the same appeal in the shrine of Juno; Juno too
answers that she cannot offend her kinswoman—and adds in
yet another legal pleasantry that it is against the law to harbour
runaway slaves.[1] It should be noted that Apuleius introduces at
this point a relationship between Venus and Psyche as mistress
and slave which is nowhere mentioned at the beginning of the
story. It is tempting to see here another minor inconsistency
resulting from a *mélange* of literary story and folk-tale, for in
the traditional oral version the wandering maiden is allowed to
remain in the house of the witch, 'usually as a servant'.[2]
Psyche now decides to surrender herself to her mistress Venus,
and at this second point of decision in her pilgrimage, Apuleius
again leaves her to transport the reader to action on the divine
plane, and to describe Venus' plans in her search for the re-
calcitrant Psyche.

Venus has now decided to enlist the aid of Jupiter. Remarkably enough, in her earlier journey the goddess had merely
to emerge from the sea to reach her 'golden chamber' for her
conversations with Cupid and with Ceres and Juno, but to
address Jupiter she has to make preparations for a more
extensive trip to heaven. It is as if Apuleius is making the
Neoplatonist distinction between the abodes of the popular
deities, who as 'demons' dwell in the lower air, and that of

---

[1] See Appendix 2 for discussion of this passage.

[2] Swahn, 29. Scholars who press literary influences compare Hercules in
the service of Eurystheus (his tasks include a journey to Hell) and draw
attention to Meleager *A.P.* 12.80.5, where Psyche is a fugitive from
Eros. There may also be a hint of the relationship of a heroine like
Anthia with the deities to whom she prays, especially Isis.

Jupiter in the 'summus aether'.[1] The picturesque account of
the procession, with Venus at the centre in her golden car, is a
sophistic set-piece in Apuleius' most witty style. The atmosphere of Jupiter's palace is suitably captured by an amusing
reminiscence of Homer. Venus requests the help of Mercury
in her search, and the reply of Jupiter is indicated in a baroque
phrase remarkable even for Apuleius, a literal reproduction
of the Homeric expression.[2] Mercury willingly performs his
task, announcing a reward from Venus of 'seven sweet kisses,
and one as honeyed as can be, *blandientis adpulsu linguae*' to
whoever lays information about Psyche's whereabouts. The
reward of Venus' kiss is a Hellenistic conceit which Apuleius
hopes his readers will recognise;[3] these readers he envisages as
Roman, for the informers are to meet Mercury at a place
recognisable only by those who know their Rome through
visitation or through literature, 'behind the *metae Murciae*'.
This assignment in the city is a typical example of how
Apuleius writes for the moment, and for the sake of one
amusing topographical reference makes nonsense of all the
previous indications that the action of the story takes place in
Greece and the Aegean.

This Olympian scene, it will be noted, has no structural
purpose beyond indicating Venus' continuing hostility.
Psyche had *already* decided to surrender herself to Venus,
though Mercury's edict accelerates her decision. The descent of
Mercury is an ornamental insertion from mythology into the
folk-tale, and makes no contribution to the development of
the third act, which has its basis in the folk-tale but is adorned
with mythological interludes.

[1] Apuleius discusses in the *De Deo Socratis* the abode of the demons. For
Jupiter's abode, see *Met.* 6.6.4, and compare Cupid's later journey at
6.22.1, 'caeli penetrato vertice'.
[2] 6.7.2. Above, p. 56.
[3] Moschus 1.4:

εἴ τις ἐνὶ τριόδοισι πλανώμενον εἶδεν Ἔρωτα
δραπετίδας ἐμός ἐστιν· ὁ μανυτὰς γέρας ἑξεῖ·
μισθός τοι τὸ φίλαμα τὸ Κύπριδος· ἢν δ' ἀγάγῃς νιν
οὐ γυμνὸν τὸ φίλαμα, τὸ δ', ὦ ξένε, καὶ πλέον ἑξεῖς...

The fourth act can be described in summary as essentially folk-tale with Venus superimposed. At the outset, Psyche in her role as runaway slave approaches Venus' door to be accosted by a handmaid Consuetudo. This incorporation of abstract and symbolic characters is one of the chief indications of how the *Märchen*-turned-*Kunstmärchen* is lent an allegorical purport.[1] Whilst Consuetudo[2] is handling Psyche roughly, Venus appears with a vulgar laugh and sarcastic greeting. She consigns the girl to her maids Sollicitudo and Tristities for the punishment appropriate to a runaway slave. (Their names clearly indicate Apuleius' emphasis on the symbolic nature of the punishment and of the victim.) When the girl is haled back into her mistress's presence, Venus witheringly rejects any expectation entertained by Psyche that Cupid is her husband; the marriage will not stand up to the requirements of Roman law!

With Venus in the role of the witch of the folk-tale, Psyche is now instructed to perform a series of four tasks. It has been claimed that in folk-tales three is the regular number of tasks imposed on the heroine, and that therefore Apuleius must have superimposed the fourth; but amongst the collected versions of our tale several, including the African, incorporate four trials.[3]

[1] Sobrietas at 5.30.3, Sollicitudo and Tristities at 6.9.2 should also be noted. It is striking that these are the only named subordinate characters apart from deities. Such abstractions are not unknown in the Greek romances; in Chariton 1.2.5 the ruler of Agrigentum seeks to arm Ζηλοτυπία against Chaereas.

[2] For habit as an ally of love, see 5.4.5, 'novitas per assiduam consuetudinem delectationem ei commendarat...'; also Lucr. 4.1283, 'consuetudo concinnat amorem'; Ovid *A.A.* 2.345, where Brandt compares Ach. Tat. 1.9.5 (I owe this reference to Mr E. J. Kenney).

[3] G. Heinrici, 'Zur Geschichte der Psyche', *Preuss. Jb.* (1897), 390 ff. (now in Binder/Merkelbach, 56 ff.): 'hier ist das Märchenhaftes abgestreift, und das Mythologisch-Mysteriöse tritt an seine Platz.' So also Friedländer, *Roman Life and Manners*, tr. Gough, IV, 88 ff. But for the four tests in the African version, see O. Weinreich, *Arch.f. Religionswiss.* (1930), 92 (Binder/Merkelbach, 298). There is something in the thesis of Reitzenstein, 'Noch einmal...' (Binder/Merkelbach, 256 ff.), who

The first two tasks are traditional 'bride's proofs' concerned with food and clothing.[1] The first test is the separation of a confused mass of cereal-grains into constituent kinds by nightfall. When Psyche gapes helplessly, an army of ants performs the work for the wife of Cupid. The type of task and the ants as helpmates are authentic folk-lore elements; but it is worth noting that Venus attributes the successful completion of the work to her son, and we are to envisage the ants as his agents in Apuleius' developed version.[2] After the completion of the test Cupid and Psyche have to endure the night under the same roof but apart, and here the influence of the love-romance may again obtrude.[3]

The second day brings the second ordeal, perhaps a mythological refinement of the traditional clothing test. Psyche is bidden to bring a lock of golden wool from the sheep in the nearby grove. She is again filled with despair—though the task as outlined seems hardly arduous except for one with mythological preoccupations![4]—and prepares for suicide. But a reed ('harundo simplex et humana') instructs her how to avoid danger by waiting till the heat of the day has passed, and

compares eastern versions to propose that the visit to the underworld is not merely a fourth task but the organic close to the story, by which Psyche gains heaven.

[1] So Bieler, *Arch. f. Religionswiss.* (1933), 258 (Binder/Merkelbach, 354): 'beide sind typische Brautproben'.

[2] Friedländer cites Grimm 17 for the ants, and in Grimm 21 doves perform a similar task. Swahn observes that in the folk-versions of our story the husband normally assists the girl, and he suggests that the incorporation of ants and other agents is 'probably Apuleius' own idea' (375). Comments at 6.10.5 f. and 6.15.1 f. support this view; these complaints by Venus of Cupid's assistance to Psyche may have been carried over from the folk-tale, where direct help is lent by a husband not seriously hurt.

[3] 6.11.3, and compare Achilles Tatius 4.1. Merkelbach would interpret this as the requirement of sexual chastity during initiation (Tib. 1.3.26; Prop. 2.28.62, etc.).

[4] Apuleius should either have indicated the difficulty of the task, or Psyche should have set out confidently and then been warned by the reed. The inconsistency suggests the adaptation by Apuleius of a more obviously hazardous task.

by taking the wool from the trees where the sheep have rubbed themselves. No close parallels from folk-tales can be adduced for this variation on the wool-task, and Apuleius may have introduced from the Argo story a more mythological flavour to superimpose on the folk-tale.[1] Nor has the talking reed a known relationship to this folk-tale; and the popularity of 'human' reeds in love-romances tempts us to believe that Apuleius drew his influence from there.[2] Psyche's success in this task is again attributed to Cupid's work.

The third task imposed on Psyche is to take a vessel to the top of a mountain and to fill it from the spring which 'waters the Stygian marshes and the harsh streams of Cocytus'. When she draws near, she realises the impossibility of the task. But the hazards of rocks and snakes and animate waters are confronted on her behalf by an eagle, the bird of Jupiter who is glad thus to repay Cupid for his services in the kidnapping of Ganymede. It has been suggested that the basic theme here is the journey for 'the water of life', which in folk-lore usually involves a visit to the realms of the dead, so that the third test is virtually a duplication of the fourth; on this view Apuleius will have translated the third trial to the realm of earth, and introduced the fourth himself.[3] But in Apuleius' version this third trial conveys no hint of a journey below the earth. The description of the waters shows that he has in mind the Ar-

[1] The nearest parallel in Swahn is the task of milking the witch's cows which turn out to be bears. In the African version feathers have to be restored to birds (Weinreich, 92 (298 in Binder/Merkelbach)). Besides the story of the golden fleece, mythology provides similar quests at Ps. Apollod. 2.5.1 (skin of Nemean lion); Ovid. *Met.* 9.188 ff. (Helm).

[2] E.g. the syrinx story in Longus 2.34, in which a maiden refuses Pan, sinks into a fen, and becomes a reed from which Pan makes a pipe. Cf. Achilles Tatius 8.6.7. Merkelbach draws attention to the reed's being the holy plant of the Nile, but this connexion with Isis is fanciful.

[3] Bieler, 247 (Binder/Merkelbach, 340): 'Was Psyche aus der Unterwelt holen soll, ist gleichfalls das Wasser des Lebens. Demnach sind die dritte und vierte Arbeit Dubletten.' The Latin at 6.16.4 f. suggests that the salve of 'formonsitas' has been used for Cupid's healing, and that Venus needs more for her own ravaged appearance.

cadian Styx described by his contemporary Pausanias,[1] and the incidental details of the trial all suggest a locale above the earth. In all probability Apuleius is here investing his folk-lore version of a third difficult test with mythological additions. The dragons on guard convey more than a hint of the visit of Hercules to the gardens of the Hesperides;[2] and the mythological model for Psyche's task may well have been Iris' journey to fetch water to the gods from the Styx for the purposes of oaths.[3] Like the reed in the second trial, the eagle seems to have been added from mythology as Cupid's agent—a touch inspired by the story of Ganymede and necessitated by the disability of Cupid in Apuleius' narrative.

The fourth and final task, Psyche's journey to Hades, is a re-creation in mythological terms of the journey to the second witch in the folk-tale. The theme of κατάβασις permits Apuleius to present Psyche's journey as a symbolic expression of Lucius' initiation into the Isiac mysteries. On to the theme of the visit to the sister-witch, now translated into the mythological Persephone, is grafted a series of mythological and literary motifs. First, Psyche is advised about her journey by a tower from which she seeks to throw herself, and this tower—surely a literary borrowing from Aristophanes[4]—is the counselling counterpart of ants, reed and eagle in the earlier tasks. Secondly, the advice to Psyche on how to deport herself in Hades is virtually a mosaic of Virgil's description of Aeneas' journey to Hell in *Aeneid VI*.[5]

Psyche duly emerges safe from the realms of the dead with the box which she is forbidden to open. But just as earlier her *curiositas* led her to contravene Cupid's instruction, so now it is the cause of her disobeying Venus.[6] She opens the box to find

---

[1] Paus. 8.17.6 ff.   [2] The point is developed by Helm.

[3] Hesiod, *Theog.* 780 ff.; cf. Apul. *Met.* 6.15.4. I must again express a debt to Mr Wright's patient schooling here.

[4] At *Frogs*, 129 ff., Heracles tells Dionysus to mount a high tower and throw himself down—in the context of a projected journey to Hades. See Dietze, 141; Helm, 204.   [5] Above, pp. 56 f.

[6] 6.20.5: 'mentem capitur temeraria curiositate...'.

within not 'formonsitas' but the sleep of the Stygian world; this motif of the box with baneful contents is present both in versions of the folk-tale and in such myths as that of Pandora.[1] In the whole of this act the literary flavour is pronounced, but the essential lines of the folk-tale are nonetheless visible.

In the final act, the folk-tale is almost wholly abandoned. True, it is in evidence when Cupid emerges in full health to rescue Psyche by restoring the Stygian sleep to its box; but then, after scolding her for her second lapse into *curiositas*, he bids her return to Venus whilst he himself wings his way up to Jupiter. In the wholly mythological finale, he resumes his *persona* of the pert and wanton child. Jupiter jocularly rebukes him for exposing the father of the gods to adulterous relationships not only undignified but also. . .contrary to Roman law![2] He then summons the gods to assembly, announcing a fine for non-attendance.[3] Addressing them in phrases parodying senatorial procedure, he intimates his approval of the marriage; he bids Venus not to be disheartened, for he will legitimise the union and make Psyche immortal. The nuptial feast follows, with Bacchus serving the wine, Vulcan cooking, Apollo singing, and Venus dancing. 'This was Psyche's solemn marriage to Cupid, and a daughter was born to them when the time was ripe; we call her Voluptas.' Though the folk-tale ends with a wedding, the whole description here is in the tradition of Hellenistic burlesque of Olympian revelry;[4] there must have

[1] For the folk-theme, see Swahn, *ad loc.*; for Pandora, Hesiod *WD* 79 ff.; Babr. *Fab.* 58; *A.P.* 10.71.

[2] For Jupiter's catalogue of the shapes assumed to seduce maidens, editors well compare Lucian, *Dial. Deorum* 7 and Ovid *Met.* 6.103 ff.

[3] Fines were frequently exacted for non-attendance at the Roman senate in the Republic and under Augustus; see Varro *ap.* Gell. 14.7.10; Dio 54.18.3, 55.3.2 ff.: Cic. *Phil.* 1.12 with Denniston's note. (I owe these references to Mr J. R. G. Wright.) Some similar proclamation may have been announced at the time of writing to make this joke topical in the later second century, when attendance was increasingly shirked.

[4] Helm, *Lucian und Menipp* (Leipzig 1906), 160 n. 2.

been other such scenes translated into the Latin of Varronian satire on the lines of Seneca's *Apocolocyntosis.*

Such, then, is the action of *Cupid and Psyche* in relation to its predecessors, and it is worth making a speculative attempt to estimate Apuleius' original contribution on the basis of his techniques of story-telling exemplified elsewhere in *The Golden Ass.* We have seen that in many of the anecdotes inserted into the Greek framework, his artistic efforts are directed towards a synthesis of different themes assembled into an ingenious but precarious unity, and the attempt to harmonise these different strands is revealed by the existence of inconsistencies and loose ends.[1] A similar procedure may be envisaged in the composition of *Cupid and Psyche,* in which our author may have synthesised a well-known folk-story with the theme of the love of Cupid and Psyche as depicted in the poetry and art (and perhaps the love-fiction) of the Hellenistic period. The fusion is suggested above all, as we have seen, in the schizoid personality of Cupid, alternating uneasily between earnest lover and wanton boy. It is likewise indicated by the loose ends in the plot, notably when Cupid is briefed by Venus to punish Psyche yet refrains from action; when the Cupid of the folk-tale flies off unhurt but is then seriously ill in the ensuing 'Alexandrian' scene; when Psyche is suddenly characterised as Venus' slave; and when Mercury's mission to find the girl is introduced without any effect on the action. A synthesis was possible because of the fundamental similarity of theme in folk-tale and Alexandrian story, yet the levels of sophistication are so different that the two component elements can be readily distinguished. The combined story is then further developed by apposite motifs from the love-romances, by reminiscences of Platonist myth, and by the evocation of well-known scenes from Greek and Latin poetry.

Having assembled his tale in its main lines, Apuleius developed the characterisation, which is one of his distinctive

---

[1] The stories include those of Socrates, Thelyphron, the death of Charite, and the two stories in Bk. 10.

contributions to *The Golden Ass* as a whole, as the portraits of Milo, Photis and Pamphile show.[1] Thus Psyche in her naïvety and curiosity, in her timidity and piety has been drawn by an Apuleius inspired by the heroines of the Greek love-romance. Venus likewise in her domineering role as mother-in-law has been developed with the aid of Alexandrian comic portraiture. So too with the minor characters. At the earthly level the portrayal of the sisters, especially in their dialogue with each other, is typically Apuleian in wit as in inconsistency; at the divine level Ceres and Juno are likewise wittily drawn, playing out their parts as embarrassed neutrals caught between their fear of Cupid and their obligation to Venus.

Beyond these techniques of synthesis, literary ornamentation, and developed characterisation, lie the plan and purpose of the whole, which is so much more than the sum of its parts. It is instructive to review a few of the allegorical interpretations of the story; though some of these go well beyond Apuleius' conscious intentions, they serve to illustrate how *Cupid and Psyche* impresses itself on minds of different generations and disciplines as a myth of archetypal stature.

In the Christian era it soon became common to exploit Greek myths to illuminate Christian truths,[2] and Fulgentius Planciades interprets *Cupid and Psyche* as religious myth. Psyche's native city is the world, and the king and queen her father and mother represent God and matter respectively. The elder sisters are the flesh and free will, and Psyche herself the soul. Venus is lust, directing desire (Cupiditas not Cupido) towards the soul. But desire can have a good or evil aim, and on this occasion instead of seducing the soul it falls in love with it, persuading it not to seek to know the delights of desire however much flesh and free will urge it to do so. But the soul is persuaded by them, and, drawing from under a bushel a lamp ('desiderii

---

[1] For the characterisation in the *Metamorphoses*, Junghanns and Paratore, 165 ff., are useful.

[2] See H. Rahner, *Greek Myths and Christian Mystery* (English edition, London 1962).

flamma'), she sees and falls in love with desire. Cupid is burnt by the oil because 'desire blazes and implants the stain of sin on its flesh'. The soul is then deserted by desire and expelled from the royal abode. (?) At this point, where Fulgentius seems to change horses in mid-stream and visualises Psyche as Adam expelled from Paradise, he casually invites the reader to round off the allegory for himself.[1] On the original interpretation, the finale would have demanded a reconciliation of the soul with lust, and the soul's eternal marriage with desire! But much Christian typology is allusive rather than sustained, and Fulgentius presumably sees the close of the myth as representing man's reconciliation with God.

Fulgentius' interpretation is very much the child of its age, and inevitably the analysis thrown up by our own post-Freudian society is psychoanalytical. A Jungian interpretation[2] visualises the whole tale as a struggle between Psyche, the psychic development of the feminine, and Venus, the symbol of fertility. Psyche's initial marriage with death expresses the primordial notion of marriage as abduction or rape by the male, and the sisters' marriages symbolise feminine slavery in a patriarchal society. Psyche in the enchanted palace surrenders herself to the sexual bondage of Eros. He is of course content with the situation, but Psyche is induced by her sisters, who are the projection of Psyche's own suppressed matriarchal tendencies, to reassert matriarchal power by killing her husband. But once she sees her husband by the light of the lamp (which represents her consciousness) she 'emerges from the darkness of the unconscious' and loves Eros, the prick of whose arrow makes her an active lover instead of a passive one. This gesture of maturity, reflecting her developing personality,

---

[1] Fulgentius, *Mitol.* 3.6 (ed. Helm): 'si quis vero in Apuleio ipsam fabulam legerit, nostra expositionis materia quae non diximus ipse reliqua recognoscit'. Another Christian interpretation of the myth is that of Calderón, who sees the three daughters as representing paganism, Judaism, and the Church wed to Christ. See Haight, ch. 4.

[2] E. Neumann, *Amor and Psyche: The Psychic Development of the Feminine* (English edition, London 1956). See C. A. Rubino, *Class. Bull.* (1966), 65 ff.

involves separation from the masculine but growth in that real love which is the striving for higher unity. The tests which she performs symbolise victory over those masculine and feminine principles which threaten her development. Her failure in opening the box represents her surrender to the feminine desire to please Eros. Thus she sacrifices the 'masculine' gains won by her labours; she requires salvation, and Eros is able to realise his manhood by saving her.

This psychological interpretation is acute, but it relates more to the wellsprings of the original folk-tale than to any conscious aims of Apuleius himself. He visualises the tale with the same Platonist–Isiac vision which shapes the adventures of Lucius.

In the different analyses of both Fulgentius and Neumann lies more than a hint of that Platonist conception which has undoubtedly affected Apuleius' telling of the story. The Platonist implications have been developed by some scholars to posit the whole tale as a philosophical myth.[1] Psyche and her sisters are envisaged as the tripartite soul of Platonist psychology—Psyche as the rational, the others as the 'desirous' and 'spirited' parts.[2] The oracle represents the divine admonition to the rational soul to break loose and dwell in purity with Eros. But after achieving this, Psyche is visited by the longing for earthly pleasures; dislodged from her union with Eros, she falls to earth. But her fall leads to the resolution to sunder herself from things of earth, and she is finally united with Eros through Orphic initiation. Her acceptance amongst the gods means that she is freed from the cycle of rebirth and death.

No one who reads the central myth of the *Phaedrus* can fail to be struck by the similarity between Plato's account of the pilgrimage of the soul and Apuleius' version of the pilgrimage of Psyche. One may—and one should—dispute the overheated imaginings by which every detail of the folk-tale is fitted into

[1] Above, p. 207 n. 1.

[2] Psyche is τὸ λογιστικόν, the sisters τὸ ἐπιθυμητικόν and τὸ θυμοειδές (Plato *Rep.* 440). I am sceptical of Apuleius' having conceived the allegory in such technical detail, especially as the 'spirited' part is not invariably opposed to the rational in Plato's scheme. The schism in Apuleius is rather between soul and body.

the philosophical scheme; but the totally opposed view that the *philosophus Platonicus Madaurensis* is completely indifferent to the symbolic implications of the story is even more foolish, especially if we recall that his master Plato used such myths as the regular vehicle of his teaching.

This Platonist interpretation can clearly be harmonised with the Isiac message which crowns the whole *Metamorphoses*. It is, however, important not to exaggerate this Isiac element. The ingenious but misguided interpretation by which the entire myth has been visualised as a detailed description of Isiac initiation[1] has tended to discredit the whole line of approach in a most unfortunate way.[2] The comprehensive attempt is wrong-headed because it presses into service basic folk-lore elements as if Apuleius had introduced them to describe Isiac belief or ritual,[3] and because the pattern of the story thus interpreted strains all credibility.[4] We have seen that the importance of the Psyche story vis-à-vis the Isiac mysteries is as a

---

[1] See now Merkelbach's *Roman und Mysterium* (München 1962), developing his article in *Philol.* (1958), 103 ff., and the earlier speculations on these lines of Kerényi and Altheim.

[2] E.g., Perry, *The Ancient Romances*, 336 n. 17: 'This is all nonsense to me.'

[3] See Merkelbach, 8 ff., where, for example, the 'funereus thalamus' of Psyche is interpreted as the mystical death and rebirth; Psyche's journey to the rock as the initiate's profession; the Zephyr as the machine of the mystery-cult; the bath in the palace as the ritual baptism; Eros' visit the *hieros gamos* of the unseen priest, and so on. The comment of Lancel, *Rev. hist. rel.* (1961), 38 n. 3, is just: 'C'est trop délibérément méconnaître l'universalité du thème dans le mythe et le folklore.'

[4] Merkelbach keeps so many balls in the air that his thesis is difficult to summarise. The line of argument by which he suggests that Psyche equals Io equals Isis (so that Psyche's wanderings symbolise the journey of Isis herself) is tenable for so long as it steers clear of the significant detail of the story. The concomitant thesis that Psyche's vision of Eros in the palace symbolises the revelation of the Isiac mystery, after which the initiate spends the rest of her life on pilgrimage in the service of the goddess, likewise falls down as soon as we remember that the whole economy of Apuleius' story, by which Psyche's disobedience is depicted *as a sin* of *curiositas*, suggests otherwise. The notion of the initiate's brief vision robs the story of its point.

parable of Lucius' own pilgrimage; in other words, the climax of Psyche's adventures, once she has submitted to Venus' dominion, foreshadows the submission and initiation of Lucius. Only in the fourth act of the story, where Psyche voluntarily undergoes her trials, does the Isiac interpretation shape the career of Psyche in detail; but the theological framework is already in position, so to say, for this climax to the tale. By verbal correspondences and motifs too close to be coincidental, Apuleius aligns the trials of Psyche with the initiation of Lucius. A close reading of the eleventh book of *The Golden Ass* enables us to see clearly how Lucius' conversion is thus prefigured in Psyche's final adventures. In this sense one may speak of *Cupid and Psyche* as a Platonist myth proceeding to an Isiac conclusion.

So Psyche, after the toils of her wanderings, prays to Ceres and then to Juno, just as Lucius prays to the Queen of heaven, who is these and all other goddesses in one.[1] When Isis reveals and describes herself to Lucius, she pronounces herself identical with the Venus of the Psyche story, showing that Venus and Isis are one deity with different roles—Venus the testing goddess and Isis the *Fortuna videns*.[2] Just as Lucius' adoration of Isis is to continue in this life and the next,[3] so Psyche achieves immortality after her pilgrimage on earth. Above all, Psyche's fourth trial, the journey to the realms of death, is visualised as a projection of Lucius' initiation. Psyche observes the necessary silence, encounters on her journey 'a limping ass and a similar groom' whom she is to ignore, and carries back a box not to be opened. In all these respects she evokes the experiences of Lucius. For him too *taciturnitas* is enjoined; the groom with his ass must symbolise Typhon, for he appears in the triumphal procession of Isis witnessed by

---

[1] 6.2–4. Note the words in the second prayer, 'in tantis exanclatis laboribus...libera', and compare 11.2.4, 'saevis exanclatis casibus'.

[2] At 11.5, where Isis describes herself as 'rerum naturae parens, elementorum omnium domina, saeculorum progenies initialis', just as Venus did at 4.30.1, she further stresses that she and Venus are one.

[3] 11.6.5: 'adusque terminos ultimi spiritus...et cum...ad inferos demearis...'.

Lucius, as does the box which is not be to opened.[1] And in general, when Lucius describes his initiation ('accessi confinium mortis, et calcato Proserpinae limine... nocte media vidi solem candido coruscantem lumine, deos inferos et deos superos accessi coram et adoravi de proxumo'),[2] the mystical death and rebirth, the communion with the gods below and the gods above echo the experiences of Psyche in the underworld and on Olympus. There she is reunited with Cupid, whom she earlier calls her *lumen in tenebris*.

The lesson to be gained from a survey of modern research is a salutary one. A series of specialised enquiries has established *Cupid and Psyche* as a folk-tale wittily retold, as the creative synthesis of a series of mythological motifs, as a sustained philosophical myth, as the re-enactment in fiction of the ritual of Isiac initiation. Frequently these theses have been urged against each other. There is an urgent need to qualify the exaggerations implicit in each, and to achieve a synthesis by the reconciliation of views which are all in part valid. The story is essentially the folk-tale of enchanted suitor and lovelorn maiden united with the Hellenistic theme of Cupid and Psyche, and the essentially simple presentation which marked the first can be glimpsed within its literary setting, and distinguished from the sophisticated Alexandrian vision of the second. In uniting the two elements, Apuleius has overlaid his whole composition with the pervasive literary reminiscences which are an inherent part of all ancient fiction. The story which emerges is at once simple and contrived, at once moving and amusing. But it is not told merely as a story for its own sake. Viewed as the projection of Lucius' career into the world of myth, the history of Psyche presents a vision of the progress of the human soul alienated from the true reality, yet searching unceasingly for it and being eventually admitted to it by initiation into the mysteries. It is in this sense that Apuleius can be said to have shaped the tale into a Platonist–Isiac myth.

[1] 6.18.4 'tacita', 11.22.1 'probabili taciturnitate'; the ass, 6.18.4 and 11.8.4; the 'cista secretorum', 6.19.7 and 11.11.2.   [2] 11.23.7.

8

'NACHLEBEN': THE ROMAN NOVEL AND THE REBIRTH OF THE PICARESQUE

But the question arises: did these innovators create in a vacuum when portraying people of their own sort, or did they operate within a tradition which was able to contribute something from an earlier time to their conceptions of realism?

MARGARET SCHLAUCH, *Antecedents of the English Novel 1400–1600*, 4

The *Satyricon* and the *Metamorphoses*, it has been suggested, begin from a common starting-point in the theory of the comic romance. Set in the Milesian tradition, they describe the sensational adventures of Encolpius and of Lucius in their travels, with satirical portraits of the persons they encounter. The *Metamorphoses*, however, differs decisively in purpose from its predecessor. The *Satyricon* was intended solely to entertain; Apuleius seeks simultaneously to entertain and to improve. This difference in conscious intention is to dictate the later history of the two novels. Petronius' fiction has never exercised a momentous influence in European letters; with the possible exceptions of Voltaire and T. S. Eliot, no major figure since the Renaissance has been an enthusiastic participator in his minority-cult. Apuleius' influence on the other hand has been considerable.[1] The tag from the *Ars Poetica* epitomising

---

[1] So M. Menéndez Pelayo, *Orígenes de la Novela*, I, 25, rightly comments: 'Petronio ha influído muy poco en la literatura moderna. Los antiguos humanistas no le citaban ni le comentaban más que en latín;... Apuleyo, en quien la obscenidad es menos frecuente y menos inseparable del fondo del libro, ha recreado con sus portentosas invenciones a todos los pueblos cultos, y muy especialmente a los españoles e italianos ...muy particularmente nuestro género picaresco de los siglos XVI y XVII, y su imitación francesca el *Gil Blas*, deben algo a Apuleyo, si no en la materia de sus narraciones, en el cuadro general novelesco, que se presta a una holgada representación de la vida humana en todos los estados y condiciones de ella.'

Apuleius' approach, 'omne tulit punctum qui miscuit utile dulci', is regularly quoted in the prefaces to the picaresque novels of Spain and France. The progress of the anti-hero, simultaneously entertaining and didactic, warns the reader against the descent into moral degeneration of a Guzmán or a Gil Blas, and, in the development of this theme of the man who experiences degradation but gains salvation at the eleventh hour, the Apuleian *asinarius* is frequently evoked.

Yet the influence of the Romans on the picaresque novel in Spain, France and Britain is by no means confined to this Apuleian didactic pattern of degeneration followed by redemption. The fact is that the structure and form of the realistic novel in Alemán, Le Sage and Fielding is essentially that of Apuleius and Petronius, and it is all too often wrongly assumed that the Roman comic romances have no place in, or influence on, the history of the picaresque. One recent study makes no mention of either Roman author from beginning to end; *Lazarillo de Tormes* is 'the first example of the genre'. For another critic, 'The modern novel is born when realism first supplants the fanciful idealistic romance, namely the novels of chivalry, and this realism is ushered in with the Spanish pícaro.'[1] Yet another critic explains how the realistic novels manifested this reaction against the chivalric romances, with the inference that writers like Alemán were unaware that their path had already been trodden in antiquity.[2] Such a view underestimates the impact on European letters of the rediscovery of Petronius and Apuleius in the Italy of the Renaissance, and ignores the respect for the Classical tradition so dominant in Spain.

The English reader may obtain the clearest notion of the essential similarity between the form of the Roman novel and that of the later picaresque by perusal of the novels of Fielding,

[1] R. Alter, *Rogue's Progress: Studies in the Picaresque Novel* (Harvard 1964): A. A. Parker, *Literature and the Delinquent* (Edinburgh 1967).
[2] H. Warner Allen, 'The Picaresque Novel—an Essay in Comparative Literature', in Mabbe's *Celestina* (London 1923). This view is predominant in modern criticism on the picaresque.

who is the author who brings the genre to its climax. A fine Classical scholar, Fielding has little time for 'the unjustly celebrated Petronius';[1] yet the structure, presentation, and indeed the whole theory of the comic novel as he expounds it reflect the Petronian practice. Take, for example, the views expressed at the outset of *Joseph Andrews*:

Now a comic romance is a comic epic poem in prose, differing from comedy as the serious epic from tragedy, its action being more extended and comprehensive, containing a much larger circle of incidents, and introducing a great variety of characters. It differs from the serious romance in its fable and action in this, that as in the one these are grave and solemn, so in the other they are light and ridiculous: it differs in its characters by introducing persons of inferior rank, and consequently of inferior manners, whereas the grave romance sets the highest before us; lastly in its sentiments and diction by preserving the ludicrous instead of the sublime. In the diction, I think, burlesque itself may be sometimes admitted, of which many instances will occur in this work, as in the description of the battles, and some other places not necessary to be pointed out to the classical reader, for whose entertainment those parodies or burlesque imitations are chiefly calculated.

This description is as relevant to the action of the *Satyricon* as to that of *Joseph Andrews*. Encolpius is precisely the comic perversion of the epic hero, encountering 'persons of inferior rank' who manifest 'inferior manners'. The basic pattern of Fielding's novels, in which the episodic adventures of the hero are interspersed with anecdotes and cultural discussions, is anticipated in Petronius. It is moreover a striking fact that Fielding was stimulated to embark on *Joseph Andrews* through exasperation at the success of Richardson's *Pamela, or Virtue Rewarded*, which ran through six editions in 1740–1; *Shamela* (1741) exposes the vulnerable facets of Richardson's novel, and *Joseph Andrews* (1742) makes the point that Fielding's characters are flesh and blood ('Every thing is copied from the Book of Nature'), unlike the unassailable Pamela so eulogised by

[1] In the *Covent Garden Journal* for 3 March 1752, Fielding remarks that the epistles of St Paul contain more wit than 'the unjustly celebrated Petronius'.

contemporary clerics.[1] Petronius likewise, it has been suggested earlier, was stimulated to write in reaction against the Greek ideal romances. Fielding was of course following the example of *Don Quixote*, which Cervantes composed as a salutary corrective to the fabulous view of life enshrined in such romances as *Amadis the Gaul*. If Cervantes pointed the way for Fielding, may not the Romans have similarly inspired the Spanish reaction?

But the most striking correspondence between Fielding and the Roman novelists lies in the literary texture. The comic introduction of mythological themes for a bombastic exordium is a favourite device of the English novelist:

Now the rake Hesperus had called for his breeches, and having well rubbed his drowsy eyes, prepared to dress himself for all night; by whose example his brother rakes on earth likewise leave those beds in which they had slept away the day. Now Thetis, the good housewife, began to put on the pot, in order to regale the good man Phoebus after his daily labours were over. In vulgar language, it was the evening, when Joseph attended his lady's orders.[2]

The technique is similar to Apuleius', but more overtly comic; Fielding likewise guys the epic simile, for example when describing in *Tom Jones* the descent of Mrs Deborah Wilkins on the parish, in search of the foundling's mother.[3]

There is a patterning after epic episodes similar to that of the Roman novel, as when Tom and Molly Seagrim retire into the thickest part of the grove like Aeneas and Dido. There they are disturbed by Fortune (who maintains her interest in the picaresque throughout its history) with the sudden arrival of Mr Thwackum the Divine and Master Blifil. Here Fielding splendidly adapts the Virgilian description:

> Speluncam Blifil, dux et divinus eandem
> Deveniunt...[4]

[1] See M. C. Battestin's Introduction to his edition of *Joseph Andrews* (Oxford 1967).

[2] *Joseph Andrews* I, 8 ('In which, after some very fine writing, the history goes on...').

[3] *Tom Jones* I, 6: 'Not otherwise than when a kite, tremendous bird, is beheld by the feathered generation soaring aloft...'.

[4] v, 1; cf. *Aen.* 4.124 f.

The dialogue which follows between Thwackum[1] and Tom has the same scholastic overtones as the dialogues of the *Satyricon*. But perhaps the best example of Fielding's classically comic style is the description of Sophia, where his romantic affections are amusingly restrained by ironical quotation:

Her eyebrows were full, even, and arched beyond the power of art to imitate. Her black eyes had a lustre in them which all her softness could not extinguish. Her nose was exactly regular, and her mouth, in which were two rows of ivory, exactly answered Sir John Suckling's descriptions in those lines

> Her lips were red, and one was thin,
> Compared to that was next her chin.
> Some bee had stung it newly.[2]

It would be misleading to suggest that this highly literary texture of Fielding's fiction is representative of the picaresque tradition as a whole; he is the most widely read of realistic novelists, and in particular an avid admirer of Lucian, so that he had a knowledge of the techniques of ancient satirical fiction. Yet the more general connexions between the Roman comic romances and the later picaresque as a whole justify a brief survey of the later fortunes of Petronius and Apuleius, and a re-examination of the extent of their influence on Spanish, French and English fiction.

Habent sua fata libelli, but the fate of the *Satyricon* and the *Metamorphoses* during late antiquity and the medieval period contains few surprises. Though the sub-literary genre receives few public acknowledgments, the two novels were widely read up to the sixth century. Petronius is quoted or mentioned by Terentius Maurus in the second century, by several grammarians and by St Jerome in the fourth, by Macrobius, Sidonius Apollinaris, Marius Mercator and sundry commentators in the fifth, and by Boethius and Fulgentius Planciades in the sixth; and even after that learned men like Isidore

---

[1] The descriptive names in Fielding are of course another point of connexion; so also in Smollett.
[2] IV, 2.

reveal their acquaintance with him.[1] Apuleius' fame is likewise signalled from the second century to the sixth. The Caesar Clodius Albinus, a fellow-African, is known to have read the *Metamorphoses* before his death in 197. In the fourth century, Lactantius, Jerome, Ausonius reveal acquaintance with the novel; Augustine repeatedly mentions it, and clearly it had a vogue in Africa. The tale of Cupid and Psyche inspired the beginning of Martianus Capella's *Marriage of Philology and Mercury* in the fifth century, and Fulgentius Planciades provides an interpretation of the myth in the sixth. Macrobius, Sidonius Apollinaris, Cassiodorus are others who mention the *Metamorphoses*.[2]

Subsequently, however, the novels are rarely in evidence during the period of the Middle Ages. Eric of Auxerre in the ninth century shows acquaintance with a poem in the *Satyricon*, the *carmen de bello civili*, and it is believed that the *codex Bernensis*, written about 850, may have been at Auxerre at that time. Most of the subsequent citations of Petronius up to the twelfth century are at second hand; in particular, the story of the inventor of unbreakable glass, whose death was ordered by a Roman emperor, is related by Guido of Arezzo and by Peter Damian in the eleventh century, and in the twelfth by Hildebert of Lavardin.[3] But there is no doubt that Petronius was known at Chartres in the twelfth century. Theodoric of Chartres, in his commentary on Cicero's *De Inventione*, quotes from the *Satyricon*—'ut ait Petronius, nos magistri in scolis soli relinquemur'.[4] John of Salisbury, whose connexions with the school of Chartres are well known, shows close acquaintance with the novel. In his *Policraticus* (1159), he quotes the verses 'grex agit in scaena...', and adds 'quod fere totus mundus iuxta Petronium exerceat histrionem'.[5] Elsewhere in the

[1] The references are gathered in Collignon, *Pétrone en France*, ch. 1; see also the fragments of Petronius in Müller's edition, 185 ff.

[2] See Haight, *Apuleius and his Influence*, ch. 4.

[3] I take these references from Manitius, *Gesch. der lat. Lit. des Mittelalt.*

[4] *Sat.* 3.

[5] This passage inspired the motto for the Globe theatre, and indirectly the Shakespearian speech 'All the world's a stage...'. See *Policr.* 3.8.

Policraticus, and in his correspondence, John shows acquaintance with the *Cena Trimalchionis*,[1] showing that there existed at Chartres a manuscript or manuscripts containing all of Petronius that we possess today. (This is the sole evidence of the existence of the *Cena* before the fifteenth century; the *codex Traguriensis*, the sole manuscript containing it, was copied then after Poggio's discovery but was once more lost until 1650).[2] There is also a school-curriculum dating to later in the twelfth century which recommends Martial and Petronius ('Both contain much that is useful, but likewise things unworthy of hearing.')[3] And in the following century Vincent of Beauvais quotes several excerpts from the *Satyricon*.[4] If *florilegia* are discounted, the total picture of Petronius in the Middle Ages is of a precarious survival in France alone until the manuscripts proliferate in the fifteenth century.

Apuleius' chief claim to fame in these medieval centuries is as magician and as Platonist philosopher; there is little clear evidence of first-hand knowledge of the *Metamorphoses* before the twelfth century. All the manuscripts that we possess are descended from one copied at Monte Cassino in the eleventh century;[5] this was the rescue-operation which gave the novel a wider currency from 1100 onward. Petrus Pictor's *De illa quae impudenter filium suum adamavit*, written about 1100, derives from Apuleius' *novella* about the infatuated step-mother. Some believe that Apuleius made his way to Britain in the twelfth century, for Geoffrey of Monmouth's account of the birth of Merlin (whose mother claims to have been visited by an invisible lover) bears some resemblance to the Cupid and Psyche story. But the claim of a directly Apuleian influence is

---

[1] *Policr.* 8.7: 'Cenam Trimalchionis, si potes, ingredere, et porcum sic gravidari posse miraberis, nisi forte admirationem multiplex ignota et inaudita luxuria tollat...'. *Ep.* 112: 'licet Mandrogerus grunniat, Trimalchio intabescat, rideat Bromius...'.

[2] See K. Müller's edition of Petronius, xxxiii f.

[3] Haskins, *HSCP* (1909), 75, attributes it to Alexander Neckam.

[4] *Speculum Historiale* 21.25.

[5] For this manuscript (F), see Robertson's Introduction to his Budé text, xxxviii.

contested,[1] for there is no evidence for a knowledge of the *Metamorphoses* in France before the mention by Vincent of Beauvais in the thirteenth century, and it is accordingly improbable that the novel was known earlier in Britain. Subsequently copies proliferate in the fourteenth and fifteenth centuries, and manuscripts survive from Italy, France and Britain.

Poggio played the vital role in restoring the fortunes of Petronius at the time of the Renaissance. His discovery of Petronian manuscripts in Britain in 1420 and at Cologne in 1423[2] occurred at a time when Petronius was unknown in Italy. Poggio tells his friend Niccolo Niccoli:

De Petronio Arbitro quod scire cupis quid tractet, lege Macrobii principium super somnio Scipionis, ubi enumerans genera fabularum dicit in eis esse argumenta fictis amatorum casibus referta, quibus multum se Arbiter exercuit. Est autem homo gravis versu et prosa constans, et ut conicio paulo post tempora Augusti.[3]

One of these two discoveries fathers a dozen manuscripts copied later in the fifteenth century, and the other is the sole manuscript of the *Cena*, which was lost, stolen or suppressed while in Niccolo's possession, and did not reappear till 1650. With the invention of printing, the *editio princeps* appeared at Milan in 1482, to be reprinted at Venice in 1499 and at Paris in 1520; an improved text by Sambucus was published at Antwerp in 1565. Meanwhile in England Daniel Rogers had written out virtually the whole of the *codex Londiniensis* in his own hand by 1572, and this was utilised by Douza, who in 1585 produced at Paris one of several editions of Petronius appearing shortly before or after 1600. One of these was the work of the Spanish scholar Gonzales de Salas, and was published at Frankfurt in 1619.

The licentious content of the *Satyricon* was thus becoming known more widely than ever before, winning notoriety for

---

[1] For the controversy, see Manitius, III, 479; Haight, ch. 4.

[2] See K. Müller's edition, VIII f., XXVIII ff.

[3] Poggio Bracciolini *Epistolae*, ed. T. de Tonellis (1832, repr. Turin 1963), 1.7. Cf. 2.3, 3.3, 4.2 ff.

those scholars working on the text. The great Scaliger was attacked in a pamphlet in 1609 by Caspar Schoppius, who accused him of studying Petronius for titillation.[1] It is clear therefore that any Western humanist with a pretence to Latin scholarship must have been aware of the nature of Petronius' novel by the end of the sixteenth century; but the fragmentary nature of the text, the absence of the *Cena*, and the scabrous content militated against a wide diffusion of the novel.

Apuleius on the other hand wins a larger public. He had already become well known in Italy during the fourteenth century through the enthusiasm of Boccaccio, who in 1355 discovered a manuscript of *The Golden Ass* at Monte Cassino and transcribed it with his own hand. The *Decameron* contains three stories from the *Metamorphoses*, and Apuleius becomes a favourite quarry in the subsequent history of the *novella*.[2] Henceforward *The Golden Ass* is to exercise a threefold influence on the history of fiction. First, it stimulates a variety of ass-stories, not only in Italy (where Bruno's *Cabala* takes as its theme that the greatest asses are the most honoured!) but also in other countries of western Europe; and the image of the picaro as ass is a frequent feature of rogue-literature. Secondly, the Cupid and Psyche story has its own remarkable history, from the version of Boccaccio in his *Genealogy of the Gods* to Walter Pater's celebrated translation in *Marius the Epicurean*. In the seventeenth century alone the theme is handled by Calderón and by Antonio de Solis in Spain, by La Fontaine and jointly by Molière, Corneille and Quinault in France, and by Thomas Heywood, by Joseph Beaumont and by Marmion in England.[3] Thirdly, other stories of Apuleius, especially those of cuckolded husbands, repeatedly find their way into the collections of *novelle* such as de la Sale's *Cent nouvelles nouvelles*,

[1] *Scaliger Hypobolimaeus* by Caspar Schoppius ('acerbissimus maledicentissimus Scaligeri obtrectator') (Mainz 1609).

[2] *Decameron*, 5.10, 7.2, 8.8; see in general Di Francia, *Novellistica* I (Milan 1924).

[3] For the later history of Cupid and Psyche, see Purser's edition, lxv ff., with more detailed bibliography.

which appeared in the fifteenth century and was rendered into English as *The Deceyte of Women* in the sixteenth.[1]

The writings of Apuleius were amongst the first classical books printed after 1465.[2] After the *editio princeps* of all his surviving works was published at Rome in 1469, further imprints appeared at Vicenza, Venice, Milan and Florence in the ensuing fifty years, and separate editions of *The Golden Ass* were produced at Bologna, Venice and Paris during the same period. The sixteenth century saw a remarkable proliferation of editions throughout Europe, and even more significantly of translations into every major vernacular. In Italy, Boiardo's translation appeared in 1508, to be reprinted several times before being overshadowed in 1550 by the version of Firenzuola, which in its numerous reissues became one of the most widely read books in Europe. In Germany, Johan Sieder's translation appeared at Augsburg in 1538. Adlington's English version was published first in 1566, and is still a source of revenue to modern publishers. There were two French versions in the sixteenth century, that of Temporal and that of Louveau d'Orléans. Most significantly of all for the later history of the picaresque novel, *The Golden Ass* becomes a great favourite in Spain, where a translation usually attributed to Diego López de Cortegana appeared as early as 1513, to be rapidly followed by two others, so that Apuleius was one of the best-known writers of fiction in the sixteenth century.[3]

---

[1] E.g., *The Deceyte*, no. 2, a development of the first story in *Cent nouvelles nouvelles*, describes how a wife in dalliance with a neighbour rushes back to her own house on the approach of her husband. 'And when that he came afore his house, he saw that there was yet light in it and knocked at the door...and she asked who was there, and he sayd: "I am he thy husband"...She set her hands in her syde, and sayde, "Thou noughty knave, this haste thou done for to prove me, and I tell thee thou art not worthy for to have so honest a wyfe."' Compare Apuleius, *Met.* 9.5.3 ff.

[2] Details in R. R. Bolgar, *The Classical Heritage* (Cambridge 1954), 276; Sandys, *History of Classical Scholarship*[3], II, 96.

[3] Medina del Campo's translation appeared in 1543, and Amberes' in 1551; see Menéndez Pelayo, *Orígenes*, IV, 260; cf. E. C. Riley, *Cervantes' Theory of the Novel* (Oxford 1962), 207.

Such is the influence of the Roman comic fiction widely diffused through Europe at the rebirth of the picaresque novel in Spain in the sixteenth century, which surely justifies this nineteenth-century assessment of its influence on Spanish rogue-literature:

Encolpius in the *Satyricon* of Petronius Arbiter has been hailed as the forerunner of Spanish rogues, and the facts that most of the Peninsular picaresque authors were classicists, and that Petronius in the sixteenth and seventeenth centuries had a special vogue, have been adduced as proving a probable bond between the *Satyricon* and the romances of roguery. But the low-life adventures of the decadent voluptuary, or the excesses of the feast of Trimalchio, have little in common with the shifts of the unfortunate rascal in service. The *Ass* of Apuleius in his changes of masters bore a closer analogy to the picaro and his vicissitudes than any other classic type; yet Lucius, the man beneath the ass's hide, was no rogue but rather the victim of unhappy chance and his own curiosity. Allowing, however, for the absence of roguery in the hero, the *Golden Ass* may be deemed an important model for the picaresque novel. Beyond the fact that its incidents were taken bodily into the Spanish and subsequent fictions, this fable undoubtedly furnished to the first romances of roguery the essential idea of describing society through the narrative of one in servitude whose passage from master to master should afford opportunities for observation and satire. The method of Petronius[1] is faithfully copied even to the insertion of anecdote and extraneous incident, and the resemblance throughout remains too strong to have been purely fortuitous. In the course of most of the Spanish novels too, the *Ass* receives honourable mention, and the *Picara Justina* expressly proposes it among others as a pattern.[2]

To express the matter more briefly and with more precision, the *Satyricon* is the first known picaresque novel, and Encolpius as peripatetic rogue is the forbear of the heroes of the Spanish, French and English picaresque traditions, being precisely 'the amusing rogue or vagabond', the 'delinquent'

---

[1] Did Chandler mean Apuleius?

[2] F. W. Chandler, *Romances of Roguery* (Columbia 1899), 3 f. It should be noted that the *Cena Trimalchionis* was unknown at the turn of the sixteenth century, and so the absence of its influence is hardly surprising! The scholar cited as espousing the theory of Petronian influence is Jan Ten Brink, *Eene Studie over den Hollandschen Schelmenroman der zeventiende eeuw* (Rotterdam 1885).

or 'offender against the moral and civil laws' which is the proper definition of the picaro.[1] But Petronius' influence is chiefly oblique; the Spanish realistic novelists must have known *about* the *Satyricon* and the kind of work it was, but they know *The Golden Ass* intimately, and the theme of the ass in service to a series of masters, many of them satirically depicted, is a reorientation of the Petronian form in the direction of fable. The first Spanish picaresque novel, *Laʒarillo de Tormes,* reveals no direct debt to Petronius but the general influence of *The Golden Ass.* Mateo Alemán on the other hand is a man of greater learning, and when we find in *Guʒmán de Alfarache* the kind of leisured discussions which are a feature in Petronius but not in Apuleius, it is reasonable to assume that Alemán (like many sixteenth-century humanists with Italian connexions) not only knew Apuleius,[2] but had also seen one or other of the Italian editions of the *Satyricon,* and was aware of its characteristics. This exploitation of the Roman tradition in no sense detracts from the originality of Alemán, for under the impetus of native religious, political and cultural circumstances he develops the literary tradition in a wholly new direction.

It is important to realise how prominently the romantic fiction of antiquity remained as a model during the later Middle Ages and the Renaissance. The first known Spanish work of fiction, *El Cavallero Cifar,* which dates from about 1300, attempts to win readers by the bogus claim that it is 'translated from the Chaldean into Latin, and from Latin into Romance'. The author of *Amadis the Gaul* claims that he corrected it 'from old originals'.[3] The Latin romance *Apollonius of Tyre* (the ultimate source of Shakespeare's *Pericles*) was a perennial favourite, and inspired (besides Boccaccio's *Filostrato* and *Fiametta* and Aeneas Sylvius' *De duobus*

---

[1] See Parker, *Literature and the Delinquent,* ch. 1.

[2] Chapelain, in his French translation of Alemán (1619), considers *Guʒmán* better than 'both its models, *The Golden Ass* and *Laʒarillo*' (quoted by Parker, ch. 5).

[3] See H. Thomas, *Spanish and Portugese Romances of Chivalry* (Cambridge 1920), 3 ff.

amantibus) Diego de San Pedro's *Arnalto y Lucenda* (1491); moreover, many of the Greek romances were translated into Latin in the sixteenth century, and it has been suggested that Heliodorus' *Ethiopian Story* is a direct influence on Alemán.[1] Cervantes' comments about the romances of chivalry demonstrate how they retain the essential structure of the ancient novel, and how they are visualised within that frame. He himself is certainly aware of the existence of 'Milesian fables' in antiquity.[2] Hence it is too doctrinaire to claim that Petronius was wholly unknown by sixteenth-century Spanish writers, but Apuleius is the really influential figure through whom is mediated the effect of the Roman tradition upon the Spanish.

Lazarillo de Tormes (1554)[3] is the story of a boy who begins life with every disadvantage, and who after serving a blind man passes successively into the service of a priest, a squire, a friar, a pardoner, a chaplain, and a constable before finally obtaining a government appointment and a wife. As in Apuleius, the humorous account of Lazarillo's adventures is synthesised with a satirical portrayal of most but not all of his masters. The capricious cruelty of the blind man is followed by the stinginess of the cleric. ('Compared with this priest, the blind man was Alexander the Great.') But the Escudero is not satirised, and in fact the strongest criticism is directed against the hypocritical religious observance of the pardoner. This social satire is clearly in reaction against the contemporary religious abuses, and the Christian writings of the previous thirty years may have encouraged the anonymous author in initiating this movement in fiction from idealism to realism.[4] Yet in Apuleius' novel too the most severe satire is directed against the bogus priests, so that *The Golden Ass* deserves more comparative study here than it appears to have received; the

---

[1] D. MacGrady, 'Heliodorus' influence on Mateo Alemán', *Hisp. Rev.* (1966), 49–53.

[2] *Don Quixote*, 1.47. But Cervantes includes romances of chivalry under this title, so that he may be referring to the ideal romances.

[3] There is an English translation by Markham (London 1908).

[4] See Parker's illuminating comments, 20 ff.

eunuch priests of Atargatis are, so to say, the pardoners of the Greek world of the second century.[1]

In Alemán's *Guzmán de Alfarache* (1599/1604),[2] the influence of Apuleius is implicit from the initial declaration. 'This Booke divides it selfe into three parts. In the first it is treated of Guzman de Alfarache's going forth of his mother's house, and the slender consideration of young men in those endevours which they attempt: and how, though their eye-sight be cleere, they will not see, precipitated and blinded with their false pleasures. . .' As this passage proceeds, one is reminded more and more of the sermon of the Isiac priest in the last book of the *Metamorphoses*, and it is interesting to note in this connexion the description in *Guzmán* of the Egyptian festival of Isis, who as in Apuleius is described as the goddess of Fortune.[3] There are moreover repeated allusions to Guzmán as an ass, suggesting that the Apuleian story had been recognised in Spain as having a symbolic significance. 'The Fraternity of Asses is a great brotherhood; for even men have beene willing to bee admitted into this companie; and have been glad to yeeld themselves to carrie unclean and heavie loades with as much patience as the silliest Asse alive.'[4] Some of the anecdotes (often told, as in the Roman novels, to while away a journey) may have been adapted from Apuleius.[5] So too in some of

---

[1] *Met.* 8.26 ff. It will be obvious that I am discussing the influences on *Lazarillo* from one aspect only here. The fact that the story begins from the author's birth ('It seemed to the author that he should not begin in the middle but quite at the beginning. . .') suggests the influence of romances like *Amadis the Gaul*. But the exordium, 'Well, your Honour must know before anything else that they call me Lazarillo de Tormes, and that I am the son of Thome Goncales and Antonia, natives of Tejares. . .', has its parallel in Apuleius. The biblical choice of name (cf. Luke 16.20 ff.) reflects the different social milieu.

[2] I quote from Mabbe's translation (1622).　　　　[3] 1.1.7.

[4] 1.2.2. So at 1.1.7 Guzmán feasts on a mule 'as if I should have devoured my own flesh; I mean by his father's side.' At 2.3.5 Guzmán and his wife are helped by a broker 'not for the Asse's sake but for the goddess borne by the Asse'. Cf. 1.3.1, 2.1.5, etc.

[5] So, for example, 1.2.8, the concealment in the cask; cf. *Met.* 9.5 ff., adapted by Boccaccio and Strapaiola (who is believed by Cros to be the

Guzmán's adventures Alemán seems to be invoking the experiences of Lucius for the amusement of his literary readers; for example, when Guzmán is in service to a cook, the cook's wife takes a dislike to him after a comic encounter at night; and, like Lucius hated by the miller's wife, 'backe I went to the Mille again'.[1] It need hardly be said that the technique of the I-narrative is taken over likewise from Roman fiction.[2] *Guzmán de Alfarache* is thus a Christianised *Metamorphoses*, but in spite of its discursive nature and oppressively edifying tone, it presents a clearer consistency of theme which sets it as an artistic achievement above the novel of Apuleius.

A similar Apuleian element is discernible in other Spanish novels of the period. In some, such as Úbeda's *La pícara Justina* (1605), the debt is acknowledged. In others, including Vicente Espinel's *Vida del escudero Marcos de Obregón* (1618), the attentive reader can detect the influence of Apuleius in such scenes as that enacted in the robbers' cave, or the story of the amorous barber snuffed out behind a screen by a spaniel.[3] But the Spanish picaresque is by this date well launched on its own course, and in Espinel, as in Quevedo's *Buscón* (1616), the Roman influence is less evident.[4] The same is true of *Don Quixote* (1605/15), whether it is considered as the last Spanish novel of chivalry or as a fusion of the chivalresque and picaresque genres; but Apuleian themes do appear, and to deny, for example, that Lucius' battle with the wineskins inspired the similar scene in Cervantes seems excessively sceptical.[5]

source here). Also 2.2.9, the story of the young woman pursued by two suitors, which bears some similarity to the story at *Met.* 8.1.5 ff.

[1] 1.2.6.

[2] Parker, ch. 2, believes that Augustine's *Confessions* is the model, but this seems improbable.   [3] 2.3.18, 1.1.4 (the dog replaces the ass!).

[4] Some parallels do suggest themselves. The hero's mother in Quevedo's story is a witch with some resemblances to Apuleius' Pamphile. The elderly clergyman met on the road from Alcala to Madrid is in the Eumolpus mould ('Here are 901 sonnets and 12 roundos made in praise of my mistress's legs.')

[5] *Don Quixote*, 1.35; *Met.* 2.32. The parallel is discounted by Menéndez Pelayo, IV, 244 ff., but accepted by Robinson Smith in his translation of *Don Quixote*[4] (N.Y. 1932).

In Spain, then, Apuleius is a key figure in the rebirth of the picaresque. In France, the rogue-novel as it develops in the seventeenth and eighteenth centuries is above all shaped by the Spanish tradition, but Petronius here achieves a greater though still restricted prominence.[1] The most interesting imitation of the *Satyricon* is the *Euphormionis Satyricon* (1603),[2] a work composed (significantly) in Latin by John Barclay, a Scot born and bred in France. In 1603 Barclay came to London to the court of King James in search of patronage, and the *Euphormionis Satyricon* was published in support. It became a best-seller, and was frequently republished in the following two hundred years.

Euphormio is a Scot resident in France, and the Petronian episodes are adapted to present a satirical vision of various facets of seventeenth-century social life. The Menippean texture of alternating prose and verses is used. The first scene is a lecture-hall in which a pompous lecturer is pronouncing on Roman law; here the Agamemnon-scene in the *Satyricon* is the model. Later scenes take up the theme of contemporary education, as Petronius had done; Barclay uses the anagram to disguise thinly the object of his satire, and Acignius here represents Ignatius Loyola, the founder of the Jesuit system. In a later scene, Labetrus is the Archduke Albert, governor of the Netherlands; the description of his Moorish retinue and his house, in which the walls depict Albert's pedigree and career, make one wonder if the memory of Trimalchio and his establishment can have been totally lost till 1650. In addition to the anagrammatic technique, Barclay also uses the symbolic title. There is a *Eumolpus redivivus* called Lucretius, whose

---

[1] On Petronius' influence in France, see A. Collignon, *Pétrone en France* (Paris 1905). There was a lively cult in the seventeenth century; the Matron of Ephesus theme was treated by Saint-Evremond (1665), by La Fontaine at the end of *Poème du Quinquina* (1682), and by sundry dramatists. Bussy-Rabutin's *L'Histoire amoureuse des Gaules* (1665) contains many imitations. But only Voltaire of the great eighteenth-century figures is a Petronius enthusiast (Collignon, 96).

[2] There is an English translation by Paul Turner (London 1954).

name attests his loyalties in the struggle of ancients versus
moderns, and who delivers a tirade against modern trends in
education and literature. These satirical vignettes are, as in
Petronius, interspersed with mimic scenes and sensational
adventures, in which episodes from both the *Satyricon* and
Apuleius' *Metamorphoses* are evoked. So in the second scene,
when Euphormio has no money to pay for his meal at the inn,
'Gallico gelu frigidior metus etiam intimum calorem tentavit'.[1]
Later at Basilium a mimic battle is enacted, described in the
language of mock-epic; and later still in Italy Euphormio is,
like Encolpius, lashed and branded. Apuleian touches include
Percas' ghost-story, a love-encounter in a cave described in the
language of soldiering,[2] and the legal scene in which a king is
selected for the Feast of Fools, recalling the Festival of
Laughter in Apuleius.

In general, however, the French realistic and comic fiction is
little affected by the Roman novels, and it is the Spanish
picaresque which is most influential.[3] The seventeenth-century
comic romances like Sorel's *Francion* (1623) and Scarron's
Roman Comique (1651/7), written like their predecessors in
Spain in reaction against the popular romances, have virtually
no direct classical borrowings.[4] This is also true of *Gil Blas*,
the picaresque novel of Le Sage which is generally lauded for
transforming the genre into something 'both French and
universal'.[5] Though Sorel and Scarron are formative fore-
runners, Le Sage was influenced above all by the Spaniards.
After translating Guevara's *Diablo cojuelo*, he exploited Cer-

[1] Cf. Petronius, 19.3.
[2] 'Non audis urbes obsidionum initio civium diligentia muniri, captas
non hostium quam suorum manibus concidisse?'
[3] Parker, ch. 5, counts 5 French translations of *Laẓarillo* by 1678, 18
French editions of *Guẓmán* by 1732, and 20 of *El buscón* in the seventeenth century.
[4] Cf. B. Guégan, *L'œuvre galante de Charles Sorel* (Paris 1924), iv: 'A
l'époque où fut écrit le *Francion*, on ne lisait que de fades et languissants
romans...le *Francion* fut fait des souvenirs d'enfance, de collège, et de
débauche.' For an isolated Petronian reminiscence, see Guégan, 89.
[5] So Warner Allen (p. 225 n. 2 above).

vantes and above all Espinel's *Marcos de Obregón* in *Gil Blas*.[1]
There is no Petronian influence in the book,[2] but it is tempting
to hazard that Apuleius was in Le Sage's mind when he composed the early scene set in the cavern of the brigands; this
Apuleian episode had already been exploited by Espinel, who
may have been Le Sage's source here as elsewhere. But the
description of the adventure in comically mythological terms
is Apuleian, and the lady in the cave, Donna Mencia, recounts
her experiences after the manner of Charite in Apuleius.[3]

From *Gil Blas* and France it is a logical step to the novels of
Smollett, but the student of the picaresque should first hark
back to an earlier essay in English, Thomas Nashe's *The
Unfortunate Traveller* (1594). It is sometimes suggested that
Nashe may have fallen under the spell of *Lazarillo de Tormes*,
but his story of Jack Wilton is told in a more ironical, almost
burlesque manner suggesting the influence of the Roman
novelists. Moreover the literary texture evocative of epic is in
the manner of Petronius and Apuleius. Sir Henrie Howard,
Jack's master, falls in love with his Geraldine at Hampton
Court, which is 'Cupid's inchaunted castle': he is told by his
lady to seek Italy 'like Aeneas': and at the climax, when Jack
and his lady Diamante escape down the Tiber from the
Countess Juliana, she reacts like 'a frantick Bacchinall'—in
other words, like Virgil's Dido. The structure of the story, in
which Jack meets a succession of characters satirically depicted,
is similar to that of the Roman novel, and some episodes are
reminiscent of Petronian or Apuleian scenes. The episode of
the Anabaptists of Munster recalls the bogus priests in Apuleius:
the speech of the university orator at Wittenberg ('it was all by
patch and piecemeale out of Tully') reminds us of the first
extant scene in Petronius: Tabitha the temptress is a latter-day

---

[1] On the sources of *Gil Blas*, see C. Dédéyan, *Lesage et Gil Blas* I (Paris
1965), 82 ff.

[2] Collignon, 46: 'Le Sage ne semble pas avoir lu Pétrone.'

[3] See Alter, *Rogue's Progress*, 19 f. The use of the ironical adjective ('Je
cédai à la nécessité...et dévorant ma douleur, je me préparai à servir
des *honnêtes* gens') is also Apuleian.

Quartilla.[1] There is a Milesian Tale of a wife who after being raped by a lustful Spaniard kills herself over her husband whom she believes dead, and in falling on him rouses him. And, most significantly, as in *Guzmán* the image of the ass is frequently employed to describe the attitude of the hero, suggesting that Apuleius' novel, already well known in Adlington's version of 1566, was being interpreted in its symbolic sense as in Spain.

Nashe's picaresque novel is an isolated Elizabethan phenomenon.[2] It is not until the eighteenth century that the genre becomes established in English with Defoe, Smollett and Fielding. Though Defoe's *Moll Flanders* is comparable to *La pícara Justina* and though the Spanish picaresque was very popular in England in the eighteenth century, Defoe seems to have drawn his inspiration chiefly from criminological cases, from life rather than from literature. Smollett's *Roderick Random* (1748) marks the first appearance on British soil of the continental picaro. The similarities to the conventions of the Roman novel are not attributable to a direct influence, for Smollett in both *Roderick* and in *Peregrine Pickle* is dominated by *Gil Blas*, which he translated in 1749. It is perfectly clear from the Preface to *Roderick Random* that neither Petronius nor Apuleius is visualised by Smollett as a forerunner; he names Cervantes as the true originator of realistic fiction, who 'by an inimitable piece of ridicule reformed the taste of mankind, representing chivalry in the right point of view, and converting romance to purposes far more useful and entertaining by making it assume the sock, and point out the follies of ordinary life.' He adds: 'The same method has been practised by other Spanish and French authors, and by none more successfully than by Monsieur Le Sage, who in his *Adventures of Gil Blas* has described the knavery and the foibles of life

---

[1] There are also, in the Petronian manner, formal descriptions of 'a summer banketting house' and of the antiquities of Rome ('I was at Pontius Pilate's house, and pist against it').

[2] But other types of Elizabethan fiction reflect Apuleian influence, especially the Euphuistic romances of Lyly, John Grange and others. And Jonson's *Volpone* (1605/6) shows that Petronius also was being read.

with infinite humour and sagacity. The following sheets I have modelled on his plan...'

Whereas Smollett looked to Le Sage's novel, Fielding as we have seen venerated Cervantes and derived from him the whole of his theory of the comic romance. *Joseph Andrews* and *Tom Jones* were not composed with the *Satyricon* and the *Metamorphoses* in mind, and there is now a decisive shift in the whole conception of the genre; the exemplary instruction is no longer a warning against taking the path of a Guzmán or a Gil Blas, but an implicit exhortation to imitate the positive virtues of an Abraham Adams, and to admire the decent humanity of a Tom Jones. Fielding is closely preoccupied with the didactic function of his fiction, which is to 'promote the cause of virtue', and 'to recommend virtue and innocence', and Petronius' purely comic purposes represent a wholly different intention. Yet we have seen that the generic resemblance in terms of theory and structure is perceptible, and testifies that the tradition to which Fielding is heir begins not in sixteenth-century Spain but in Neronian Rome.

Fielding is perhaps the last author in whom the classical tradition is still visible. Our own generation is sufficiently anti-chivalric to be a fertile ground for fresh developments in the picaresque, and Thomas Mann's *Memoirs of Felix Krull*, Joyce Cary's *The Horse's Mouth*, John Wain's *Hurry On Down*, and Saul Bellow's *The Adventures of Augie March* indicate that the genre has not died.[1] Now that Petronius and Apuleius are once more being widely read in translation, and Petronius is being presented by Fellini on the wide screen, it would certainly be premature to pronounce the last rites over their influence upon creative literature.

---

[1] Alter in his final chapter discusses some contemporary contributions to the picaresque.

THE DATE OF THE 'SATYRICON'

This subject has been exhaustively treated by several recent scholars. The purpose of this appendix is to summarise the arguments favouring a Neronian date, as this has been assumed throughout.

Though the date of the *Satyricon* has been a topic of controversy since the Renaissance,[1] the weight of recent opinion strongly favours the identification of the author with the Petronius described at length by Tacitus, and mentioned more briefly by the elder Pliny and by Plutarch.[2] The manuscripts of the *Satyricon* accord no *praenomen* to the author; in Tacitus at the second mention he is Gaius, but in Pliny and Plutarch he is Titus. As all three clearly refer to the same person, the problem is merely to decide who has made the mistake. It seems probable that the name in Tacitus is incorrect, and that the Petronius described in his pages is Titus Petronius Niger, consul in 62 or thereabouts.[3] This identification is not challenged by the fact that almost all the manuscripts, as well as Macrobius and Marius Victorinus, label the author of the *Satyricon* Petronius Arbiter, for Arbiter is not a *cognomen* proper but the sort of soubriquet common in ancient clubs and sodalities. So Tacitus' description *elegantiae arbiter* alludes to his nick-name at court.[4]

The arguments favouring a Neronian date for the novel, which are necessary to make persuasive the identification with the Petronius described by Tacitus, may be summarised as follows.[5] First, references to contemporaries. Second, the economic factors. Third, the literary considerations. Fourth,

---

[1] See the amusing survey of K. F. C. Rose, *Arion* (1966), 275 ff.
[2] Tac. *Ann.* 16.18 f.; Pliny, *N.H.* 37.20; Plutarch, *Moralia* 60D.
[3] See Rose, *Latomus* (1961), 821 ff.
[4] P. Veyne, *RPh* (1963), 258 f.; G. Bagnani, *Arbiter of Elegance*, 6.
[5] See Rose, *CQ* (1962), 185; Sullivan, *The Satyricon*, 22 ff.

a reference to buried treasure which may be connected with an abortive treasure-hunt in A.D. 65. Fifth, some legal evidence. Once these arguments are accepted, one may note the striking correspondences between the ethos of the novel and the character of Petronius as described by Tacitus.

Amongst the contemporaries mentioned, particularly important are the gladiator Petraites and the lyre-player Menecrates; it is surely no coincidence that men with these names were well-known performers in Nero's day.[1] There is also a reference to Apelles by Plocamus, a guest at Trimalchio's dinner, when he is recalling the heyday of his youth; now there was a well-known entertainer of that name in the reign of Gaius, and that would well accord with a dramatic date for the *Satyricon* in the Neronian age.[2] Also in the *Cena* is Hermeros' claim to be a king's son, and this may well comically refer to the suggestion that Pallas, the outstanding freedman-administrator under Claudius, was of royal blood.[3] These references depend for their comic point on their topicality, and on the ability of Petronius' contemporaries to recognise them.

Secondly, the economic conditions described in the novel reflect those of the mid-first century. Trimalchio makes his money out of wine—'tunc erat contra aurum'[4]—and this harmonises better with the situation in the first century than later.[5] Again, there are several references to the extent of *latifundia* and the exclusive use of slave-labour. This situation is most apposite to a first-century date, as the elder Pliny's celebrated lament ('latifundia perdidere Italiam') and the later growth in numbers of free tenants suggest.[6] And in general the *Cena* is a satire on *nouveaux-riches* freedmen, who become especially prominent in the Italy of the later Julio-Claudians;

---

[1] Petraites, 52.3; for the archaeological parallel, see H. T. Rowell, *TAPA* (1958), 14. Menecrates, 73.3; cf. Suet. *Nero* 30.2.

[2] 64.4; cf. Suet. *Cal.* 33.

[3] 57.4; cf. Tac. *Ann.* 12.53.2 f. So R. Browning, *CR* (1949), 28 f.

[4] 76.3.

[5] When Gallic and Spanish wine began to flood the market. See H. Schnur, *Latomus* (1959), 790 ff.

[6] Rostovtzeff, *SEHRE*, 190 ff.

the satire would lose much of its point if it were aimed at the circumstances of a previous generation.

Thirdly, there are the literary arguments. There is clear evidence that Petronius' poem *De Bello Civili* contains deliberate echoes of Lucan.[1] The end of the two poems is strikingly similar—a strong presumption that Petronius was writing between Lucan's death in April 65 and his own death about a year later, for again such parody may lose its edge if directed at a poet of an earlier age. Moreover, Eumolpus' discussion of the nature of epic is directed to a contemporary situation. A similar argument holds good for the echoes of Senecan philosophy.[2]

Fourthly, the legal arguments suggest a pre-Hadrianic date. Two passages report the summary execution of a slave by his master. Mithridates the slave is crucified 'quia Gai nostri genio male dixerat', and Glyco sends his steward into the arena to face the wild beasts because he has been discovered in adultery with his mistress.[3] These punishments *tout court* would have been impossible after Hadrian's reign.[4] In the same principate the gold ring ceased to be the symbol of equestrian rank; now Ascyltus' wearing of it is taken by Hermeros as meaning that Ascyltus is boasting equestrian rank.[5]

Finally there is the curious matter of the buried treasure. Some verses in the *Satyricon* read as follows:

> nocte soporifera veluti cum somnia ludunt
> errantes oculos effossaque protulit aurum
> in lucem tellus; versat manus improba furtum
> et mentem timor altus habet, ne forte gravatum
> excutiat gremium secreti conscius auri...[6]

There is a striking parallel with Tacitus' account[7] of how in the year 65 Caesellius Bassus, a Roman knight, dreamt of

---

[1] Above, p. 49.

[2] Above, pp. 136 f.   [3] 53.3, 45.7.

[4] *SHA Hadrian* 18.7 f. This is one of Bagnani's main arguments favouring a Neronian date.

[5] 58.10; cf. R. Browning, *CR* (1949), 12.

[6] *Sat.* 128.   [7] *Ann.* 16.1 ff.

buried treasure left by Dido in an African cave, and how he persuaded Nero to dispatch an expedition to find it, but with abortive results.

All this evidence suggests that the *Satyricon* was being composed about A.D. 65. We have no knowledge of how long it took to compose, and it is legitimate to assume that the earlier episodes may have been written earlier. This kind of speculation is greatly affected by theories of the length of the work and of the artistic pains devoted to it. My own view is that it was much shorter than is popularly supposed, and that it could have been completed within a few months or even weeks.

THE CAREER OF APULEIUS AND THE DATE OF THE 'METAMORPHOSES'[1]

Apuleius was born about 125, as three facts indicate. He was considerably younger than Pudentilla his wife, whose age of forty at the trial of Apuleius was attested by documents. The trial is to be dated 158/9; Pudentilla's birth was accordingly about 118.[2] Apuleius was a school contemporary of Aemilianus Strabo, consul in 156; the minimum age for the consulship was at that time thirty-two, or a year or two less for a candidate with children. Strabo must have been born in 126 or earlier.[3] Thirdly, Apuleius was a student at Athens with Pontianus, son of Pudentilla, 'arto postea contubernio intime iunctus'; in view of his mother's age Pontianus can hardly have been born before 133, and in view of his later career not long after that year. As he addresses Apuleius as 'parens, dominus, magister', he was clearly a younger contemporary.[4] Hence Apuleius was born considerably after 118 and considerably earlier than 133, and was at school with a man born in 126 or earlier. A range of about 123–8 for his birth is reasonable.

After schooling under the grammaticus and rhetor at Carthage, where he also learnt some philosophy, he resumed his education at Athens, where he studied for some years.[5] He

---

[1] There are good accounts in Butler/Owen's edition of the *Apologia* (Oxford 1914), vii ff.; and in P. Vallette's Budé edition of the *Apologia* and *Florida*² (Paris 1960), v ff.

[2] Apuleius younger, *Apol.* 27, etc.; Pudentilla's age, *Apol.* 89; date of trial, see Syme, *REA* (1959), 316 f.

[3] Strabo's consulship, *Act. arv. ann. 156* (Henzen, clxxi): age for consulship, M. Hammond, *The Antonine Monarchy* (Rome 1959), 290.

[4] Pontianus' friendship, *Apol.* 72; Pontianus *adultus* and *uxori idoneus* by 155, *Apol.* 69 f. (for interpretation, see Butler/Owen, xix ff.); Pontianus younger than Apuleius, *Apol.* 97.

[5] Philosophy at Carthage, *Flor.* 18.15; Athens, *Apol.* 23.2: 'longa peregrinatione et diutinis studiis'. He was still there not many years before 158–9 (*Apol.* 72.3).

also lived at Rome, and it is natural to assume that like Pontianus he went there after his Athenian period.[1] He may have
returned to Carthage and his birthplace Madaura subsequently,
but no evidence of a return to Africa predates his arrival at Oea
(Tripoli) in the winter of 155/6.[2] Already, at the age of thirty,
he is a literary celebrity.[3]

The history of his residence at Oea, marriage to Pudentilla,
and indictment on a charge of magic needs no elaboration. He
was obviously acquitted, and must have returned to reside at
Carthage shortly afterwards. Excerpts from the *Florida* reveal
his determination to spend the rest of his life there.[4] These
speeches and set pieces composed on diverse occasions reflect
his prominence in the Carthage of the 160s—delivering the
farewell oration to the proconsul Severianus, and another to
the proconsul Scipio Orfitus. One speech mentions that his
oratory has been celebrated at Carthage for six years.[5] He
accepts from the Carthaginian senate the honour of a public
statue, and the priesthood which designates him leading
citizen.[6]

From this time onward (about 170), nothing further is
heard of Apuleius. To what period can the *Metamorphoses* be
ascribed? The external evidence is limited and negative; the
absence of reference to the book at Apuleius' trial, its absence
too in the catalogues of his writings in the *Florida* have led some
to infer that the romance was composed after he had settled at
Carthage. These arguments are precarious.[7]

---

[1] *Flor.* 17.4.

[2] *Apol.* 72. The date, 'abhinc ferme triennium', *Apol.* 55.

[3] *Apol.* 73.2.

[4] *Flor.* 16.3: 'ita institui omne vitae meae tempus vobis probare, quibus
me in perpetuum firmiter dedicavi.' Cf. *Flor.* 18.14.

[5] Severianus, *Flor.* 9 (see §40 for the date between 161 and 169); Orfitus,
Flor. 17 (163/4); *Flor.* 18.16.

[6] Statue, *Flor.* 16.1 ff.; priesthood, *Flor.* 16.38.

[7] *Flor.* 9.27 ff., 20.5 ff. For reservations, Bernhard, 358. The evidence of
Julius Capitolinus, *Albinus* 12.12, provides a terminal date of 197. This
is a citation of a letter of Severus to the senate, complaining at the favour
shown to Albinus; '...maior fuit dolor, quod illum pro litterato

More positive are the internal indications. Some parts of the *Metamorphoses* certainly correspond to Apuleius' own experiences. Lucius' trial at the Festival of Laughter, and the offer of the citizens to erect a statue to him, seem to make a comic reference to Apuleius' own trial and the citizens' offer of a statue at Oea.[1] So also the fact that Lucius was initiated into various mysteries in Greece reflects Apuleius' own history.[2] Then there is the journey of Lucius to Rome in the final book.[3] These autobiographical touches in the narrative make it reasonably certain that the romance can be dated after 160.

Secondly there are suggestive legal passages. Above all, there is the plea of Juno that she cannot harbour Psyche because of 'the laws which forbid runaway slaves belonging to others from being harboured against their masters' will'. Venus makes Mercury go to earth to describe Psyche's appearance so that none can plead ignorance, and a little earlier Psyche begs to stay in Ceres' shrine 'for only a few days', and is refused.[4] Now in the *Digest* there is a joint rescript from Marcus Aurelius and Commodus directing officials to compel property-owners to deliver up runaways; Ulpian indicates that this was to tighten existing legislation by no longer allowing the twenty days' grace previously permitted. The whole passage may well have been written by Apuleius with the more stringent regulation in mind, and the date would then be after 177.[5]

laudandum plerique duxistis, cum ille neniis quibusdam anilibus occupatus inter Milesias Punicas Apulei sui et ludicra litteraria consenesceret.' Clodius Albinus died in 197; 'consenesceret' suggests that he read the *Metamorphoses* in the 190s.

[1] *Met.* 3.11.5; Augustine, *Ep.* 138.19.
[2] *Met.* 3.15; cf. *Apol.* 55.
[3] On this and other allegedly autobiographical elements (not all persuasive) see M. Hicter, *Ant. Class.* (1944), 95 ff.; (1945), 61 ff.
[4] 6.4.5, 7.4, 2.6: 'patere vel pauculos dies delitescam'.
[5] See G. W. Bowersock, *RhM* (1965), 282 n. 31. Hesky, *WS* (1904), 71 ff., cites 1.6.2, 'liberis tuis tutores iuridici provincialis decreto dati', as evidence that the book was written after 163/4 (cf. *SHA Ant. Phil.* 11.6), and the many references to Caesar (not 'Caesares'; 3.29.2, etc.) to suggest a date after 169. But the arguments are insecure; see Purser, xvi n. 1, and Vallette at *Met.* 1.6.2.

Thirdly, there is the mention of Sextus with Plutarch among the older relatives of Lucius.[1] It can reasonably be argued that Apuleius would never have cited a living celebrity as kinsman of a fictitious hero. Though Plutarch was probably dead before Apuleius was born, the philosopher Sextus was the teacher of Verus, and was therefore alive and alert in the middle of the century. This too suggests a date of composition much later than the period of Apuleius' stay in Rome.

Apart from the fact that nothing is heard of Apuleius after 170 (and this may be attributable to the chance survival of only the earlier speeches and pieces in the *Florida*), there is no argument against a date as late as 180 or 190. The arguments put forward in support of composition in the 150s, during Apuleius' stay in Rome, are wholly subjective. Emphasis is laid on topographical references such as the *metae Murciae* and the *Tullianum*: on the profusion of legal jokes, alleged to be particularly apposite to the period of a legal training: on the many references to senatorial procedure: and on the racy content and ebullient style, the alleged work of a young author.[2] These points certainly argue for a man young in heart writing for Roman readers; they are nugatory in the problem of establishing the date of composition.

[1] *Met.* 1.2.1. For Sextus as teacher of Verus, *SHA Verus*, 2.5.

[2] For a summary of the arguments, see Bernhard, 357 ff., who inclines to a date during Apuleius' Roman period (as also Rohde, Purser, Haight and others) but finally enters a judgment of *non liquet*. As a spokesman for the more widely held view of composition at a later date in Africa, see Paratore, *La novella*[2], 81 ff.

THE ISIAC ARETALOGY
FROM KYME

It has been earlier suggested[1] that, in creating an original ending for his novel, Apuleius was inspired by the conventional endings of love-romances, and that, in developing the role of Isis as saviour, he has exploited an Isiac aretalogy. This is especially obvious in the prayer addressed to Isis by Lucius before his reformation to human shape, and in the words addressed to him by the goddess at her epiphany.[2]

The fullest Isiac aretalogy which we possess was found on a marble *stele* in the temple of Isis at Kyme. The text is as follows:[3]

(1) Εἶσις ἐγώ εἰμι ἡ τύραννος πάσης χώρας καὶ ἐπαιδεύθην ὑπ[ὸ] Ἑρμοῦ καὶ γράμματα εὗρον μετὰ Ἑρμοῦ, τά τε ἱερὰ καὶ τὰ δημόσια γράμματα, ἵνα μὴ ἐν τοῖς αὐτοῖς πάντα γράφηται.

(2) Ἐγὼ νόμους ἀνθρώποις ἐθέμην καὶ ἐνομοθέτησα ἃ οὐθεὶς δύναται μεταθεῖναι.

(3) Ἐγώ εἰμι Κρόνου θυγάτηρ πρεσβυτάτη{ι}.

(4) Ἐγώ εἰμι γ[υ]νὴ καὶ ἀδελφὴ Ὀσείριδος βασιλέως.

(5) Ἐγώ εἰμι ἡ κάρπον ἀνθρώποις εὑροῦσα.

(6) Ἐγώ εἰμι μήτηρ Ὥρου βασιλέως.

(7) Ἐγώ εἰμι ἡ ἐν τῶ τοῦ Κυνὸς ἄστρῳ ἐπιτέλλουσα.

(8) Ἐγώ εἰμι ἡ παρὰ γυναιξὶ θεὸς καλουμένη.

(9) Ἐμοὶ Βούβαστος πόλις ᾠκοδομήθη.

(10) Ἐγὼ ἐχώρισα γῆν ἀπ᾽ οὐρανοῦ.

(11) Ἐγὼ ἄστρων ὁδοὺς ἔδειξα.

(12) Ἐγὼ ἡλίου καὶ σελήνη[ς] πορέαν συνεταξάμην.

(13) Ἐγὼ θαλάσσια ἔργα εὗρον.

(14) Ἐγὼ τὸ δίκαιον ἰσχυρὸν ἐποίησα.

(15) Ἐγὼ γυναῖκα καὶ ἄνδρα συνήγαγον.

[1] Above, p. 175.

[2] 11.2, 11.5. I must again record my debt to Mr Stephen Ryle here.

[3] I reproduce the text from A. Salač, 'Inscriptions de Kymé d'Éolide, de Phocée, de Tralles', *BCH* (1927), 379 f. This article usefully demonstrates the close connexion between this and other Isiac aretalogies.

(16) Ἐγὼ γυναικὶ δεκαμηνιαῖον βρέφος εἰς φῶς ἐξενεγκεῖν ἔταξα.
(17) Ἐγὼ ὑπὸ τέκνου γονεῖς ἐνομοθέτησα φιλοστοργεῖσθαι.
(18) Ἐγὼ τοῖς ἀστόργοις γονεῦσιν διακειμένοις τειμω(ρί)αν ἐπέθηκα.
(19) Ἐγὼ μετὰ τοῦ ἀδελφοῦ Ὀσίριδος τὰς ἀνθρωποφαγίας ἔπαυσα.
(20) Ἐγὼ μυήσεις ἀνθρώποις ἐπέδε[ι]ξα.
(21) Ἐγὼ ἀγάλματα θεῶν τειμᾶν ἐδίδαξα.
(22) Ἐγὼ τεμένη θεῶν ἱδρυσάμην.
(23) Ἐγὼ τυράννων ἀρχὰς κατέλυσα.
(24) Ἐγὼ φόνους ἔπαυσα.
(25) Ἐγὼ στέργεσθαι γυναῖκας ὑπὸ ἀνδρῶν ἠνάγκασα.
(26) Ἐγὼ τὸ δίκαιον ἰσχυρότερον χρυσίου καὶ ἀργυρίου ἐποίησα.
(27) Ἐγὼ τὸ ἀληθὲς καλὸν ἐνομο[θέ]τησα νομίζε[σ]θαι.
(28) Ἐγὼ συγγραφὰς γαμικὰς εὗρον.
(29) Ἐγὼ διαλέκτους Ἕλλησι καὶ βαρβάροις ἔταξα.
(30) Ἐγὼ τὸ καλὸν καὶ αἰσχρὸ[ν] διαγεινώσκεσθαι ὑπὸ τῆς φύσεως ἐποίησα.
(31) Ἐγὼ ὅρκου φοβερώτερον οὐθὲν ἐποίησα.
(32) Ἐγὼ τὸν ἀδίκως ἐπιβουλεύοντα ἄλλοις ⟨ἄλλω⟩ ὑποχείριον τῷ ἐπιβου[λ]ευομένω παρέδωκα.
(33) Ἐγὼ τοῖς ἄδικα πράσσουσιν τειμωρίαν ἐπιτίθημι.
(34) Ἐγὼ ἱκέτας ἐλεᾶν ἐνομοθ[έ]τησα.
(35) Ἐγὼ τοὺς δικαίως ἀμυνομένους τειμῶ.
(36) Παρ' ἐμοὶ τὸ δίκαιον ἰσχύει.
(37) Ἐγὼ ποταμῶν καὶ ἀνέμων [κ]αὶ θαλάσσης εἰμὶ κυρία.
(38) Οὐθεὶς δοξάζεται ἄνευ τῆς ἐμῆς γνώμης.
(39) Ἐγώ εἰμι πολέμου κυρία.
(40) Ἐγὼ κεραύνου κυρία εἰμί.
(41) Ἐγὼ πραΰνω καὶ κυμαίνω θάλασσαν.
(42) Ἐγὼ ἐν ταῖς τοῦ ἡλίου αὐγαῖς εἰμί.
(43) Ἐγὼ παρεδρεύω τῇ τοῦ ἡλίου πορεία.
(44) Ὅ ἂν ἐμοὶ δόξη, τοῦτο καὶ τελεῖτα[ι].
(45) Ἐμοὶ πάντ' ἐπείκει.
(46) Ἐγὼ τοὺς ἐν δεσμοῖς λύω{ι}.
(47) Ἐγὼ ναυτιλίας εἰμὶ κυρία.
(48) Ἐγὼ τὰ πλωτὰ ἄπλωτα ποι[ῶ ὅ]ταν ἐμοὶ δόξη.
(49) Ἐγὼ περιβόλους πόλεων ἔκτισα.
(50) Ἐ(γ)ώ εἰμι ἡ θεσμοφόρος καλουμένη.
(51) Ἐγὼ ν(ή)σ{σ}ους ἐκ β[υ][θ]ῶν εἰς φῶν (sic) ἀνήγαγον.
(52) Ἐγὼ ὄμβρων εἰμὶ κυρία.
(53) Ἐγὼ τὸ ἱμαρμένον νικῶ.
(54) Ἐμοῦ τὸ εἱμαρμένον ἀκούει.
    Χαῖρε Αἴγυπτε θρέψασά με.

SELECT BIBLIOGRAPHY

A. GENERAL

Barns, J. W. B. 'Egypt and the Greek Romance', *Mitteil. aus d. Pap.-samml. d. Öst.-Nat. Bibl.* (1955), 29 ff.

Beare, W. *The Roman Stage*[3] (London 1964).

Bonner, S. F. *Roman Declamation* (Liverpool 1949).

Bornecque, H. *Les déclamations et les déclamateurs* (Lille 1902).

Bürger, K. 'Der antike Roman vor Petronius', *H* (1892), 345 ff.

Castiglioni, L. *Stile e testo del romanzo pastorale di Longo* (Milan 1928).

Cèbe, J. P. *La caricature et la parodie dans le monde romain antique* (Paris 1966).

Chassang, F. *Histoire du roman dans l'antiquité grecque et latine*[2] (Paris 1862).

Courtney, E. 'Parody and Literary Allusion in Menippean Satire', *Philol.* (1962), 86 ff.

Dalmeyda, G. Budé edition of Longus (Paris 1934).
  Budé edition of Xenophon of Ephesus (Paris 1926).

Duff, J. W. *Roman Satire* (Berkeley 1936).

Haight, E. H. *Essays on Ancient Fiction* (N.Y. 1936).

Helm, R. *Der antike Roman*[2] (Göttingen 1956).
  Lucian und Menipp (Leipzig 1906).

Henriksson, K. E. *Griechische Büchertitel in der röm. Lit.* (Helsinki 1956).

Highet, G. *The Anatomy of Satire* (Princeton 1962).

Kleinknecht, H. *Die Gebetsparodie in der Antike* (Stuttgart 1937).

Knoche, U. *Die römische Satire*[2] (Göttingen 1957).

Lavagnini, B. *Le origini del romanzo greco* (Pisa 1921).
  Studi sul romanzo greco (Florence 1950).

Oltramare, A. *Les origines de la diatribe romaine* (Lausanne 1926).

Perry, B. E. *The Ancient Romances* (Berkeley 1967).

Reich, H. *Der Mimus* (Berlin 1903).

Reitzenstein, R. *Hellenistische Wundererzählungen*[2] (Darmstadt 1963).

Rohde, E. *Der griechische Roman und seine Vorläufer*[3] (Leipzig 1914, repr. 1960).

Rooy, van, C. A. *Studies in Classical Satire and related Literary Theory* (Leiden 1965).

Rudd, Niall. *The Satires of Horace* (Cambridge 1966).

Tarn, W. W. and Griffith, G. T. *Hellenistic Civilisation*[3] (London 1952), ch. 8.

Todd, F. A. *Some Ancient Novels* (London 1940).

Trenkner, S. *The Greek Novella in the Classical Period* (Cambridge 1958).

Weinreich, O. 'Der griechische Liebesroman', *Heliodor, die Abenteuer der schönen Chariklea* (Hamburg 1962), 233 ff.

B. PETRONIUS

Texts and Editions of the *Satyricon*: Bücheler (Berlin 1862), Ernout[4] (Paris 1958), K. Müller (Munich 1961; revised in Müller/Ehlers' Tusculum edition, Munich 1965), Paratore (Florence 1933), Sage (N.Y. 1929). Of the *Cena*: Friedländer[2] (Leipzig 1906; repr. Amsterdam 1960), Maiuri (Naples 1945), Marmorale (Florence 1947), Perrochat[2] (Paris 1952), Lowe (London 1905), Sedgwick[2] (Oxford 1950). Translations: Arrowsmith (Ann Arbor 1959), Sullivan (London 1965), Dinnage (London 1953), Heseltine (London 1913).

Abbott, F. F. 'The use of language as a means of characterisation in Petronius', *CP* (1907), 43 ff.
  'The origin of the realistic romance among the Romans', *CP* (1911), 257 ff.
Arrowsmith, W. 'Luxury and Death in the Satyricon', *Arion* (1966), 304 ff.
Auerbach, E. *Mimesis* (English edition, Princeton 1953).
Bagnani, G. *Arbiter of Elegance* (Toronto 1954).
  'And Passing Rich', *Essays in honour of Gilbert Norwood* (Toronto 1952), 218 ff.
  'Trimalchio', *Phoenix* (1954), 77 ff.
  'The house of Trimalchio', *AJP* (1954), 16 ff.
Baldwin, F. T. *The Bellum Civile of Petronius* (N.Y. 1911).
Boissier, G. *L'opposition sous les Césars* (Paris 1875), ch. 5.
  Tacitus and other Roman Studies (English edition, London 1906), 197 ff.
Browning, R. 'The date of Petronius', *CR* (1949), 12 ff., 28 ff.
Cahen, R. *Le Satiricon et ses origines* (Paris 1925).
Cameron, Averil. 'Petronius and Plato', *CQ* (1969), 367–70.
Carratelli, G. P. 'Tabulae ceratae Herculanenses', *PP* (1946), 381.
Ciaffi, V. *La struttura del Satyricon* (Turin 1955).
Cichorius, C. 'Petronius und Massilia', *Römische Studien* (Leipzig 1922), 438 ff.
Collignon, A. *Etude sur Pétrone* (Paris 1892).
Crum, R. H. 'Petronius and the emperors', *CW* (1951/2), 161 ff., 197 ff.
Faider, P. *Etudes sur Sénèque* (Ghent 1921).
George, P. A. 'Style and Character in the *Satyricon*', *Arion* (1966), 336 ff.
Grimal, P. 'Note à Pétrone, Satiricon XXVI', *RPh* (1941), 19 f.
Grube, G. M. A. *The Greek and Roman Critics* (Toronto 1965).
Heinze, R. 'Petronius und der griechische Roman', *H* (1889), 494 ff.
Heitland, W. E. Preface to Haskins' edition of Lucan's *Pharsalia* (Cambridge 1887).

Highet, G. 'Petronius the Moralist', *TAPA* (1941), 176 ff.

Kroll, W. *Studien ʒum Verständnis der römische Literatur* (Stuttgart 1924), 224 ff.

'Petronius', *RE* 19, 1201.

Marmorale, E. V. *La questione petroniana* (Bari 1948).

Perry, B. E. 'Petronius and the Comic Romance', *CP* (1925), 31 ff.

Preston, K. 'Some sources of the comic effect in Petronius', *CP* (1915), 260 ff.

Raith, O. *Petronius, ein Epikureer* (Nuremberg 1963).

Révay, J. 'Horaz und Petron', *CP* (1922), 202 ff.

Rose, K. F. C. 'The author of the *Satyricon*', *Latomus* (1961), 821 ff.

'The date of the *Satyricon*', *CQ* (1962), 166 ff.

'The Petronian Inquisition: an Auto-da-Fé', *Arion* (1966), 275 ff.

Rosenblüth, M. *Beiträge ʒur Quellenkunde von Petronius' Satiren* (diss. Berlin 1909).

Rowell, H. T. 'The Gladiator Petraites and the Date of the Satyricon', *TAPA* (1958), 12 ff.

Schur, H. C. 'The Economic Background of the Satyricon', *Latomus* (1959), 790 ff.

Schuster, M. 'Der Werwolf und die Hexen', *WS* (1930), 149 ff.

Shero, L. R. 'The *Cena* in Roman Satire', *CP* (1923), 126 ff.

Sinko, T. 'De famis et libidinis in fabula Petroniana momento', *Eos* (1935), 385 ff.

Sochatoff, A. F. 'The Purpose of Petronius' *Bellum Civile*: a Re-examination', *TAPA* (1962), 449 ff.

Stubbe, H. *Die Verseinlagen im Petron* (*Philol. Suppl.* XXV H.2; Leipzig 1933).

Sullivan, J. P. 'Realism and Satire in Petronius', *Critical Essays on Roman Literature: Satire* (ed. Sullivan: London 1963), 73 ff.

The Satyricon of Petronius (London 1968).

Süss, W. *De eo quem dicunt inesse Trimalchionis cenae sermone vulgari* (Dorpat 1926).

Thomas, E. *Pétrone*[3] (Paris 1912).

Veyne, P. 'Arbiter Elegantiae', *RPh* (1963), 258 f.

'Le "Je" dans le Satiricon', *REL* (1964), 301 ff.

Vreese, de, J. G. W. M. *Petron 39 und die Astrologie* (Amsterdam 1927).

Walsh, P. G. 'Eumolpus, the *Halosis Troiae* and the *De Bello Civili*', *CP* (1968), 208 ff.

Westerburg, M. 'Petron und Lucan', *RhM* (1883), 92 ff.

C. APULEIUS

The major texts of the *Metamorphoses* are discussed in the Introduction to D. S. Robertson's great Budé edition. A modern Commentary is conspicuously lacking. Amongst editions of *Cupid and Psyche* worthy of mention are Purser (London 1910), Beck (Groningen 1902), Fernhout (Groningen 1949), Paratore (Florence 1948), Grimal (Paris 1963). Amongst translations, Graves' (London 1950) is witty if free. Pater's version of *Cupid and Psyche* in *Marius the Epicurean*, ch. 5, is a classic.

Abt, A. *Die Apologie des Apuleius von Madaura und die antike Zauberei* (Giessen 1908).

Anderson, W. 'Zu Apuleius Novelle vom Tode der Charite', *Philol.* (1909), 537 ff.

Angus, S. *The Mystery-religions and Christianity* (N.Y. 1925).

Babbitt, F. C. Loeb edition of Plutarch's *Moralia*, vol. 5 (London 1957).

Bernhard, M. *Der Stil des Apuleius von Madaura*² (Amsterdam 1965).

Berreth, J. *Studien zum Isisbuch in Apuleius' Metamorphosen* (Diss. Tübingen 1931).

Bieler, L. 'Psyches dritte und vierte Arbeit bei Apuleius', *Arch. f. Religionswiss.* (1933), 242 ff. (= Binder/Merkelbach, 334 ff.).

Binder, G. and Merkelbach, R., eds. *Amor und Psyche* (Darmstadt 1968).

Bowersock, G. W. 'Zur Geschichte des römischen Thessaliens', *RhM* (1965), 277 ff.

Brotherton, B. 'The Introduction of Characters by Name in the *Metamorphoses* of Apuleius', *CP* (1934), 36 ff.

Bürger, K. *De Lucio Patrensi* (diss. Berlin 1887).

Butler, H. E. and Owen, A. S. *Apulei Apologia* (Oxford 1914).

Callebat, L. 'L'archaïsme dans les *Métamorphoses* d'Apulée', *REL* 1964, 364 ff.
Sermo Cotidianus dans les Métamorphoses d'Apulée (Caen 1968).

Ciaffi, V. *Petronio in Apuleio* (Turin 1960).

Cocchia, E. *Romanzo e realtà nella vita e nell'attività letteraria di Lucio Apuleio* (Catania 1915).

Dietrich, B. C. 'The Golden Art of Apuleius', *GR* (1966), 189 ff.

Dieze, J. 'Zum Märchen von Amor und Psyche', *Philol.* (1900), 136 ff.

Dornseiff, F. 'Lucius und Apuleius' *Metamorphosen*', *H* (1938), 222 ff.

Ferguson, J. 'Apuleius', *GR* (1961), 61 ff.

Festugière, A.-J. *Personal Religion amongst the Greeks* (Berkeley 1960).
'A propos des arétalogies d'Isis', *HThR* (1949), 209 ff.

Forbes, C. A. 'Charite and Dido', *CW* (1943/4), 39.

Friedländer, L. 'The Story of Cupid and Psyche', *Roman Life and Manners*, IV, tr. Gough (London 1913), 88 ff. (= Binder/Merkelbach, 16 ff.).

Haight, E. H. *Apuleius and his influence* (N. Y. 1927).

Hammer, S. 'De narrationum Apulei *Met. X* insertarum compositione et exemplaribus', *Eos* (1923/4), 6 ff.

'De Apulei arte narrandi novae observationes', *Eos* (1925), 51 ff.

Harder, R. 'Karpokrates von Chalkis und die memphitische Isispropaganda', *Abh. Preuss. Akad.* (1943), no. 14.

Heinrici, G. 'Zur Geschichte der Psyche', *Preuss. Jb.* (1897), 390 ff. (= Binder/Merkelbach, 56 ff.).

Helm, R. Edition of *Florida* (Leipzig 1910), Introdn.

'Das "Märchen" von Amor und Psyche', *NJb* (1914), 170 ff. (= Binder/Merkelbach, 175 ff.).

Herrmann, L. '*L'âne d'or* et le christianisme', *Latomus* (1953), 188 ff.

Hesky, R. 'Zur Abfassungszeit der *Metamorphosen* des Apuleius', *WS* (1904), 71 ff.

Hicter, M. *Apulée, conteur fantastique* (Brussels 1942).

'L'autobiographie dans *L'âne d'or* d'Apulée', *Ant. Class.* (1944), 95 ff.; (1945), 61 ff.

Jonge, de, B. J. Edition of *Metamorphoses II* (Groningen 1941).

Junghanns, P. *Die Erzählungstechnik von Apuleius' Metamorphosen und ihrer Vorlage* (*Philol. Suppl.* XXIV H.1; Leipzig 1932).

Kroll, W. 'Das afrikanische Latein', *RhM* (1897), 569 ff.

Labhardt, A. 'Curiositas': notes sur l'histoire d'une notion', *Mus. Helv.* (1960), 206 ff.

Lancel, S. '"Curiositas" et préoccupations spirituelles chez Apulée', *Rev. Hist. Rel.* (1961), 25 ff. (= Binder/Merkelbach, 408 ff.).

Lesky, A. 'Apuleius von Madaura und Lukios von Patrai', *H* (1941), 43 ff.

McLeod, M. D. Loeb edition of Lucian VIII (London 1967).

Médan, P. *La latinité d'Apulée dans les Métamorphoses* (Paris 1926).

Merkelbach, R. 'Eros und Psyche', *Philol.* (1958), 103 ff.

Roman und Mysterium in der Antike (München 1962).

Mette, H. J. 'Curiositas', in *Festschr. Bruno Snell* (München 1956), 227 ff.

Mold, M. Edition of *Metamorphoses I* (Groningen 1938).

Monceaux, P. *Apulée, roman et magie* (Paris 1888).

Müller, D. 'Ägypten und die griechischen Isis-Aretalogien', *Abh. Sächs. Akad.* (1961), H.1.

Neumann, E. *Amor and Psyche* (English edition, London 1966).

Nock, A. D. *Conversion* (Oxford 1933).

Norden, E. *Die antike Kunstprosa* (Leipzig 1909), II, 588 ff.

Norden, F. *Apuleius von Madaura und das römische Privatrecht* (Leipzig 1912).

Norwood, F. 'The Magic Pilgrimage of Apuleius', *Phoenix* (1956), 1 ff.

Oldfather, W. A., Canter, H. V., Perry, B. E. *Index Apuleianus* (Middletown, Conn. 1934).

Paratore, E. *La novella in Apuleio*² (Messina 1942).

Perry, B. E. 'Some Aspects of the Literary Art of Apuleius', *TAPA* (1923), 196 ff.

'An Interpretation of Apuleius' *Metamorphoses*', *TAPA* (1926), 238 ff.

'On Apuleius' *Metamorphoses*', *CP* (1929), 394 ff.

Reitzenstein, R. *Das Märchen von Amor und Psyche bei Apuleius* (Leipzig 1912: = Binder/Merkelbach, 87 ff.).

'Noch einmal Eros und Psyche', *Arch. f. Religionswiss.* (1930), 42 ff. (= Binder/Merkelbach, 159 ff.).

'Eros und Psyche in der Ägyptische-Griechischen Kleinkunst', *Sitz. Heidelb. Akad.* (1914), 3 ff. (= Binder/Merkelbach, 159 ff.).

Riefstahl, H. *Der Roman des Apuleius* (Frankfurt 1938).

Robertson, D. S. 'A Greek Carnival', *JHS* (1919), 110 ff.

Roussel, P. 'Un nouvel hymne grec à Isis', *REG* (1929), 137 ff.

Rubino, C. A. 'Literary Intelligibility in Apuleius' *Metamorphoses*', *Class. Bull.* (1966), 65 ff.

Scazzoso, P. *Le Metamorphosi di Apuleio* (Milan 1951).

Schaller, W. *De fabula Apuleiana* (diss. Leipzig 1911).

Schissel, O. 'Die Ethopoiie der Psyche', *H* (1941), 106 ff.

Souter, M. '"Zatchlas" in Apuleius', *JTS* (1936), 80.

Stephenson, W. E. 'The Comedy of Evil in Apuleius', *Arion* (1964), 87 ff.

Swahn, J. Ö. *The Tale of Cupid and Psyche* (Lund 1955).

Syme, R. 'Proconsuls d'Afrique sous Antonin le Pieux', *REA* (1959), 316 ff.

Thibau, R. 'Les *Métamorphoses* d'Apulée et la théorie platonicienne de l'Eros', *Stud. philos. Gand.* (1965), 89 ff.

Vallette, P. Budé edition of *Apologie/Florides*² (Paris 1960).

Walsh, P. G. 'Lucius Madaurensis', *Phoenix* (1968), 143 ff.

Weinreich, O. 'Eros und Psyche bei den Kabylen', *Arch. f. Religionswiss.* (1930), 88 ff. (= Binder/Merkelbach, 293 ff.).

Witt, R. E. 'Isis–Hellas', *Proc. Camb. Phil. Soc.* (1966), 48 ff.

Wittmann, W. *Das Isisbuch des Apuleius* (Stuttgart 1938).

17-2

INDEXES

1. INDEX OF PASSAGES CITED

Achilles Tatius
(1.1.13), 197; (1.4.4), 206; (1.9.5),
212; (1.13.2), 202; (1.15), 203;
(1.15.2), 64; (2.8), 23, 152; (2.11 f.),
170; (2.15.3), 64; (2.25), 206; (2.34),
163; (2.36 ff.), 23; (3.7), 202; (3.15),
155; (4.1), 213; (4.2), 23; (8.6.7), 214

Ad Herennium
(4.19.26), 65

Aeschylus
P.V. (658 ff.), 53; (747 f.), 53
Suppl. (291 ff.), 53

Anthologia Palatina
(5.7), 207; (5.8), 207; (9.157), 195;
(9.325), 195; (9.449), 195, 199;
(10.71), 216; (12.48.1), 202; (12.80),
196; (12.80.5,) 210; (12.144.1), 202;
(16.195 ff.), 195; (16.199), 195;
(16.200), 195; (16.201), 196;
(16.210), 195

(Ps. Apollodorus)
Bibl. (2.1.3), 53, 209; (2.5.1), 214;
(3.5.5), 60

Apollonius Rhodius
(3.36 ff.), 209; (3.90 ff.), 209;
(3.129 ff.), 201

Apuleius
Apol. (4), 152; (12), 183; (23.2), 248;
(27), 248; (29 ff.), 152; (33.7), 61;
(34.3), 61; (43.2), 184; (55), 184,
249, 250; (56.2), 183; (56.3 ff.), 185;
(63.3), 185; (63.6), 133; (69 f.), 248;
(72), 152, 248, 249; (72.3), 248;
(73.2), 249; (89), 248; (97), 248
De Deo Socratis (6), 184
Flor. (6.1), 183; (9.27 ff.), 2, 249;
(9.40), 249; (15.14 f.), 249; (16.1),
249; (16.3), 249; (16.9), 65; (16.38),
249; (17), 249; (17.4), 249; (18.3 f.),
65; (18.14), 249; (18.15), 248;
(18.16), 249; (18.38 ff.), 185;
(20.5 ff.), 2, 249
Metamorphoses 1 (1.1), 3, 7, 145, 202;
(1.6), 7, 145; (2.1), 182, 251; (3.1 ff.),
180, 192. (6 ff;), 14; (6.2), 250; (7.9),

177; (8.1), 177; (8.4 ff.), 178, 184;
(9.1 ff.), 153, 178; (10.2), 60; (12.7);
149; (13.1), 14; (13.2), 149; (13.8),
14; (14.2), 14; (15.2), 31; (16),
31; (16.2), 150; (20.5), 48, 150;
(21), 31; (21.5), 151; (21.7), 151;
(22.2), 151; (22.6 f.), 151; (23.1 ff.),
151; (23.6), 60; (24 f.), 88; (25.6),
151, 156; (26.1), 151
2 (2.1), 178; (4), 64, 178; (5.4 ff.), 178;
(6.1 ff.), 178; (6.8), 62; (7.1), 62;
(8.2 ff.), 152; (10.2), 178; (11.5),
178; (11.6 ff.), 180; (13.3 ff.), 179;
(16 f.), 153; (16.5), 62; (17.1), 61,
(17.3), 61; (20.1), 179; (20.7), 153;
(21.2), 153; (22.3), 153; (24.3), 61;
(26.8), 60; (28), 183; (29.6), 156,
(31.1), 153; (32), 238; (32.6), 155
3 (1 ff.), 155, 192; (1.1), 57; (3 ff.), 29;
(3.2 ff.), 59; (4.3 ff.), 59; (11.5),
155, 250; (12.3), 179; (15), 250;
(15.7 ff.), 156; (17.3 ff.), 156;
(18.1), 65; (18.6 f.), 60; (19.1), 60;
(19.4 ff.), 180; (22.2), 156; (23.3, 156;
(24.3 f.), 156; (26.5), 63; (27.1),
63; (29.2), 250; (29.3), 159; (29.7),
157
4 (1.4 ff.), 157; (3.10), 157; (4.5), 63;
(6.1), 58; (8.7 f.), 158; (9 ff.), 157;
(21.6), 59; (29.3), 202; (30.1), 55,
222; (30.4 f.), 199, 201; (32.3), 205;
(32.5), 53; (32.6), 53, 202; (33), 74;
(33.3), 202; (35.4), 203
5 (1), 203; (4.3 f.), 204; (4.5), 212;
(4.6), 204; (5.2), 205; (6.6), 192;
(6.7), 205; (9.1), 156; (9.8), 205;
(10.1 f.), 205; (11.3), 205; (11.5),
192; (11.6), 192; (12.4), 205; (13.5),
205; (14.5), 205; (15.4), 192; (18.4),
192; (19.3), 192; (19.5), 192; (21.2),
208; (21.4), 206; (23.1), 192; (23.4),
207; (24.1), 56, 207; (24.3), 192;
(24.5), 208; (25.1), 53; (28), 53;
(28.1), 56; (28.3), 208; (29.2), 209;
(29.5 f.), 62, 209; (30.3), 212

Apuleius (*cont.*)
  6 (2 ff.), 222; (2.5), 65; (2.6), 250;
    (4.5), 62, 250; (6.4), 211; (7.2), 56,
    211; (7.4), 250; (9.2), 212; (9.6), 62;
    (10.5 f.), 213; (10.6), 57; (11.3),
    213; (13.4), 57; (15.1), 213; (15.3),
    192; (15.4), 215; (16.4 f.), 214;
    (18.1), 202; (18.2 ff.), 56; (18.4),
    223; (18.8), 57; (19.3), 56, 57;
    (19.7), 192, 223; (20.5), 192, 215;
    (21.4), 192; (22.1), 211; (22.4), 62;
    (26.9), 159; (27.5), 60; (28.2), 160;
    (28.3), 159; (29.5), 160; (30.6), 156;
    (31), 159; (31.2), 58; (32.1), 17
  7 (2.4 f.), 181; (3.1), 181; (3.3), 159;
    (3.4), 159; (5.2), 161; (6.2 ff.), 162;
    (8.1), 161; (11.4 ff.), 161; (13.1),
    58; (13.3), 159; (16.1), 181; (17.1),
    181; (24.3 ff.), 163; (25.3), 181;
    (25.8), 160; (27.5), 59; (28.4), 60
  8 (1.4), 57; (1.5 ff.), 238; (1.5), 164;
    (6.4), 54; (7.5), 164; (8.6), 54; (9.1),
    54; (12), 54; (13.2 ff.), 54; (24),
    165; (24.1), 181; (24.2), 165; (24.4),
    61; (25.1), 160; (26 ff.), 237;
    (26.1 f.), 165; (27.6), 165, 181;
    (28.1), 165; (28.6), 165; (29), 165;
    (29.2), 165; (29.5), 159; (31.1), 166
  9 (2.3), 166; (5 ff.), 237; (5.3 ff.), 233;
    (7), 167; (9.3), 167; (11 ff.), 168;
    (11.2), 63; (14 ff.), 14; (14.3 f.),
    168; (14.5), 183, 187; (15.4 f.), 187;
    (17 ff.), 14; (22.3), 156; (23 ff.), 14,
    28; (23.2), 168; (24.3), 31; (26 ff.),
    14; (32.1), 58; (33 f.), 58; (39),
    31
  10 (2), 28; (2.4), 171; (2.7), 55; (4.3),
    171; (5.3), 172; (12.5), 172; (13.7),
    159; (14.4 ff.), 172; (19.3), 60;
    (21.2), 65; (22.3), 17; (22.4), 60;
    (23 ff.), 173; (24.2), 173; (25.2),
    173; (33.1), 182; (33.4), 159
  11 (2), 252; (2.1), 182; (2.4), 222;
    (5), 252; (5.1), 201, 222; (5.2 ff.),
    185; (5.5), 188; (6.2), 187; (6.5),
    188, 222; (6.7), 188; (8.4), 223;
    (9.2), 65; (10.1), 188; (11.2), 223;
    (15), 181; (15.1 ff.), 177; (15.4),
    189; (19.3), 188; (21.7), 192; (22.1),
    223; (23.3), 188; (23.7), 192, 203;
    (24.5), 192; (27.9), 184
Aristides, Marcianus
  Apol. (12.3), 187

Aristides Milesius
  (Soph. fr. 449 Pearson), 17
Aristophanes
  Ranae (129 ff.), 215
  Vesp. (262), 178
Aristotle
  Rhet. (2.26), 59
Athenaeus
  Deipnosoph. (614D), 10
Augustine
  C.D. (8.14); 184; (18.18), 143
  Ep. (138.19), 155, 250

Babrius
  Fab. (58), 216
Bion
  (fr. 9 Gow), 202; (fr. 16 Gow),
    33

Caesar
  B.G. (6.11), 58
Callimachus
  Aitia (3 fr. 75 Pfeiffer, 20 ff.),
    202
Callistratus
  (1.4,) 207
Carmina Priapeia
  (37.8 ff.), 79
Cassius Dio
  (54.18.3), 216; (55.3.2 ff.), 216
Catullus
  (66.52 ff.), 203
Chariton
  (1.1.2), 55, 107; (1.2.5), 212;
    (1.14.1), 55; (2.3.6), 55, 107; (5.6 ff.),
    58
Cicero
  Att. (9.19), 104
  Cael. (65), 27
  Fin. (5.87), 96
  Phil. (1.12), 216
  Pis. (67), 132

Digest
  (3.2.2), 63
Diogenes Laertius
  (7.180), 96

Euripides
  Medea (1042 ff.), 206

Fulgentius
  Mitol. (3.6), 198, 219

Gellius, Aulus
 (6.16.2 ff.), 112; (13.11.1 ff.), 112;
 (14.7.10), 216; (16.7), 27

Heliodorus
 (3.7 f.), 206
Hermas
 Pastor (29.1 ff.), 188
Herodotus
 (1.6), 200; (1.34 ff.), 53, 163; (3.102), 33
Hesiod
 Theog. (780 ff.), 215
 WD (179 ff.), 216
Homer
 Il. (1.348 ff.), 36; (1.528), 56;
  (18.478 ff.), 93
 Od. (4.43 ff.), 203; (4.71 ff.), 203;
  (12.184), 38; (24.1 ff.), 79
Horace
 Ep. (1.2), 20; (1.5.2), 115; (1.12.12 f.),
  96
 Sat. (1.5), 21; (2.3.281 ff.), 41; (2.4),
  115; (2.5), 40; (2.8), 38, 115; (2.8.1),
  39; (2.8.4 f.), 39; (2.8.6), 39; (2.8.16),
  39; (2.8.26 ff.), 39; (2.8.45), 39;
  (2.8.61 ff.), 39; (2.8.77 ff.), 39;
  (2.8.93 ff.), 39

Justin Martyr
 1 *Apol.* (6), 189; (15), 188; (61 ff.), 188
Juvenal
 (1.13 f.), 47; (1.94), 116; (1.142 ff.),
  116; (5), 112; (5.98), 40; (7), 94;
  (10.163 ff.), 45; (10.346 ff.), 41;
  (10.356), 97; (12.93 ff.), 40;
  (15.114), 108

Livy
 (1.7.2), 88; (9.8.13), 58; (21.7 ff.),
  108; (21.35.8), 49; (21.36.8), 49;
  (21.62), 58; (22.1.8 ff.), 58;
  (22.53.10), 45; (23.30), 108; (24.3),
  104; (28.39.19), 63; (30.17.14), 63;
  (31.14.12), 58; (34.45.4), 104;
  (39.13.13), 203; (40.8 ff.), 59
 Epit. (59), 108
Longus
 Daphnis and Chloe (1.4.2), 64; (1.7),
  170; (1.7.2), 64; (1.10), 33; (1.14),
  33; (1.17), 33; (1.18), 33; (1.31),
  33; (2.3 ff.), 197; (2.34), 64, 214;
  (3.2), 33; (3.25.2), 33; (4.2 f.), 203;
  (4.12.2 f.), 64; (4.14.1 f.), 64

Lucan
 (1.8), 45; (1.57 f.), 49; (1.81 ff.), 49;
  (1.110), 49; (1.330 f.), 49;
  (1.405 ff.), 74; (5.30), 49; (7.180),
  49; (7.473), 49
Lucian
 Dial. Deorum (7), 216
 Menippus (1), 48
 Vera Historia (1.1), 3; (1.16), 33;
  (1.20), 34; (2.18), 34, 96; (2.19),
  34; (2.20), 34
 Vitarum Auctio (23), 96
(Ps. Lucian)
 Erōtes (1), 3, 15
 Onos (4), 180; (5), 61; (8 ff.), 152;
  (10 ff.), 153; (10), 61; (11), 155;
  (15), 176; (16), 157, 159; (17), 157;
  (18), 157; (21), 157; (23), 60; (25),
  17; (26), 160, 161; (33 f.), 162; (35),
  165; (41), 167; (42), 168; (43 ff.),
  170; (43), 169; (51), 60; (56), 176
Lucilius
 (fr. 94 ff. Warmington), 21
 (fr. 489 f. Warmington), 112
Lucretius
 (3.888 ff.), 51; (3.978 ff.), 51;
  (4.353 ff.), 50; (4.962 ff.), 51;
  (4.1283), 212; (5.1161 ff.), 110

Macrobius
 In Somn. Scip. (1.2.8), 3
 Saturnalia (1.21.10), 155
Martial
 (1.59.3), 118; (2.14.11), 118; (3.60),
  112; (6.42), 118; (12.95.2), 11
Moschus
 (1.4), 211; (1.27), 33; (6), 207

Ovid
 Amores (1.8.9 f.), 42; (2.1.23 f.), 42;
  (3.7.37), 42; (3.7.69), 42; (3.7.80),
  42
 A.A. (1.437), 106; (2.345), 212;
  (3.619), 106
 Fasti (3.327 ff.), 100
 Met. (2.1 ff.), 203; (2.531 ff.), 209;
  (5.365 ff.), 201; (6.103 ff.), 216;
  (9.188 ff.), 214
 Tristia (2.104 f.), 90; (2.413 f.), 16;
  (2.443 f.), 16

Pausanias
 (8.17.6 ff.), 215

Persius
    (1.13 f.), 41; (1.26), 41; (5), 105;
    (6.24), 116
Petronius
    (2.1 ff.), 85; (2.7), 63; (3.3 ff.), 40, 85;
    (3.4), 126; (5.1 ff.), 85; (6 ff.), 77;
    (6.1), 86; (7.1), 31; (7.2), 87; (7.4),
    81; (9.5), 43, 87; (9.8 ff.), 87
    (10.1), 83; (10.2), 83; (11.2), 83; 11.4,
    88; (12.5), 75; (13.4), 75; (16 ff.),
    76, 77; (17.2), 81; (17.5), 79, 91;
    (17.6 ff.), 75; (17.6), 90; (17.8), 76,
    90; (17.9), 79, 91; (18.2), 81; (19.1),
    24; (19.3), 81, 240
    (25.4), 91; (26.1), 91; (26.7 ff.), 114;
    (26.9), 133; (27.3), 119; (27.4),
    140; (28.3), 137; (28.4), 138; (28.6),
    140; (29.1), 118; (29.8), 138; (29.9),
    118
    (30.1 f.), 118; (30.3), 119; (30.4), 139;
    (30.5), 129, 132, 140; (30.7), 130;
    (30.10), 131; (31.7), 24 f.; (31.8),
    135, 140; (31.9 f.), 119; (32.1), 139,
    140; (32.2), 138; (32.3), 132; (32.4),
    138; (33.4), 39; (33.5), 25; (34.2),
    130; (34.3), 119; (34.5), 129 f., 135,
    140; (34.6), 117; (34.8 f.), 133, 140;
    (34.10), 128; (35), 132; (35.1), 140;
    (35.6), 25; (36.1), 116; (36.3), 39,
    119; (36.5 ff.), 125, 137; (37 f.), 123;
    (37.2 ff.), 120; (37.5), 123; (37.7), 123;
    (37.8), 123; (37.9), 129; (38.1), 123;
    (38.5), 39; (38.7 ff.), 121; (38.11 ff.)
    121; (39 ff.), 81; (39.3), 125;
    (39.4 ff.), 135; (39.8), 139;
    (39.11 ff.), 126; (39.13), 31
    (40.1), 119, 126, 140; (40.3), 39;
    (41.5), 81; (41.7), 125, 130;
    (41.9 ff.), 122; (41.9), 39; (41.10 ff.),
    122 f.; (42.2), 123; (42.7), 123;
    (43.1 ff.), 121; (44), 135; (44.17 f.),
    97; (45.1), 121; (45.3 f.), 123; (45.6),
    123; (45.7), 246; (45.10), 123;
    (46.1), 123; (46.7), 122; (46.8),
    121, 123; (47 f.), 81; (47.2), 134;
    (47.4), 139; (47.8), 116; (47.11),
    135; (47.12), 129, 131; (48), 137;
    (48.1), 39; (48.2 ff.), 131, 136;.
    (48.2), 117; (48.4 ff.), 135; (48.7 f.),
    126
    (50.1), 130, 140; (50.4 ff.), 135; (50.5),
    126; (52.1 ff.), 119. 127, 135; (52.3),
    245; (52.4), 130; (52.7), 85; (52.9),

    134; (52.10), 120; (53.1 ff.), 130;
    (53.2), 129; (53.3), 246; (53.9), 129,
    131; (54.1), 138; (54.2), 120, 129;
    (54.3), 130; (55.1), 39, 140; (55.3),
    128; (55.5 ff.), 127; (56), 81;
    (56.1 ff.), 127; (56.7 ff.), 125;
    (56.8 ff.), 139; (57.1 ff.), 120, 123;
    (57.1), 83, 140; (57.4), 245; (57.6),
    128; (58.1), 140; (58.8), 122;
    (58.10), 246; (59.3 ff.), 127; (59.4),
    126
    (60), 137; (60.1), 119, 140; (60.7), 131;
    (60.9), 131; (61.1), 97; (61.4), 122;
    (61.6 ff.), 14; (62.5), 14; (62.6), 14;
    (62.10), 14; (64.2), 121; (64.4),
    245; (64.7), 134; (64.10), 119;
    (64.13), 129; (65), 40; (65.1), 116;
    (65.2), 125; (65.5), 121; (65.9 ff.),
    122; (66.1 ff.), 39, 134; (66.6), 125;
    (67.2), 120, 134; (67.4 ff.), 120;
    (67.7), 125; (67.13), 120; (68.2),
    125; (69.7), 116; (69.8 ff.), 39
    (70.1 ff.), 129; (70.3), 130; (70.7),
    140; (70.8), 119; (70.10), 120;
    (70.11), 135; (71.5 ff.), 132; (71.12),
    135, 137; (72.6), 116; (73.2), 80,
    118; (73.3), 25, 134, 245; (73.5),
    119; (74.1), 132; (74.6), 129;
    (74.9 ff.), 120; (74.13 f.), 120, 124;
    (75.3 ff.), 124; (75.10 ff.), 131;
    (76.3), 245; (76.9), 136; (76.10 ff.),
    132; (77.4 f.), 117; (78.5 ff.), 133;
    (78.5), 80; (78.8), 39; (79.9), 83;
    (80), 82; (80.1), 92; (80.3), 43, 92;
    (80.9), 23, 25, 92, 93; (81.1), 36;
    (81.3), 28; (81.4), 83; (82), 31;
    (82.1), 37; (83.7), 94; (83.9 f.), 94;
    (84 ff.), 94; (85 ff.), 13; (88.2), 96;
    (89), 46
    (90.3), 95; (90.6), 95; (91.2 ff.), 81;
    (91.2), 83; (91.8), 82; (92.9), 83;
    (94.1), 98; (94.8 ff.), 31, 150; (94.9),
    82; (94.15), 25; (95.5), 27; (95.8),
    27; (96 f.), 82; (96.4), 81; (96.7),
    94; (97.5), 43; (98), 31; (98.5), 43;
    (98.6), 79; (99.3), 99
    (100.1 ff.), 81; (101.1), 78; (101.4),
    101; (101.7), 43, 95; (102.10), 43;
    (104), 74; (104.1), 76, 79, 100;
    (105.5 ff.), 74; (105.9), 74; (105.10),
    43; (106.1), 25, 100; (106.2), 74;
    (106.3), 78 f., 101; (106.4), 75, 101;
    (107), 28, 94; (107.1), 74; (107.5),

Petronius (*cont.*)
74; (107.11), 74; (108.9 ff.), 44;
(108.14), 45; (109.1 ff.), 45; (109.8),
95
(110.1), 95; (111 f.), 11; (113), 82;
(113.7), 102; (113.8), 74; (114.1),
37; (114.4 f.), 101; (114.8), 78;
(114.11), 82; (115.2 ff.), 95;
(115.3 ff.), 94; (115.5), 95; (115.6),
37; (115.7 ff.), 37, 51; (115.12 ff.),
81; (115.16), 103; (115.20), 94;
(116), 108; (116.1), 37 f.; (116.6),
103; (117.2), 104; (117.3), 75;
(117.4), 25, 104; (117.10), 25;
(118.2), 72; (118.3), 35; (118.6),
48; (119 ff.), 49
(124.2 ff.), 40; (124.2), 105; (125.2),
78; (125.3), 40; (125.4), 22;
(126 ff.), 38; (126.18), 73; (127 ff.),
42; (127.2), 77; (127.3), 79, 107;
(128), 246; (128.1), 42; (128.5),
78; (129.8), 42
(132.10), 42; (132.11), 44; (132.15),
106; (133.2), 77; (134.12), 42; (137),
23; (139.2 ff.), 77; (139.4), 107
(140.6), 108; (140.12), 79; (141.2 ff.),
40; (141.5), 108
(fr. 1 Müller), 74; (fr.4), 73; (fr.6), 75;
(fr.8), 58, 75; (fr.25), 51; (fr.27),
110; (fr.29), 50; (fr.30), 51; (fr.37
Bücheler), 74
Phaedrus
(Appendix *Fab.* 15 Perry), 11
Philodemus
Peri Kakiōn (4.27 ff.), 135; (7.12 ff.),
135; (15.5 ff.), 135; (17.1 ff.), 135;
(18.11 ff.), 135; (18.35 ff.), 135
Plato
Phaedrus (248 c), 56, 207; (249 d),
33; (251 e), 56; (255 d), 33
Rep. (440), 220; (586 a), 183
Symp. (180 e), 196; (181 a), 196;
(212 d–e), 40
Tim. (49 a), 185; (51 a), 185
Pliny, elder
(8.80), 122; (10.49), 132; (10.51),
107; (10.78), 118; (18.357), 178;
(34.37), 97; (34.58), 97; (36.194 f.),
117; (37.20), 244
Pliny, younger
(1.15), 115; (2.6), 112; (2.17), 117;
(2.20), 11; (2.20.1), 143; (2.20.2 ff.),
108; (2.20.12), 108; (3.5.5), 71;

(5.5.2), 108; (8.21.2), 16; (10.96.5),
131
Plutarch
Caes. (49), 43
Crass. (32), 11
Moralia: De Curiositate (515 B–23 B),
182
Moralia: De Disc. Adul. et Am.
(60 D–E), 69, 244
Moralia: De Iside (355 D), 183;
(362 F), 183; (371 A–B), 183;
(371 C), 183; (372 E), 183, 185
Moralia: Mul. Virt. (1.1.(243 A)), 2;
(20(257 E–58 C)), 53, 164
Polybius
(32.26.5), 67
Porphyrion
on Hor. *Sat.* (2.4.1), 20
Probus
on Virg. *Ecl.* (6.31), 19
Propertius
(2.28.9), 200; (2.28.62), 213; (2.34.85),
16; (4.3), 106
Publilius Syrus
(104), 48

Quintilian
(3.9), 59; (9.4.52), 64; (10.1.46 ff.), 2;
(10.1.100), 27

Sallust
B.C. (5), 164; (14 f.), 164
B.J. (12), 13; (17.1), 58; (95.2), 58
Sappho
(105 L–P), 33; (130), 202
SHA Albinus (12.12), 249
Ant. Phil. (11.6), 250
Hadr. (18.7 f.), 246
Heliog. (30), 116
Verus (2.5), 251
Seneca, elder
Contr. (1 *pr.* 7), 84
Seneca, younger
Agam. (406 ff.), 47
Medea (893 ff.), 206
Apocol. (8), 35; (14.2), 69
Brev. Vit. (2.20.3), 137
Ep. (10.4), 97; (12.8), 137; (15.3), 137;
(27.5), 136; (41.7), 136; (47.6), 137;
(47.10), 130; (56.2), 137; (73.6 ff.),
101; (76.4), 94; (86.4), 117; (89.20),
137; (90.15), 137; (90.39), 137;
(94.27), 24; (95.18), 116; (108.8),

Seneca, younger (*cont.*)
26; (114), 37; (114.2 ff.), 84; (115.10 ff.), 96; (123.7), 138
Sidonius Apollinaris
Carm. (23.155 ff.), 73
Sophocles
Antigone (891 ff.), 202
Statius
Silvae (1.5), 118
Suetonius
Aug. (74), 116, 139; (75), 139; (78), 11; (92.2), 139; (94.12), 139
Cal. (33), 245
Claud. (32), 139
Nero (6.4), 138; (12.2), 138; (12.4), 138; (28.1), 138; (30), 138; (30.2), 245; (51), 138; (52), 71
De Gramm. (23), 95
Vita Lucani, 70, 71
Vita Persii, 41

Tacitus
Ann. (6.47.2), 75; (12.53.2 f.), 245; (13.25.4), 25; (14.16.1), 71; (14.16.3), 95; (14.21.7), 25; (14.40), 109; (14.51.6), 68; (14.52.1), 68; (14.52.3), 71; (14.63.2), 90; (15.37.9), 91; (15.40.3), 130; (15.44), 187; (15.49.3), 71; (15.49.5), 69; (15.52.2), 138; (16.1 ff.), 246; (16.18 f.), 2, 68, 80, 244; (16.19.4), 130
Dialogus (34 f.), 84
Hist. (5.3 ff.), 186
Tertullian
Apol. (1), 188; (6), 185; (9), 188; (13), 188; (16), 187; (17 ff.), 188; (24), 189; (37), 186
Theocritus
(1), 33; (1.52), 33; (1.74 f.), 33; (11.10), 33; (23.4), 199
Theophrastus
Char. (3.2), 39, 134; (3.3), 134, 135; (4.10), 134; (4.13), 134; (6.3), 134; (16), 136; (20.6), 134; (27.2), 10

Thucydides
(5.18), 34; (6.103), 158
Tibullus
(1.3.26), 213

Varro
(fr. 43 Bücheler), 20; (fr.63), 20; (fr.71), 20; (fr.122), 20; (fr.126), 20; (fr. 137), 20; (fr.144), 21, 41; (fr.181), 19, 41; (fr.190), 19; (fr.242), 20; (fr.252), 20; (fr.276), 21; (fr.313), 20; (fr.385), 20; (fr.447), 20; (fr.497), 19; (fr.507), 22; (fr.516), 21; (fr.524), 20
Virgil
Aen. (1.88 f.), 37; (11.77), 37; (1.306ff.), 37; (1.419 f.), 38; (1.482), 44; (2.13 ff.), 46; (2.206 ff.), 55; (2.314), 37; (2.316), 37; (2.528), 37; (2.595), 37; (2.671 f.), 37; (2.745), 37; (2.761), 37; (4.29), 44; (4.65 f.), 54 f.; (4.68 ff.), 54; (4.124), 227; (4.242 ff.), 79; (4.298 f.), 54; (4.300 f.), 54; (4.460), 54; (4.607), 54; (4.646 ff.), 54; (4.659), 54; (5.670), 45; (6.258 f.), 90; (6.269), 57; (6.299), 57; (6.314), 57; (6.327), 57; (6.337 ff.), 57; (6.369), 57; (6.413 f.), 57; (6.417 f.), 57; (6.420 f.), 57; (6.469 f.), 44; (6.535), 57; (6.595), 57; (7.26), 57; (7.568 f.), 57; (8.115), 45; (9.139 f.), 45; (9.296 ff.), 98; (9.436), 44; (9.641), 98
Ecl. (3.83), 44; (5.16), 44; (10.7), 56; (10.19), 56
Georg. (1.108), 56; (1.391), 178; (3.430 f.), 55; (4.458), 55

Xenophon
Anabasis (3.1.4), 200
Xenophon of Ephesus
(1.1), 55; (1.2.7), 55, 107; (1.6), 202; (1.6.2), 74; (2.5), 206; (2.9), 201; (3.11), 175; (4.3.4), 175; (4.6.2 ff.), 159; (5.13.4), 175

GENERAL INDEX

Abraham Adams, 243
Abroea and Byrrhena, 152
Academics, satirised in Lucian, 34
Achilles, and Encolpius, 36 f.; shield of, 93
Achilles Tatius, 23, 93; date of, 176;
  style of, 64
Actaeon, 178
Actium, 162
Adam, 219
Adlington, 233, 242
Adrastus, 163
Aeaea, 38
Aemilianus Strabo, 248
Aeneas and Encolpius, 28, **36 ff.**, 44,
  87
Aeneas Sylvius, 235 f.
Aeschylus in Apuleius, 53
Aesculapius, 185
Afranius, 127
Africa, religious climate in, 144
Agamemnon in Homer, 36
Agamemnon (character of Petronius),
  23, 40, 75, 96, 126 f.; as satirical
  target, 40 f., **83 ff.**
Aithiopika of Heliodorus, 72 n. 2
Ajax, 60, 127
Albert, 239
Albinus, 249 n. 7
Albucia, 75, 77
Alcibiades and Habinnas, 40 n. 1
Alcimus, 158
Alemán, 225, 235 f.
Alexander Neckham, 230 n. 3
Althaea, 60 n. 5
Amadis the Gaul, 227, 235 f.
Anabaptists of Munster, 241
Andreas Capellanus, 203 n. 2
Andromeda and Psyche, 202
Anna, 12
Anthia, 55 n. 2, 159, 175, 200, 201 n. 3,
  210 n. 2
Antigone, 202
Apelles, 245
Aphrodite, 55, 79, 174, 196; *see also*
  Venus
Apocolocyntosis, see Seneca
Apollo, 93, 202
Apollonius, 166

Apollonius of Tyre, 1, 235
Apollonius Rhodius in Apuleius, 209
Apology of Apuleius, 183, 185; style of,
  63
Apuleius, career of, **141** f., **248 ff.**; religious practices, 185; Platonist,
  182 ff.; programme for romance,
  32; Latinity, 63 ff.; and comic
  romance, 18, 30; and declamations,
  28 f.; and love-romance, 9, 55,
  161 f., 163; and Milesian Tales,
  13 ff., 16 f., 30 f.; and mime, 27 f.,
  30 f.; and Petronius, 30 f., 146 n. 3;
  and travelogue, 10; literary evoca-
  tion in, 52 ff.; of Aeschylus, 53;
  Virgil, 53 ff.; parody of genres,
  57 ff.; legal jokes, 61 f., 173, 210,
  212, 216
Arbiter as soubriquet, 244
Archestratus, 111 n. 2
Arete, 13 f., 168
Arion, 160
Aristides of Miletus, 1, **10** ff., **15** ff.
Aristides, Marcianus, 187
Aristofontes, 197
Aristomenes, 14, 31, 60, **149** f., 152,
  177 f.
Aristophanes, 209; in Menippus, 34; in
  Cupid and Psyche, 215
Armorum Iudicium of Varro, 20
Artemis, 55 n. 2, 106
Asclepiades, 207 n. 2
Asconius Pedianus, 111
Ascyltus, 26, 36, 39 f., 43, 75 ff., **82 ff.**,
  87, 98, 246
Asianic influence on Apuleius, 64
Atargatis, 165
Athenaeus, 10, 111
Athens, 248 f.
Atys, 53, 163
Augustine, St, 229
Augustus, 116; in *Apocol.*, 35; and
  Trimalchio, 139
Ausonius, 229
Auxerre, 229

Barbarus, 13 f., 168
Barclay, 239 f.

Bargates, 94 n. 5, 98
Basilium, 240
Beaumont, 232
Bellona, 185
Bellow, Saul, 243
Beroea, 164
Bion, 33
Boccaccio, 167 n. 2, 232, 235, 237 n. 5
Boethius, 228
Boiardo, 233
Briseis, 36
Bruno's *Cabala*, 232
Burrus, 68
Byrrhena, 145, 148, **152** ff., **178** f.

Caesellius Bassus, 246
Calderon, 219 n. 1, 232
Callimachus, 60 n. 1, 93 n. 2, 190
Callirhoe, 159; and Psyche, 55, 200
Calvisius Sabinus, 136
Camma, 53, 163 f.
Cannae, 58
captatores, 40, 76, 104 ff., 108 f.
Carpus, 137 f.
Carthage, 63, 141 f., 248 f.
Cary, Joyce, 243
Cassandra, 127
Cassiodorus, 229
Catiline, 163
Catius, 115
Cato, 65
Catullus, 190
Celsus, 188
Cena Trimalchionis, 21, 27, 29, **111** ff.; reflecting court-life, 81 f.
Cenchreae, 174
Cerberus, 60
Ceres, 185, 209 f., 218, 222
Cervantes, 4, 32, 227, 236, 238, 242
Chaereas, 212 n. 1
Charite, 30, 58, 148, 157 f., **159** ff., **163** ff., 175, 190, 241; and Dido, 53 f., 164; and Widow of Ephesus, 164
Chariton, 12 n. 1, 32, 58, 79, 106, 155, 174, 199 f.; date of, 176
Chartres, 229 f.
Chesterton, 189 n. 2
Choerilus, 104 f.
Christianity, 186 ff.
Chrysanthus, 121
Chryseros, 158
Chrysippus, 96

Chrysis, 105, 107
Cicero, 27, 63, 86, 127, 229
Circe, 38, 44, 77, **105** ff.; evoking Ovid, 42; as heroine of love-romance, 106 f.
Claudius, in *Apocol.*, 34 f., 67 n. 2; and Trimalchio, 139
Cleanthes, 20
Cleon, 209 n. 1
Clitophon, 23
Cocytus, 214
Colophon, 202 n. 3
comic romance, 10 ff.
comic travelogue, 9 f.
Commodus, 250
Consuetudo, 212
Corinth, 10, 142, 164 n. 5, 172
Corneille, 232
Crinagoras, 195 n. 2
Crispus, Vibius   68
Croesus, 114, 138 n. 5
Croton, 22, 25, 27, 37, 48, 76, 103 f.; scene of climax in *Satyricon*, 76, 79
Ctesias, 33 n. 5
Cumae, 69
Cupid, 53, 64, **190** ff., **192** ff., 199
Cupid and Psyche, literary reminiscence in, 54 ff.; related to *Met.* as whole, 146, 148, **157** f., **190** ff.; love-romance elements in, 175; structure of, 198 f.
Cybele, 185
Cynicism in Varro, 19 f.

Daedalus in myth, 93 n. 2, 127
Daedalus, Trimalchio's cook, 130
Dama, 121 f.
Daphnis and Chloe, see Longus
De Bello Civili, 23, **48** ff., 95
Decameron, see Boccaccio
declamation, influence of, 28 f., 100
de Cortegana, 233
Defoe, 242
de la Sale, 232
Delphi, 53
Demochares, 158
Democritus, 96
Demosthenes, 84, 87
de Salas, Gonzales, 231
de San Pedro, 236
de Solis, Antonio, 232
Diana, 178, 185

Dido, 38, 44, 93 n. 2, 247; in *Widow of Ephesus*, 12; and Charite, 53 f., 164; and stepmother, 54 f., 171
Diogenes, philosopher, 34
Diogenes, friend of Trimalchio, 120 f.
Diomede, 127
Dionysus, 215 n. 4
Diophanes, 170
Dipsas, 42
Dirce, 60
Dodona, 53
Domus aurea, 138 n. 5
Don Quixote, 227, 238
Doris, 73
Douza, 231

Echion, 121 ff.
Echo, 207 n. 5
Egypt, 174; religion of, in Plutarch, 183; in Apuleius, 183
Elagabalus, 116
El Cavellero Cifar, 235
Eliot, T. S., 76 n., 224
Encolpius, 10, 15, 22, 24, 25, 27, 28, 39 f., 46 f., 74 ff., **80** ff.; as epic hero, **36** ff., 43, 76; liaison with Giton, 77
Ennius, 19, 111
ephebus at Pergamum, 13
epic, evocation of, 28, 45 f.
Epicureanism in Petronius, 50 f., 82, 100 n. 3, **109** f., 135 n. 7
Epicurus, 109 f.
Eric of Auxerre, 229
Eros, 195 ff.; *see also* Cupid
Erōtes of Ps. Lucian, 15 f.
Espinel, 238, 241
Eteocles, 43
Eudoxus, 96
Eumolpus, 11, 13, 25, 27, 28, 35, 40, 46 ff., 82, **94** ff., 246; target for satire, 41
Euphormio, 240
Euphuism, 66 n. 1
Euripides, 53 n. 8, 84, 206
Europa, 160
Eurystheus, 210 n. 2
Euscius, 75

Fellini, 243
Festival of Laughter, 148, **154** f., 180, 240, 250
Fielding, 8, 32, 67, 111, 225 ff., 243
Finnegan's Wake, 66

Firenzuola, 233
Florida, 141 f., 249
Fortunata, 119 f., 124, 134
Fortuna in Petronius, 78, 100, 102; in Apuleius, 176, 181
Fronto, 63, 65
Fulgentius, 197 f., 218 f., 228 f.
Fundanius, 39

Gadara, 19
Gaius, emperor, 245
Ganymede, mythological, 93, 127, 214 f.
Ganymede, friend of Trimalchio, 121, 134
genus deliberativum, 58
genus demonstrativum, 59
genus iudiciale, 29
Geoffrey of Monmouth, 230
Geryon, 60
Gil Blas, 225, 240 ff.
Giton, 10, 25, 27, 36, 43, 74 ff., 80, **82** f., 87, 89, 97 ff.
Glyco, 246
Golden Ass, meaning of, 143 n. 1
Gorgias, 108 f.
Granius, 112 n. 2
Guido of Arezzo, 229
Guzmán de Alfarache, 225, 235, **236** f.

Habinnas, 39, 120 f., 132, 134; and Alcibiades, 40 n. 1
Habrocames, 175
Hades, Psyche in, 56 f., 215
'Haemus', 160 ff.
Halosis Troiae, 23, **46** f., 95, 97
Hannibal, 49, 101, 126
Harpocrates, 202 n. 2
Hazlitt, 6
Hecale, 60
Hecate, 185
Hedyle, 74, 77
Helen, 127, 173
Heliodorus, 236
Helios, 203
Hephaestio, 166
Hera, 53
Herculaneum, 117
Hercules, 60, 210 n. 2, 215
Hermeros, 120 ff., 245
Hermes, 187
Herodas, 27 n. 5
Herodotus, 33 n. 5, 53
Hesperides, 215

Heywood, 232
Hilaria, 155, n. 5
Hildebert of Lavardin, 229
Hipparchus and Milo, 150
Hippolytus, 171 f.
Homer, 87; in Apuleius, 56, 211; in Lucian, 34; in Menippus, 34; in Petronius, 36 f.
Horace, 20, 41, 111, 115; in Petronius, 36, 112, 115 n. 1
Horos, 202 n. 2
Hyacinth, 93
Hylas, 93
Hypata, 10, 142, 149 ff., 179
Hyperides, 84
Hypnophilus, 166

Iambulus, 33 n. 5
Icarus, 138
Ignatius Loyola, 239
Io model of Psyche, 52 f., 202 n. 3, 207
Iris, 215
Isiac aretalogy, 252 f.
Isiac elements in Apuleius, 144, 202 n. 2, 221 ff.
Isidore, 228
Isis in Apuleius, 142 ff., 174 ff., 185, 192, 252; in Petronius, 101; in Xenophon of Ephesus, 79

Jack Wilton, 241
Jerome, St, 228 f.
John of Salisbury, 24, 229 f.
Joyce, James, 143
Julia, 90
Julius Capitolinus, 249 n. 7
Juno, 185, 209 f., 218, 222, 250
Jupiter, 56, 210 ff., 216
Justin, 187

Kinsey, 16
Kyme, 252

Laberius, Decimus, 27 f.
Lactantius, 229
Laenas, 118
La Fontaine, 232
Lamachus, 158
Lazarillo de Tormes, 4, 225, 235, 236 f., 241
legacy-hunters, *see captatores*
legal pleasantries in Apuleius, 61, 173, 210, 212, 216, 251

Le Sage, 225, 240 ff.
Lichas, 28, 43, 74, 76, 94 n. 5, 99 ff.; and Orontes, 37; satirised, 41 f.
Livy in Petronius, 43, 44 f., 49; in Apuleius, 57 f., 164, 170
Logomachia of Varro, 20
Longus, 32 f., 79, 93, 174, 197; date of, 176; style of, 64; literary evocation in, 33
Louveau d'Orléans, 233
love-romance, Greek, 4, 7 ff.; burlesqued by Petronius, 18, 78 f., 102; influence on Apuleius, 52, 55, 154, 154 f., 159, 174, 175; in *Cupid and Psyche*, 197, 199 f., 202, 206, 209 f., 218
Lucan, 45, 70 f.; his epic criticised, 48, 104 f.; and *De Bello Civili*, 49 ff., 70, 105, 246
Lucian, 3, 4, 9, 16, 30, 32, 48, 85, 145, 176; literary allusions in, 33 f.
Lucilius, 19, 21, 111 f.
Lucius, 15, 31 n. 1, 57 ff., 142 ff.; Corinthian turned Madauran 184, 187; and Psyche, 191 f., 201 n. 1, 215, 221 ff.
Lucius or the Ass, 7, 144 ff.; authorship, 145 f.; and Aristides Sisenna, 17
Lucretia, 12, 143, 164
Lucretius in Petronius, 50 f.; in Apuleius, 55, 201; in Barclay, 239 f.
Lycurgus, 75
Lyly, 66 n. 1
Lysippus, 96 f.

Macaulay, 112 n. 1
Macrobius, 3, 228 f., 244
Madaura, *Madaurensis*, 184, 187, 249
Maecenas, 40, 111 n. 1
Mann, Thomas, 243
Manto, 201 n. 3
Marathon, bull of, 60
Marcellus, Eprius, 68
Marcus Aurelius, 65, 250
Marianus Scholasticus, 196
Marius Mercator, 228
Marius Victorinus, 244
Marmion, 232
market-episodes, 88, 151 f.
Marseilles, 73, 75
Marsyas, 119
Martial, 11, 230
Martianus Capella, 229
Medea and Psyche, 206

Meleager, 195 f., 207 n. 2
Menecrates, 25, 134, 245
Menelaus in Homer, 203
Menelaus, Petronian character, 83
Menippean satire, 1, 7, 19 ff.; influence
    on Petronius, 4, 21 ff., 48
Menippus of Gadara, 19, 21; literary
    allusion in, 34
Mercury in Petronius, 79, 106, 107; in
    Apuleius, 56, 211
Meroë, 14, 60, 149 f., 177 f.
Messeniaka, 72 n. 2
metae Murciae, 211, 251
Metamorphoses, Greek, model of
    Apuleius, 145 f.; length of, 146
Metamorphoses of Apuleius, 141 ff.; date
    of, 248 ff.; purposes of, 142 ff.;
    structure of, 146 ff.; as entertain-
    ment, 144 ff.; as fable, 176 ff.;
    characterisation in, 145
metaphor in Apuleius, 61
Milesian tales, 1, 3, 10 ff., 15 ff., 30, 149
    n. 2, 236, 242; in Petronius, 11 ff.,
    122; in Apuleius, 4, 7, 13 ff., 30,
    151, 167, 168
Miletus, 16, 33, 53, 202
Milo, 60, 145, 150 ff., 160, 178 f.
mime, influence of, 24 ff., 98 f., 100, 104,
    106
Minerva, 185
Minucius Felix, 63
Mithridates, 130 f., 246
Molière, 232
Monaco, 74 f.
Monte Cassino, 230, 232
Moschus, 33
Myrmex, 13 f., 168
Myron, 96 f.
Myrtilus, 166
Mytilene, 33

Nashe's *The Unfortunate Traveller*,
    241 f.
Nasidienus and Trimalchio, 38 ff., 115 ff.,
    136
Nasta, 130 n. 6
Nemesis, 185
Nero, 25, 68, 71, 86, 93, 245, 247; and
    Trimalchio, 70, 137 ff.
Neronian court, 5, 25, 70
Niccolo Niccoli, 231
Niceros, 14, 31 n. 1, 121 f.
Ninus romance, 8 n.3, 174

Niobe, 127
Numantians, 108

Octavia, 90
Odysseus and Encolpius, 28, 36, 38
Odyssey 9; in Petronius, 43
Oea (Tripoli), 152, 155, 249 f.
Oenomaus, 166 n. 3
Oenothea, 78, 105; and Dipsas, 42
oracles in romance, 202
Orontes and Lichas, 37, 101
Orpheus, 60
Ovid, 16, 36, 61, 90, 203; in Petronius,
    42, 106
Oxyrhynchus mime, 26, 41

Pacuvius, 137
Palaestra and Photis, 61, 152
Palinurus, 57, 101
Pallas, 245
Pamphile, 145, 151 ff., 155 f., 178 ff.
Pan, 53, 56, 79, 174, 207, 214 n. 2
Pandateria, 90
Pandora, 216
Pannychis, 89, 91
Panthia, 149 n. 2
Paris, 173, 182
parody of genres, in Petronius, 44 ff.;
    in Apuleius, 57 ff.
Parthians, 11
Pasiphae, 60, 171
Pater, 232
Pausanias, 215
Pelops, 166 n. 3
Pentheus, 60
Pergamum, 13 n. 3
Persephone, 192, 215; *see also* Proserpina
Persius, 41, 72, 104 f.
Petelians, 108
Petraites, 245
Petronii at Herculaneum, 133
Petronius, identity of, 67 ff.; career of,
    68 f.; habits of, 81; and Apuleius,
    30 f., 146 n. 3; and love-romance,
    7 ff., 18, 78, 102; and Lucan, 49 ff.,
    70 f.; and Milesian tradition, 10 ff.;
    and mime, 24 ff., 98 f., 100, 104;
    and Seneca, 84, 97, 99, 101 n. 5, 103
    n. 2, 117 n. 5, 130; and comic
    travelogue, 9 f.; and Varro, 21 ff.;
    general literary evocation in, 36 ff.
Petronius, P., 69 n. 2
Phileros, 121

Philesitherus, 13 f., 168
Philetas, 197 n. 2
Philodemus, 135 f.
Philomela, 107
Philostratus, 64 n. 1
Photis, 30, 60 f., 145, 148, 151, 152 f., 175, 177 f., 180
Phrixus, 160
Pindar, 84
Plato, 84, 111, 141, 185; *Phaedrus* evoked in Longus, 33; in Apuleius, 55 f., 195, 206 f., 220; *Republic* in Lucian, 34; *Symposium* in Petronius, 40 n. 1; in Marianus Scholasticus, 196
Pliny, elder, 71, 96 n. 3, 244, 245
Pliny, younger, 115, 117, 131
Plocamus, 121, 245
Plotina, 161 f.
Plutarch, 2, 11, 244; as relative of Lucius, 182, 251; *De Iside*, 182 f.
Poggio, 230 ff.
Polyaenus, pseudonym of Encolpius, 38, 42, 106
Polyneices, 43
Pompeii, 117
Pontianus, 248 f.
Praxiteles, 106
Priapeia, theory of lost, 17 f.
Priapus, anger of, 18, 38, 76 ff., 105, 107
Proculus, 121
Prometheus, 53, 207
Propertius, 61
Proselenus, 105
Proserpina, 185
prosimetric form of Menippean satire, 21
Protesilaus of Euripides, 53 n. 8
Ps. Clement, 1
Psyche, 30, 190 ff., 250; modelled on Io, 52 f., 202 n. 3, 207; and Lucius, 190 ff., 201 n. 1, 215, 221 ff.
Publilius Syrus, 127
Pudentilla, 141, 247 f.
Puteoli, 76
Pythagoras, 91
Pythias, 151

Quartilla, 24, 75, 88 ff.
Quevedo, 238
Quinault, 232
Quintilian, 2, 27, 64 n. 4

Rabelais, 141, 143
Reate, 19

Recognitions of Ps. Clement, 1
religious sentiment mocked by Petronius, 78 f., 100, 107
Richardson, 226
Rogers, 231
Rome, Apuleius at, 249 f.
Rufinus, 1

Sabrata, 141
Saguntum, 108; confused with Troy, 126 n. 4
Sallust, 65; and Apuleius, 57 f.
Sambucus, 231
Sappho, 33
Satyricon, meaning of, 22, 72; date of, 67; length of, 73; plot of, 77; purpose of, 71 ff., 79 f., 109 f.; *see also* Petronius
Scaevinus, Flavius, 69
Scaliger, 232
Scarron, 240
Schoppius, 232
Scintilla, 40 n. 1
Scipio Africanus, 117
Scipio Orfitus, 249
Scylax, 134
Second Sophistic, 64
Seleucus, 121 ff.
Seneca, younger, 23, 27; political fortunes, 68, 71; *Apocol.*, 21, 34 f., 217; plays, 70, 206; on Roman cultural decline, 84; and *Halosis Troiae*, 47 f., 70; and Trimalchio, 136 ff.; satirised by Petronius, 84, 97, 99, 101 n. 5, 103 n. 2, 117 n. 5, 130, 246
Serapa, 132
Severianus, 249
Sexagesis of Varro, 21
Sextus, 251
Sibyl and Quartilla, 89
Sicily, 131
Sidonius Apollinaris, 228 f.
Sieder, 233
Sinatus, 163
Sinorix, 163 f.
Sisenna, 3, 11, 16, 65 n. 4, 202 n. 1
Skiamachia of Varro, 20
Smollett, 67, 241, 242
Socrates, 14, 148, 149 f., 177
Sollicitudo, 212
Sophocles, 84
Sorel, 240

Sporus, 138 n. 5
Stoicism, attacked by Varro, 20; by Lucian, 34; defended by Lucius, 178
Strabo, 9
Strapaiola, 237 n. 5
Styx, 215
superstitio, 41 f., 100 f.
Sybaritici libelli, 11
Sychaeus, 44, 54
Syracuse, 158

Tacitus, 2, 95, 109; on Petronius, 68 ff., 244; on Roman cultural decline, 84; on Octavia, 90
Tantalus, 51
Tarentum, 98, 131
Tarquinius, Sextus, 163
Tarracina, 131
Temporal, 233
Terentius Maurus, 228
Tertullian, 63, 185 ff.
Thebes, 158
Thelyphron, 31 n. 1, 60, 148, **153** f., **179**
Theocritus, 33
Theodoric of Chartres, 229
Theophrastus, 10, 111, 133 ff.
Theseus, 60
Thessalonica, 164 n. 5, 170, 172
Thetis, 37, 56
Thiasus, 145, 172
Thrasyleon, 59, 158
Thrasyllus, 54, 163 f.; and Catiline, 164
Thucydides, 84; in Longus, 33; in Lucian, 34
Tigellinus, 68 f., 130 n. 6
Tityus, 51
Tlepolemus, 161, 163
Tom Jones, 227 f., 243
Trasimene, 58
Trimalchio, 24, 26, 80, 85 f., **109** ff.; and Maecenas, 137 n. 5; and Nasidienus, 38 ff.; and Nero, 70, 128, **137** ff.;
as Roman emperor, 128 ff.; as landowner, 131 f.; superstition and morbidity, 114, 132 f.; vulgarity, 114 ff.; ignorance, 125 ff.; arrogance, 128 ff.
Tristities, 212
Tryphaena, 26, 45, 74 f., 77, 82, **99** ff.
Tullianum, 167, 251
Typhon, 183, 184, 187

Úbeda, 238
urination, 14 n. 4

Varius, 40
Varro of Atax, 16
Varro of Reate, **19** ff., 41, 111 f., 127; literary allusion in, 34
Venus in Petronius, 107; in Apuleius, 53, 55 f., 61, 173, **183** f., 185; in *Cupid and Psyche*, 92, 200 f., 208 ff., 218
Verus, 251
Vibidius, 40
Vincent of Beauvais, 230 f.
Virgil in Petronius, 12, 36, 43 f., 45, 49, 106; in *Halosis Troiae*, 46; in Apuleius, 55 ff.; pictorial representation in, 93
Voltaire, 49 n. 4, 138 n. 6, 224

Wain, John, 243
Widow of Ephesus, **11** ff., 43 f., 48 n. 3, 99 f.; and Charite, 31, 164
Wittenberg, 241

Xenophon, historian, 111
Xenophon of Ephesus, 12 n. 1, 106, 159, 174 f.; date of, 176

Zachlas, 179
Zephyr, 203 f., 208
Zeus, 53